ART FOR ALL THE CHILDREN

ART FOR ALL THE CHILDREN
APPROACHES TO ART THERAPY
FOR CHILDREN WITH DISABILITIES
Second Edition

By

FRANCES E. ANDERSON, ED.D., A.T.R., H.L.M.

Distinguished Professor of Art
College of Fine Arts
Illinois State University

With Contributions by

Doris Arrington, ED.D., A.T.R.
Audrey Di Maria, M.A., A.T.R.
Marcia Rosal, PH.D., A.T.R.
Betty Jo Troeger, PH.D., A.T.R.

With a Foreword by

Judith A. Rubin, P.H.D., A.T.R., H.L.M.

CHARLES C THOMAS • PUBLISHER
Springfield • Illinois • U.S.A.

Published and Distributed Throughout the World by

CHARLES C THOMAS • PUBLISHER
2600 South First Street
Springfield, Illinois 62794-9265

© *1992 by* CHARLES C THOMAS • PUBLISHER

ISBN 0-398-05797-4

Library of Congress Catalog Card Number: 92-7087
FIRST EDITION, 1978

With THOMAS BOOKS *careful attention is given to all details of manufacturing
and design. It is the Publisher's desire to present books that are satisfactory as to
their physical qualities and artistic possibilities and appropriate for their particular
use.* THOMAS BOOKS *will be true to those laws of quality that assure a good
name and good will.*

Printed in the United States of America
SC-R-3

Library of Congress Cataloging-in-Publication Data
Anderson, Frances E. (Frances Elisabeth), 1941–
    Art for all the children : approaches to art therapy for children
with disabilities / by Francis E. Anderson ; with introduction by
Doris Arrington ; with a foreword by Judith A. Rufin. — 2nd ed.
    p.   cm.
    Includes bibliographical references and index.
    ISBN 0-398-05797-4 (cloth)
    1. Handicapped children—Education—Art.
LC4075.A54   1992
371.9'0445—dc20   92-7087
                                                         CIP

CONTRIBUTORS

MARCIA ROSAL, Ph.D., A.T.R.
Associate Professor of Expressive Therapies
The University of Louisville
Louisville, Kentucky

BETTY JO TROEGER, Ph.D., A.T.R.
Associate Professor of Art Education
School of Visual Arts
The Florida State University
Tallahassee, Florida

AUDREY DI MARIA, M.A., A.T.R.
Art Therapist, Paul Robeson School for
Growth and Development
Adjunct Assistant Professor
The George Washington University
Washington, D.C.
Visiting Faculty Member
Vermont College of Norwich University
Montpelier, Vermont

DORIS ARRINGTON, Ed.D., A.T.R.
Director, Art Therapy Program
College of Notre Dame
Belmont, California

This revised edition is dedicated to all of us who struggle with our own disabilities (especially C.P.P.). It is this triumph of the human spirit and the Creative Spirit in each of us that shines brightly in the darkest night that I wish to celebrate in this book.

FOREWORD

Once a month I meet with a group of mothers. We have been getting together regularly for a long time, first weekly, then bi-weekly, now monthly. Each of these mothers has a multiply handicapped child, along with one or more "normal" ones. They have inspired me, through their consistent determination, to find the best growth experiences for their disabled youngsters. I met them when they each brought in one of their children for individual art therapy. The youngsters have finished their treatment, at least for the time being. But for the mothers, parenting these children is a lifetime burden, full of fear for the unknown future.

In my own first experiences as an art therapist, I was asked to see what might be possible with children who had fairly severe disabilities. Hospitalized schizophrenics, institutionalized physically impaired, multiply handicapped blind, retarded, and deaf children — each of the groups described in Doctor Anderson's book. I recall vividly the skepticism, of those who knew the children better than I, about whether or not they would be able to use art materials appropriately or creatively. The doubts were enormous, as were the anxieties of other professionals about the possible negative impact of art activities.

Psychiatrists and child care workers worried that the schizophrenic children would become more psychotic and disorganized. Teachers and administrators feared accidents and injuries in those who were physically handicapped. Those in charge worried that the blind children would make terrible messes, that the retarded children would regress uncontrollably, that the deaf children would become confused and hyperactive. Happily, that was not the case. Children in each of these groups, treated as individuals and with appropriate adjustments for their disabilities, were able to create and to express themselves in art, well beyond even my fondest hopes. But it was an uphill battle at the time, and I remember it well.

Old attitudes die hard. Despite a new appreciation of the creative potential in the disabled person and of the value of art, there are many who have yet to learn. Although the situation has indeed improved since the first edition of *Art For All The Children* was published in 1978, there are still children who are excluded from both art and therapy, because they are thought to be too handicapped to benefit from either. The creative adaptations throughout Doctor Anderson's book can make both growth processes possible for even the most damaged child.

Even if art and/or therapy are provided, they may still be offered in such a prescriptive and inhibiting fashion that the true self of the youngster cannot develop freely. Misunderstandings of behavioral, cognitive, and developmental approaches to art therapy can greatly limit what might be possible, given more depth and ingenuity. The many examples provided in this book by Doctor Anderson and her collaborators allow the reader to imagine ways of helping which vary tremendously, yet which consistently respect the child's uniqueness.

As Doctor Anderson states clearly and repeatedly throughout the book, a child with disabilities is—first and foremost—a child. Although art therapists have always worked with those whose problems are primarily social and emotional, relatively little attention has been paid to youngsters with cognitive, sensory, and physical impairments.

A heightened consciousness on the part of parents of children with disabilities, like the mothers with whom I meet, has led to significant legislation, described in detail by the author. Not only are school districts now required to provide appropriate educational programming for youngsters with handicaps; they are mandated to do so in a fashion which suits the needs of each individual child.

While art and other child therapists are accustomed to thinking in terms of individual needs, educators have most often taught and thought in terms of groups. The requirement for Individualized Educational Programs (IEPs) for each and every child with a disability has made possible more personally meaningful planning, a rich soil for the growth of programs in therapeutic art.

Fortunately, art therapy is one of the related services mentioned in the landmark legislation (PL 94-142), making it possible to educate the public and the schools about its benefits for exceptional children. While a child's primary disability may be something physiological, it is almost inevitable that emotional and social problems will accompany any major handicapping condition. They often interfere with the child's ability to take advantage of what the school itself has to offer. Almost always, they depress the child's self-concept, an area to which Doctor Anderson pays much attention.

This second edition of her book comes at a welcome time and with very helpful additions to the first. The time is ripe, because parents and teachers and therapists need to know what can be accomplished for the disabled through art therapy in order to press for its inclusion in a child's program. The book is full of useful information, not only about atypical children and about development, but, most exciting, it contains many examples of actual art therapy programs with children who have disabilities, most of them in public school settings.

Doctor Anderson's invitation to those who have contributed case examples, methods of assessment, and modes of work with children, has added a great deal for the reader. Doctor Rosal's comprehensive chapter on different approaches to art therapy with children is especially helpful, as is Doctor Arrington's case study of a child who suffered sexual abuse. Doctor Anderson's modesty is reflected not only in having invited such contributions but also in her frequent references to those from whom she has learned and her acknowledgment that no single book can include everything on such a broad topic.

This second edition of one of the first books to focus on art for children with disabilities is a welcome addition to the literature for those in art and special education and in art therapy. Hopefully, friends and parents of the disabled will also learn of its existence, for it is through their efforts that more such opportunities may be made available to more such children. Perhaps, as is implicit in the title, authentic art will be possible some day for all.

J.A.R.

Judith A. Rubin is Clinical Assistant Professor of Psychiatry, University of Pittsburgh Faculty, Pittsburgh Psychoanalytic Institute. She is also the author of *Child Art Therapy: Understanding and Helping Children Grow Through Art* (2nd Ed.) (New York: Van Nostrand Reinhold, 1984), *The Art of Art Therapy* (New York: Brunner/Mazel, 1984), and *Approaches to Art Therapy: Theory and Technique* (New York: Brunner/Mazel, 1987).

INTRODUCTION

IN THE DECADE since the first edition of this book was published there has been an enormous shift in attitudes toward children with disabilities and a tremendous explosion of information about children, art, art therapy, art education and special education. No longer are children with disabilities hidden and invisible. No longer is art therapy an unknown treatment modality.

Now all of us are likely to encounter daily at least one person with a disability. Now there are over 100 schools that offer courses in art therapy, and the American Art Therapy Association has given approval status to more than 25 academic, clinical and institute training programs in this country and Canada. Now there is a growing acceptance of the use of art to remediate learning and social problems, to facilitate growth, development and expression in all of us no matter what our age or disability.

And, yes, there is even some hard data research (Anderson, 1983; Anderson, 1988; Anderson, 1991; Anderson, Ash & Gambach, 1982) that supports what we who have been practicing art therapy have always known: **art is essential to the quality of life.** Art is also a major means to facilitate academic learning. Art is a means to help us express our inner chaos, to bring order and control over our inner turmoil as well as our outer chaotic worlds. Artistic activity is intrinsically healing, centering and strengthening. Art connects us all to ourselves and to our inner children no matter what our ages are.

The first edition of this book was written for art therapists, art teachers, special educators and other adults who had the responsibility for the art programming of children with disabilities. The field of art for children with disabilities has grown so much that one book cannot cover the necessary material. The focus of this revised edition is on approaches to art therapy for children with disabilities. It has been written specifically for art therapists in training and for in-service professionals in art therapy, art education and special education who have children with disabilities as a part of their case/class load. Another book geared specifically to approaches to art for children with disabilities and written for preservice art and special education teachers and undergraduate art therapy students is under development.

This revised edition is grounded in reality and research and based on my own experience of three decades of work with children with visual impairments, hearing impairments, physical disabilities, mental retardation, learning disabilities and behavior disorders/emotional disturbance. I (and the other contributors) have tried to integrate research with practice and theory with reality. I hope that the outcome is a coherent whole and yet is so ordered that one can dip into its waters at specific points—or proceed through it in a linear way.

The first two chapters of the book lay a foundation in understanding disabilities and normal artistic development of children. These chapters are followed by an overview of four approaches to child art therapy buttressed with case material. These three chapters provide a knowledge base for the rest of the book.

Since Individualized Education Programs are a major means to avail children with disabilities of appropriate, meaningful and therapeutic art experiences, Chapter 4 is devoted to this topic. Also included in this chapter are several ways to assess children on their art skills. Finally, a segment focuses on the Miami, Florida, Dade County Clinical Art Therapy Program. As of this writing there were 15 art therapists working in public schools in Miami with learners who are seriously emotionally disturbed.

A detailed case of art therapy with a public school child is discussed in Chapter 5. This treatment was funded through legislation in California that is complimentary to Public Law 94-142 (now IDEA). If there is a healthier economy in this country in the years to come, I predict that more and more public school districts will have art therapists working with children who are disabled.

These chapters are followed by an extensive discussion of adaptative approaches to art for children with disabilities. I profoundly believe that art is indeed for **all the children.** So, one of the major goals in this book is to demonstrate the many ways that art can be adapted so that **ALL** children (with or without disabilities) can have a meaningful encounter with art. Chapter 6 covers in some detail many approaches to adapting art for children. Safety issues and health hazards related to art media are also covered.

The book concludes in Chapter 7 with a discussion of what research tells us about the effectiveness of the use of art to build more positive self-concepts in children. This information is followed by illustrations of ways to foster and encourage the development of a positive self-concept in children through appropriate art experiences. Chapter 7 also provides a model for sequencing art experiences into a coherent series that moves from simpler art experiences (and simple body concepts) to more complex art experiences (and more complex conceptual materials related to body concept). Additionally, each art experience discussed in Chapter 7 is followed by suggested ways to adapt the activity for children with the six major disabilities covered in Public Law 94-142 (1975). This format is presented as a model to help the reader begin to understand specifically what needs to be adapted so that children with mental retardation, learning disabilities, behavior disorders, physical disabilities, hearing impairments and visual impairments can participate in the art experience.

I hope that the reader will have a better understanding of art therapy and how it can be used (in the best sense) to remediate academic, social and emotional problems of children with disabilities. With the information provided, I also hope that the reader will be better prepared to understand children, their art, their disabilities and how to adapt art to meet their needs.

As I complete this revised edition, I am reminded of the story of the building of a stone wall in the orient. In completing this structure, the laborers always placed one stone upside down to insure the wall had imperfections, for the gods would be angry if the stone wall were perfect. No human is permitted perfection. So I am very aware of my many stones in this work that are not perfectly placed. (I speak only of the parts which I have written.) I ask your tolerance and understanding. And *I know the gods will not be angry.*

REFERENCES

Anderson, F. E. (1983). A critical analysis of *A Review of the Published Research Literature on Arts with the Handicapped: 1971–1981.* with special attention to the visual arts. *Art Therapy, 1*(1), 26–35.

Anderson, F. E. (1988). *A review of the published research literature on arts with children with disabilities.* Unpublished manuscript. Illinois State University, Normal.

Anderson, F. E. (1991). *A review of the published research literature on arts with children with disabilities.* Unpublished manuscript. Illinois State University, Normal.

Anderson, F. E., Ash, L., and Gambach, J. (1982). *A review of the published research literature on arts with the handicapped: 1971–1981.* Washington, DC: National Committee, Arts with the Handicapped.

Public Law 94-142, 1975.

ACKNOWLEDGMENTS

This revised edition is very much a collaborative effort. I want to gratefully acknowledge the contributions of the following colleagues who so willingly permitted their work to be a part of this manuscript:

- Doris Arrington, Ed.D., A.T.R., Director, Master of Art Therapy Program, College of Notre Dame, Belmont, CA and Director, American Art Therapy Association.
- Audrey Di Maria, M.A., A.T.R., Art Therapist, Paul Robebon School for Growth and Development, Washington, D.C., and Adjunct Assistant Professor, Graduate Art Therapy Program, George Washington University. Visiting Faculty Member, Vermont College of Norwich University, Montpelier, Vermont.
- Marcia Rosal, Ph.D., A.T.R., Associate Professor, Expressive Therapies Department, the University of Louisville, KY, Contributing Editor, *Art Therapy,* and member Education and Training Board, American Art Therapy Association.
- Betty Jo Troeger, Ph.D., A.T.R., Associate Professor of Art Education, The Florida State University, and Contributing Editor, *Art Therapy.*

I wish to thank the following publishers and professional organizations for permitting the reprinting of materials: The American Art Therapy Association, Mundelein, Illinois; The Florida Diagnostic and Learning Resource System South, Miami, Florida; Houghton Mifflin Company, Boston, Massachusetts; The International Collection of Child Art, The University Museum, Illinois State University; MacMillan Publishing Company, New York; Charles Merrill Publishing Company, Columbus, Ohio; and Prentice-Hall, Englewood Cliffs, New Jersey.

I am deeply appreciative of the review and critique of parts of this manuscript by Doctor Richard A. Salome. His feedback was essential to the success of this endeavor. I also wish to thank Doctor Barry Moore, Curator of the International Collection of Child Art, for his assistance in finding appropriate examples of children's art to be included in this book.

Thanks go to Victoria Foster and Robert Mechtly for their help in creating many of the illustrations in this book.

For the support of Illinois State University in granting me a sabbatical leave thus providing needed time to write, I am most grateful. I am also grateful to the Art Department at Illinois State University for providing some released time for research so necessary to the completion of this book. I must also thank the Art Education Department of the School of the Visual Arts at The Florida State University for providing the scholarly environment in which a major part of the writing of this manuscript was accomplished.

I have had excellent assistance with copy editing from Eileen Bularzik, Susan Swartwout and Mary Leen. Thanks also go to Roxanne Moss for her dedicated and careful word processing.

Acknowledgment and gratidute also go to the following colleagues from the Department of Specialized Educational Development at Illinois State University: Doctor Mack Bowen, Doctor Paula Crowley and Doctor Lanny Morreau.

Also, I wish to thank the children and their parents who so willingly permitted me to include case material and artwork in this book. Without their cooperation, there would have been no second edition.

Finally, I wish to thank my family, my family of choice and friends for their prayers, support and encouragement during the four years of my work on this book. (I Chronicles, XXIX:11–14.)

One can never pay in gratitude: one can only pay "in kind" somewhere else in life.
Ann Morrow Lindberg.

CONTENTS

ART FOR ALL THE CHILDREN

With regard to the use of non-sexist language, the author has throughout this book in the chapters, as well as segments in chapter 1, alternated the use of the pronouns he and she, her and him, and himself and herself.

Chapter 1

CHILDREN WITH DIFFERENT WAYS OF LEARNING ARE CHILDREN FIRST AND FOREMOST!

A DISCUSSION OF DISABILITIES

Introduction

Children with disabilities may have strange-sounding labels like osteo-genesis imperfecta, athetoid cerebral palsied, multi-disabled, hearing impaired, socially maladjusted, and on and on, but mainly they are children. In fact, since 1975 there has been a trend (Kirk & Lord, 1975) **not** to label or categorize special children because such labels can become stigmas. Labels perpetuate negative and erroneous stereotypes about disabilities and mostly focus on what a child is unable to accomplish or do (Blandy, 1989).

Since the 1975 federal mandate (PL 94-142) to place children with disabilities in the least restrictive educational environment, two related approaches have emerged. These are the ecological and normalization approaches which are to some degree extensions of the mainstreaming concept.

In the ecological approach, children are viewed in terms of their abilities and how these interrelate with their sociocultural background, environs, and the significant persons in the learners' world. Teachers, counselors, and therapists are part of a team in equal partnership with the learner, and together they determine learning outcomes and set goals and objectives (Blandy, 1989).

Normalization is governed by the principle that underscores the "utilization of means which are as culturally normative as possible in order to establish and/or maintain personal behaviors and characteristics which are as culturally normative as possible" (Wolfensberger, 1979, p. 28). In normalization, art experiences would occur in a context that is as near the age norm as possible. The key here is a chronological, age-appropriate context in terms of art media used and art activities provided in a typical classroom environment (Blandy, 1989).

NOTE: Some material in this chapter has been taken from Daniel P. Hallahan and James M. Kauffman, *Exceptional Children: Introduction to Special Education*, 4th ed. Adapted by permission of Prentice-Hall, Inc., Englewood Cliffs, New Jersey; also, Kirk, S.A., *Educating Exceptional Children*, 4th ed., 5th ed., & 6th ed. Adapted with permission of Houghton Mifflin Company, Boston, MA.

Some art teachers and art therapists philosophically prefer not to know the details of a child's disability before personally having the opportunity to work with that child. Indeed, many would agree with Blandy (1989) that a normalizing and ecological approach is optimal in working with all children; however, there are some very good reasons to be aware of what disabilities a child may have. One reason is very pragmatic. Unless a child in a school setting has been assessed and his disabilities fall within those cited in Public Law 94-142, that child cannot qualify to receive special education services. Secondly, there are disabling conditions that require special interventions and assistance—and in some cases, unless the professional is knowledgeable about those conditions, the child might be physically or psychologically harmed or be placed in unsafe situations. This is especially true with children who are physically disabled, epileptic, and/or on medication. So it is best to be well-informed about a child's disability. Such information can insure the child's physical safety and enable informed planning of appropriate treatment modalities. This information may be confidential; art therapists and art teachers do have a "right to know" (Thorne, 1990) because they are responsible for the direct instruction and provision of services to these children. The individual child's classroom teacher can also be consulted by the art teacher or art therapist. Mainly, this should be done to check on medical issues, safety guidelines and possible allergies.

With these factors in mind, a discussion of the major categories of disabilities follows. The special education student or teacher may already know what all the labels and descriptions mean. The student or teacher of the visual arts, the art therapist, or regular classroom teacher, however, may not understand all these categories.

Who then are these children and what are the disabilities that they have? There are several ways to describe their disabilities—in fact, the variations in descriptions and definitions can cause some confusion and problems (Anderson, Ash, & Gambach, 1982). Therefore, for the purposes of our discussion here and elsewhere in this book, the definitions and descriptions that are included in the Regulations governing Public Law 94-142 and those that have been changed in the Individuals with Disabilities Education Act (IDEA) (PL 101-476 which is the reauthorization bill for PL 94-142) will be used.

> The term "children with disabilities" means children—
> (A) with mental retardation, hearing impairments including deafness, speech or language impairments, visual impairments including blindness, serious emotional disturbance, orthopedic impairments, autism, traumatic brain injury, other health impairments, or specific learning disabilities, and
> (B) who, by reason thereof need special education and related services. (IDEA, 20 U.S.C. Chapter 33 as amended by Public Law 101-476, 1990).

Recent trends in the field of professional special education and in disabled special-interest groups have resulted in determining that the terms *handicapped, handicapping condition, impairment* and *mentally* or *physically challenged* are inappropriate, euphemistic and unrealistic. These professionals and special-interest groups prefer to describe children as having a disability and/or to use the specific disability such as mentally retarded or emotionally disturbed (LIFE–CIL, n.d.; Research & Training Center on Independent Living, 1987). This trend in the use of descriptors for disabilities will be honored throughout this book. Further, the current way to use descriptors of disabilities is to phrase these descriptions so that they **follow** the words child, children, learner, person, and individuals. Thus, the term *disabled child* becomes **child with disabilities** or **child with mental retardation**. The reasoning behind this rephrasing is that the child comes first and then his disability descriptor. Attempts to honor this phrasing have been made throughout this book. However, there are instances when to do so would result in extremely awkward language, so there will be occasions where the descriptor of the child's disability does not follow but precedes the noun. This usage is not meant in any way to trivialize the child or to detract from the concept that the child is what is most important in our discussions. Because the following disabilities are most prevalent and likely to occur with greater frequency, this chapter will focus on children with the following six types of disabilities: mental retardation, hearing impairments, visual impairments, behavior disorders/emotional disturbance, physical disabilities, and learning disabilities.

Some information about ways art activities might be tailored for children having these disabilities is also included. More specific information about adaptations for art are further addressed in a chapter devoted solely to this topic (Chapter 6). Additionally, suggested art adaptions are included as part of every art activity discussed in Chapter 7. In reading the material that follows, please keep in mind that in spite of labels and descriptors, **children with disabilities are CHILDREN FIRST AND FOREMOST!**

CHILDREN WITH MENTAL RETARDATION

The term *mentally retarded* is defined in the regulations governing PL 94-142 (now IDEA) as "significantly subaverage general intellectual functioning existing concurrently with deficits in adaptive behavior and manifested during the developmental period, which adversely affects a child's educational performance" (PL 94-142, Reg. 300.5).

The American Association of Mental Deficiency (AAMD) uses four classifications under the general term *mentally retarded:* mild retardation with ranges of intelligence scores from 50–55 to about 70; moderate retardation with ranges of intelligence test scores from 35–40 to about 50–55; severe retardation with ranges of intelligence scores from 20–25 to 35–40; and profound retardation with intelligence scores below 20 to 25. The AAMD emphasizes that several indicators of intellectual functioning should be used, including some provision for social adaptability (Grossman, 1983).

Identification

The majority of students in the retarded grouping fall into the mildly retarded category. It is only after they enroll in school that the retardation appears as they fall behind in school assignments. It is often not until the second or third year of formal schooling that these children are identified as being mildly mentally retarded, and the classroom teacher is often the first to suspect that a child has mental retardation.

There are two major means of determining mental retardation: individual standardized tests of intelligence and assessment of the child's ability to socially adapt. Students scoring two standard deviations below the mean on standardized intelligence tests are considered below normal in intelligence. There are two assessment tools of social adaptability widely in use: the AAMD Adaptive Behavior Scale (ABS) (Lambert et al., 1975) and the Adaptive Behavior Inventory for Children (ABIC) (Mercer & Lewis, 1978).

Causes of Mental Retardation

According to the AAMD, the causes of retardation fall into nine groups: "infection and intoxication, trauma or physical agents, metabolism or nutrition, gross brain disease, unknown prenatal influences, chromosomal abnormalities, gestational disorders, psychiatric disorders, environmental influence" (Grossman, 1983, p. 11).

Most children who fall into the mild retardation group are considered culturally-familial retarded, which means the condition is caused more by "poor social-environmental conditions" (Hallahan & Kauffman, 1988, p. 51) than heredity. This means that there is no evidence of brain damage, and the individual has been raised under conditions of poor nutrition and inadequate learning opportunities (Kauffman & Hallahan, 1988).

Moderate retardation is most likely caused by brain damage or genetic factors (MacMillan, 1982). Two more common genetic causes are Down's syndrome and phenylketonuria, although there are over 100 identified genetic disorders. Down's syndrome accounts for one to two births out of every thousand. Down's syndrome is caused by one added chromosome in the genetic code (47 instead of the standard 46). The result is either mild or moderate mental retardation (10 percent of all Down's syndrome children are moderately or severely mentally retarded) (MacMillan, 1982). Added physical problems are related to the heart, the skeleton and/or the ears, and physical appearance.

Phenylketonuria is caused by a genetic defect resulting in the inability of the blood to process a chemical in the body (phenylalanine). If not treated by strict diet in the early years, the result is severe retardation. However, the condition can be treated by adherence to a strict diet.

Brain disease can also occur due to infections or environmental hazards which may result in mental retardation. Infections transmitted by the mother to the fetus include rubella syphilis and herpes simplex. Two infections occurring in children that also cause brain damage are meningitis, which attacks the brain covering, and encephalitis, which is an inflammation of the brain. These infections can cause microcephalus which is a small size head and sloping forehead, and hydrocephalus, which is a buildup of cerebrospinal fluid in or around the brain.

Included in the group of environmental hazards are head injuries, radiation, and toxic substances (alcohol, drugs, caffeine and food additives transmitted from the mother to the fetus). Ingestion of these poisons by the mother (such as heavy amounts of alcohol or other drugs) can cause damage to the fetal central nervous system. Ingestion of lead through eating leaded paint and absorption of lead from toxic fumes can also cause damage to the developing nervous system and brain.

Polygenic Inheritance

An individual's genetic makeup is the result of complex interactions of genes. The intellectual capacities are also the result of the polygenic inherited qualities, as well as the result of environmental influences (Kirk & Gallagher, 1986).

CHILDREN WITH MILD MENTAL RETARDATION

The most obvious characteristic of the child who is mentally retarded is his lesser ability to learn. This decreased learning ability impacts on four aspects of thinking: memory, attention, language, and academics.

The child with retardation must continually focus his attention—attending to tasks is not an automatic process. Moreover, this child must garner more energy to remain on tasks than nonretarded children and therefore has less resources for other thinking processes such as recall, memory, attention to details, and blocking out unimportant or distracting elements that relate to the specific task.

Memory is processed at several levels at the same time. The child with mental retardation has trouble with the deep processing of memory tasks (Craik & Tulving, 1975). Therefore, the more complete the memory tasks, the more difficulty the retarded child has with it (Shultz, 1983). Individuals with mental retardation have trouble efficiently using various learning strategies including rehearsal and clustering to remember lists and numbers. The nonretarded person does not have these problems and can also develop the ability to automatically use these learning modes.

Also, the person with mental retardation may not select the most efficient learning method to solve a problem. He lacks the ability to self-monitor his performance and thus cannot tell if the method chosen works (Sternberg & Spear 1985). This process of selection, monitoring, and evaluation of the learning approach is termed *executive control processing* and is at the core of special education programs for students with mental retardation.

The child with mental retardation has a lower self-concept than nondisabled children (Leahy, Bella & Zigler, 1982). He often has other behavior problems including disruptiveness and a short attention span (Polloway, Epstein & Cullinan, 1985). He often has a preset expectation to fail. Children with mental retardation generally feel less in control of their environments and of things that happen to them — they feel more acted or imposed upon than able to control the life events that seem to control them. Mentally retarded persons, therefore, are less willing to become involved in challenging tasks and tend to give up quickly when a problem occurs they think they cannot solve. Those learners who are mentally retarded often generally lack persistence as they engage in all kinds of tasks.

Language Use and Acquisition

Language shapes our thinking and our social interactions and is crucial to so many other successful life experiences. There are two types of language use — descriptive and interpretative. Descriptive language is a lower-level language use that is employed in labeling and classification. Interpretative language is necessary for employing logical sequences, determining relationships and consequences, and modifying ideas. The development of interpretative language is influenced by practice and social input and is much less developed in individuals with mental retardation.

Persons with mental retardation will have problems with sound formation and articulation and may have voice problems and stuttering. The overall level of language will be below the mental age. Speech patterns are similar to the nonretarded individual, but they may well lack expressive qualities of the speech of nondisabled children. The frequency and level of speech and language problems relate to the overall general level of retardation.

Motor and Physical Abilities

Many children with mild mental retardation do not have underdeveloped motor or physical abilities. In short, they are more similar to their nondisabled classmates than not. However on a case-by-case basis, one may well encounter some children with poor fine motor skills, underdeveloped strength in their limbs, or some limited perceptual abilities. This is because mildly retarded learners do have an increased incidence of hearing, visual, and neurological problems over nondisabled students.

Social Behaviors

Because of their history of failure, children with mental retardation have a lower tolerance for frustration and a shorter attention span than nondisabled children. This results in inappropriate behaviors in the classroom and impacts negatively on classmates and teachers. Additionally, the delayed language development of mentally retarded students impairs social interactions and relationships. Inability to focus on tasks, a characteristic of learners with mental retardation, results in disruptive behaviors, shortened time spent on learning tasks, and a lessened ability to learn and remember things.

Educational Implications

The preschool programs for children with mild mental retardation focus on readiness skills and training that can take two to three years. Since art has an intrinsic motivating aspect, it is a natural activity to help develop motor skills, language development, stimuli discrimination, and peer interaction. Specific activities will focus on exploration of various media (paint, finger paint, clay, crayons, and markers). Since children in preschool programs will most likely be functioning at the scribbling stage of artistic development (Lowenfeld & Brittain, 1987), children should not be expected to do realistic or representational artwork (drawing recognizable objects using symbols that an adult can identify). These children can learn correct ways of holding drawing and painting tools and can gain kinesthetic pleasure from scribbling on paper, finger painting, and manipulating brushes, paint, and clay. Throughout these sorts of art activities, language related to them can be reinforced. Following directions and teaching other vocabulary such as position words can also be achieved through art activities. For example, children can be shown how to push the clay or pull the brush toward them. Cutting and pasting activities would also be appropriate for these children as would simple printmaking activities. Finally, the activities related to shape discrimination and textural awareness described in Chapter 7 would be most appropriate for preschool programs. One thing must be emphasized: the focus must be on the process, not on producing a beautiful product from an adult perspective. A more detailed discussion of children's artistic development may be found in Chapter 2.

The primary school programs for children with mild mental retardation are generally an extension of the preschool programs with an increased focus on language and concept development, and increased focus on the development of social skills. These children range in age from 6 to 10 years chronologically but have mental ages of from four to six years of age.

The elementary intermediate classes focus on functional academics—i.e., reading to survive in the world, using phone books and newspapers, and completing job applications, as well as the ability to make change and to read labels. These classes are the most prevalent because most children are not identified as having mental retardation until they are in school for one or two years. These students range in chronological age from 9 to 13 years with a mental age of from six to nine years. This child develops at a rate that is one-half to three-fourths that of an average child. He remains longer at each developmental stage and is slower in learning.

The child who is mentally retarded may not begin reading until he is eight years old (or older). For example, it takes about 17 repetitions for a typical child to learn a word in a primer; it takes between 25 and 30 repetitions for the mildly mentally retarded child to complete the same task (Telford & Sawrey, 1977). The reading program focuses on function/survival skills, which include being able to identify traffic signs, exit signs, restroom signs, and traffic signals. Reading and math are taught using a unit or thematic approach such as the community and all basic skills of reading, spelling, arithmetic, and writing are integrated into the unit centering around the major theme. Arithmetic concepts are related to needs in the environment such as using money and telling time.

Developing socially appropriate behaviors is an important part of the curriculum for children with mental retardation. These children have problems transferring information from one context to another. Special educators recommend a social learning curriculum that combines conceptual objectives and behavioral approaches.

In prevocational skill development the focus is on developing self-help skills and appropriate social behaviors. These in turn develop good work habits and cooperative skills, an awareness of the world of work. The specific vocational skills are taught which lead to specific job-related skills development, such as assembly-line concepts, how to complete specific tasks, how to actually get around the community, and how to find information from a newspaper. It is interesting to note that in secondary schools mainstreaming may be counterproductive to development of vocational skills for the mentally retarded student because regular classes do not include a focus on these skills (Kirk & Gallagher, 1986).

The child with mental retardation may have formal schooling ending with the completion of the academic equivalent of between the second and sixth grades. This child is below the normal child in motor abilities, reading, and social development. However, the interests of the mentally retarded child are similar to normal children of comparable chronological age.

Behavior problems such as short attention span and easy frustration occur when expectations that are too high are placed on children with mental retardation. This often occurs when they are in a regular class. When these children are placed in special classes (usually between 9 and 13 years), they seem to adjust better socially. Sometimes such classes are resource rooms, and the child will be integrated for special subjects such as art, home economics, and music.

Strategies Utilized by Special Educators

One of the major goals for the education of children with mental retardation is to assist them in developing behaviors and social skills that facilitate learning and social interactions and to reduce behaviors that inhibit social relationships and knowledge acquisition. One of the major means of doing this is through behavior modification. Behavior modification is grounded in work done by Skinner (1953) who discovered that positive rewards following a behavior tend to increase the incidence of that behavior being repeated, while negative reward (punishment) tends to extinguish or eliminate unwanted behavior. The absence of rewards or reinforcements (be they negative or positive) results in the disappearance of a behavior. Thus, the fastest way to make a behavior disappear is to ignore it while rewarding a more desirable behavior. This is the basis for the Premack principle (1959) which, simply stated, is if you eat your spinach, then you can have your favorite dessert.

Behavior modification takes several forms in the special education classroom. In differential reinforcement the unacceptable behavior (hitting, outspokenness) is ignored and the intervals between these unacceptable behaviors are rewarded—and rewarded increasingly as the time intervals increase.

At times a child may be removed physically from a situation. This removal is called a *time-out* and usually occurs just after the child has demonstrated a negative or inappropriate behavior response. The child is separated and is allowed to return to the class group when he feels he is again in control of his behaviors. This technique seems to work effectively with children who have disruptive, acting out, aggressive, and other negative social behaviors. Sometimes a token economy or contingent social reinforcement is used. In this situation children are rewarded for appropriate behaviors by being given a token. Later, these tokens can be turned in for something the child wants (food, a particular toy, a game). If the child acts inappropriately socially, then tokens are taken away. This token economy seems to be effective in self-contained classes of learners with disabilities and in some mainstreamed situations. While behavior modification techniques do work, there is some debate on their efficacy because the child may not internalize the needed response, and the child is controlled with external factors (Kirk & Gallagher, 1986).

A variant of behavior modification that has had some success is cognitive behavior modification. In this approach, the child models his behaviors after that of an adult. The adult undertakes some task or performs some behavior while talking to himself (however, in the model the adult talks out loud). Later, the child repeats the steps until the overt out loud self-talk becomes silent self-talk. Self-talk is used in a specific sequence to self-modify behaviors. First the problem is identified, attention is focused on the problem, and a response is planned. Next self-praise is used, followed by a self-evaluation of how the child is doing on the task. Finally, errors are corrected (Meichenbaum & Goodman, 1971). This approach seems also to be effective in working with children who have learning and behavior disabilities.

Another strategy that is very helpful in working with children who are mentally retarded is task analysis. In a task analysis, a complicated task is broken down into its simplest parts, and each part is taught separately, then as a whole operation. Task analysis is discussed in more detail in Chapter 6.

With respect to organizing the art learning, the art specialist should be aware that children with mental retardation learn at a slower rate. Mildly mentally retarded children have trouble abstracting and generalizing. These children do not pick up skills and concepts incidentally, but need to be taught specifically in each situation. The teacher should not assume that they can carry over learning from prior experiences (*Insights,* 1976). It is important that the children have some success from each art experience and lesson.

Implications for the Art Program

It may be necessary to build longer involvement in art activities over time. Shorter art encounters which focus on one key skill and/or concept which the children can master with little frustration will be most meaningful. The children need a lot of feedback as they work on their art. This feedback should be encouraging and positively reinforcing. It also will be important to incorporate repetition of new words and skills through several art sessions. Artistic processes should be broken down into small-step increments which allow the children to focus on only one step at a time. It is also very important to provide, over time, a sequence of activities that proceed from easier to more difficult tasks. Such a sequence should include repetition of processes and ideas so that concepts and generalizations can be built.

Providing a cafeteria selection of many different art materials and processes can do more to confuse the children than to improve their expressive abilities and knowledge of art processes and skills. At the same time, some materials and situations in the art lesson need to be varied to provide maximum involvement and motivation. For example, a lot of time may be spent on developing body concepts in art. The media and situations in which body concepts are being accomplished may shift from completing drawings of figures to executing a personalized life-size portrait. The concepts of body awareness and naming body parts are the same throughout, but the materials may vary according to the children's interests and skills. This approach is used in Chapter 7.

Finally, it will be important to discover a good match between skills and concepts being taught and the children's ability to grasp them. Additionally, working as a team with other teachers can provide a united educational effort for each child. Key academic concepts can then be integrated into art learnings, and consistent classroom management can be maintained. These basic guidelines will also be useful in work with moderately mentally retarded children.

CHILDREN WITH MODERATE MENTAL RETARDATION

Children with moderate mental retardation do have learning potential. They can develop self-help abilities and the social adjustment necessary to be at home in their family environment and in the immediate neighborhood.

These children develop at between one-fourth to one-half of the rate of the normal children. Moderately mentally retarded children reach a final mental age of between three and seven years. They will not be able to read but will be able to recognize key words. These children will be able to count up to 10, and older students will be able to write numbers. Some will be able to tell time, understand the calendar, comprehend some money concepts, and recall some telephone numbers.

Educational Programs

Preschool programs emphasize early stimulation and concept and language development. Speech and physical therapists may be part of these programs because many children with moderate mental retardation have multiple disabilities. The elementary and secondary classes focus on functional academics, especially on vocational and self-help skills (dressing, toileting, eating, hygiene) and socialization skills. The curriculum will include using drama to act out stories, singing songs to get across key ideas, discussing pictures, and listening to stories. Older students will also learn prevocational and vocational skills such as cooking, sewing, and gardening.

Learners with moderate mental retardation can be expected to understand quantitative concepts, such as large and small or more and less, and to be able to count up to 10. In secondary school the moderately mentally retarded student can usually be able to write from 1 to 10, to tell time, and to read a calendar. Some can also recall phone numbers and simple money usage. In the math curriculum, as in the reading curriculum, learning is tied directly to the needs of daily living.

Children with moderate mental retardation have even slower development in language than the child with mild mental retardation. This is due to many factors including actual physical brain damage, and often in Down's syndrome children, hearing impairment is a factor which impedes language development. In developing language and communication skills, the focus is on the home and the community—holidays, weeks, months, and transportation are all a part of the curriculum. The focus is on being able to describe objects and feelings in a detailed way. An active learning approach is used, with role playing and dramatization being important parts of the teaching methods utilized (Kirk & Gallagher, 1986).

One of the problems that children with moderate mental retardation have is delayed and poor motor skills. They often lack fine motor skills, have a stiff movement pattern when walking, and lack general coordination (Kirk & Gallagher, 1986).

The general characteristics in terms of deficits in social adaptability in the mildly mentally retarded child are more pronounced with the moderately retarded child. These children have a greater tendency toward impulsive behavior and hyperactivity. Additionally, they have a greater tendency to become more childlike in stress-provoking situations and to use this as an inappropriate means of coping.

Finally, students with moderate mental retardation who have been placed in institutionalized residential environments tend to have fewer typical life experiences. Thus, they are less able to cope when confronted with a variety of life situations, such as getting on buses, shopping in stores, and making change.

An art program should focus on basic art skills, such as proper use and care of art media, tools, and materials. Once children have mastered the basic use of artistic media, they can use these skills for expression. The art teacher and art therapist must realize the developmental lag that these children have. Therefore, a child who is scribbling is probably only functioning at an artistic developmental stage of a typical two-year-old. Such children cannot be expected to draw, paint, or use art media in the same way as their counterparts in the regular classroom who may be the same chronological age.

The art program will be similar to that of a preprimary art curriculum, with a focus on manipulative and sensory approaches. Assuming they are beyond the scribbling stage, it is important to allow time for children to develop their own expressive abilities with art materials. Time to work with drawing and painting media should be provided. Sometimes certain art media such as paint are too fluid and too hard for some children to control and they get frustrated. The therapist and teacher must be sensitive to this and to a child's possible frustration resulting from being offered too many choices. A limited choice of materials and activities is encouraged, but some choice should be a part of such activity. Simple (but not simplistic) activities that provide for frequent repetition of basic ideas and key concepts are helpful. It must be remembered that these children have a short attention span and limited recall.

The art teacher and art therapist will want to work closely with the other adults who are a part of the education team for the child with moderate mental retardation. This cooperation will provide important carry-over of management programs and academic concepts. Integrating the art activities with classroom activities may be an important means of emphasizing key concepts and motivating these children. All staff must respond consistently to each child.

Older students with moderate mental retardation can be taught art skills that may be used in a sheltered workshop setting. These skills have been used by mentally retarded persons in at least two such facilities (Creative Growth in Oakland, CA and Le Fil D'Ariane in Montreal, Canada).

CHILDREN WITH SEVERE AND PROFOUND MENTAL RETARDATION

Children with severe and profound mental retardation are included in the provisions of PL 94-142 (now IDEA), and educational programming must be provided for this segment of the mentally retarded population. The focus of programs is on self-help and survival skills.

Programming for persons with severe and profound mental retardation stresses the importance of using age-appropriate materials. This means that the selection of art materials must take into consideration both the mental and chronological ages of the students. Using child art media and processes such as finger paint and crayons are not appropriate for students who are high school age. More appropriate materials might be paintbrushes instead of finger paint and markers instead of crayons.

Learning objectives for students who are severely and profoundly mentally retarded must be as specific as possible. Activities that are grounded in the real world are strongly recommended. There will be a need for extra prompting when directing actions. For example, one should point to the scissors while saying "pick up the scissors." Individualized education programs should be reviewed regularly and short-term and intermediate goals updated more often because long-range goals are harder to establish for this group of students.

As with all good educational environments, there is a need for consistency in scheduling daily activities and in room setup. There is a need for a total program approach involving all staff who have interaction with each student. Art teachers and art therapists need to understand and be willing to use behavior modification or token economies. The art teacher and art therapist may not be familiar with the use of behavior modification and should work closely with other staff to maintain consistency in what is used to reward appropriate behaviors for each student. Task analysis is strongly recommended as a teaching methodology and is discussed in detail in Chapter 6.

Programming should include work with small groups of students to build social skills. It is also recommended that exposure and association with nondisabled persons be a regular part of educational programming. Family involvement in educational programs is also strongly recommended (Bates et al., 1981).

Art activities can help in many aspects of the educational programming for the profoundly and severely mentally retarded child and adult. Art can facilitate sensorimotor stimulation, development and integration in many ways. Sight and muscular response are all facilitated by art activities such as holding a drawing instrument or a brush. The textural activities discussed in Chapter 7 can assist with the sensoristimulation at the preschool level and with sensorimotor development at the school level.

If the individual with severe/profound mental retardation develops beyond the scribbling stage of artistic development, there are numerous other art activities that can assist with sensorimotor integration. Art also can play an important role in developing physical dexterity and in providing the motivation and skills for leisure activities.

Art can assist in language development at all levels. At the preschool level language development can occur simply by identifying the names of art media and tools that the child may be using. Art can facilitate language development in school by being used in the best sense to teach position words and simple commands. For example, the student could be asked to put the paint on the left or to fill the top part of the paper with color. The child could be asked to paint a wood sculpture from the top to the bottom. In working in clay, the child would be asked to pull a lump of clay from the ball or flatten the clay ball. In weaving, the child could be asked to follow directions such as "put the red thread over the green thread, pull the red thread through," etc. In fact, every art activity could focus on following simple directions and developing language. Finally art activities can greatly facilitate social interactions and self-directed work. There are many group art activities such as mural making, group sculpture, and printmaking that can facilitate both social interactions and self-direction in work.

Postscript

All children grow up—including those who are mentally retarded. Adults with mild mental retardation do hold down jobs and often have a better record of low job turnover. Individuals with moderate mental retardation can also function in sheltered workshops where they learn simple tasks and where the workshops produce piecework or other salable products. Workers receive wages for pay. There are a few exemplary workshops around the country in which artwork is produced for sale. Two such workshops are Creative Growth in Oakland, California and Le Fil D'Ariane in Montreal, Canada.

Founded in 1973, Creative Growth has as its major purpose the provision of a creative outlet for the adult who is physically, emotionally and mentally disabled. The facility has the following goals:

Artistic development and integration of the personality through creative experi-
    ences in the visual arts
Enhancement of self-image and self-esteem
Prevocational training
Independent living experiences
Normalization and prevention of institutionalization
Appreciation by the public of the creativity of the handicapped
Professional training-undergraduate, graduate, continuing education
Research on creative art of the handicapped (Brydon, n.d.)

The program is funded from several local and state programs including the California Arts Council. In addition to running an open studio in print-making, sculpture and painting, there are educational programs that focus on independent living skills. Also, Creative Growth runs an art gallery where the participants display and sell their artwork. The Creative Growth Gallery's exhibitions have had critical acclaim from art critics in the Oakland area (Killen, 1983; Ross, 1982).

The visual arts have also been found to be an important means of breaking down barriers between disabled and nondisabled adults. The 1987 Arts for Transition program (Appel & Krammer, 1987), conducted by Macro Systems, Inc. and funded by the National Institute for Disability and Rehabilitation Research, developed a model for the participation of disabled and nondisabled individuals in a variety of community arts events and experiences. The model was developed and tested at two sites: Wright State University in Dayton, Ohio, and Trinity College in Washington, DC. The project documented that all the arts could be vehicles for social integration and mainstreaming of disabled and nondisabled persons. Additionally, participation in the program resulted in increased self-esteem and self-confidence.

Summary

There are four major divisions of mental retardation based on IQ: mild, IQ 50–55 to 70; moderate, IQ 35–40 to 50–55; severe, IQ 35–40 to 50–55 and profound, IQ below 20–25. Intelligence quotient and/or social adaptability is used as a means of identifying mentally retarded children.

Children with Mild Mental Retardation

The major causes of mild mental retardation are: cultural/familial retardation or poor nutrition. The abilities of someone with mild retardation develop up to one-half to three-fourths that of the average child. It takes two times as long to learn and to complete tasks for a child with mild mental retardation than a child without mental retardation. There will be less developed motor abilities, delayed language development, lower self-esteem, shorter attention spans, inhibited social interactions, inappropriate social behaviors and speech problems for persons with mild mental retardation. Primary school children will have a mental age of four to five years and a chronological age of six to ten years. These children are mentally about two to four years below their chronological agemates who are of average intelligence.

In intermediate programs reading may not occur until the child is chronologically eight years of age. The rate of development at this level is also one-half to three-fourths that of average children. Generally, these mildly mentally retarded students will be 9 to 13 years of age chronologically and six to nine years of age mentally. It will take about two times as many repetitions to learn a task as that needed for an average child. This means that it will take 17 repetitions to learn a concept, fact or task for an average child and 25 to 30 repetitions for a mildly mentally retarded child. Socially appropriate behaviors are one major educational goal. Prevocational and vocational skills will also be a priority for the educational program. Teaching strategies may include task analysis, behavior modification, token economies and contingent social reinforcement.

In the art program, consideration must be given to the slower learning rate of the child and the fact that abstracting and generalizing will be difficult. Also, skills and concepts must be specifically taught. Positive reinforcement and experiences that permit a high degree of success in a short time period will be important components of the art program. Limited choices of materials and activities will decrease frustration. Art experiences that incorporate academic concepts being covered in other subjects will provide added reinforcement of ideas and opportunities for repetition so necessary to learning for the mild mentally retarded child. In planning art experiences, social level, chronological age level, mental age and level of artistic development must be considered.

Children with Moderate Mental Retardation

The major causes of moderate mental retardation are genetic and brain damage. This child develops at between one-half to one-fourth the rate of a normal child. He may reach a final mental age somewhere between three and seven years. He will be able to identify key words but may not be able to read. This child will be able to count up to ten and may eventually be able to write numbers. He also may understand time, money concepts, and be able to remember telephone numbers.

Preschool programs focus on concept and language development and on providing lots of sensory stimulation. Elementary and secondary programs focus on vocational and self-help skills. Language development is at a slower rate than that of the mildly mentally retarded child. Poor and delayed motor skills are major problems. These problems result in a stiff walking pattern and in a lack of general motor coordination. This child has a greater deficit in social adaptability than students with mild mental retardation. Also, these children tend to have impulsive behaviors, hyperactivity, and may regress when placed in stressful situations.

The art program should stress basic art concepts and skills and mastery of cutting, drawing, pasting and painting abilities. The art teacher must plan art experiences that match the child's artistic developmental level which also motivate the child. This means taking into account the chronological age and the social and mental age of the child. In planning art experiences, a limited palette is recommended. Also in planning art experiences it will be important to consider the child's short attention span, current art skills, and need for repetition to learn.

Creative Growth in Oakland, California and Le Fil d'Ariane in Montreal are two examples of sheltered workshops for moderately mentally retarded adults where they work as artisans and artists.

Children with Severe and Profound Mental Retardation

Children with severe and profound mental retardation also can benefit from an educational program. Programming will focus on self-help and survival skills. The art program will be very similar to that appropriate for very young children who are in the scribbling stage of artistic development. Sensory awareness will be a major component of both the art and educational program.

CHILDREN WITH LEARNING DISABILITIES

Children with *learning disabilities* have a *specific disability* in the development of their ability to speak, perceive, read, think, write, spell, and/or calculate. These disabilities are not caused primarily by visual, auditory, physical, mental, or behavioral disorders or by environmental disadvantages. Children with learning disabilities may appear normal in all but one area of information processing, communicating, or expressing. Thus, one particular child may not be able to read but can learn by listening. Another child may have problems following verbal instructions but have no problem following a visual demonstration. Every individual learns best through one of four learning modes: looking, listening, touching, or moving.

There are numerous definitions of learning disabilities. For our purposes we will use the federal definition advocated in PL 101-476, the IDEA:

> The term "children with specific learning disabilities" means those children who have a disorder in one or more of the basic psychological processes involved in understanding or in using language, spoken or written, which disorder may manifest itself in imperfect ability to listen, think, speak, read, write, spell, or do mathematical calculations. Such disorders include such conditions as perceptual disabilities, brain injury, minimal brain dysfunction, dyslexia, developmental aphasia. Such term does not include children who have learning problems which are primarily the result of visual, hearing, or motor disabilities, of mental retardation, of emotional disturbance, environmental, cultural, or economic disadvantage. (Public Law 101-476, Individuals with Disabilities Education Act, 20 U.S.C. Chapter 33 section 1401, 15, October 30, 1990).

Some experts in the area of learning disabilities group this disability into two major classifications: developmental and academic. Developmental disabilities include problems in perceiving, attending, remembering, thinking, expressing and receiving language, and perceptual motor difficulties. Academic learning disabilities are problems in the four main academic areas— abilities to read, spell, write, and do math. Academic disabilities are identified when children are performing below their academic potential on school subjects. Evaluating children with academic learning disabilities is a process by exclusion—the focus is one of eliminating environmental causes, or determining that the child is not mentally retarded or does not have serious behavior problems or visual or hearing impairments (Kirk & Gallagher, 1986).

Incidence

The number of children identified as having learning disabilities has grown in recent years. The number is twice what it was in 1976, and in 1985–86 the number was put at 43 percent of all identified students with disabling conditions. One concern about this large (and growing) number is that it may be difficult to obtain ongoing federal support and services to children having this disabling condition, simply because of the numbers of children being identified as having learning disabilities.

Origins of Learning Disabilities

There are three possible major origins: biological and organic, environmental, and genetic. Hallahan and Kauffman (1988) present convincing arguments against the existence of organic and biological causes for learning disabilities.

There is, however, some evidence that learning disabilities are related to genetic factors and seem to cluster in families. Whether these family traits are purely genetic or also due to environmental influences has yet to be determined.

Causes of learning disabilities due to environmental factors are also hard to document. There is some evidence that culturally disadvantaged or environmentally disadvantaged persons tend to exhibit more learning disabilities—but whether this is due to genes or to poor instruction has not been determined. There is some evidence that poor instructional practices in early education years contribute to the presence of learning disabilities in students (Hallahan & Kauffman, 1988).

Diagnosis

Initial indicators that a child may have a learning problem are usually discovered by parents if the child is a preschooler. The most often identified preschool learning disability is in the area of language. Once in school it is the classroom teacher who first notices discrepancies in the child's potential for learning and her actual performance (Kirk & Gallagher, 1986).

Acquisition of preacademic skills is one good predictor of whether a child will have problems later and be classified as learning disabled. Preacademic skills include counting as well as shape, color, number, and letter identification.

The key in remediating learning disabilities is in assessing the child in terms of a resulting prescription for instruction. There are four areas of testing utilized:

1. standardized achievement tests
2. process tests
3. informal reading inventories
4. formative evaluation methods (Hallahan & Kauffman, 1988, p. 109)

Since academic learning problems are one of the major characteristics of children with learning disabilities, the standardized achievement test is one of the major ways children are assessed. There are many general achievement tests such as the California Achievement Test and the Iowa Test of

Basic Skills. There are also standardized tests of math and reading achievement. The important aspect of these tests is how the results are used. Some standardized tests permit an analysis of just where students are deficient.

Another approach in the assessment of children with learning disabilities is process testing in which psychological processes are evaluated and then appropriate remediation is planned. Linguistic and perceptual processing are the most frequent abilities assessed. The underlying assumption is remediation of the basic processing problem rather than the specific academic deficiency—i.e., the perceptual processing problem is evaluated, not just reading deficiencies. The two most commonly used process tests are the Illinois Test of Psycholinguistic Abilities (ITPA) (Kirk, McCarthy, & Kirk, 1961, 1968) and the Marianne Frostig Developmental Test of Visual Perception (FDTVT) (Frostig, Lefever, & Whittlesey, 1964).

The ITPA assesses three modes of processing: visual, auditory, motor and vocal channels of receiving information; abilities to internally manipulate concepts and linguistic information and to express or transmit information; and the ability to think symbolically as well as habitually (automatically). These three modes—communication, psycholinguistic process, and organizational levels—are tested in the ITPA through twelve subtests (Kirk, McCarthy, & Kirk, 1961, 1968).

The FDTVP assesses five areas of visual perception: eye-hand coordination (the child must draw figures within certain boundaries and guidelines), figure-ground (tests in perceiving complex figure-ground configurations), shape constancy (a series of geometric shapes is presented in different contexts and the ability to perceive is assessed), perceived figures (tests in perceiving different spatial positions and in perceiving shapes in reversal form), and finally spatial relationships (the child must copy a variety of lines and forms). The DTVP results are aimed at locating a child's specific perceptual deficit or deficits (Frostig, Lefever, & Whittlesey, 1964).

Another evaluative approach is for the teacher to use an informal test of the children's reading skills. An informal reading inventory (IRI) is a test made up by the individual teacher. It may include having the children read either passages or lists of words. The children are then asked questions about what they have read. Each child is assessed on the ease or difficulty in completing these reading tasks.

Formative evaluation methods are being used more and more by teachers. In formative evaluation approaches, the teacher does the assessment, and the material assessed directly relates to the student's classroom curriculum and performance. The teacher takes several measures of the student's performance within a two- to three-week period of time. Also as part of formative evaluation, the teacher sets instructional and educational goals for the child and uses the formative evaluation results to make shifts in instructional strategies for the particular student being evaluated. These approaches have an advantage in that they are related specifically to the child's performance in the classroom as opposed to performance on more general achievement tests. Also, the child's performance can be compared more readily to other students in the class and in the school. Formative approaches include assessment of the student on several occasions as opposed to a "one-shot" approach represented by standardized achievement tests (Hallahan & Kauffman, 1988).

Characteristics

The literature is full of numerous descriptors of children with learning disabilities. Clements (1966) reviewed the literature and identified the ten most often cited characteristics:

1. Hyperactivity
2. Perceptual-motor skills
3. Emotional lability (frequent shifts in emotional mood)
4. General coordination deficits
5. Disorders of attention (short attention span, distractibility, perseveration)
6. Impulsivity
7. Disorders of memory and thinking
8. Specific academic problems (reading, arithmetic, writing, spelling)
9. Disorders of speech and hearing
10. Equivocal neurological signs and electroencephalographic (EEG) irregularities (Hallahan & Kauffman, p. 113)

Coordination Abnormalities, Perceptual and Perceptual-Motor Problems

Children with learning disabilities will more often have problems with the organization and interpretation of visual stimuli than children who read on an average or above average level. These children also have problems with auditory perception, although auditory problems are not as prevalent. Learning disabled children do not always have auditory problems or visual problems that are associated with difficulty in reading, and vice versa.

Children who are learning disabled tend to have problems with both fine and gross motor skills. They have been described as being "all thumbs."

Hyperactivity is a somewhat pervasive problem for children with learning disabilities. The estimates of the prevalence of hyperactivity in children with learning disabilities range from between 80 percent (highest estimate) to 33 percent (lowest estimate).

Attention problems are closely associated with hyperactivity and they will frequently be parallel problems. Indeed, research has noted that attention deficits are more generic than hyperkinesis and are a primary difficulty for hyperkinetic children.

Hallahan and Kauffman (1988) note three kinds of attention problems: (a) focusing attention—getting around to attending to tasks presented to the student—difficulty sorting out the important factors to which they should be giving their attention; (b) making decisions—impulsively choosing the first or second alternative and not being able to consider all alternatives before making a decision; and (c) keeping on task—attention wanes at a faster rate through longer tasks than with nondisabled children.

Problems with Memory and Thinking Processes

Children with learning disabilities often have problems with remembering both visual and auditory stimuli. These children may have only one or two means for remembering information, and lack methods and conventions for remembering items that nondisabled children have in their repertory. Poor verbal memory may be due to poor skill in language which would make recalling auditory information more difficult.

Thinking

Thinking in this context is defined as problem-solving ability and the capacity to conceptualize. An important aspect of thinking is metacognition which includes two parts: knowledge of what methods and abilities are necessary to undertake a task successfully, and the capacity to self-monitor during a task to determine how performing the task is progressing, shifting strategies in process as needed during the performance of the task when problems arise (Baker, 1982). Metacognition breaks down into metalistening, metamemory, and metacomprehension. Learning disabled children have problems in each of these areas.

Adjustment to Social Situations

Evaluations by peers, teachers, and parents seem to affirm that children with learning disabilities have problems relating socially and are less often chosen by nondisabled peers as friends. In addition to problems relating to others socially, learning disabled students tend to have greater shifts in their moods which makes it more difficult to relate to them. The learning disabled child tends to have a negative self-concept in terms of the ability to perform academically. The extent to which this negative self-concept pervades all aspects of the learning disabled child's daily life is unclear.

The child with learning disabilities seems to have difficulty empathizing with others, tends to be less attentive in social interactions, and tends to be a poorer communicator of thoughts and feelings. One study noted that learning disabled children tend to have very little direct eye contact during social interchanges, which was perceived as a negative mannerism and tended to "put others off" in social interactions (Byran, Sherman, & Fisher, 1980).

Motivational Problems

Students with learning disabilities tend to feel that they are passive in their worlds and are more "done unto" than masters of their own fates. They tend to lack the feeling that they could succeed at tasks and tend to take it too personally when they could not perform academically. There seems to be a pervasive feeling of learned helplessness (Seligman, 1975) on the part of many learning disabled children which means they tend to throw in the towel too quickly in the face of difficult tasks. Thus, they do not have faith in their own abilities.

There is hope for this inactive learner, however. Research has shown that the learning disabled student can be instructed in effective metacognitive methods (Hallahan & Kauffman, 1988).

Problems in Academic Achievement

Were there no identified academic achievement problems, there would be no such thing as a student with learning disabilities. Some have problems in all academic areas, others in only one.

Problems with Spoken Language

Spoken language problems fall into five components: phonology (ability to break down sounds and combine them to make words), grammar or syntax (following the fixed rules of language usage), morphology (the way words are changed by the addition or deletion of some part of the word), semantics (the meaning of language) and pragmatics (the understanding of how to use language in social interactions). Learning disabled children have been found to have more problems in these areas of spoken language than nondisabled children.

Problems with Reading

Teachers of children with learning disabilities spend more time on reading than other subjects. Most reading problems relate to the previously noted problems with spoken language (specifically semantics, morphology, syntax, and phonology).

The three most often used descriptors for children with reading problems are dyslexic, remedial reader, and corrective reader. The term *dyslexia* has medical origins and overtones. Generally, dyslexia implies severe reading problems that may be due to neurological difficulties and will require intensive remediation.

The term *remedial reader* is more associated with education than with medicine. Children who are remedial readers have problems with reading comprehension, speed, accuracy, and fluency. Students with learning disabilities who have reading problems will have problems similar to those who are termed remedial readers.

The term *corrective reading* is also an educational term. Students who are corrective readers have less intense problems with reading but will also have problems with comprehension, speed, accuracy, and fluency (Hallahan, Kauffman, & Lloyd, 1985).

Problems with Written Language

Often students with learning disabilities have problems with written language (handwriting, spelling, and composition). Learning disabled students may be slow writers and their handwriting may often be unreadable. Good spelling requires that one know the relationship between sounds (phonemes) and written letters (graphemes). This ability is not well developed in children with learning disabilities.

Problems with Mathematics

There is increasing attention to students with learning disabilities who have problems with mathematics. These problems stem in part from problems with reading and attention deficits. This may explain why many learning disabled students have particular trouble solving story mathematical problems. Additionally, some children with learning disabilities seem to have problems in applying correct problem-solving methods to mathematical problems.

Treatment Strategies

There are seven main categories of educational treatment utilized with learning disabled children. These are: "Process training, multisensory approaches, structure and stimulus reduction, medication, cognitive training, behavior modification, and direct instruction" (Hallahan & Kauffman, 1988, p. 129).

Process Training

The underlying concept with process training is to remediate the cognitive processing problems associated with the academic learning problem. If a child has problems with reading, and process testing reveals a perceptual motor problem, then the child is given specific stages of perceptual motor drills and tasks (not tasks related specifically to reading). Process training takes into account the child's strengths and weaknesses in planning remediation strategies. Hallahan and Kauffman (1988) report that the research thus far does not support the effectiveness of process training for remediating learning disabilities.

Aptitude-treatment intervention (ATI) is a related form of process training. ATI utilizes both the child's strengths and weaknesses in planning remediation. The basic premise of ATI is to identify the method best suited to each child vis-à-vis particular learning strengths or weaknesses.

Art is especially helpful for children who have perceptual-learning disabilities because perception is a learned behavior (Lerner, 1972; McFee, 1972) and a great deal of art focuses on perceptual development. Children with perceptual-learning problems may see only total configurations (gestalts) and not parts of items. Other children may have trouble with part-whole perception and have problems seeing gestalts, seeing instead only parts of objects. Both abilities are necessary. A child who does not see total wholes may color parts of objects instead of the whole thing. For example, a shirt may have one sleeve at the fold colored green and the rest of the sleeve colored blue (Lerner, 1972).

Children also may have trouble with figure-ground differentiation and may not be able to distinguish an object from its background. In discussing artwork, the art teacher or art therapist may need to emphasize those parts that are background and those parts that are figures.

When children have trouble with visual closure, they cannot identify an item when part of it is missing. Starter sheets described in Chapter 7, can assist with this problem. Three-dimensional artwork may help children who have problems with spatial relationships and with seeing an item surrounded by space. The abilities to visually identify an object (object recognition) and to distinguish one object from another by sight (visual discrimination) can be helped by many art activities. An example of such art activities is the texture sequence described in Chapter 7.

Visualization is the capacity to remember what has been seen and touched and to see it with the mind's eye. Visualization is a very important and complex perceptual ability. Many basic drawing and painting activities based on memory of either immediate past events (this morning's field trip) or several months ago (last summer's activities) can help the child to visualize. Visually expressing what the child plans to do in the future also helps the child visualize.

Multisensory approaches

Multisensory approaches are similar to process training except that remediation involves academic tasks not underlying process tasks and more than one sense is always involved in the treatment. The standard approach was advocated by Fernald. His Visual Auditory Kinesthetic and Tactile (VAKT) strategy is the prototype of multisensory approaches (Fernald, 1943). This

VAKT approach means that the teacher would show the child a word, say the word and have the child repeat it, and then have the child touch the word and trace it.

In art instruction it is easy to implement a multisensory approach. It may be helpful to use both verbal and visual demonstrations of the art activities that children are to undertake. At times, it may be important to combine as many as four senses in presenting an art lesson. For example, in presenting a lesson on basic geometric shapes, the teacher can visually present the various shapes and play a shape identification game with the children in which the children must verbally identify various geometric shapes as they are held up. Next, the children can tactually explore cardboard shapes and identify them while they are hidden in a bag. Finally, the children can form these shapes with their bodies.

There is a note of caution with this multisensory approach. Sometimes using several sensory channels for instruction may provide an overload of stimuli for some learning disabled children.

Structured and Stimulus Reduction Approaches

Structured and stimulus reduction strategies are used with learning disabled children who are hyperactive and have attention problems. This approach involves a teacher-directed structured strategy because these hyperactive and easily distracted children are not able to make decisions independently unless specifically taught to do so. A part of this program is the reduction of stimulation from the classroom environs, including limited displays, closed bookshelves, study carrels, opaque windows, soundproofing and carpeting to reduce distracting auditory stimuli. Finally, teaching materials can be highlighted by use of intense or bright colors to help attract and hold the child's attention.

Hyperactive children may need more active learning experiences and/or times when they can be moving around the art room. In this situation, establishing specific rules and maintaining a consistent structure will help. Hyperactive children are easily distracted, and a classroom environment that is free from a lot of distracting and changing stimuli may be necessary. This means that the art room with its often changing visual environment and many, many visual stimuli can contribute to a child's distractibility. The art teacher and art therapist must be sensitive to this potential problem and alter the visual environs accordingly.

During an art lesson there may be a need to separate the easily distractible children and put them into learning carrels or seating that has fewer distractions, especially during the working part of the art experiences.

Hypoactive children may need to do some active learning before getting down to the art task. Perhaps having these slower-moving children stand for a while during the start of the lesson or having them do some related movement activities can help (*Insights*, 1976).

Drugs

There is a lot of debate and controversy over the use of drugs to control overactive behaviors of children with learning disabilities. Ritalin is one drug that has been used to reduce hyperactivity. One concern is that drugs can become addictive and can be used as an excuse for good teaching. Children on drugs need to be carefully monitored because there are often side effects.

Cognitive Training

Cognitive training involves changes in the individual's inner or covert thoughts. This approach, which was developed by Meichenbaum (Meichenbaum & Goodman, 1971), is becoming increasingly accepted and used as an intervention strategy. The strategy emphasizes self-involvement of the children in a self-instructional mode and as such can assist the children to surmount their learning helplessness and passive approach to learning. It also provides some specific learning approaches for problem solving. Finally, cognitive training seems especially appropriate for children with hyperactivity and distractibility difficulties. Cognitive training also has been termed cognitive behavior modification, or metacognitive strategy instruction.

Three major techniques in the cognitive training approach are self-instruction, self-monitoring, and reciprocal teaching. In self-instruction, instruction is first modeled by an adult and the adult talks through the task. Next the child models this same behavior. Then the child repeats the task while whispering the instructions and finally repeats the task while saying the instructions silently.

This approach lends itself quite readily to much of the way art activities are presented. The teacher or therapist demonstrates the art activity and verbally explains the steps involved. The children can be asked then to model the behavior, first whispering the steps involved and finally saying the steps involved to themselves.

When children are engaged in self-monitoring, they keep track of whether they are staying on task and performing particular behaviors. An example of how this approach is taught is as follows. A child is given a task and is placed near a tape recorder that has random tones placed at random intervals on it. When not paying attention, the child hears the tone and records this on a sheet. Keeping track of how much the child is paying attention empowers the learner with the perception of being in more control of attending behaviors.

Rosal (1985a, 1985b, 1986, 1987) found cognitive art therapy to be a viable treatment for children with learning disabilities, behavior problems and poor self-control. Chapter 3 includes a discussion of cognitive approaches to art therapy with children.

Reciprocal Teaching

Reciprocal teaching has as its focus the metacognitive skills for reading comprehension. Its major component has the teacher structuring the instruction and then gradually giving more and more responsibility to the student for the actual instruction.

Behavior Modification

Behavior modification has been discussed at some length in the section on children with mental retardation. It has been found to be useful in working with learning disabled children when they are placed on a token economy and given actual rewards for specific attending behaviors.

The art teacher and/or the art therapist should check to see if any of the students with learning disabilities are on a special behavior modification program. For behavior modification to be effective the entire treatment team should consistently use the rewards that have been established. Additionally, behavior modification can be used in the art room to reinforce appropriate social as well as artistic behaviors. The special classroom teacher can assist in planning such a system of positive reinforcement for the learning disabled child.

Direct Instruction

In direct instruction the focus is on the material to be taught and a logical analysis of the concepts rather than emphasizing the child's particular learning problems. It does share some of the basic tenets of behavior modification such as rewarding correct responses.

As noted above, a preschool child's ability (or inability) to count and to identify colors, shapes, numbers, and letters, and lack of mastery of other preacademic skills can be an indicator of future learning problems. Art programs are inclusive of many of these so-called preacademic skills and can be easily geared to provide reinforcement of skills (and direct instruction) in these areas.

Microcomputers

Microcomputers are being used in the educational programs of learning disabled children. There are several distinct advantages to the use of microcomputers including that they are noncritical of errors in performance; they provide individualized programs and permit the child to proceed at her own pace; they may include game formats for learning; and they have infinite patience (Kirk & Gallagher, 1986).

Game Strategies

Many art concepts can be presented in a game format. An example of a game that has been used is texo, in which a series of texture cards each with a different type of texture are used to play a game very similar to dominos. Another game includes a series of descriptors of physical characteristics. Players are divided into teams and draw five descriptors to go with a body part. The descriptors include words such as *courageous, prickly, vibrant.* The team then draws a person with the body part having the descriptors they have drawn. The game encourages visualization abilities and cooperation (Cardinale & Anderson, 1979).

Another game that encourages visual memory and spatial relationship is played like *Concentration.* The difference is that the configurations that players must match are pairs of art reproduction postcards.

Placement

Most often children with learning disabilities spend most of their day in the regular classroom and part of the day in a resource room. The major goal is for the children to spend as much of their time in the regular classroom as possible. This regular classroom placement depends on how proficient the regular teacher is in dealing with special needs students.

Teaching Hints

Care should be taken to insure instructional tasks are matched to the level of learning disabled students. Since children with learning disabilities are of normal intelligence, there may be a tendency to gear instructional tasks to this level—but because of the learning disabled students' learning problems, they may not be functioning at normal levels in many instructional areas.

Directions given to students with learning disabilities need to be presented in an extremely clear way. Often these students may appear to understand directions when they do not. One way of checking whether a student understands directions is to have the child repeat back to you, in different words, the directions you have given.

There may be a need to separate the easily distractible children and put them into learning carrels or seating that has fewer distractions. The teacher may want to reduce visual and auditory stimuli around these children.

These children may exhibit behavior and emotional problems, and these need to be addressed in much the same way as the problems of children who are identified as emotionally disturbed.

The child with learning disabilities may easily grasp many cognitive concepts but may need extra help and practice with fundamental skills such as cutting paper and pounding nails. Art can provide some of the basic remediation in these areas.

Some children with learning disabilities may have problems with laterality; this means they shift hand preference by sometimes using the right hand, sometimes the left. A choice of handedness should be made and consistently reinforced by the teacher.

Some children may have problems with sequencing and visual and/or auditory memory. Art can reinforce sequencing abilities because many art activities require following instructional steps in a specific order.

Socially poor development in children with learning disabilities usually means that they have a negative self-image and their body concepts are poorly developed (Harris, 1963). The art experiences in Chapter 7 are all designed to assist the child with building a positive body image.

Because many children with learning disabilities tend to be passive learners, they may have trouble working independently and will need encouragement and situations in art where they must work on their own. Finally, children with social development problems need a clear distinction between the real world and the world of fantasy. Since art can often deal with the imagined or with fantasy, it will help to continually underscore what things are imagined and what things are a part of the real world.

Some children with learning disabilities may have a perseveration problem. Perseveration means that the child dwells conceptually or physically on one task or subject and cannot shift without help from the teacher. Perseveration needs to be stopped and the child's attention shifted to something else.

It is important to remember that children with learning disabilities may frustrate easily. It helps to provide some choices and limits within which the child can work in an art activity.

There are many, many learning problems which children with learning disabilities may have. Such children must each be treated on an individual basis. The art teacher and art therapist must be sensitively attuned to the specifics of each child's learning disability. This will mean spending time consulting with the classroom or resource teacher and spending time looking in files before planning specific art experiences and adaptations.

It also will be important to be aware of which treatment approach or approaches are being used for each learning disabled child who enters the art room. Art experiences can be tailored to parallel the treatment approaches being used in the child's special Individualized Education Program.

Summary

Two approaches to identifying children with learning disabilities are developmental and academic. A child with developmental learning disabilities will have problems with her ability to perceive, attend, remember, think, express and understand language. There will also be problems in perceptual motor development. A child with academic learning disabilities will have problems in reading, spelling, writing and math. Learning disabilities are identified when performance in school falls below normal expectations and the child is neither mentally retarded nor has serious behavioral, visual or hearing problems. Forty-three percent of all children identified as having a disability are learning disabled. There are three major causes: biological and organic, environmental and genetic. Most evidence points to genetic and environmental causes. Learning disabilities are identified by standardized achievement measures (California Achievement Test or the Iowa Test of Basic Skills), process testing (Illinois Test of Psycholinguistic Abilities, Frostig Developmental Test of Visual Perception), informal reading assessment, and formal evaluation (specifically tailored to a particular student and done over a period of several days with repeated measures).

The child with learning disabilities may exhibit one or more of the following characteristics: hyperactivity, perceptual motor problems, frequent mood shifts, lack of motor coordination, short attention span/easily distracted/perseverated, impulsive, problems with memory and thinking, problems with reading, math, writing, spelling, speech and hearing problems, abnormal neurological patterns, social problems (unpopular with classmates), and learned helplessness.

Treatment methods include: process training (perceptual motor drills including art), multisensory methods (several senses called on for task completion—art activities may be important methods, as art most often involves at least two senses), structure and stimulus reduction (teacher-directed tasks and a class environs in which few distractors are present), drugs, cognitive training (self-instruction, self-monitoring and reciprocal teaching), behavior modification (token economies and positive rewards for attending behaviors), direct instruction, and microcomputers (noncritical of mistakes, individualized instruction enables the child to work at her own pace).

Teaching strategies include matching the level of learning to the ability of the student (which may vary depending on the subject and learning involved), clear directions (having student verbally repeat directions can help her understanding of tasks), separating easily distracted students using carrels, reducing the audio and visual stimuli, making extra help available for motor tasks. The teacher should also encourage the child to use the same hand for most tasks—i.e., encouraging consistent use of either the left or right hand. It will also help to provide many positive learning opportunities that result in high degrees of success which in turn can build positive self-attitudes. Perseveration should be interrupted and limits and limited choices in learning activities should be provided. It will be important to be aware of each child's specific learning disability. Finally, it will help to synchronize teaching and treatment methods with those used by other teachers who instruct the same child.

The Art Program

In addition to applying the aforementioned teaching strategies to the art program, it will be important to provide opportunities for mastery (that is, successful mastery of skills as opposed to frustrating tasks that are difficult to master) with art materials which in turn can build positive self-concepts. Art can aid in learning sequencing and teaching independent learning skills. Art experiences, because of their inherently individualized nature, can be tailored to fit the specific strengths of each child. Often art can provide an ongoing successful experience of great value to a child with learning disabilities who may rarely encounter such success in other subjects.

CHILDREN WITH BEHAVIOR DISORDERS/EMOTIONAL DISTURBANCE

The terms used for this disability are in transition and there is a general lack of agreement on an accurate definition and/or description of children with behavior problems. This is due in part to the several treatment approaches used with these children which have origins in differing theoretical positions. The situation is further complicated because there is a lack of a precise, economical and easily utilized assessment tool that can discriminate between children who have behavior problems and those who do not. Also, environmental and sociocultural influences impact differently on children, which further complicates the assessment process.

With these issues in mind, the definitions included in PL 94-142 will be used.

(i) the term ("Seriously emotionally disturbed") means a condition exhibiting one or more of the following characteristics over a long period of time and to a marked extent which adversely affects educational performance:
    (A) An inability to learn which cannot be explained by intellectual, sensory, or health factors;
    (B) An inability to build or maintain satisfactory relationships with peers and teachers;
    (C) Inappropriate types of behavior or feelings under normal circumstances;
    (D) A generally pervasive mood of unhappiness or depression; or

(E) A tendency to develop physical symptoms or fears associated with persons or school problems.

(ii) The term includes children who are schizophrenic *or autistic.* (Later this group was placed under the category "other health impaired.") The term does not include children who are socially maladjusted unless it is determined that they are seriously emotionally disturbed. (*Federal Register,* August 23, 1977, p. 42478)

In the IDEA of 1990 the term "autism" was taken out of this definition and is now considered a separate disability category. Because there is a moratorium on regulations, no definition for "autism" has been developed (PL 101-476).

One aspect that this definition lacks is the inclusion of children who do not have problems with schoolwork or problems generally exhibited in school—that is, some children only exhibit problem behaviors outside of the classroom (Morse, 1985).

In attempts to classify children with behavior disorders, the systems used would ideally be consistent over time, could be used by a number of different persons with consistent results, and the classification would remain constant under differing circumstances. However, this just is not the case.

While it might be helpful to be able to link the causes of emotional disturbance and behavior disorders to specific cases, there is no firm evidence that this can be done (Kauffman, 1985). Also, classifying according to legal definitions is problematic because these terms have different meanings in different legal jurisdictions. Attempts at adapting adult classifications of psychiatric and psychological disorders have also been lacking because they have not taken into account the issue of appropriateness of behaviors at differing ages—that is, developmental issues and age-appropriate behaviors.

Four Clusters of Problem Behaviors

One way of handling the definition issues and the difficulties in describing children with behavior problems is through a statistical analysis of all available descriptors used in the research literature. In 1979, Quay did this and was able to identify four major groupings of problem behaviors. This analysis was further confirmed with research relying on ratings of children's behaviors by parents and teachers as well as life histories of children and children's own responses to questionnaires (Hallahan & Kauffman, 1988). These four clusters identified children who had conduct disorders, those who were anxious and withdrawn, those who were immature, and those who were socially aggressive.

Conduct Disorder

Conduct disorders include descriptors such as disobedience, possessiveness, outspokenness, and destructiveness. Life reviews of persons with conduct disorders reveal problems with authority and inordinate guilt feelings. When responding to questionnaire items, children who had conduct disorders reveal pictures of children who do just as they please, who are generally mistrustful of others, and who generally consider themselves "tough" (Hallahan & Kauffman, 1988).

There also was a tendency for children with conduct disorders to be hyperactive. Hyperactivity does tend to disappear with age, but children who are impulsive and antisocial will not outgrow this and will have problems in adulthood. There is a tendency for problems to run in families and go from one generation to another.

Anxious/Withdrawn

Children characterized as being anxious and withdrawn report they have strong inferiority feelings, are self-conscious, depressed, and anxious, and feel sad and guilty (Hallahan & Kauffman, 1988). They are also characterized as being dependent and sensitive, have an excessive shyness or timidity, and are reclusive. The children with these characteristics tend to have families who are overly protective and who are from above average socioeconomic levels. They tend to remain in tight control of feelings, desires, and impulses no matter where they are or in what environment they find themselves. Rigidity and lack of spontaneous behaviors are typical. There is a learned helplessness or victim stance that characterizes the world view of these children. Low self-esteem in these children makes it especially difficult for them to deal with failure in school or in social situations, and it adds to poor academic performance. The children tend to have a chronic anxiety stemming often from stressful home environments in which there is little or no warmth or accepting, loving responses from parents. One outcome of ongoing anxiety is depression and resultant self-destructive tendencies (Kirk & Gallagher, 1986).

Immature

The immaturity category is characterized by children who have problems attending to tasks, are clumsy or passive, daydream, prefer playmates younger than themselves, and exhibit other general behaviors expected of children who are chronologically younger (Hallahan & Kauffman, 1988). Children who are immature tend to be slothful, have attention problems, are slow, and lack interest in school. Their behaviors are similar to children who are autistic.

Socially Aggressive

Children who are characterized as socially aggressive are those who tend to associate with antisocial children and are active in groups with histories and current reputations of delinquency. Belligerent and destructive behaviors that result in lawbreaking are also typical behaviors.

Prevalence

Since 1986 the U.S. Department of Education has noted that children who are behavior disordered and/or emotionally disturbed represent a " 'traditionally underserved' category of special education students whose needs are particularly complex" (Hallahan & Kauffman, 1988, p. 170). Currently, only about one percent of the school-age population in the United States has been singled out as having serious emotional disturbance—however, other very conservative studies estimate that the actual figure worldwide falls somewhere between six and ten percent. The ratio of boys to girls in this group is five to one.

A recent study conducted by the Bank Street College of Education (*Education of the Handicapped,* 1990) reports that only 10 to 30 percent of students with behavior disorders/emotional disturbance have been identified by the public schools and the services offered by schools are often inadequate. The researchers concluded that thousands of students with behavior disorders are not receiving the services they deserve.

The problem is compounded because in some schools (public schools in Northern California, for example), students with behavior disorders cannot receive special education services because, in order to receive proper services and special education, these students must be labeled as learners with "serious emotional disturbance." School psychologists are faced with a dilemma for students who do have behavior disorders cannot receive services if they are given this label. Only students with "serious emotional disturbance" can be served. Therefore many learners are continuing in the school system without receiving the special education they need (C. Arrington, personal communication, July 11, 1991).

Students classified as juvenile delinquents complicate the prevalence picture. It is estimated that about three percent of the school age children are involved in a juvenile court every year. Some experts feel that all children who are juvenile delinquents should also be classified as having behavior disorders/emotional disturbance (Murphy, 1986). Other experts prefer the classification of children with social maladjustment (not serious behavior disorders) as an appropriate descriptor for these students who have problems with the law.

Causes

There is rarely only one single cause for behavior problems. It is impor-

tant to understand that one or more of four key components contributen to behavior disordered/emotionally disturbed children. The idea of "contributing
factors" is helpful in understanding both the causes and the ways that behavior problems can be remediated (Hallahan & Kauffman, 1988, p. 171).
The four major factors are biological, familial, cultural, and school related.

Two major conceptual models represent two ends of a continuum in terms
of the relative importance of determining the causes of emotional disturbance.
In the psychoanalytical model there is great importance in determining the
root cause of the child's problem, because, unless the root of the problem is
uncovered and dispensed with, the child will simply continue the behaviors
or may drop one inappropriate behavior and substitute another. Therefore,
treating the superficial behaviors does not really deal with the problem. At the
other end of the continuum is the behavioral model in which dealing with
the immediate problem behavior is the primary treatment method in which
behavior disorders are treated. The behavior model focuses on manipulating the child's environment to change the child's problem behaviors. If this
approach does work, then spending time on eliminating the underlying
roots or root causes of the problem behaviors will not be an important aspect
of the treatment.

In reality, no one conceptual model (psychodynamic, behavioral, or
developmental) has met with sufficient success in dealing with problem
children to warrant total adherence to the exclusion of the others.

Biological Factors

Biological factors include genetic, neurological or biochemical components or some mixture of these. For those children classified as having
moderate or mild behavior problems there is no clear link between biological factors and their behavior. On the other hand, there is some evidence
that points to a link between biological factors and children having severe
and profound behavior problems (i.e., psychosis and/or schizophrenia).
Genetic factors are related to schizophrenia, and neurological impairments
are prevalent in children who are autistic and/or psychotic.

Familial Factors

It is not clear from the empirical studies exactly how family factors impact
on children's behavior problems. Some psychoanalytic theorists posit that
all emotional problems stem primarily from the early years of life and from
the interactions between child and mother. Hallahan and Kauffman (1988)
state that empirical evidence has not borne this theory out. There is a
complex interaction between problem children and their parents, and each
influences the other.

There are many ways to be effective parents. Good parenting involves being sensitive to the needs of the child; providing positive rewards for appropriate behaviors which include encouragement, praise and attention; and love-pervasive ways of dealing with inappropriate behaviors. Delinquent and aggressive children are the products of homes in which parents are inconsistent in discipline, hostile, rejecting and generally cruel to the child. Parents with histories of unlawful behaviors or those who are generally violent often have children who are delinquent. Additionally, children who come from abusive family situations are at risk for having emotional disturbance.

Cultural Factors

There are numerous cultural factors that influence behavior. The core family culture and the larger community and school cultures have sets of expectations which can conflict with one another. Threat of war, terrorism and the amount of violence in the media all have been shown to influence behavior. In one interesting study researchers found that disturbed children thought violence on television was real. Another study reported that disturbed children were more likely to engage in belligerent acts as a result of experiencing television violence (Spraftkin, Gadow, and Dussault, 1986). Other cultural influences on behavior include alcohol and drug use, teenage suicides, teenage pregnancy, and the high incidence of teenage runaways and violence in the schools.

The school is itself a subculture, and there are many potential situations in which a child can end up in trouble. Teachers may be insensitive to problems children might have. Negative behaviors can be rewarded via undue attention to them. Children can be radicalized due to violence that exists in ever-increasing levels in schools. Peer pressure can have negative influences on children. Withdrawn children can be totally ignored. Children have behavior problems that can interfere with their being able to conform to school rules and being able to learn and have meaningful learning experiences. Children who exhibit inappropriate or negative behaviors often receive negative responses from classmates and adults (Kauffman, 1986).

There are some obvious causes of behavioral problems. Being poor, under- or malnourished, neglected, abused, having a family in conflict and school failure are all contributors to behaviorally disordered/emotionally disturbed factors. Early intervention can help, especially when one realizes that negative behaviors from children elicit negative behaviors from peers and teachers. Intervention programs that have been effective include teaching specific social skills, such as how to interact with peers (how to compliment another), role playing, how to solve problems, teaching children to be less impulsive in actions—to think before they act (Weissberg and Allen, 1986).

Approaches to the Identification
of Children with Behavior Problems

Children who exhibit conduct disorders (are disruptive and act out) are the ones most often identified as having behavior problems, and the child who is withdrawn and anxious is less likely to be identified. Additionally, some children do not exhibit behavior problems in the classroom and thus may not be identified by their teachers as having serious problems. Finally, younger children are not as easily identified as having behavior problems (Hallahan & Kauffman, 1988).

There are five major categories of tests and screening instruments that are in use to identify children with behavior problems. These are interviews, behavior observation, behavior checklists, objective tests and projective tests. The Thematic Apperception Test (TAT) and the Rorschach Ink Blot Test (RIBT) and sentence completion tests are examples of projective tests. The person tested is presented with stimuli (visual, verbal) that are unclear or ambiguous in an effort to detect the individual's perceptions and underlying emotional content and needs. The tests require very skilled and well-trained clinicians to administer and to interpret them. Examples of objective tests are the Coopersmith Self-Esteem Inventory (Coopersmith, 1968), the Piers-Harris Children's Self-Concept Scale (Piers & Harris, 1969) and the Tennessee Self-Concept Scale (Fitts, 1971). These are paper and pencil tests that necessitate the individual's ability to read and to give honest responses. The answers are compared to those of children and adults who have been identified as having emotional disturbances.

Examples of behavior checklists would be the Quay-Patterson Behavior Problem Check List or the Walker Problem Behavior Identification Check Lists. These rely on parents or teachers to observe and identify specific key behaviors. The checklists necessitate accurate observations and consensus of what are understood to be key behaviors. Checklists do not take into account behavior intensity or frequency (Hallahan & Kauffman, 1988).

The McKinney SCAN (Feagans & McKinney, 1981) is an example of a behavior observation tool. With the Mckinney SCAN the child's behaviors are recorded in the classroom. The child's behaviors outside of school are not taken into account. Also, a large sampling of behaviors is necessary to achieve a diagnosis and there is no benchmark or preestablished group of behaviors against which current observations are compared.

The Vineland Social Maturity Scale is an example of an interview tool. The Vineland relies on information obtained from parents. The interview is based on a preestablished group of questions, and the skill of the interviewer is directly related to the usefulness of the information obtained (Kirk & Gallagher, 1986).

Intelligence Issues

It is a myth that children with behavior problems are bright or above average in intelligence. The reality is that the majority of children with behavior problems are slow learners or have mild mental retardation. There is some evidence that the intelligence tests themselves are biased and tend to result in lower scores for children with emotional disturbance. Most children with behavior problems, while capable of achievement at the same level as their nondisabled age group, are often underachievers.

Those children with severe or profound emotional disturbance or behavior disorders often lack even the most basic of academic skills and cannot read or do math. Many also lack adequate self-help skills and have difficulty even feeding and dressing themselves.

Peer Acceptance

The child with behavior disorders/emotional disturbance is not usually accepted or liked by his peer group. This is especially true of children who are aggressive and act out. This group is characterized by children who tease, yell, hit, fight, exhort, destroy, cry, and generally do not comply with adult requests. Sometimes these children are termed hyperactive or characterized as having brain damage. Some of these children also have been termed sociopathic due to their tendency to inflict pain or hurt on others without having any sense of doing something wrong. These children are scolded so often that punishment has little or no impact on them. The issue is not just the behavior of the child but the interaction of this behavior with the behavior of the others which the child encounters.

Aggression as a Learned Behavior

There is a growing body of research to support the idea that aggressive behavior is learned (Bandura, 1973; Patterson, 1982; Patterson, Reid, Jones & Conger, 1975). Children learn by seeing-/modeling the behaviors of others. When they see aggressive behaviors exhibited by others who are admired or have a high status or do not get punished for the aggressive behavior, the other children will perceive aggression as a behavior with positive outcomes. If children are able to rationalize the aggressive behaviors, such as by detaching themselves from the victim and not considering the victim as human, they are more likely to exhibit belligerent behaviors. Under some circumstances punishment can even reinforce aggressive behaviors. This is especially true when the punishment is inconsistent or not carried out immediately or when the child perceives he can inflict further aggression through counterattacking the punisher—or when there is no positive counterpart to the aggressive negative behaviors being exhibited.

Research does not support the notion that one should just let the children act out their aggressive behaviors. Rather, social learning theorists and behavior researchers advocate offering models of nonaggressive reactions to aggressive behavior, offering positive reinforcers for passive (nonaggressive) behavior, giving the child opportunities to rehearse nonaggressive responses and offering punishment that is not aggressive in nature such as offering a time-out room or socially separating the child from others for a short time.

A child who has serious aggressive behaviors has a problem that should not be underestimated. Such a child is most likely to continue to have problems throughout his lifetime—and may have real difficulty completing school, holding a job, and staying out of jail or off the police rolls.

Externalizing/Internalizing Characteristics

Another way to describe behavior problems in children is to characterize them as externalizing or internalizing characteristics. Those who show external traits are characterized by traits similar to conduct disorders and socialized aggression. The traits of immaturity and anxiety/withdrawal are internalizing characteristics. The traits of conduct disorder, withdrawal, immaturity, and socialized aggression are not discrete categories, and children may have characteristics from several of these general groupings.

Extreme cases of internalizing behaviors are child schizophrenia and infantile autism. The immature withdrawn child has few friends, rarely interacts or plays with age peers, and just does not have the social skills necessary to enjoy himself and others and to have fun. The result is that this child often withdraws into daydreams or fantasies. Frequently, this child invents ways of avoiding participation in typical daily activities. The child also demands continual attention and assistance. Or the child may appear depressed with no obvious cause.

Some will plead illness to avoid participation, and others regress to more immature behaviors to avoid active involvement in daily activities and human interactions. While there are many ways of explaining withdrawn behaviors, the social learning perspective has the most hard data support (Kauffman, 1985).

Social learning approaches attribute causes of withdrawn behaviors to poor environmental factors including overcontrolling parents, rewards for inappropriate social responses, and few, if any, opportunities to learn and practice skills appropriate for social interactions. Research supports the notion that children can be taught the social skills they lack by providing practice for these skills, by showing models of appropriate social interaction and by offering positive rewards for more appropriate social behavior.

Depression is now recognized as a serious problem for children and youth. Indicators of depression include dramatic weight loss or gain, sleep disturbances (either too sleepy or not able to sleep), extremes of energy levels (too little or too much activity), feeling constantly tired, not able to enjoy life or have fun, low self-esteem and feelings of being worthless, inability to concentrate, no motivation, a pessimistic outlook on life, avoidance of social interactions, bed-wetting, encopresis, fear of school, school failure, suicide talk, and attempts. Suicide is now among the leading causes of death in children and youth, and there is a real link between depression and suicide attempts. Depression can be caused by external factors such as divorce, peer rejection, abusive home life, and the death of a family member or some other person significant to the child. There also may be a physiological cause of depression, and medication can be helpful if there is a biological basis for the problem. There has been some success in treating depression using the social learning model in which children are taught special skills in how to socially interact, how to control their own behaviors and how to have a more positive self-perception.

Children with Severe and Profound Emotional Disturbance

While there is disagreement about some of the labels for children with extreme disturbances, two terms frequently used are schizophrenia and autism or early infantile autism. Schizophrenia generally means that an individual has a loss of contact with the real world, has bizarre thinking processes and excessive inappropriate behaviors. The autistic person (this condition is also sometimes referred to as early infantile autism) is extremely withdrawn socially, engages in self-stimulation, and had language problems and thinking disorders which appeared prior to 2½ years of age. Schizophrenia does not appear until a child is five years of age and often shows up in later childhood or during the adolescent years.

Other general characteristics of children who are severely and profoundly disturbed include the lack of basic dressing, feeding and toileting skills. They are unable to communicate and are often erroneously thought to be deaf or blind because they seem to be totally unaware of what is happening around them. They fail to respond to noises or lights in the usual way. The general impression is that these children do not seem to be able to comprehend events in their daily environs.

Many extremely disturbed children cannot be given intelligence tests, or if they can, their scores fall in the range of children with mental retardation. Some exhibit characteristics of the idiot savant and appear quite gifted in selective areas such as memory or mathematics, but they cannot apply this ability to other daily tasks.

The child with severe emotional disturbance seems unable to respond to significant others as people but rather as physical objects. He seems unable to give or receive physical affection.

Some of these children have no expressive speech or seem unable to understand others' spoken words. Echolalia, which is a parroting of what someone says, is also common in these children as is mistaken use of pronouns and spoken gibberish as well as strange-sounding voice quality.

Self-stimulatory behaviors such as thumb sucking, head beating, twirling objects, and patting some part of the body are common in these children. These behaviors are very difficult to extinguish and those who hit themselves, scratch or scrape themselves must be put into restraints to prevent them from inflicting self-injury. Finally, these children may be very aggressive and have intense temper tantrums which can be very harmful to themselves and others.

The outlook is not good for treatment of children with severe and profound emotional disturbance unless very early intervention occurs. Research has shown that with intensive treatment consisting of 40 hours or more of one-to-one instruction per week that begins prior to the child's reaching 3½ years of age, about half of these autistic children may recover completely (Lovos, 1982). Autistic children who receive less intensive treatment begun after they are 3½ years old will most likely be psychotic adults.

Treatment Approaches

Finally, the severity of the behavior problems is also an important issue in designing treatment programs for children. Those children with mild or moderate behavior problems (neurotic) are those whose behaviors can be handled effectively by teachers and parents with assistance from mental health specialists. Children with severe and profound disturbance (psychotic or autistic) are those who need intense and long-term intervention in special classes or residential facilities.

There are several different educational approaches utilized in the education of children with behavior disorders/emotional disturbance. These will be discussed only briefly here.

Psychoanalytical Approach

In this approach which is based on a medical model, the child is perceived as having problems with his origins in the imbalance of the dynamic portions of the mind (the id, ego and superego). The focus in treatment and education is to reveal the underlying pathology and thus to ameliorate the child's psychological functions and his behaviors and achievements. Thus, in a classroom with this approach the teacher would have a very open and permissive atmosphere in which the child feels safe enough to act out his impulses no matter how inappropriate they may be. The teacher is assisted by therapists who work with the child and his family, and their aim is to bring to light the hidden mental conflicts. There is not an emphasis on attempting to change the child's behaviors or on academic instruction in this approach.

Behavioral Approach

The behavioral approach is based on the assumption that all behavior is learned (Ullman and Krasner, 1969). Children with behavior problems therefore have learned inappropriate behaviors. What is learned can be unlearned or modified, provided the appropriate rewards are included. The key intervention is based on careful measurement of the child's inappropriate behaviors and careful manipulation of the responses to these behaviors to produce changes.

According to behavioral approaches, there are two basic types of learned responses (conditioning): respondent (classical) and operant. In classical conditioning, responses (respondents) are learned by their preceding stimuli. For example, a child may be presented with a loud noise (something already causing a right response in the child) paired with a red tulip. After doing this a number of times, the red tulip is presented without the noise and the child gives the same frightened response. The fear reaction can be changed by presenting the red tulip along with a pleasurable stimuli (something the child really likes). This is done a little at a time and at a distance at first. Gradually, the child is encouraged to move closer and closer until he is desensitized and no longer gives a frightened response.

Operant conditioning (learning) is based on the premise that a person's actions are a function of his consequences. For example, to get a child to stop talking without raising his hand, the child is not recognized or attended to unless his hand is raised. Therefore, his attempts at getting attention are not rewarded (reinforced). Behavior that is inappropriate is analyzed, including the events that are rewarding this behavior. The environs and events that are rewarding the inappropriate behavior are reordered so that the rewards no longer affect the child's behavior.

Sometimes the child is placed on a specific reward system called a token economy. In this arrangement, the child is given points or some other token for an appropriate response and behavior. At the end of the period or lesson, the child is told specifically when and how his behavior was appropriate, and his points are added up. These points can then be turned in for other rewards, such as toys or snacks at the end of the day.

Psychoeducational approach

This approach combines some aspects of the psychoanalytical approach and also attempts to modify inappropriate behaviors and to attain educational goals. It acknowledges psychoanalytic origins for much of the child's behaviors but also concerns itself with changing the child's external problem behavior.

More specifically, the psychoeducational approach is concerned with why a child does something (similar to the psychodynamic strategy) and what the child is doing (similar to the behavior modification approach). The psychoeducational strategy aims at breaking the frustration/failure cycle that a child with behavior disorders may have as he fails to measure up to school expectations. These are expectations in terms of classroom behavior and academic performance and the consequent nonacceptance the child receives from peers and teachers. To intervene, it is important to consider the expectations and pressures on the child and his coping skills in the situation. Key factors in the intervention program are also the child's relationships with peers and the teacher, his motivation for the inappropriate behavior, and his self-image.

The teacher has at least four ways of coping with the child's inappropriate behavior. The teacher can reorder the learning situation to prevent disruptions. Certain behaviors can be permitted at certain appropriate times, such as on the playground. The teacher can tolerate some of the inappropriate behavior until the child can gain self-control. It is important that the child be told after control is gained that his behavior is expected to improve. Finally, the teacher may also choose to interrupt a behavior when one or more children are endangered or the class is totally disrupted (Long & Newman, 1965; Long, Morse & Newman, 1980). The arts often play a central role in educational programming in the psychoeducational approach (Hallahan and Kauffman, 1988).

Humanistic Approach

Beginning with Maslow (1962) and Rogers (1969), this approach was also called the open educational approach or movement. The focus in this approach is to have children get in touch with their own feelings and to help them to obtain emotional pleasure from learning. Also, children are encouraged to be self-directed and to self-monitor feelings and emotions. In the humanistic approach the teacher and the child work as a team in the learning encounter.

Ecological Approach

This approach considers the interaction of the child with the environment. The goal is to alter the environs sufficiently so as to facilitate more desirable behaviors in the child that will continue long after the intervention stops. This approach considers the child's family, neighborhood and the community as important factors in the treatment and intervention.

Combined Approaches

Current thinking in the area of treating disturbed children focuses on a combination of factors that cause a child to modify his behavior. One approach called cognitive psychology has seemed successful. In this approach there are four components which are a blend of learning and developmental approaches. These include monitoring one's own behaviors, self-talk or self-instruction where one teaches/talks oneself through a problem, self-evaluating one's behaviors or performance and self-stroking or reinforcing the performance or behavior through compliments or self-rewards.

Educational Considerations

The child with severe and profound emotional disturbance requires very intense and individual instruction. There is a trend toward the deinstitutionalization of this group of children. Hallahan and Kauffman (1988) recommend a behavioral modification approach in teaching these youngsters.

For children and young persons with moderate and mild emotional disturbance, basic academic skills are essential to the curriculum. Basic social skills and communication are not just learned incidentally by this group of students; the curriculum must actively teach these skills as well as the academic basics.

The Mainstreamed Child with Emotional Disturbance/ Behavior Disorders and the Art Program

The mainstreamed child will need special attention to manage his behaviors. The art teacher and art therapist will need to consult closely with the special education teacher and the other mental health professionals involved with that child to insure consistent follow-through on the discipline and classroom management techniques that the regular teacher is using. Additionally, the art teacher and art therapist should set specific behavior limits and clearly communicate these early to the child.

The emphasis should be on appropriate and consistent outcomes for behavior. Both positive and desirable behaviors should be noted and rewarded immediately by use of praise and social approval. Undesirable behaviors should be ignored or negatively rewarded—heavy punishment should be avoided as it can have the effect of rewarding the inappropriate behaviors. The focus should be on public approval of desirable behaviors and private correction of negative behaviors.

Realistic expectations about the child and his artistic and academic behaviors are important and necessary. Tasks should be planned with the child's abilities in mind and the work should not be either too easy or too hard for the child to accomplish. Expectations of behaviors should be done as clearly and firmly as possible and the child should always know what is expected of him and the consequences of inappropriate behaviors. This is true whether the child is alone or in a group.

The art therapist and art teacher should be sensitive to factors in the disturbed child's world that have contributed to his problems and whether specific factors can be identified. If these factors can be pinpointed, then some attention toward dealing with them might be centered in the classroom. For example, a child with a highly critical parent at home may benefit from lots of encouragement in the art room.

A consistent routine will be important in terms of getting ready, presenting the activity, working, sharing time, and cleaning up. It may be helpful to provide choices so that unnecessary power plays with authority are eliminated. Setting up specific limits may help the child know where he stands. Using a game format for some of the art activities can also help motivate children and set some of these limits (Morse, 1976; Cardinale & Anderson, 1979). The classroom teacher can help in determining some of these boundaries. The learning encounter itself can provide structure. For example, the teacher may establish a working policy in which everyone tries the activity or picks one of several choices. Just sitting quietly and watching might be one of the choices. It will be important to accept the child's efforts and to provide, at least at the start of the term, brief lessons with a high success factor.

Good work habits and efforts should be encouraged and praised. Not reacting at all to poor efforts may be best. The focus should be on rewarding best efforts and withholding reinforcement of poorer efforts. This is a more constructive approach than punishing a child for poor use of materials or an apathetic response. Such negative attention can become a positive reinforcement to the child, who thus may continue the inappropriate behavior.

Teachers and therapists need to be aware of the low frustration tolerance and short attention spans that many children with behavior disorders have. A second activity can be planned for those with attention problems. For many it will be important to provide a positive outlet for feelings, and such expression should be encouraged. Until the child's limits and abilities are apparent, whatever attempts are made should be accepted.

It will be important to encourage cooperation and sharing of materials.

Group work can build social skills. However, there may also be problems in having children working in groups. Groups need to be carefully chosen.

The art therapist has many treatment options that she can use with a particular child, including psychoanalytic, developmental, adaptive and cognitive. Chapter 3 provides a brief overview of approaches to art therapy with children.

The very nature of the artistic process can be a source of therapy and healing. This happens in the classroom or wherever the child produces art. The teacher should be aware of this therapeutic treatment aspect of art. He must also be aware that specific art therapeutic treatment is **not** his responsibility. Such responsibility rests with the professionally qualified art therapist. (The exception would be that unique individual who is trained and certified as both a teacher and a therapist.)

Summary

Children with Mild and Moderate
Behavior Disorders Emotional Disturbance

There are four clusters of problem behaviors: conduct disorders (hyperactivity, disobedience, outspokenness, destructiveness, possessiveness, disrespectfulness to authority and distrustfulness of others); anxious/withdrawn (depression, self-consciousness, feelings of inferiority, dependence, sensitivity, timidity, reclusion, highly controlled feelings, rigidity, learned helplessness, victim stance, poor academics and self-destructiveness); socially aggressive (truancy, delinquency, petty thievery, belligerence); and immaturity (clumsiness, passivity, short attention, slow learning in completing tasks, preference for younger age children as friends, lack of interest in school).

One percent of the school age group has behavior disorders and there are five times more boys as girls in this category. There is no one cause but four contributing factors: biological (genetic, neurological, biochemical); familial (abrasive parents, unlawful parents, inconsistency in disciplining children); cultural (violence in environs, drug and alcohol use in subcultures, teenage suicide, pregnancy, runaways); and school related (violence in schools, drug use in schools and nonsupportive teachers).

Identifying the child with behavioral disorders can be done through screening and testing (behavior checklists, interviews, objective tests, projective tests and behavior observations). Additional indicators include learners who are below average in intelligence and those who underachieve in school. The child with behavioral disorders may not be liked by peers, may be sociopathic and amoral.

There are internal and external characteristics associated with behavior

disordered children. Internal characteristics include immaturity, introspectiveness, depression, avoidant personalities, and infantile autism (an extreme
example). External characteristics include social aggressiveness, outspokenness,
disrespectfulness, truancy, and belligerence.

Treatment of Children with Mild or Moderate
Behavior Disorders and Emotional Disturbance

There are two major models utilized: the medical model (psychoanalytical
approaches) and the educational model (behavioral approaches). In the
psychoanalytic approach within the classroom there is a very open and
permissive atmosphere. There is no direct attempt to change behaviors or to
provide academic instruction. The focus is on uncovering underlying causes
of behavior problems. In the behavior approach it is believed that children
have learned their inappropriate behaviors. These behaviors are analyzed
and the consequences (rewards) for displaying these behaviors are noted and
changed. Token economies are implemented.

Under the general behavioral approaches there are four categories:
psychoeducational, which combines some aspects of the psychoanalytic and
the behavioral approach; humanistic, which involves a team of the teacher
and the child who work toward greater self-directed behaviors on the part of
the child; ecological approach in which the interaction of the child and his
environs is important and these environs are altered to enhance more
desired behaviors; and the combined approach which focuses on cognitive
psychology involving monitoring behaviors, self-talk, self-evaluation and
self-reinforcement.

Teaching Strategies

The educational focus is on basic academic skills as well as direct instruction
in basic social skills and communication. All teachers and school personnel
that interact with the child must be a part of a team so that there is consistency in handling problem behaviors. Positive and desirable behaviors need
immediate rewards and praise while negative behaviors may be ignored.
This strategy may be summed up by public approval for good/appropriate
behaviors and private correction of inappropriate behaviors.

Realistic expectations of what the child can do will help as well as
individualization of tasks whenever possible. An awareness of specific contributing factors to the child's behavior problems may help create a better
learning situation for the child.

Art Strategies

In addition to those noted above, art approaches may need to be structured
with clear detailing of expected behaviors and consequences for inappropri-

ate behaviors. Consistency is important and includes a regular class routine. Game formats for instruction may be particularly motivating. Activities with a high success factor will be important. The focus should be on rewarding best efforts and withholding reinforcement of poorer efforts. Group work and cooperation as well as sharing of abilities on group projects can foster better social interaction in these children.

Children with Severe/Profound Emotional Disturbance

Included in this group are those children with early infantile autism prior to 2½ years of age and schizophrenia which may appear after five years of age or not until adolescence. Early infantile autism is characterized by being withdrawn, out of contact with the real world, a tendency to self-stimulatory behaviors, and language and thinking problems.

Both groups of children have problems with self-help skills, toileting, feeding, and they fail to respond to noises and lights. It may be impossible to test their intelligence. These children are unable to give or receive affection and may lack speech or the ability to understand others. They may have intense temper tantrums and may speak in jibberish or exhibit echolalia.

The treatment of children with severe and profound emotional disturbance focuses on intense and long-term special classes. The educational focus is on a concentrated individual approach and a behavioral modification approach is advocated. Many may be housed in a residential facility.

An art program for children with severe and profound emotional disturbance will focus primarily on awareness activities and pre-art experiences. If the child develops beyond the scribbling stage of artistic development, it will be possible for him to engage in art experiences more typical of children functioning at more developed artistic levels (such as the preschematic, schematic, or even the gang age).

CHILDREN WITH PHYSICAL DISABILITIES

Children with physical disabilities are a large heterogeneous group who have physical problems (excluding primary visual or auditory disabilities) that interfere with learning or participation in regular school classes and whose disabilities require special equipment, training, or materials. Because of the medical and health problems of these children, a team approach is used that includes medical personnel and special educators (Hallahan & Kauffman, 1988).

Again, we turn to the *Federal Register* for the legal definition of physical disabilities and health impairments (PL 94-142 now IDEA).

"Orthopedically Impaired" means having a severe orthopedic impairment. The term includes an impairment caused by a congenital anomaly (e.g., clubfoot, absence of some member, etc.), an impairment caused by disease (e.g., poliomyelitis, bone tuberculosis), and an impairment from any other cause (e.g., cerebral palsy, amputations, and fractures or burns which cause contractures). (*Federal Register,* August 4, 1982, p. 33846)

In the general category of physical disabilities we will also include part of the *Federal Register* definition of "other health impaired." Under "other health impaired" the federal definition includes

Limited strength, vitality or alertness, due to chronic or acute health problems such as a heart condition, tuberculosis, rheumatic fever, nephritis, asthma, sickle cell anemia, hemophilia, epilepsy, lead poisoning, leukemia, or diabetes." (*Federal Register,* August 4, 1982, p. 33847)

This group of "other health impairments" will be included in our discussion of children with physical disabilities. The term "traumatic brain injury" has been removed from this definition and made a separate category of disability in the IDEA of 1990 (PL 101-476, the reauthorization bill for PL 94-142). As noted elsewhere in this chapter, the regulations for the IDEA have not been developed due to a moratorium on all regulations. In the absence of regulations providing a definition of "traumatic brain injury", this category will not be discussed.

Children may be born with physical disabilities (congenital anomalies) or develop these disabilities as a result of accidents or diseases after birth.

Screening

Naturally, most physical problems are identified well before children enter school. Medical staff are the ones most often involved in determining these conditions. However, unless parents are sensitive observers of their children, some medical problems can be overlooked. The other adult who has the most contact with children is the classroom teacher. It is this adult who is often the one to note physical problems. For example, a parent or teacher may note a child staring which might indicate petit mal seizures. Teachers are also the ones who are most likely to accurately report effects of medication on health conditions such as seizures or hyperactivity.

Incidence

Approximately 0.5 percent of the school-age population are physically disabled. Of this number, about half or 100,000 have cerebral palsy and half have other health impairments that necessitate special education. Recent figures from the U.S. Department of Education (1986) suggest that there are three major categories under which students with physical disabilities are being provided with special education: about 59,000 are classified as orthopedically disabled, 69,000 are classified as "other health impaired," and 72,000 are grouped as multi-disabled. The overall number of students with physical disabilities is increasing. This is due to improvements in medical treatment permitting longer life spans for many with chronic health problems.

For our purposes children with physical disabilities will be discussed in four groupings: neurological impairments, musculoskeletal problems, congenital malformations, and other physically disabling conditions.

Children with Neurological Impairments

Damage to the brain or spinal cord—i.e., the central nervous system—is one of the more common causes of physical disabilities in children. Brain damage may be very localized (focal) or very diffuse. Those with brain damage may exhibit many problem behaviors including retardation, perceptual or learning problems, emotional problems, and speech and language problems as well as uncoordinated motor behaviors and attention deficits. Also, a child with brain damage may have paralysis and/or seizures.

Children who have spinal cord damage may lose feeling or control in their extremities and be unable to move parts of the body. Whatever the particular cause of the nervous system damage, weak muscles and/or paralysis is most often one of the symptoms (Hallahan & Kauffman, 1988).

Cerebral Palsy

Cerebral palsy can develop as a result of damage to the brain during its development in the womb or during the birth of the baby. Also, any disease or infection to the mother can cause brain damage to the developing fetus. Lack of oxygen to the fetal brain is one of the main causes of cerebral palsy. Other plausible causes of cerebral palsy include poisoning, bleeding in the cerebral region, or direct brain trauma. In about 40 percent of the cases the actual cause of cerebral palsy is unknown (Batshaw & Perret, 1986).

Cerebral palsy and other motor paralysis can be grouped according to the extent of the involvement of the body. If either half of the right or left side of the body is affected, the condition is termed hemiplegia and accounts for about 35 to 40 percent of the cerebral palsy cases (Denhoff, 1976). In 10 to 20 percent of the cases the legs are affected more than the arms, and this condition is termed diplegia. If all four limbs are affected the condition is termed quadriplegia and accounts for 15 to 20 percent of the cases. Finally, if only the legs are affected the condition is called paraplegia and accounts for 10 to 20 percent of the cases (Denhoff, 1976).

Another way of classifying types of cerebral palsy is according to type of brain damage and the resulting type of motor disability. The three groupings are pyramidal (spastic), extrapyramidal (choreoathetoid, rigid, and atonic), and mixed. In the pyramidal type, the damage is to the motor cortex or the pyramidal tract of the brain. And the result is stiff, tense muscles and voluntary movement that is inaccurate. Spasticity occurs in about half of the cases of cerebral palsy. In the extrapyramidal type the brain damage occurs outside of the pyramidal tract. The resulting motor behaviors are described as quick movements that are involuntary. There is difficulty in maintaining posture (choreoathetoid). Also, there may be atonic (muscle tone that is floppy) or rigid muscles (stiffness or rigidity that is malleable). This condition occurs in about 25 percent of the cerebral palsy cases. In the mixed type, which accounts for about 25 percent of the cases of cerebral palsy, the damage occurs in both the pyramidal and extrapyramidal parts of the brain. The individual with this type has a mixture of motor effects which may be manifested as spasticity in the arms and rigidity in the legs—or vice versa (Hallahan & Kauffman, 1988).

Batshaw and Perret (1986) report that about 0.15 percent of the child population have cerebral palsy. Also, more white than black and more male than female children have the disability.

There is a multi-disabling condition associated with many who have cerebral palsy. A large number of children with the condition also have impairments in hearing, vision, perception, speech, mental processing, and behaviors—or some combination of these impairments. Children with cerebral palsy also may drool and have contorted facial conditions. While some children with this condition have above average intelligence, Hallahan and Kauffman (1988) report that the average intelligence scores of these children is below the norm. The educational implications for children with cerebral palsy include a team approach with specialists to assist the several disabilities which many with cerebral palsy exhibit.

Seizure Disorders

When an abnormal discharge of electrical energy occurs in certain brain cells, the result is a seizure with the effect being involuntary motion of limbs and/or strange sensory phenomena. Interestingly, seizures seem to occur before six years of age or in old age. Seizures are commonly due to lack of oxygen or low blood sugar. Physical trauma and infection can also cause seizures. There are two main types of seizures: generalized and partial. As the terms indicate, the generalized seizure occurs in a large part of the brain, and the partial seizure involves only a small part of the brain. Epilepsy is related to repeated seizures and occurs in 0.5 percent of the population in general. Seizures may last for several minutes or only a few seconds and may occur only one time a year or every minute or so. Many things can trigger a seizure. Triggers may be predictable stimuli or totally unrelated to the external environs. There may be minor motor movements such as a twitch in the face or major convulsions. High fever, poison, or trauma may cause a seizure, but often the cause is unknown. Drugs can totally or partially control seizures. About half the children who have epilepsy have normal or average intelligence. Also, children with epilepsy who are not mentally retarded tend to have a larger than average incidence of learning problems. Children with epilepsy tend to have a greater than average number of behavior and emotional problems (Hallahan & Kauffman, 1988).

In grand mal epilepsy, there is sometimes a warning (aura) that a seizure is coming. This aura may be in the form of strange sounds, visual phenomena, or an internal feeling. Initially, there is a tonic phase to the seizure in which muscles are rigid and then a clonic stage where there are jerky muscular convulsions. This clonic stage lasts about three minutes and then the child falls into a deep sleep. Often, grand mal epilepsy is controlled by medication. This medication can slow the child's other responses and thinking processes.

Teachers and art therapists should know specifically how to deal with a child who has a major epileptic seizure. When a child has a seizure, it is important to remain calm and be sure that the child lies on one side and that the tongue has not been swallowed. Sometimes it may help to hold the child to avoid injury to the head or other parts of the body during the clonic phase. It will be important to explain to the other children in the class that the child is just temporarily ill. The child should rest after the seizure, and parents and medical staff should be notified.

In petit mal epilepsy, there is a brief unconscious seizure stage that lasts only a few seconds. The child's head may nod and eyes blink. Children who have petit mal attacks often outgrow them (Anderson, 1978). Children who have brief seizures may need to have instructional information repeated and may need more time to complete educational tasks.

Spina Bifida

During early development of the fetus the bony spinal column fails to close resulting in a congenital midline defect. The defect can occur anywhere along the spinal column from the head to the tailbone. With an open spinal column the nerves are exposed, and the result may be paralysis or loss of function or sensation below the site of the defect. One condition often associated with spina bifida is lack of bladder and bowel control. Surgery can correct the defect in many cases and is performed in early infancy.

Often the head is enlarged in cases of spina bifida because of pressure caused by cerebrospinal fluid. This condition is termed hydrocephalus. While hydrocephalus is associated with mental retardation, the condition in spina bifida alone does not cause retardation.

Multiple Sclerosis

Multiple sclerosis does not manifest itself until adolescence and adulthood. Multiple sclerosis is a disease that affects the central nervous system, and the protective cover of certain nerves is scarred or hardened. Many accompanying sensory problems are associated with the disease including problems with vision, muscle weakness, speech problems, spastic movements, emotional problems, and walking problems. The cause is unknown and the disease gets progressively worse. Also, there are periodic remissions or periods when the symptoms are in remission.

There are other neurological impairments that are caused by heredity and rare diseases. Accidents also cause neurological impairment. One neurological problem caused by disease has been practically eliminated due to a medical vaccine—poliomyelitis. However, polio does occasionally occur in isolated areas where children fail to receive the vaccination (Hallahan & Kauffman, 1988).

Children with Musculoskeletal Conditions

Musculoskeletal conditions are physical disabilities that can occur due to muscle or bone disease or defects. Musculoskeletal conditions include amputation and burns that can result in amputation or decrease of the muscles. Arthritis, muscular dystrophy, and scoliosis are examples of musculoskeletal conditions. Most children with musculoskeletal conditions have problems with mobility and motor control that result in problems walking, standing, sitting, or hand use. Musculoskeletal conditions can be caused prenatally or by disease or accidents after birth (Kirk & Gallagher, 1986; Hallahan & Kauffman, 1988).

Children who have musculoskeletal conditions caused by injuries may have an even more difficult time accepting the status quo. There is a period of mourning over the lost ability, and the degree to which the child can cope depends on many factors including prior coping patterns, family support, and the importance of the ability that has been lost (Heinemann & Shontz, 1984). Additionally, the physical appearance of children with musculoskeletal conditions causes considerable emotional/social discomfort and can interfere with peer interactions and developing friendships.

Kirk and Gallagher (1986) note that there are twelve steps in the adjustment to a physical handicap: "shock, anxiety, bargaining, denial, mourning, depression, withdrawal, internalized anger, externalized aggression, acknowledgement, acceptance, and adjustment" (pp. 471–472).

Among other things, supportive adults and family can help the child deal with the reality of the disability. Achieving some sense of control over the disability as well as acquiring new skills or mastery can be helpful in the child's acceptance of the disability.

Muscular Dystrophy

One of the most common of the muscular and skeletal problems is muscular dystrophy. Children whose muscles are weakening or progressively deteriorating caused by neurological damage or nerve degeneration have a condition termed atrophy. When the muscle weakness or wasting away is not caused by neurological impairment or disease, the condition is termed myopathy. When the condition is progressive myopathy and caused by heredity, it is termed dystrophy. Muscular dystrophy is a disease with a hereditary cause that has the characteristic of progressively weaker muscle fibers. There are two types of muscular dystrophy. One type (pseudohypertrophic or Duchenne form) is limited to males. In this condition the muscles atrophy and are replaced by fat tissue. Rarely do those who have this form of muscular dystrophy live into adulthood. Children with the Duchenne form tend to have below average intelligence scores in the verbal area.

The other form of muscular dystrophy (facioscapulohumeral or Landouzy-Dejerine form) begins in adolescence and both males and females can contract the disease. In the facioscapulohumeral form, muscle weakness involves the upper body, the arms and shoulders, and the face. The disease progresses at a slower rate than pseudohypertrophic forms, and many live a normal length of life. Some are totally disabled (Hallahan & Kauffman, 1988).

Arthritis

Arthritis is the other major musculoskeletal condition. Arthritis is a general term for conditions associated with pain in and surrounding joints. Contrary to the stereotype, arthritis occurs in all ages including children. The most common form is rheumatoid arthritis, and the cause is unknown. Interestingly, there is a 0 to 80 percent remission rate in juveniles having rheumatoid arthritis. About 0.08 percent of persons under 17 years of age have this form of the disease (U.S. Department of Health, Education and Welfare, 1974). A larger number of females than males acquire the condition. Symptoms range from mild swelling to profoundly debilitating situations in which joints are deformed. Fever and problems with the heart, lungs and eyes can occur as the result of arthritis.

Osteoarthritis is the most frequent form of arthritis in children with disabilities. In osteoarthritis, cartilage surrounding a joint is affected, the available space between bones shrinks, and lubrication diminishes with the resulting movements becoming either impossible or very painful. When there is a dislocated joint, osteoarthritis may develop. Surgery can repair a dislocated joint and lower the danger of acquiring arthritis (Batshaw & Perret, 1986).

Other Conditions Affecting the Musculoskeletal System

There are other conditions affecting the musculoskeletal system including osteogenesis imperfecta, scoliosis, osteomyelitis, arthrogyposis, clubfoot, and Legg-Calve-Perthes disease. In osteogenesis imperfecta, bones are improperly formed and break very easily. In scoliosis the spine has an abnormal curve to it. With osteomyelitis the individual has a bacterial bone infection. In arthrogyposis the muscles in the limbs may be missing, smaller or weaker than normal. The child whose foot is turned at the ankle in the wrong angle has a clubfoot. With Legg-Calve-Perthes disease there is a flattening of the femur, hipbone, or head.

With musculoskeletal conditions the major aim is to make the educational experience as normal as possible and to assist the child with mobility. There may be periods in which the child is absent from school. The teacher must see to it that the child's education continues during out-of-school confinements (Hallahan & Kauffman, 1988).

Children with Congenital Malformations

While spina bifida is a congenital malformation, we have discussed that condition in the section on neurological impairment. Here we shall discuss defects of the heart and lungs and of the extremities. Defects that are congenital and those that are discovered in the first year affect about six percent of the population (Bigge & O'Donnell, 1977).

One common defect is congenital dislocation of the hip which occurs in 1.5 of every 1,000 births. Interestingly, females are eight times more likely to have the problem than are males (Hallahan & Kauffman, 1988).

Congenital malformations of the extremities include webbed feet and hands or partial arms and legs. Sometimes this is due to hereditary defects. Or it can be caused by chemical substances, viral infections, or radiation. These teratogens adversely affect parental chromosomes and thus normal prenatal development. One well-known teratogen is thalidomide. Thalidomide use by mothers resulted in babies who had very short or missing limbs or hands and feet directly attached to their bodies.

The most commonly used teratogenic drug is alcohol. Recent research has linked ethanol (alcohol used in spirits) to birth defects, mutations, and even cancer. A baby whose mother drank heavily during pregnancy may have fetal alcohol syndrome. Fetal alcohol syndrome or alcohol embropathy can result in retardation of the growth of brain cells, heart problems, facial anomalies, and hyperactivity (Wisniewski & Lupin, 1979).

Congenital defect of the head and face can cause damage to the brain, eyes, ears, mouth, and nose. Additionally, these craniofacial abnormalities may result in serious deformities of the facial features as well as visual, auditory, gastronomic, mental, and speech disabilities.

Children Disabled by Accidents and Other Physical Disabilities

Many children are disabled in a variety of accidents ranging from auto or vehicle accidents to poisoning, falling, and burning. Injuries of the spinal cord occur at a high rate in persons ages 15 to 24 (Rutledge & Dick, 1983).

There are other physical conditions that impact on a child's physical abilities. Among these are the following: cancer, rheumatic fever (occurring after scarlet fever or strep throat in which joints are swollen and inflamed — the fever can spread to the brain and heart), hemophilia (a condition inherited in which blood does not clot resulting in excessive bleeding internally when bruised and externally when bruised or cut), sickle cell anemia (a hereditary disease of the blood predominantly occurring in blacks in which blood cells are malformed and fail to circulate properly), nephrosis and nephritis (kidney diseases and disorders caused by infection, poisoning, burns, and accidents and other diseases), and diabetes.

Cystic fibrosis and asthma are sometimes grouped under a heading called cardiopulmonary conditions which also includes children with heart defects and circulation problems. Cystic fibrosis is an inherited chronic respiratory disease that causes problems in breathing and digestion. Asthma is a chronic respiratory disability resulting in difficulty in breathing, especially in exhalation. Children with breathing problems, heart defects, or circulatory problems may even have trouble walking from one class to another, and ordinary physical education activities are totally out of the question. Teachers should be aware of the child's lack of mobility and realize that children with these problems should have frequent rest periods. Also, key academic instruction must be scheduled to coincide with each child's peak energy period during the school day.

The most recent addition to this list of other physical disabilities is AIDS, which is a terminal viral illness that attacks the individual's natural immune system. It was estimated in 1987 that one million people in the United States had the infection which is transmitted primarily through sexual activity, intravenous drug use, and transfusions of contaminated blood. Church (1986) noted that children with the disease might have to be segregated in school because of the need to monitor any bodily secretion (other possible means by which the disease is transmitted) that might remain on food trays and toys. Additionally, some children exhibit uncontrolled biting and scratching behaviors which could result in the transmission of the disease.

Child Abuse and Neglect

Child abuse and negligence can result in physical disabilities. Abuse can be physical, emotional, or sexual. Physical abuse can result in permanent brain damage, internal injuries, deformed skeleton and faces, and impairment of the senses. Children may be abandoned for long periods of time, left unsupervised and thus unprotected at home. Children can also be neglected medically and nutritionally. They may not have appropriate clothing or shelter. Their emotional needs and their physical needs may be ignored.

Indicators of child abuse include: a child who appears fearful especially of parents, has repeated injuries or injuries that are not properly treated, seems malnourished, is poorly clothed for weather or climatic conditions, is aggressive or irritable, frequently cries, and tries to meet parent needs or to protect parents. Children with disabilities are at greater risk for abuse than their nondisabled peers. Because disabled children are less independent and less able to defend themselves, they can be easy targets for abuse (Hallahan & Kauffman, 1988). Deske (1987) reviewed the research on child abuse as it relates to art and art therapy, and concluded that art can be a major means of intervention for children who have been both physically and emotionally abused.

Personality Characteristics of Children with Physical Disabilities

Children with physical disabilities have as varied personalities and intellectual abilities as their nondisabled age-mates. Their school performances may vary due to longer than usual periods of absence caused by their particular physical problem. The key in the education and treatment of physically disabled children is in treating them like other children, accepting their disabilities as minor limitations to learning, and seeing beyond the disability to the person underneath (Hallahan & Kauffman, 1988).

Physically disabled children may also have a greater need for acceptance because they may be quite deformed. This is a vicious circle because these children may already have experienced frequent rejection due to their disability. These children will need experiences which help build positive self-images and body images. They will also need experiences which build their feeling of independence and enable them to work on their own with little help from others, especially from adults (Anderson, 1978).

There has been an increasing acceptance by the general public of persons with physical disabilities, and there has been an increase in hiring of persons with all kinds of disabilities (Satz, 1986). At the same time there remains prejudice and unacceptance—often in proportion to the severity of the disability or deformity (Hallahan & Kauffman, 1988).

Children with physical disabilities may have a greater degree of shyness and be less extroverted and more self-conscious than other children. The children probably live in a more restricted environment because of their disabilities. In addition, many families may be overprotective of their physically disabled members. Disabled children may have problems accepting their limited abilities, and there may be a gap between what they desire to accomplish and what they are realistically able to do. Their frustrations may show up in terms of verbally aggressive behaviors, regression to more childish modes of acting, and withdrawal into fantasy. It will be important to help these children set realistic immediate and long-term goals (Anderson, 1978).

Generally, children with disabilities have lower self-concepts. Harvey and Greenway (1984) noted this was generally true for children with physical disabilities and reported that these children had a lower sense of self-worth and a disintegrated view of themselves as compared with nondisabled children. Kirk and Gallagher (1986) also noted this general lower self-concept and self-esteem that individuals with physical disabilities have and that this seems to persist into adulthood.

Family Issues of Children with Physical Disabilities

There is great family stress—financial and psychological—when there is a physically disabled sibling. As much as 25 percent of a family's disposable income may be spent on the care of their disabled child (Hobbs, Perrin, Ireys, Moynahan & Shayne, 1984). Moreover, there is a great deal of guilt, and denial, on the part of parents. Families may totally indulge their disabled child—creating an extremely dependent or infantile person—or ignore the needs of their disabled child. Finding the right balance in caring for a disabled family member is a very difficult, stress-inducing issue.

Interestingly, children will react to their own disabilities in much the same way that their families do. There is a difficult period of adjustment which includes denial and the desire/fantasy to be "normal." However, most children do move to an acceptance of their situation with the help of concerned, caring adults.

Adaptive Devices

There are two major types of devices that can assist physically disabled individuals—a prosthesis and an orthosis. When a missing body part such as an arm, hand, or leg is replaced by an artificial one, it is called a prosthesis. When a specific function that is no longer present is replaced by an artificial device, it is called an orthosis. There are numerous other devices that are utilized to assist the disabled child in performing daily functions. Examples of these adaptations would be special handholds on cups and spoons, and special helmets that hold a wand or pointer that can be used to type or can be replaced by a pencil or brush so that the children can draw, write, or paint using their heads instead of their hands. Further examples of some of these adaptative devices can be found in Chapter 6. It is essential to realize that when at all possible (and pending medical approval), disabled children should be encouraged to make whatever use possible of their arms, legs, etc. Disuse of limbs can result in a quicker deterioration of muscles and limb function. This lack of total or partial reliance on prosthesis and orthosis can foster greater independence in the child as well (Hallahan & Kauffman, 1988).

High Technology and the Physically Disabled

In addition to adaptive devices such as prostheses and orthoses and simple adaptive tools, personal computers and other high technology have been instrumental in improving the quality of life of disabled individuals and in assisting them to live more normal lives. Even computer software that enables students to produce graphic images has contributed significantly to the normalization of physically disabled children. This software enables the user to draw a line with the touch of a key on the computer keyboard, thus eliminating the need for fine motor skills and permitting a child using only one finger or a mouth-held or helmet-held pointer to direct the lines of the drawing.

Instructional Issues

Much of the educational programming for children with physical disabilities is individualized. A lot of vicarious and firsthand experiences are important, as these children's disabilities may have precluded such encounters outside of school. This means that many have not been on field trips, ridden public transportation, gone out trick-or-treating, flown a kite, or made a snowman. Classroom experiences must take this fact into consideration and provide as near normal as possible these typical life experiences. It must also be realized that children with physical disabilities may be educationally behind their nondisabled classmates simply because they have not been able to personally experience much of the world.

In the education programs, emphasis is on developing self-sufficiency and on language and speech remediation. As much as possible, physically disabled children will be mainstreamed for at least part of their school day. Teachers must also realize that the education of children with physical disabilities will definitely be a team effort with physical therapists, speech therapists, psychologists, and other medical and instructional specialists being involved.

Another issue that must be faced with children with physical disabilities is that they may have shortened life spans. This is true for some forms of muscular dystrophy and with cancer, diabetes, and cystic fibrosis. This means that teachers and therapists must deal with grief, loss, and death issues personally, so that they can deal with these same issues with the children affected and with their classmates and parents.

Art therapists and teachers must have a real understanding of the child's disabilities including the medical aspects, limitations, and implications, and they should communicate these aspects to classmates. It is important to know precisely how to help a physically disabled child and when it is not appropriate to intervene. For example, picking up a child who keeps falling is not recommended (unless medical staff advise differently) because it can instill a sense of dependence in that child. It is also strongly recommended that whenever possible children should be encouraged to do their own work— even if it may take much longer as in the case of some art experiences because in so doing children build that important sense of mastery. New skills are acquired that can enhance self-esteem and build independence. Art experiences in which children have control and art skills which children can master result in an increased sense of control and empowerment—which is very important to children who may have a real sense of powerlessness in so many other areas of their lives.

Issues Related to Preschool Children with Physical Disabilities

Two major concerns for teachers of young preschool physically disabled children are early identification so that intervention can begin as soon as possible and the development of good communication between the children and adults. There are two other concerns that relate to both preschool physically disabled children and are also issues for physically disabled children who have developmental delays. These concerns are handling of the children (how they are to be lifted, held, carried and generally physically assisted) and positioning (offering support to the body and making instructional and play materials available). Muscle tone is affected by handling and positioning. Some children have spastic muscles and their limbs are in a flexed or extended position all the time. Without intervention to counter the flexed or extended muscles, the children may have long-lasting shortened muscles and connective tissue that cause further malformations and disabilities. This condition is called contractures. Other children have uncontrolled movement caused by fluctuating muscles and muscle tone. These children must have some restraint on their movement. Finally, some children have hypotonic muscles (weak and flaccid muscles). Children with hypotonic muscles may not learn how to hold their heads up, sit, or stand.

In handling and positioning, the key points which influence muscle tone in the extremities and control movement that is voluntary should be known. Special positioning equipment may be used and is easily adapted from existing pallets and from rubber pillows and blocks. The focus for preschool programs is on gross motor activities such as sitting, standing, walking, and head control. Fine motor skills including grasping and releasing, and self-help skills including feeding, dressing, and toileting are also primary foci of the instructional programming. These goals are in addition to other typical goals for preschool programs including social skill development, communication, and cognitive skills (Hallahan & Kauffman, 1988).

Issues Related to Art

In the art program, working closely with the special teacher and with each of the children is essential. Often the children are the best source of information about what can or cannot be accomplished and the best ways to arrange work areas. It will be important to develop an atmosphere of acceptance and a willingness to explore and try new processes. Unless the children have full use of their hands, art activities should be developed which do not require fine, detailed work.

Physical adaptations of art media may be required. For example, handles of drawing and painting tools may need to be thickened and shortened. A piece of foam rubber, rubber-banded to the handles, will probably thicken handles so they can be easily grasped. Paper should be taped down, and water containers and paint containers should be weighted so that they will not spill.

If it is medically permissible, it may be best to move the children from their wheelchairs and let them work on the floor. Children who cannot use their hands to hold art tools may use their feet or may be able to grasp art tools in their teeth. Sometimes art tools can be attached to a helmet for use.

Many children need large working areas. If they cannot be moved from their wheelchairs, large drawing boards can be clamped on their chairs.

With children who have osteogenesis imperfecta or hemophilia, it will be important to plan activities and arrange the class environment so that they do not bump or bruise themselves. Materials that require a lot of pounding (clay, hammers, and nails) and sharp tools should be avoided and adaptations developed. For example, glue may be used instead of nails in constructing activities. Children who have these conditions have a high rate of absenteeism due to medical treatment for broken bones and blood clotting. This high rate of absenteeism must be considered in planning appropriate art experiences for these children. This may mean it will be difficult to have the child engaged in art projects that take several weeks to complete.

Other specific adaptations are discussed in Chapter 6 and the art adaptations sections of Chapter 7.

Summary

Those persons with physical disabilities are defined as having severe orthopedic impairments due to disease, genetics, birth defects, amputations, fractures or burns, and other health impairments resulting in limited strength, vitality or alertness. Included in other health impairments are heart conditions, asthma, hemophilia, epilepsy, lead poisoning, diabetes, leukemia, nephritis, and rheumatic fever. Most physical problems are identified prior to formal schooling. Teachers also play a role in the identification of physical disabilities which a child may have.

Incidence

The incidence of physical disabilities is about 0.5 percent of school-age children. Of this number about half (100,000) have cerebral palsy. Special education provides services in three major groupings: 72,000 multi-disabled, 69,000 other health impaired, and 59,000 orthopedically disabled.

Major Groupings

There are four groupings of physical disabilities: neurological impairments, musculoskeletal conditions, congenital defects of lungs, heart and extremities, accidents and other physical disabilities. Neurological impairments are caused by brain or spinal cord damage. Brain damage may result in one or more of the following: retardation, learning or perceptual difficulties, emotional problems, speech and language problems, and motor and attention problems. Cerebral palsy is the largest group of neurological impairments caused by lack of oxygen to the fetal brain. Motor problems are major problems along with impairments in hearing, sight, speech and mental processing. Also included in the neurological impairment grouping are epilepsy, spinal bifida and multiple sclerosis.

Musculoskeletal conditions are physical disabilities occurring because of defects or disease in muscles or bones. Included in this grouping are: amputations, burns, arthritis, muscular dystrophy, scoliosis, osteogenesis imperfecta and clubfoot.

Congenital defects of lungs, heart and extremities include hip dislocation, congenital malformations such as webbed feet, malformations caused by viral infections, and drugs (including alcohol) taken by the mother during pregnancy. Cardiopulmonary conditions, cystic fibrosis and asthma are also included in this grouping.

Accidents and other causes include auto accidents, poisoning, falling, and burning. Other physical conditions impacting a child are cancer, scarlet fever, hemophilia, rheumatic fever, asthma, cystic fibrosis, diabetes, and kidney disease.

Child abuse and neglect can cause physical disabilities. Children who have physical disabilities are at greater risk for being abused than children without physical disabilities.

Familial and Psychological Issues

Children with physical disabilities have as varied personalities and intellectual abilities as any group of children. Acceptance of children who are quite deformed is an issue and rejection may occur. Self-esteem and positive self-concept are major issues that need to be addressed. The physically disabled child may have fewer broad life experiences because of her restricted environment. The child may have problems with accepting her limitations. Frustrations may appear in aggressive and/or abusive language as well as regression to younger, immature behaviors. Fantasy may be an escape for these children.

Children with physical disabilities place financial and psychological stress on their families. Families may be overprotective or overly indulgent of their disabled member. This can result in a very dependent or infantile child.

Adaptative devices such as a prosthesis can be developed to replace a missing limb or body part. An orthosis is a device specifically developed to replace a particular function that has been disabled or is missing. Additionally, there are many other types of adaptive devices that are used including special handholds on cups, spoons and pencils, and helmet devices that can hold writing and drawing tools. Computers and other high-technology devices are available to assist the disabled child in having a more normal life.

Educational Implications

The educational goal is to help the child have a schooling experience that is as normal as possible. Absenteeism is a major problem and provisions must be made for these school absences. Early intervention is essential for children with physical disabilities. Most programming is individualized. Since most physically disabled children have fewer real life experiences, many more firsthand experiences must be provided in the classroom. Educational programs focus on speech and language remediation, and self-sufficiency. Teachers will be a part of a team that includes physical therapists, speech pathologists, occupational therapists and psychologists. Teachers and therapists must be knowledgeable of each child's physical and medical limitations in planning instructional activities.

Art Programming

The art teacher or art therapist must work with the physically disabled child as a team. Together, the child and the adult will discover the best ways of setting up work stations and adapting art media and tools. Handles of tools and brushes may need to be thickened using foam rubber. Velcro may be used to assist the child in holding art tools and in anchoring paint, water and glue containers. Some children may need to have drawing boards fastened to their wheelchairs to provide a work surface. Projects requiring heavy pounding and strength (such as claywork, stapling and nailing) may not be appropriate, and the art activity may need to be amended. Children with frequent absenteeism may not benefit from art activities that may take several art periods to complete.

CHILDREN WITH HEARING IMPAIRMENTS

As with our discussion of the other major disabilities, here we shall use as our primary definition of hearing impairments the one included in Public Law 94-142 (now IDEA). In the provisions of this law there are two categories under the major descriptor of hearing impaired. These two categories are deaf and hard of hearing.

> "Deaf" means a hearing impairment which is so severe that the child is disabled in processing linguistic information through hearing, with or without amplification, which adversely affects educational performance.

> "Hard of hearing" means a hearing impairment, whether permanent or fluctuating, which adversely affects a child's educational performance but which is not included under the definition of "deaf" in this section. (*Federal Register* Aug. 4, 1982, p. 33845)

Special educators also use definitions that relate to the specific physiology and educational implications for a child with a hearing impairment. The physiological perspective focuses on the measured degree of loss of hearing. Deaf children are those who have a hearing loss of 90 decibels (db) (a decibel is an index of "relative loudness of sounds" [Hallahan & Kauffman, 1988, p. 269]). Hard-of-hearing individuals have a loss of less than 90 db. Normal hearing registers at zero decibels which is the level at which the slightest sound is heard.

Educational definitions involve the extent to which the loss of hearing affects one's ability to talk and one's capacity for language development.

According to the Executive Committee of the Conference of Educational Administrators Serving the Deaf (Brill, MacNeil, & Newman, 1986), a *deaf* person is one whose hearing loss does not permit language processing by means of hearing even with a hearing aid. A *hard-of-hearing* person is one who with the assistance of a hearing aid can process language by means of hearing.

There is a relationship of the age at which hearing loss occurs and the accompanying delay in language development. The later the hearing loss, the less disabled the individual is in language development. The following four terms are often used to describe types of deafness. Congenitally deaf individuals are born deaf, and adventitiously deaf persons are those whose deafness occurred some time later than birth. Prelingually deaf is a term that describes a child who is deaf from birth or who becomes deaf prior to language or speech development. Postlingually deaf describes a hearing loss that occurs after the individual has developed language and speech abilities.

Brill, MacNeil, & Newman (1986) have advocated a range of hearing thresholds related to the extent to which the loss affects speech and language. Mild hearing loss is 26 to 54 db, moderate hearing loss is 55 to 69 db, severe hearing loss is 70 to 89 db, and profound hearing loss is 90 db and higher. This definition cuts across educational and physiological perspectives. Hallahan and Kauffman (1988) feel it is important to classify individuals more on language ability than on the individual's loss of hearing level.

Incidence and Ways of Testing for Hearing Loss

About 0.17 percent of children from 2 years to 16 or 17 (high school seniors) have a hearing loss and are in special education programs. There is also an unidentified number of children with some hearing loss that could be helped through special education but who are not receiving these services (Hallahan & Kauffman, 1988).

Initial screening of children for hearing loss may occur in the classroom. This may be done by using a watch and having the child indicate when the ticking is heard and from which ear. Another test is to stand behind the child and quietly whisper a name or some other direction. If the child does not hear the ticking watch or the whispered words, then there is a high probability that the child may have a hearing loss. Hearing capacity is measured in three main ways: special testing for very young children or those who are difficult to test, pure tone audiometry, and speech audiometry. In testing for hearing capabilities and hearing loss, the audiologist tries to determine the intensity of sound (decibel is the unit of measure of sound intensity) that can be heard and the different frequency levels at which the sound can be heard. Frequency levels of sound are measured in hertz. These tests utilize pure tones or speech that have been prerecorded. Young children or those who may have some difficulty in being tested using either speech audiometry or pure tone audiometry may be tested by observation and measurement of the Moro reflex (this is a response which a child has at birth). The Moro reflex is a response to a loud sound. The response may be seen in the face, in moves made by the arms, legs, or body, or in the blinking of the eyes. The orienting response occurs in babies or infants when they turn their heads in the direction of a sound. Play audiometry is an audiometric test of a child who is about 2½ years old where the actual testing is done in a game format so the child responds to sounds as though playing a game.

Causes of Hearing Loss

Hearing losses are grouped according to the location of the problem in the individual's auditory system. Conductive hearing losses occur when there are problems with the ability to transfer sound along the ear's conductive path. Conductive problems occur in either the outer or middle ear. Hearing problems occurring in the inner ear are termed sensorineural impairments. Individuals who have hearing problems involving both sensorineural and conductive losses are described as having a mixed impairment.

Outer ear impairments are caused by external canal infections, ear wax buildups, tumors, items put into the ear, and punctures of the eardrum. Middle ear problems occur due to a failure of one or more of the ossicles to function properly. The ossicles are three small bones (the mallcus, incus, and stapes) located in the middle ear. The most prevalent problem in the middle ear is otitis media (a middle ear space infection). Otitis media occurs more frequently in children with cleft palate and Down's syndrome. Allergies cause the eustachian tube to enlarge resulting in malfunction. Tumors and blows to the head can also result in middle ear problems.

Inner ear problems are considered the most severe impairments and often are inherited. Other hearing losses that are acquired are lack of oxygen at birth, prenatal infections such as maternal rubella and maternal venereal diseases (syphilis), and other infections of the child including meningitis, mumps, and measles.

Noise is also considered a cause of hearing loss. Long exposure to loud engine noises such as jets, to cassette player music, and to skeet shooting can cause hearing loss. The degree of hearing impairment is related to the cause of the loss.

The greatest degree of hearing impairment in school-age children is due to meningitis, hereditary factors, or maternal rubella. Over half of the children with hearing losses due to these three factors have profound hearing losses.

Psychological and Behavioral Issues

Deafness is a much greater disabling condition than blindness or physical disabilities. Being deaf, especially from birth, can socially isolate the individual and seriously impair both the individual's ability to communicate verbally and to comprehend others in the environment. This is especially true in today's society in which so much interaction depends on the ability to understand English and to speak the language. While the blind person can verbally communicate and thus is not isolated, the deaf person lives in a world of silence, one that can be very limited in terms of human interaction.

Children with profound hearing loss from birth have severe problems in English language development. Research shows that at the age of eight months, deaf children stop babbling. This is due in part to lack of sound reinforcement both from their own sounds and from adults in the environment.

There is controversy over whether spoken language is necessary for thought and concept development, and whether the inability to speak a language influences concept and intellectual development. Some recent research using intelligence measures that do not rely on verbal and language processing abilities (i.e., nonverbal intelligence tests) has shown that there is no difference in performance between hearing and hearing impaired children (Sullivan, 1982; McConnell, 1973). In terms of other abilities, Silver (1966) studied the artistic abilities of hearing-impaired children and also found no difference between their abilities and that of their hearing peers.

Social Issues

Because human interactions rely strongly on verbal communication, it is this area of social relationships in which hearing-impaired children have the most difficulty. These children may grow up in virtual isolation, and there is a general tendency to limit social interaction to other hearing-impaired individuals. The extent of hearing-impaired children's familial acceptance of the disability can strongly influence their own self-acceptance and self-concept. If there is only one family member who is deaf, that child will probably be left out of much of the family activities. Making friends is difficult. Hearing-impaired individuals tend to limit social interaction to other hearing-impaired people, thus forming a deaf community which is fairly close knit in adulthood. There may be a need to specifically teach social abilities including engaging in small talk, posing questions and answers, learning how to deal with criticism and how to give and receive compliments.

Educational Issues

Children with hearing impairments may begin school as early as two years of age. In addition to the regular school program, emphasis is on reading, language, speech, and speech reading. The curriculum includes many concrete experiences, demonstrations, and dramatizations. There is also a heavy reliance on visual learning and imitation. Deaf children are usually three to five years behind their nondisabled peers in educational achievement, and as they grow, this gap grows.

Students with hearing impairments (especially profound deafness) have the greatest difficulty in reading comprehension. The average reading level for a deaf person is at the third grade level, but 10 percent of the deaf can read at the ninth grade level or higher (Telford & Sawrey, 1977). This low reading level perhaps would be expected because reading depends a great deal on language skills. There is some promise that, if intensive special instruction begins at early ages (six to eight years of age), students with hearing impairments would be only about a year behind hearing peers in reading (Moog & Geers, 1985).

There is less of a lag in arithmetic, spelling, and motor skills. In fact, hearing-impaired learners demonstrate a high level of achievement in mathematics, but this is typically at the eighth grade level for adults of age 20. These lags in academic skills do **not** mean that children with hearing impairments are less intelligent than their hearing peers.

Communication Issues

As would be expected, the major educational issue centers around communication. For some time there has been a debate between oral and manual methods of communication for the hearing-impaired person. The oral method relies on making the most use of whatever residual hearing the individual has and learning to speak orally with enough clarity to be able to communicate with nonhearing-impaired individuals. The manual method is based on the conclusion that few children with hearing impairments have enough residual hearing to really be able to speak at a level to be understood by others. Manual communication approaches focus on sign language that can be readily used to communicate with others who also learn the signs. Since the mid-1970s, most deaf educators have shifted to a focus on total communication, which is a combination of oral and manual approaches. In this approach the individual mouths or speaks the words and signs or finger spells the same words simultaneously. Oral techniques include auditory training and speechreading. There are three goals of auditory training: becoming aware of sound, being able to differentiate among various sounds in the environment, and fostering an ability to differentiate various speech sounds.

Speechreading focuses on teaching the use of visual cues and environmental and nonverbal cues to comprehend what is being said. The visual cues from the person speaking are processed either analytically (looking for cues in syllables that are then put together) or synthetically (focusing on the general meaning as opposed to the individual separate words). Nonverbal cues mostly come from various facial expressions that relate to the content of the words spoken.

Manual techniques include the use of sign language and finger spelling. Perhaps the most utilized sign language is American Sign Language (Ameslan). Recently, Ameslan has begun to be recognized as a *true language* with a specific grammatical structure and the capacity to convey both abstract as well as concrete ideas.

Finger spelling is a system of finger movements (one for each letter of the English alphabet). Manual communication relies mostly on signs for words but interjects finger spelling for words for which there may not be a known sign. It is now the communication method most often used in working with hearing-impaired children. It offers both a visual series of cues (signs and manual alphabet) as well as spoken cues (residual hearing, contextual cues, and mimed cues in the form of words through lip and mouth movements).

Classroom Placements

About sixty percent of the school-aged children with hearing impairments are still taught in special classes or schools. The current pattern in nonresidential special schools is for hearing-impaired students to be housed in a special classroom and integrated when possible with nondisabled peers.

Technology Issues

COMPUTER–ASSISTED INSTRUCTION. Computer-assisted instruction holds great promise for use in the education of students with hearing impairments. Computers can provide the much needed individualization of instruction and important visual cues necessary for learning. There are now programs available that can form sentences and at the same time provide a picture of that sentence and the signs for the sentence (Prinz & Nelson, 1985; Prinz, Pemberton, & Nelson, 1985).

CAPTIONING AND TELETEXT. Closed captions came into their own in the early 1980s and can be used for viewing television programs. Captions appear on only specially equipped television sets. Teletext enables viewers to read news and cultural and community calendars via televised texts.

TELETYPEWRITER AND SUPERPHONE. The teletypewriter (TTY) enables persons with hearing impairments to use a telephone and to communicate via typed text. The superphone permits anyone with a push-button phone to communicate with a hearing-impaired person. The message is punched out on the push buttons and then translated into text by the teletypewriter. The superphone permits hearing persons to communicate with individuals who are hearing impaired.

HEARING AIDS. Contrary to popular myth persons with all types of hearing loss can benefit from some sort of hearing aid. With the rapid advancement of electronic technology, hearing aids are getting more powerful and much smaller. Unfortunately, finding the best type of hearing aid for an individual is still often a matter of trial and error.

Early Intervention Issues

Public Law 94-142 has mandated that early intervention programs be available for many disabling conditions including children with hearing impairments. Early deaf education programs are especially helpful if family members are included and manual communication becomes a natural part of the family's interactions. Early intervention also can provide a sort of head start on language development for children with hearing impairments.

Vocational Issues

As a group the deaf population are generally underemployed and underrepresented in the professional ranks. In 1965 the National Technical Institute of the Deaf (NITD) was established in connection with the Rochester Institute of Technology with federal funding. Among the goals of NITD was an effort to increase the training and consequent job opportunities for persons with hearing impairments. Since 1965 there has been an expansion of postsecondary training programs, and a guide to training was published in 1986 by Gallaudet University (the only major liberal arts college for hearing-impaired students, located in Washington, DC). NITD listed 145 programs (Hallahan & Kauffman, 1988).

Art can be an important vocation for a person with a hearing impairment. In fact, in a study of occupations for deaf persons (Schein & Marcus, 1974), the second-highest percentage (21.3%) made their living as craftspersons.

General and Art Classroom Issues
with Mainstreamed Hearing-Impaired Students

1. Attend to the frequency of social interactions between hearing-impaired and nondisabled.

2. Encourage independence and peer teaching (nondisabled with hearing impaired) and help the children to not always depend on the teacher for assistance.

3. Be sensitive to seating of students with hearing impairments. The students should be in front of the classroom about six feet from the instructor. They should be permitted to move their seats whenever needed.

4. Environmental noise should be kept at a minimum to avoid distracting the hearing-impaired learner. Such noise also interferes with reception of sounds from hearing aids.

5. Be sensitive to the fact that visual information can also be distracting to students with hearing impairments.

6. Talk in a natural manner to facilitate speechreading.

7. If the teacher does not have manual communication skills, use gestures, facial expressions, visual demonstrations, and simple written explanations to communicate.

8. In talking with a hearing-impaired child, establish eye contact first.

9. Always face the student when talking and avoid turning the head away from the student who is hearing impaired. Avoid backlighting of the teacher's face, and avoid talking while facing the chalkboard.

10. If possible, provide an interpreter, which can be invaluable with two-way communication. This is especially true with younger children who

have not developed reading and writing skills. Students who use manual or total communication will greatly appreciate the teacher and/or therapist who learns and uses some signs. Such effort will be a concrete demonstration that the therapist and/or teacher is really trying to communicate.

11. Be aware that many students with hearing impairments are self-conscious about reciting or answering questions out loud in front of others. Allowing single-word answers to questions can help, as well as having the hearing-impaired students become part of a class team to answer or participate in discussions. Also, it may help to have students with hearing impairments recite short selections initially.

12. Often, the hearing-impaired students mimic other students when they really may not understand what is happening (laughing with others or raising hands with others without knowing the answer or the reason for laughing). When there is a class discussion, it will help for the teacher to orally name the student who is answering each time a response is made.

13. Consider repeating instructions using different words since some words are more easily speechread.

14. Use as many visual aids as possible in instruction. Giving a written outline to students with hearing impairments before the instruction occurs is helpful as is continually writing out questions either on the chalkboard or using the overhead projector. Also providing written summaries of what has been covered in class may help. Having a hearing peer take notes using carbon paper and giving the hearing-impaired peer the copy is useful.

Other Helpful Hints for the Art Teacher or Art Therapist

In planning art experiences, the teacher or therapist should be sensitive to the imitative way (learning by modeling) which many children with hearing impairments learn. These children will probably be inclined to copy and imitate either the teacher's examples or another student's work. This is especially true when the child may not fully understand a lesson. Encourage the children to work independently and foster unique solutions to art problems.

Children with hearing impairments have difficulty learning abstract concepts. For example, it is relatively easy to teach the concept and word for clay, paper, or paintbrush because these are concrete items that the child can touch, pick up, and use. It is far more difficult to explain the concepts of harmony and rhythm or emotions such as love, happiness, or sadness because these are much more abstract. This does not mean that children with hearing impairments cannot use abstractions or do not have the ability to use their imaginations. It does mean that they may need more practice in thinking abstractly and in using their imaginations (Kunkle-Miller, 1990).

Sometimes children will too quickly generalize from one or two experiences.

For example, if they once painted in trays, the children may erroneously assume that every time trays appear in the art class they will paint in them. This kind of behavior is called a *deafism*. To help the children make appropriate generalizations, many experiences should be provided in building concepts.

When possible, concrete examples should be used in instruction. Working closely with the classroom teacher will help in planning art experiences that reinforce or build on a concept, especially vocabulary, already being developed in the classroom. Instructional language should be geared to the language level of the children. The art teacher or art therapist should use brief sentences and define all key words that the children may not know. Students should be encouraged to use full sentences.

Often combining art and drama facilitates expression and communication. In fact, many children with hearing impairments have not learned how to play and they need to be taught specifically how to play. Further, play "is a primary language for children with language and communication disorders, as play provides a better opportunity for a range of feelings than does art alone" (Kunkle-Miller, 1990, p. 37). Hearing-impaired children also enjoy face painting and dramatizing parts of their artwork.

At times these children may not have the words to express an experience, but they can visually draw that experience. Also, it may help to have some simple illustrations of types of feelings (sad, angry, happy) and other simple drawings related to the art activity in which the child is engaged so that he can just point to the drawing to express what he is feeling or needing at the time. Kunkle-Miller (1990) states that asking questions during the art-making part of the session may be disruptive as the child has to stop and free his hands to answer questions if total communication is used. In these situations questioning the child *after* the artwork is completed is a better approach to use.

Kunkle-Miller (1990) has found that children with hearing impairments prefer three-dimensional media such as wood and clay. They seem to prefer plasticine because hands do not get "dirty." If one is working with groups of children, it is best to have a large round table at which all can sit and work. Then everyone can see what is being said (and signed) to everyone else.

The expressive channel of art is very important and necessary to healthy educational and emotional development. The artistic development of children with hearing impairments will be no different from that of hearing children, provided their environment is not deprived (Silver, 1966).

Summary

A hearing impairment is defined as an impairment in hearing that interferes with a child's language processing through the auditory channel (with or without an amplification device) which impairs educational performance. Hearing loss of 90 decibels means that child is deaf. A loss of less than 90 decibels means the child is hard of hearing. From the perspective of education, deafness and hard of hearing involve the extent to which the loss impacts the ability to talk, to understand language and to build the capacity for language development. The earlier the hearing loss to a child, the greater that child is slowed in his language development.

The largest degree of hearing impairment in children of school age is due to maternal rubella, hereditary factors or meningitis. The child who is deaf from birth has a serious impairment in terms of social interaction because of his delayed language development. The classroom may be the place where children are screened for hearing loss or it may be done by an audiologist. Young children may be difficult to test because their hearing loss may mean their language development is significantly slowed.

Educational Implications

Schooling may begin as early as two years of age. Sixty percent of children who are hearing impaired are in special classes. Programs emphasize speech, speechreading or sign language, and reading. There is a three- to five-year lapse for the deaf child in achievement compared with the normal hearing child. This gap increases with age. The typical reading level for an adult who is deaf is at the third grade level. The student with hearing impairments tends not to be as far behind in math, speaking and motor skills as in reading skills. A child who has a hearing impairment is *not* less intelligent than hearing peers.

Social interactions tend to be limited to other hearing-impaired persons because of the verbal communication upon which relationships in the hearing world heavily rely. There is widespread underemployment of persons with hearing impairments.

Computer-assisted instruction is helpful for the learner with a hearing impairment. Other high-technology advances that help are closed captioning, superphones, the teletypewriter and the teletext.

Art Programming

Art abilities of children with hearing impairments tend to be on a par with nondisabled students of the same age. Helpful approaches include monitoring social interactions with nondisabled peers, fostering independence, and peer teaching (by hearing peers). Seating hearing-impaired students in the front of the class enables them to see what the teacher is saying and reduces environmental noise and visual distractions. If the art teacher or art therapist talks slowly, the student can speechread. Also, using gestures and simple written directions and talking only after getting eye contact with the hearing-impaired student can be helpful. Using an interpreter and being sensitive to the self-consciousness of learners with hearing impairments when they are asked to answer questions out loud in front of the class will also be effective. Finally, using as many visual aids as possible in instruction will enhance communication with the hearing-impaired student. Art teachers and art therapists must also be aware that students with hearing impairments have difficulty thinking in abstractions, and concrete examples will be helpful. Art experiences must often include explanations of many of the vocabulary words used to insure all students understand what is being asked of them.

CHILDREN WITH VISUAL IMPAIRMENTS

One child out of every ten entering school has some visual impairment. Most of these can be corrected with glasses and therefore are not considered visual impairments. However, one child of every thousand has a visual impairment that cannot be corrected and will need special education and special adaptations for functioning in the classroom (Kirk & Gallagher, 1986).

There are three definitions associated with visual impairment: legal, educational, and the definition from PL 94-142 (now IDEA). The legal definition has as its basis the conditions under which a person can legally qualify for benefits. This definition states that a legally blind person has visual acuity of 20/200 or less in the eye that is better even when glasses are used. Additionally, the term *legally blind* is used when a person has a narrow field of vision that is not greater than 20 degrees. (This is a sort of tunnel vision.) Those persons whose vision in the better eye with correction is between 20/70 and 20/200 are termed partially blind or partially sighted.

The educational definition centers around the inability of individuals to read without relying on Braille methods or using audiotapes and records. Thus, someone who is educationally blind must rely on Braille or aural methods to read, and partially sighted individuals are those who must use large-print books or magnifying glasses to read regular print (Hallahan & Kauffman, 1988).

The definition under the mandates of PL 94-142 (now IDEA) states that "Visually Handicapped means a visual impairment which, even with correction, adversely affects a child's education performance. This term includes both partially seeing and blind children" (Public Law 94-142, Education of All Handicapped Children Act of 1975 and *Federal Register,* August 23, 1977).

Three main causes of visual impairments are infections and diseases, accidents, and heredity. Rubella, which seems to occur in seven-year cycles, is one major cause of blindness when the mother is infected early in her pregnancy. About thirty percent of those who are severely visually impaired are under 65 years of age and the rest (about one million) are over 65 years of age (Kirk & Gallagher, 1986).

The visual problems which are most common are myopia (nearsighted), hyperopia (farsighted), and astigmatism (blurred vision). Mostly, these problems can be corrected with glasses.

Glaucoma, cataracts, and diabetes are more serious visual impairments and occur mostly in adults. However, cataracts and visual problems due to diabetes also occur in children. Glaucoma is caused by too much pressure in the eyeball and, if untreated, can result in lack of blood being supplied to the optic nerve resulting in blindness. An early symptom of glaucoma is that lights seem to have a halo around them.

Children who have cataracts have a condition called congenital cataract. The lens of the eye is clouded which causes blurred vision. Surgery can usually correct the condition.

Diabetes can result in an interruption of the blood supply to the retina with the result being a condition called diabetic retinopathy.

About 64 percent of the visual problems in children who are school age occur prenatally (United States Department of Health, Education and Welfare, 1970) and a large number of these problems are due to heredity. Cataracts and glaucoma can occur prenatally. Two other congenital eye conditions are colomba and retinitis pigmentosa. Colomba is a disease of the retina in which either the periphery or the central area of the retina are not completely formed. This condition causes problems in visual acuity and the visual field. Retinitis pigmentosa is heredity in origin and is a disease that destroys the retina. Other prenatal causes of visual problems are measles (rubella) and sexually transmitted diseases such as syphilis.

Retrolental fibroplasis (RLF) is a condition caused by too rich an oxygen presence in incubators of premature babies. It results in scarring of the tissue behind the lens of the eye. Once the cause of RLF was identified in the 1950s, it was practically eliminated. In recent years it has been reoccurring due to the increased number of premature babies that have survived, but have required higher levels of oxygen for survival.

Improper muscle function in the eye causes strabismus (crossed eyes) and nystagmus (involuntary eye movements). If not treated, strabismus can result in blindness because after a period of time the brain rejects signals from an eye that deviates. Surgery and exercise can correct most strabismus.

Nystagmus can result in nausea and dizziness and may indicate brain mal-function or problems with the inner ear.

Incidence

Visual impairment is the lowest incidence of all the disabling conditions. While estimates vary partly due to age and the way the condition is defined, the U.S. Department of Education has noted that 0.07 percent of the population ages 2–17 years are receiving special education under the term or category of visually impaired (Hallahan & Kauffman, 1988).

Identification

Early identification of visual problems and treatment can eliminate visual impairments in some cases. Regular classroom teachers are the primary detectives in the identification of children who may have visual problems (Kirk & Gallagher, 1986).

The method used most often to test for vision problems is the Snellen Chart with which we are all familiar because it is used almost universally by eye doctors in standard eye examinations. The chart does not assist in identifying problems associated with inability to read large print at close proximity or associated problems with near vision. A special adaptation of the Snellen Chart for use at a range of 14 inches is now in use. Additionally, another test of near vision problems is the Jaeger chart which consists of a variety of reading materials in differing sizes of type. Barraga et al. (Barraga, 1983; Barraga & Collins, 1979; Barraga, Collins & Hollis, 1977) have created the Diagnostic Assessment Procedure (DAP) to assess a person's ability to function visually. The DAP, which includes eight components, shows promise as a valid assessment tool. A curriculum has been developed to accompany the DAP to assist in remediating identified visual problems (Beria, Rankin, & Willis, 1980).

Characteristics of the Visually Impaired

Language

After an extensive review of the research, Hallahan and Kauffman (1988) concluded that the language development of blind children is not significantly different from that of sighted peers. A strong case has been put forth by Cutsforth (1951), a blind psychologist, that blind persons demonstrate verbalism. *Verbalism* is a verbal unreality in which words that are not directly associated with an individual's experience are used—that is, the language and phraseology of the sighted are overutilized instead of a reliance on experience that reflects the blind person's world exploration through the olfactory, auditory, and tactual senses. The issue is still being debated; however, Hallahan and Kauffman (1988) conclude that it is more appropriate to use the language of the surroundings and those in it, the majority of whom are sighted. Thus, verbalism may be very appropriate if the blind person is to feel more like sighted peers than different from them.

Intellectual functioning

It is the general consensus that persons who are blind do not perform significantly lower than sighted individuals on standardized verbal intelligence tests. Research does indicate that the conceptual ability of blind children is lower and less developed than that of sighted peers. Abstract thinking abilities are less developed in children who are blind, and these children tend to deal with their surroundings in concrete terms. However, this difference seems to be due to lack of specific training and education, and when specific training on Piagetian tasks was provided, blind children's ability to perform on classification tasks equaled sighted children's performance (Hallahan & Kauffman, 1988).

Children who are blind from birth have much more difficulty in grasping some concepts than children who are adventitiously blinded (blinded after experiencing some sight). Thus, the age at which the child loses sight and/or the amount of visual impairment can influence the ease or difficulty that the child has in thinking conceptually.

Spatial concepts

Spatial concepts are the most difficult for blind children to grasp. Spatial concepts are acquired by children who are blind primarily through tactile and kinesthetic senses. It is often only through analogy and extrapolation from objects in the individual's immediate environment or actual experience that some spatial concepts such as planets or germs can be explained to the blind person.

Tactile Perception

Tactile perception is extremely important to children who are blind. It is the major way that the children experience their world. There are two types of tactile perception: synthetic touch, which is one's direct tactile experience of the world through experiences with items that are small enough to be held in one hand or enclosed in both hands, and analytic touch, which is tactile experiences of parts of objects too large to be held in the hand or hands and the mind attempts to form some sort of composite. It is interesting that for the sighted person it is the sense of sight that helps one form an integrated concept of objects that are experienced via the other senses. The person who is blind lacks the integrative function that sight provides.

Moreover, when one experiences the world through touch, as it is accomplished successively and not simultaneously, it is with the ability to see. In other words, sight is a unifying factor in experiencing objects in the world, and it occurs simultaneously, not successively as when one explores objects tactilely. Finally, tactually exploring an object necessitates much more effort than merely looking at something.

Like the development of perceptual abilities, the development of tactile abilities is facilitated by using a variety of methods. Like good visual perception, good tactile perception is linked to the capacity to focus on the areas or points of maximal information (Salome, 1964; Davidson, 1972) which helps to identify those features that are unique about an object.

Traits of Persons With Visual Impairments

For the purpose of our discussion we shall group those who are blind and those who have some partial sight into a category called visually impaired. Like other disabling conditions, persons with visual impairments are a heterogeneous group. Research has revealed some interesting traits which individuals who are visually impaired have. They tend to be better able to focus on tasks, seem to perform better at listening tasks, and score high on measures of creativity (Halprin, Halprin, & Torrance, 1973; Halprin, Halprin, & Tillman, 1973; Tinsdale, Blackhurst, & Marks, 1971). On the other hand, there is no research to support the notion that visually impaired individuals have extraordinary music abilities or a "sixth" sense in knowing when obstacles are in their paths (Hallahan & Kauffman, 1988).

There is no truth to the stereotype that the persons with visual impairments have heightened senses of hearing or touch. This theory of sensory compensation holds that when one sense is weak or nonexistent, the other senses develop to a greater extent. Research has not supported this hypothesis with persons who are visually impaired (Kirk & Gallagher, 1986).

What the individuals who are visually impaired do have is a heightened acuity in their listening skills that enables them to distinguish more readily the changes in the sound patterns as sound waves reflect off objects. This is a phenomenon called the Doppler effect, which is an established physics principle. That is, sound waves get louder the closer one comes to an object. (Sound echoes bounce off objects more loudly the closer one is to an object.) However, there is no research that supports the myth that persons who are blind have a specially developed acuity in all their other senses. What they may do is to better utilize the information they obtain from other senses. Also, while many blind persons do have careers in music, there is no truth to the myth that a person who is blind has special musical talents (Hallahan & Kauffman, 1988).

Academic Achievement

Hallahan and Kauffman (1988) reviewed the research on the academic achievement of children with visual impairments and concluded that they are generally a little behind their sighted peers when mental age was held constant. Also, it appears that the academic achievement of children who are visually impaired is not as affected by this disabling condition as children with hearing impairments. Apparently, having a hearing impairment makes it more difficult to learn academic concepts than having a visual impairment. Lowenfeld (1971) has concluded that with more use of auditory learning approaches, blind students are now not as far behind in their academic achievement as once was the case.

Mobility

Mobility is a major issue for persons who are visually impaired. The ability to be independent in getting around one's environment is essential to one's adjustment to the world. There are two major ways a visually impaired individual processes spatial information thus enabling mobility. The person uses either a sequential map or a cognitive map. If the sequential approach is used, then there is only one route to be used to get from point A to point C. If a cognitive map of these points is used, then the person can use several different routes to get to point C. It is as though one were lost in a strange city and only knew one way to get to work. If an accident blocked that route, then one would just have to wait for that accident to be cleared away before proceeding—this person has a sequential map of the route to work. However, if one knew in one's head the cognitive map of the workplace and all routes leading to that place, one could merely take a detour around the accident by taking an alternative route to work.

Social Skills

While individuals with visual impairment are generally well-adjusted, they have difficulty learning many social skills because visual feedback is a part of how one relates to another person (i.e., facial expressions and learning via modeling someone else). Thus, visually impaired students may need to be taught specific social skills. Also, some persons with visual impairments have stereotypic behaviors or stereotypes (in former years these behaviors were called blindisms). Stereotypes include rocking movements or rubbing the eyes. These stereotypic behaviors may be caused by one or more of the following: self-stimulation because of low level of sensory stimulation coming from the environment (or no environmental stimulation—i.e., total sensory deprivation), a similar reaction because of limited or no social stimulation, and a regression to more habitual behaviors when under stress (Hallahan & Kauffman, 1988).

Educational Issues

The sense of touch and hearing are the major ways that the child with visual impairment learns. To facilitate learning, as many concrete objects and experiences as possible must be used. There is a need for many direct experiences because simulations are not as powerful vehicles for instruction as direct encounters with the real world. Therefore, direct experience is preferable, unless that experience may be dangerous for the visually impaired child (Kirk & Gallagher, 1986).

There is general agreement that educational methodologies will be generally the same for children with visual impairments as for their sighted peers. Special adaptations are needed in four areas: Braille, use of available sight, skills in listening, and training in mobility.

Braille

Braille was introduced by a blind Frenchman (Louis Braille) in the nineteenth century. Originally, the system was based on an alphabet invented by Charles Babier, an army officer who wanted to be able to **read** messages at night. Braille is an alphabet based on a rectangular cell that contains from one to six raised dots. In the thirties the braille system was standardized. There are two ways of writing in Braille: the Perkins Brailler, which is like a typewriter with six keys that can be depressed at the same time, and the slate and stylus, which is manually operated. It is more difficult to *read* Braille than standard type because Braille is presented in terms of single letters or contractions of words. One must *read* sequentially and often cannot grasp words all at once as in reading standard text. Braille also takes more time to read than standard type (Hallahan & Kauffman, 1988).

Use of Available Sight

The current emphasis in the classroom with visually impaired students is to utilize and maximize whatever sight the students may have. Large-print books and magnification devices are the two major means to assist visually impaired students to maximize their available vision. Magnifying devices include hand-held lenses and glasses, as well as television scanners that are held in the hand and enlarge images from normal size books and project them onto a screen (Hallahan & Kauffman, 1988).

Skills in Listening

Children who are visually impaired do not automatically have better listening ability. Good listening skills must be consciously taught. Obtaining information auditorily is a much more efficient method than using Braille or large-print books. Recorded methods include direct recorded text played at a normal speed, recorded text played at a faster speed, and recorded materials using compressed speech. With compressed speech the so-called "Donald Duck" effect that occurs when speech is played back at a faster speed is eliminated. Compressed speech eliminates small parts of words randomly. Compressed speech recordings are the most efficient way of acquiring information, while using Braille and large print are the slowest ways of obtaining information. Tuttle found that compressed speech was three times faster than listening to a normal speed recording, and a normal recording was two times as fast as the use of Braille in transmitting information (Tuttle, 1974, cited in Hallahan & Kauffman, 1988, p. 329).

Training in Mobility

The ability of a person with visual impairments to function as an independent person is greatly dependent on the mobility ability. As noted earlier, mobility refers to one's capacity to get around the environment on one's own without relying on some other person as a guide. Mobility can be enhanced by using guide dogs, a Hoover cane, or an electronic device. Mobility necessitates both a mental orientation to space and space obstacles (one that can be facilitated by raised maps or mental memory) and physical orientation.

Guide dogs are rarely recommended because they must be cared for like any other pet, and they only help to prevent the people with visual impairments from entering dangerous areas—the individuals must already know where they are going. Guide dogs also require extensive training.

The Hoover cane is the familiar long white cane that is the most often used mobility tool. It is used by tapping the ground ahead of the person, thus detecting obstacles ahead.

Two mobility devices now in use are the Laser cane and the Sonicguide. The Laser cane is like the Hoover cane except that it puts out three beams of infrared light, one straight ahead, one up, and one down. These three beams of light emit sounds when an obstacle is encountered. The Sonicguide is worn on the head and ultrasonic sounds are emitted. When reflections from objects are encountered, these reflections are translated into audible sound. An individual can locate objects by the intensity and level of the sounds that are emitted from the guide. Both electronic devices require extensive training for effective use, which can be a drawback (Hallahan & Kauffman, 1988).

New legislation has also helped remove barriers in the environment. The

Architectural Barriers Act (Wardell, 1980) has mandated that public buildings must be accessible, and hence there must be handrails on steps,
Braille symbols in elevators, and accessible telephones (Kirk & Gallagher,
1986).

Technological Instructional Aids

Instructional aids have been developed for learners with visual impairments using high technology. These are the Optacon, the Kurzweil Reading
Machine, the Interactive Classroom Television System, the Portable Braille
Recorder (PBR), the Speech Plus Talking Calculator and computer automa-
tion. The Optacon is a camera device that translates printed text into
readable vibrating pins. It does broaden the printed world available to the
blind person, but the fingers can read only at a rate of 5 to 11 words per
minute.

The Kurzweil Reading Machine is actually a computer that takes printed
text and translates it into electronically spoken words. Thus, the blind
individual can read at a rate equal to the standard rate of the spoken word.
This device is expensive and it is used most frequently in schools and
institutions of higher education.

The Interactive Classroom Television System is designed for use by the
partially sighted person. Both the teacher and the student have television
sets and monitors at their work stations, which enable the child to better
"see" what is written on the chalkboard or what visuals the teacher uses for
instruction.

The PBR enables Braille to be recorded onto tape cassettes, and these
cassettes can be played back on the machine's reading board at a later time.
The PBR has an added advantage over the traditional Braillers because its
recorded information takes up less space (Hallahan & Kauffman, 1988).

The Speech Plus Talking Calculator announces entries into its system. In
using this hand-held device, the blind person is told what numbers are in
the display and what the results are of various calculations.

The Massachusetts Institute of Technology has developed a computer
device that translates ink text into Grade 2 Braille. The MIT Braille Embosse
is a more sophisticated version which is utilized in conjunction with a
teletypewriter.

Placements

The individual with visual impairments will either be placed in a resource
room, a special class, or a residential school, or will be served by a traveling
teacher while enrolled in regular classes. There is a trend away from the use
of residential schools and a move toward a combined approach where
academics are provided in public schools and specialized needs such as

mobility training and self-help skills are provided in the residential facility. Because of the low incidence of this disability, the itinerant teacher model is gaining in popularity. In this situation, the teacher travels to several schools, consults with regular teachers and provides specialized training to their students with visual impairments. Where there are enough visually impaired students to warrant it, a public school may have a resource teacher who has a classroom in the school where the visually impaired students spend part of their school day. Students with visual impairments who have other disabling conditions are the ones now most likely to be enrolled in a residential facility (Hallahan & Kauffman, 1988).

Early Childhood Issues

It is essential that babies who are blind receive early mobility and sensory stimulation. It is generally established that children blind from birth are at much greater risk to have severe delays in their cognitive development starting at about the eighteenth month. These blind children are less likely to reach for objects that they hear and will crawl at a later age than normal sighted peers (Hallahan & Kauffman, 1988).

For the blind child's first five years it is the quality of experiences that are essential to future development. Normal children learn a great deal just from observation, but blind children do not have the opportunity to do this. Visual experiences must be replaced by many more interactive experiences in which holding and touching are a major component. In this way strong emotional bonds are formed between children who are blind and their parents. It is the emotional bonding that is essential for learning and for future development. As can be implied, the parents play a major role in the early development of a blind child and set the stage for further learning (Barraga, 1983). Mobility training should begin at the preschool level with a consistent work period of about 20 minutes that includes bending, stretching, and small motions that are built up into larger muscle activity (Hallahan & Kauffman, 1988).

Adolescent and Adult Educational Issues

Both adolescents and adults with visual impairments have difficulty in independent living and the procurement and maintenance of gainful employment. Often, sighted persons inadvertently contribute to the dependency of visually impaired persons. Rickelman and Blaylock (1983) offer some of the following suggestions to sighted persons when they interact with persons who are blind.

1. Offer assistance before actually helping an individual who is blind.
2. Do not hesitate to interact with blind persons. Identify yourself before initiating conversations.
3. Be careful to talk in normal voice tones and do not increase your volume unless the person who is blind requests you to do so.
4. Announce when you are leaving the presence of the blind person.
5. In guiding a person who is blind, let her take your arm and be sure you walk slightly ahead of the individual needing guidance.

Independent living skills (cooking, eating, dressing) are essential for visually impaired persons and should be covered during adolescence. There are many misconceptions about sex and sexual issues for the person with visual impairments. Special attention must be given to sex education with this group of disabled persons (Kirk & Gallagher, 1986).

Personal appearance and appropriate social behaviors are also important issues. Appearance must be a consideration, and visually impaired individuals must be taught tactile methods to check to be sure appearance is acceptable. (Sighted persons do this almost unconsciously just by looking in a mirror or by picking up on visual cues from others around them.) Socially appropriate behaviors must be taught, and students must learn to eliminate rocking and other blindisms that typically occur unless interventions are consciously planned (Kirk & Gallagher, 1986).

Employment Issues

Unfortunately, only about one third of persons who are blind who can work are in the work force. They often are underemployed and overqualified for the jobs they hold. Recent research suggests that job training and job skills should begin at the elementary level. On-the-job training is the most potent for the blind individual because many simulations omit realities such as the noise of the workplace, the reactions of sighted workers, and the physical obstacles present in every workplace, ones that are unique to each work situation and that cannot be approximated in the school classroom (Storey, Sacks & Olmstead, 1985).

Classroom Issues

For the sighted person it is the ability to see that unifies the learning experience. Children with visual impairment do not get this unified whole from their experiences, and it is the teacher's task to literally show relationships of parts to the whole and to take the time to explicate relationships.

Visually impaired children learn best by learning actively—by doing and by manipulating objects. They do not naturally pick up objects and explore them, so teachers must motivate these children to explore and to reach for objects. Sometimes this can be done by engaging the child's other senses (i.e., sounds, smells, and touch).

The teacher must be aware that learning takes more time for the child with visual impairments. This child must develop to the fullest the ability to listen and remember (Kirk & Gallagher, 1986).

All students should care for their own school materials. Sighted peer teaching is helpful as long as the visually impaired child does not become dependent on the peer. The teacher should have the same expectations for all the students in a class, regardless of visual impairment. Maximum participation in all class activities should be encouraged before making special exceptions for the visually impaired students. All students should participate in assigned tasks such as pet care or plant care in the classroom (Hanninen, 1975).

Other helpful hints include making sure that partially sighted children sit near the chalkboard and have as much light as possible. Glossy pictures may cause problems, so these should be avoided. Distracting background should be avoided in visuals that are used for instruction, and large clear lettering is essential in all illustrations. The teacher also must be sensitive to the need that students with visual impairments may have to rest more often because of the increased visual attention these students use to accomplish any task.

Class notes can be taken for visually impaired children by sighted peers. Carbon paper can also be used to make second copies of class material.

Teachers should repeat orally what is written on visuals and on the chalkboard. Additional time may be necessary for children with visual impairments to complete tasks. The American Printing House for the Blind provides embossed maps to assist in teaching geography to the visually impaired learner (Hanninen, 1975).

A lamp with a rheostat can be helpful to provide just the right amount of light for a child with visual impairments. Also helpful are large-print books, and spacing between letters and lines can help with readability. Raised-line paper can help students to stay on the line. Cassette tape recorders are very helpful to children who have difficulty taking notes because the children can play back instructional information as needed. Visually impaired children generally need more time for completing their work. A good rule of thumb is to allow 1½ times as long for children with visual impairments to finish tasks than sighted children (Kirk & Gallagher, 1986).

Learning to read Braille can be essential for blind students, but a good Braille reader works at a rate of two to three times slower than regular readers. A Braillewriter, a typewriter that types Braille, can also be helpful to the blind student. Learning to use a regular typewriter is an essential educational skill, and instruction should begin at the third grade level (Kirk & Gallagher, 1986).

Scott (1982) further recommends that children with visual impairment sit where they can be monitored by the teacher. Special equipment that the students use should have a specific location in the classroom. Special assistance and needs should be discussed with the teacher when other students are not present. The teacher should reinforce independent action and continually set up situations in which the visually impaired children can work and act independently. Peers who are in proximity should be identified by name to encourage social interaction. The student should be encouraged to ask for explanations if things are unclear and to listen closely to information and directions.

Considerations for Art Programming

The art program must be tailored to each individual child. Art activities can be an important avenue for expression. Not only partially sighted but also blind children can become deeply involved in art (Rubin & Klineman, 1974; Fukurai, 1974). Naturally, three-dimensional and textured media will be a major part of such a program. Children who are blind can also paint and draw. Their interests will parallel those of their sighted peers.

The language used to present art experiences and to discuss art processes and products needs to be embellished with analogies and metaphors that go beyond visual experiences and rely on all the other senses. For example, colors could be associated with objects or experiences in the environment. Blue could be described as associated with the feel of water, red with heat or hot-tasting spices such as chili or red peppers. Metallic paper could be described not only as shiny but as being like the tin foil used to wrap food for baking (Pazienza, 1984).

Some adaptations will be necessary in planning art activities. Adaptations might include the consistent setup of a work area, different-sized containers for different paint colors, or consistent placement of paint in Braille-marked, spill-resistant, weighted containers. Having the child paint or draw on a tray with shallow edges will provide working space limits. Sometimes it may help to put a dab of glue, a piece of masking tape, or tear a piece out of the drawing paper to provide an orientation point. Both the tray and the paper should be secured to the worktable with C-clamps and/or tape. Sometimes it helps to place a sheet of window screen under the drawing paper. The screen will help produce a textured path as the child draws with a crayon. Scented markers can be used in drawing. These will help the child to identify colors, since each has a different color-related aroma. Scents (such as food flavorings like lemon for yellow, strawberry for red, etc.) can also be added to tempera colors to help the child to distinguish between them.

When new media are being introduced, the children should explore each material in a sequence. In presenting a new art activity, it can be very helpful to have some completed examples to enable the children to grasp the total concept tactually before beginning their own work. The children may need encouragement to become involved in messy materials. The art environment should allow the children maximum mobility and enable their rapid orientation to materials and their location. Such materials should be consistently stored and easily accessible to the children so they can work as independently as possible.

Summary

One child out of ten entering school has some visual problem. There are three types of definitions: legal, educational and that specified in PL 94-142. Three major causes of visual impairments are diseases/infections including rubella and diabetes, accidents and heredity. Most frequently occurring visual problems include nearsightedness, farsightedness and blurred vision. Most of these problems can be helped with glasses. Visual impairment is the lowest occurring of all the disabling conditions. Seven-tenths of a percent of the population aged from 2 to 17 years receive special education because of visual disabilities. Regular classroom teachers may be the first to notice visual problems in children.

Intellectual and language development is not significantly different from that of sighted children. The ability to think abstractly is not as developed as with sighted peers. Synthetic and analytic touch are the major ways a child with visual impairments experiences the world. There will be difficulty in forming integrated concepts of objects and events in the world because sight plays a major role in integrating concepts.

It is the quality of experiences during the first five years that are essential to the future development of a child who is blind. Persons with visual impairments are a heterogenous group. However, they are better able to focus on tasks and to listen more intently than their sighted peers. There is no hard data to support notions that the visually impaired individual has a heightened sense of hearing, touch or musical ability.

Educational Programming

Mobility is a major issue. Mobility is accomplished by means of a sequential map or a cognitive map. Students with visual impairments lag slightly behind sighted peers on academic achievement. Social skills are hard to learn because there is no visual feedback for things like facial expressions. Socially appropriate behaviors must be specifically taught and appearance must be checked for acceptability. Visually impaired persons may exhibit rocking movements or may tend to rub themselves frequently. These mannerisms may interfere with social interactions with sighted persons.

Generally, the student with visual impairments will be mainstreamed for most of the day and spend some time in a resource room or a special class. Some visually impaired students attend a residential school or are taught by a traveling teacher. Educational programs stress the use of available sight, listening skills, mobility training and Braille training. Most of the rest of the educational program will parallel that of same-aged peers.

Technological contributions include the Laser cane, the Sonicguide, the MIT Braille Embosse, the Speech Plus Talking Calculator, the Kurzweil Reading Machine, the Interactive Classroom Television System, the Portable Braille Recorder, and the Opticon.

Hints to follow when interacting with a person who is visually impaired include: offering help before actually helping, identifying oneself prior to engaging in a conversation, talking in a normal voice, letting the visually impaired person take your arm when being led, and being sure you walk slightly ahead of the person.

Art Programming

Active learning will be an important method to use in the art room. Activities requiring motor skills and learning in general will take more time for the visually impaired person than her sighted peers. Children who are partially sighted need to sit near the chalkboard and should have as much illumination as possible for their workspaces. Glossy pictures should be avoided because of glare. Distracting backgrounds should also be eliminated in visuals. Large, clear lettering will be important in all visuals used. There should be ample opportunities to rest between and during tasks. Peer teaching and notetaking by sighted classmates can help. All visuals that include text should be read aloud by the teacher.

The art room should have fixed areas where materials are stored. Paint colors should have Braille labels. Orientation points should be provided and paper should be secured to the work area. Textured materials are recommended. As many items as possible should be easily accessible to the visually impaired child to foster independence and self-directed work. While three-dimensional materials will probably be the mainstay of the art program, children with visual impairments can also benefit from working in two-dimensional art media.

REFERENCES

Anderson, F. E. (1978). *Art for all the children: A creative sourcebook for the impaired child.* Springfield, IL: Charles C Thomas.

Appel, L. S., & Krammer, M. J. (1987). *An enriching experience.* Arlington, VA: Macro Systems, Inc.

Baker, L. (1982). An evaluation of the role of metacognitive deficits in learning disabilities. *Topics in Learning and Learning Disabilities, 2*(1), 27–35.

Bandura, A. (1973). *Aggression: A social learning analysis.* Englewood Cliffs, NJ: Prentice-Hall.

Barraga, N. C. (1983). *Visual handicaps and learning* (rev. ed.). Austin, TX: Exceptional Resources.

Barraga, N. C., & Collins, M. E. (1979). Development of efficiency in visual functioning. Rational for a comprehensive program. *Journal of Visual Impairment and Blindness, 73,* 121–126.

Barraga, N. C., Collins, M., & Hollis, J. (1977). Development of efficiency in visual functioning. A literature analysis. *Journal of Visual Impairment and Blindness, 71,* 387–391.

Bates, P., Renzaglia, A., & Wehman, P. (1981). Characteristics of an appropriate education for severely and profoundly handicapped students. *Education and Training of the Mentally Retarded, 16,* 142–149.

Batshaw, M. L., & Perret, Y. M. (1986). *Children with handicaps: A medical primer.* Baltimore: Paul H. Brookes.

Blandy, D. (1989). Ecological and normalizing approaches to disabled students and art education. *Art Education, 42*(3), 7–11.

Beria, E. P., Rankin, E. F., & Willis, D. H. (1980). Psychometric evaluation of the low vision diagnostic assessment procedure. *Journal of Visual Impairment and Blindness, 75,* 297–301.

Bigge, J., & O'Donnell, P. (1977). *Teaching individuals with physical and multiple disabilities.* Columbus: Charles E. Merrill.

Breaking Down the Barriers. (n.d.). Normal, IL: Living Independence for Everyone (LIFE–CIL) Center for Independent Living.

Brill, R. G., MacNeil, B., & Newman, L. R. (1986). Framework for appropriate programs for deaf children. *American Annals of the Deaf, 131*(2), 65–77.

Bryan, T. H., Sherman, R., & Fisher, A. (1980). Learning disabled boy's nonverbal behaviors with a dyadic interview. *Learning Disability Quarterly, 3,* 65–72.

Brydon, I. (n.d.). *Creative growth: A center dedicated to artist growth.* Unpublished paper (available from Creative Growth, 355, 24th Street, Oakland, CA 94612).

Cardinale, R., & Anderson, F. E. (1979). Art games and learning problems-or-What does a courageous prickly ear look like? *Art Education, 32*(1), 17–19.

Church, J. A., Allen, J. R., & Stichm, E. R. (1986). New scarlet letter(s), pediatric AIDS. *Pediatrics, 77,* 423–427.

Clements, S. D. (1966). *Minimal brain dysfunction in children: Terminology and identification.* NINDB Monograph No. 3. Washington, DC: U.S. Department of Health, Education and Welfare.

Coopersmith, S. (1968). Studies in self-esteem. *Scientific American, 218,* 96–102.

Craik, F. I. M., & Tulving, E. (1975). Depth of processing and the retention of words in episodic memory. *Journal of Experimental Psychology: General, 104,* 268–294.

Cutsforth, T. D. (1951). *The blind in school and society: A psychological study.* New York: American Federation for the Blind.

Davidson, P. W. (1972). The role of exploratory activity in haptic perception. Some issues, data and hypothesis. *Research Bulletin; American Foundation for the Blind* (No. 24), 21–27.

Denhoff, E. (1976). Medical aspects. In W. M. Cruickshank (Ed.), *Cerebral palsy: A developmental disability* (3rd rev. ed.) (pp. 230–270). Syracuse, NY: Syracuse University Press.

Deske, K. (1987). *A survey on the use of art in programs of domestic violence in the state of Illinois.* Unpublished master's thesis, Illinois State University, Normal, IL.

Education of the Handicapped. (1990). Study says schools don't serve thousands with behavior disorders. *16*(11): 7–8.

Feagans, L., & McKinney, J. (1981). The pattern of exceptionality across domains in learning disabled children. *Journal of Applied Developmental Psychology, 1,* 313–328.

Federal Register, August 23, 1977, p. 42478.

Federal Register, December 29, 1977, p. 65083.

Federal Register, August 4, 1982, p. 33846.

Fernald, G. M. (1943). *Remediation techniques in basic school subjects.* New York: McGraw-Hill.

Fitts, W. H. (Ed.). (1971). *The self-concept and self-actualization. Dede Wallace Center Monograph III.* Nashville, TN: Counselor Recordings and Tests.

Frostig, M., Lefever, D. W., and Whittlesey, J. R. B. (1964). *The Marianne Frostig developmental test of visual perception.* Palo Alto: Consulting Psychology Press.

Fukurai, S. (1974). *How can I make what I cannot see?* New York: Van Nostrand Reinhold.

Goldstein, H. (1974). *The social learning curriculum.* Columbus, OH: Charles E. Merrill.

Grossman, H. (Ed.). (1983). *Manual on terminology and classification in mental retardation.* Washington, DC: American Association on Mental Deficiency.

Hallahan, D. P., & Kauffman, J. M. (1988). *Exceptional children: Introduction to special education* (4th ed.). Englewood Cliffs, NJ: Prentice-Hall.

Hallahan, D. P., Kauffman, J. M., & Lloyd, J. W. (1985). *Introduction to learning disabilities.* Englewood Cliffs, NJ: Prentice-Hall.

Halprin, G., Halprin, G., & Tillman, M. H. (1973). Relationships between creative thinking, intelligence, and teacher-rated characteristics of blind children. *Education of the Visually Handicapped, 5,* 33–38.

Halprin, G., Halprin, G., & Torrance, E. P. (1973). Effects of blindness on creative thinking abilities of children. *Developmental Psychology,* 268–274.

Hanninen, K. A. (1975). *Teaching the visually handicapped.* Columbus: Charles E. Merrill.

Harris, D. B. (1963). *Children's drawings as measures of intellectual maturity.* New York: Harcourt Brace Jovanovich.

Harvey, D., & Greenway, A. (1984). The self-concepts of physically handicapped children and their non-handicapped siblings: An empirical investigation. *Journal of Child Psychology and Psychiatry, 25,* 273–284.

Heinemann, A., & Shontz, F. (1984). Adjustment following disability: Representative case studies. *Rehabilitation Counseling Bulletin, 28*(1), 3–14.

Hobbs, N., Perrin, J. M., Ireys, H. T., Moynahan, L. C., & Shayne, M. W. (1984). Chronically ill children in America. *Rehabilitation Literature, 45,* 206–213.

Insights: Art in special education. (1976). Millburn, N.J.: Art Educators of New Jersey.

Kauffman, J. M. (1985). *Characteristics of children's behavior disorders* (3rd ed.). Columbus, Ohio: Charles E. Merrill.

Kauffman, J. M. (1986). Educating children with behavior disorders. In R. J. Morris & B. Blatt (Eds.), *Special education: Research and trends.* New York: Pergamon.

Killen, W. (1983). "Creative Growth" artwork is a display of overwhelming talent. *The Montclarion,* November 22.

Kirk, S., & Gallagher, J. J. (1986). *Educating exceptional children* (5th ed.). Boston, MA: Houghton Mifflin.

Kirk, S. A., McCarthy, J. J., & Kirk, W. D. (1961; 1968). *Illinois test of psycholinguistic abilities.* Urbana: University of Illinois Press.

Kunkle-Miller, L. Potentials and problems in establishing an art therapy program in a residential school for children who are deaf. *American Journal of Art Therapy, 29,* 34–41.

Lambert, N., Windmiller, M., Cole, L., & Figuoroa, R. (1975). Standardization of a public school version of the American Association of Mental Deficiency Adaptative Behavior Scale. *Mental Retardation, 13,* 3–7.

Leahy, R., Balla, D., & Zigler, E. (1982). Role taking, self-image, and imitation in retarded and non-retarded individuals. *American Journal of Mental Deficiency, 86,* 372–379.

Lerner, J. W. (1972). *Children with learning disabilities.* Boston: Houghton Mifflin.

LIFE–CIL. (n.d.). What to write/say when reporting/talking about people with disabilities. Normal, IL: Living Independence for Everyone (LIFE–CIL)–Center for Independent Living.

Long, N. J., Morse, W. C., & Newman, R. G. (Eds.). (1980). *Conflict in the classroom* (4th ed.). Belmont, CA: Wadsworth.

Long, N. J., and Newman, R. G. (1965). Managing surface behavior in school. In N. J. Long, W. C. Morse, and R. G. Newman (Eds.), *Conflict in the classroom.* Belmont, CA: Wadsworth.

Lovos, O. I. (1982, September). *An overview of the Young Autism Project.* Paper presented at the annual convention of the American Psychological Association, Washington, DC.

Lowenfeld, B. (1971). Psychological problems of children with impaired vision. In W. M. Cruickshank (Ed.), *Psychology of exceptional children and youth* (3rd ed.). Englewood Cliffs, NJ: Prentice-Hall.

Lowenfeld, V., & Brittain, W. L. (1987). *Creative and mental growth* (8th ed.). New York: MacMillan.

MacMillan, D. L. (1982). *Mental retardation in school and society* (2nd ed.). Boston: Little Brown.

Maslow, A. (1962). *Toward a psychology of being.* New York: Van Nostrand.

McConnell, F. (1973). Children with hearing disabilities. In L. M. Dunn (Ed.), *Exceptional children in the schools: Special education in transition* (2nd ed.). New York: Hold, Rinehart, and Winston, pp. 220–260.

McFee, J. K. (1972). *Preparation for art.* Belmont, CA: Wadsworth.

Meichenbaum, D., & Goodman, J. (1971). Teaching impulsive children to talk to themselves: A means of developing self-control. *Journal of Abnormal Psychology, 77,* 115–126.

Mercer, J., & Lewis, J. (1978). *System of multicultural pluralistic assessment.* New York: Psychological Corporation.

Moog, J., & Geers, A. (1985). EPIC: A program to accelerate academic progress in profoundly hearing-impaired children. *The Volta Review, 87*(6), 259–277.

Morse, W. C. (1976). The education of socially maladjusted and emotionally disturbed children. In W. M. Cruickshank & G. O. Johnson (Eds.), *Education of exceptional children and youth* (3rd ed.). Englewood Cliffs, NJ: Prentice-Hall.

Murphy, D. M. (1986). The prevalence of handicapping conditions among juvenile delinquents. *Remedial and Special Education, 7*(3), pp. 7–17.

Patterson, G. R. (1982). *Coercive family process.* Eugene, OR: Castalia.

Patterson, G. R., Ried, J. B., Jones, R. R., & Gonger, R. E. (1975). *A social learning approach to family intervention: Vol. 1. Families with aggressive children.* Eugene, OR: Castalia.

Pazienza, J. (1984). Mainstreaming in art education: A case of the blind leading the blind. *Art Education, 11,* 20–21, 38.

Peter, I. J. (1965). *Prescriptive teaching.* New York: McGraw-Hill.

Piers, E., and Harris, D. (1969). *The Piers-Harris Self Concept Scale.* Nashville, TN: Counselor Recordings and Tests.

Polloway, E. A., Epstein, M. H., & Cullinan, D. (1985). Prevalence of behavior problems among educable mentally retarded students. *Education and Training of the Mentally Retarded, 20,* 3–13.

Premack, D. (1959). Toward empirical behavior laws: I. Positive reinforcement. *Psychological Review, 66,* 291–333.

Prinz, P. M., & Nelson, K. E. (1985). A child-computer-teacher-interactive method for teaching reading to young deaf children. In D. Martin (Ed.), *Cognitive education and deafness: Directions for research and instruction* (pp. 124–127). Washington, DC: Gallaudet University Press.

Prinz, P. M., Pemberton, E., & Nelson, K. (1985). The ALPHA Interactive Microcomputer System for teaching reading, writing and communication skills to hearing-impaired children. *American Annals of the Deaf, 130*(4), 441–461.

Public Law 94-142, 1975.

Quay, H. C. (1979). Classification. In H. C. Quay & J. S. Werry (Eds.), *Psychopathological disorders of childhood* (2nd ed.). New York: Wiley.

Research and Training Center on Independent Living. (1987).

Rickelman, B. L., & Blaylock, J. N. (1983). Behaviors of sighted individuals perceived by blind persons as hindrances to self-reliance in blind persons. *Journal of Visual Impairment and Blindness, 77,* 8–11.

Rogers, C. (1969). *Freedom to learn.* Columbus, Ohio: Charles E. Merrill.

Rosal, M. L. (1985a). *The use of art therapy to modify the focus of control and adaptive behavior of behavior disordered students.* Unpublished doctoral dissertation. University of Queensland, Brisbane, Australia.

Rosal, M. L. (1985b). *The use of personal construct drawings as an art therapeutic outcome measure.* Paper presented at the Annual Conference of the American Art Therapy Association, New Orleans, LA.

Rosal, M. L. (1986). *The rating of personal construct drawings to measure behavior change.* Paper presented at the Annual Conference of the American Art Therapy Association, Los Angeles, CA.

Rosal, M. L. (1987). *Cognitive approaches in art therapy with children.* Paper presented at the Annual Conference of the American Art Therapy Association, Miami, FL.

Ross, J. (1982). An artist interprets raw emotion. *Oakland Tribune/Eastbay Today,* Tuesday, June 22, 1982.

Rubin, J., & Klineman, J. (1974). They opened our eyes. *Education of the Visually Handicapped, 6,* 106–113.

Rutledge, D. N., & Dick, G. (1983). Spinal cord injury in adolescence. *Rehabilitation Nursing, 8*(6), 18–21.

Salome, R. A. (1964). The effects of perceptual training upon the two-dimensional drawings of children. *Studies in Art Education, 5*(1): 18–33.

Satz, J. (1986). Another first: The National Park Service opens summer work programs to students with disabilities. *The Exceptional Parent, 16*(2), 19–22.

Schein, J. D., & Marcus, I. D., Jr. (1974). *The deaf population of the United States.* Silver Springs, MD: National Association of the Deaf.

Scott, E. P. (1982). *Your visually impaired student: A guide for teachers.* Baltimore, MD: University Park Press.

Seligman, M. E. (1975). *Helplessness. On depression, developmental, and death.* San Francisco: W. H. Freeman.

Shultz, E. E., Jr. (1983). Depth of processing by mentally retarded and MA-matched nonretarded individuals. *American Journal of Mental Deficiency, 88,* 307–313.

Silver, R. A. (1966). *The role of art in the conceptual thinking, adjustment and aptitudes of deaf and aphasic children.* Unpublished doctoral dissertation, Columbia University, New York.

Skinner, B. (1953). *Science and human behavior.* New York: Free Press.

Spraftkin, J., Gadow, K. D., & Dussault, M. (1986). Reality perceptions of television: A preliminary comparison of emotionally disturbed and nonhandicapped children. *American Journal of Orthopsychiatry, 56,* 147–152.

Sternberg, R. J., & Spear, L. C. (1985). A triarchic theory of mental retardation. In N. R. Ellis (Ed.), *International review of research in mental retardation* (Vol. 13, pp. 301–326). New York: Academic Press.

Storey, K., Sacks, S. Z., & Olmstead, J. (1985). Community-referenced instruction in a technological work setting: A vocational education option for visually handicapped students. *Journal of Visual Impairment and Blindness, 79,* 481–486.

Sullivan, P. M. (1982). Administration modifications on the WISC–R Performance Scale with different categories of deaf children. *American Annals of the Deaf, 127,* 780–788.

Telford, C. W., & Sawrey, J. M. (1977). *The exceptional individual* (3rd ed.). Englewood Cliffs, NJ: Prentice-Hall.

Thorne, J. H. (1990). Mainstreaming procedures: Support services and training. *NAEA Advisory.* Reston, VA: The National Art Education Association.

Tinsdale, W. J., Blackhurst, A. E., & Marks, C. H. (1971). Divergent thinking in blind children. *Journal of Educational Psychology, 62,* 468–473.

Tuttle, K. D. (1974). A comparison of three reading media for the blind: Braille, normal recording, and compressed speech. *Research Bulletin: American Foundation for the Blind.* (No. 27-230)

Ullman, L., and Krasner, L. P. (1969). *A psychological approach to abnormal behavior.* Englewood Cliffs, NJ: Prentice-Hall.

U. S. Department of Health Education and Welfare. (1974). *Prevalence of chronic skill and musculoskeletal conditions — United States 1969.* Vital and Health Statistics, No. 92, Series 10.

Wardell, K. (1980). Environmental modifications. In R. Walsh and S. Blasch (Eds.), *Foundations of orientation and mobility* (pp. 427–524). New York: American Foundation for the Blind.

Weissberg, R. P., & Allen, J. P. (1986). Promoting children's social skills and adaptive interpersonal behavior. In B. A. Edelstein & L. Michelson (Eds.), *Handbook of prevention.* New York: Plenum.

Wisniewski, K., & Lupin, R. (1979). Fetal alcohol syndrome and related CNS problems. *Neurology, 29,* 1429–1430.

Chapter 2

AN OVERVIEW OF CHILDREN'S NORMAL DEVELOPMENT IN ART

In this chapter, information about normal children's development in art is covered. This information is included to facilitate planning appropriate art experiences for children with disabilities.

In assessing a child's strengths in art and in planning appropriate art experiences it will be important to consider the child's mental and chronological age. Some children whose mental age is different from their chronological age will probably produce artwork representative only of their mental age. Therefore, a child with a mental age of three years and a chronological age of 10 will create art that is comparable to that of an average three-year-old. It will also be important to have some framework within which to explain children's artwork. The framework selected in this book is a developmental one. If one views children's art from a traditional developmental perspective, all children, disabled or not, go through developmental stages.

Since some classroom teachers and art therapists may not be familiar with children's typical artistic development, a brief summary will be included here. A synoptic evaluation chart for assessing growth at each level is also included. For further information the reader is urged to study other original sources (Harris, 1963; Kellogg, 1970; Lansing, 1969; Lowenfeld & Brittain, 1975, 1987; McFee & Degge, 1980; Wilson & Wilson, 1977; Gardner, 1990).

SUMMARY OF NORMAL CHILDREN'S ARTISTIC DEVELOPMENT

The most widely utilized framework to explain children's normal artistic development is that provided by Viktor Lowenfeld (Lowenfeld & Brittain, 1975, 1987). There are many others who have researched this basic area (Kellogg, 1970; Lindstrum, 1964; Lansing, 1969; Salome & Moore, 1979a; Salome & Moore, 1979b), but because Lowenfeld's chronologizing of the artistic stages of development is the most widely known, it is his theory which will be discussed in detail. Some other research on the art abilities

Some information for the discussion of childrens artistic development has been adapted from *Creative and Mental Growth*, 8th edition by Vikor Lowenfeld & W. Lambert Brittain. © 1987 by the MacMillan Publishing Company. Used by permission of the publisher.

of normal children will also be described later in the chapter and summarized in charts. Most developmental approaches covered seem to share at least some similar characteristics that Lowenfeld identified in his determination of artistic developmental stages. As each developmental level is described in this section some suggestions about drawing and painting activities are also discussed.

In using the research of Lowenfeld, the reader must be aware that since many children are now a part of the television generation, their perceptual development seems to be accelerated. This acceleration may be reflected in their artistic development, and children may be progressing through the Lowenfeldian developmental stages at a more rapid rate than would have been expected even a decade ago. One should utilize the artistic developmental stages documented by Lowenfeld as broad *guidelines* and benchmarks of growth.

Scribbling Stage (*18 Months to 4 Years Typically*)

The typical child has been learning about himself and the world around him from his first breath. However, the eye-hand coordination necessary to pick up a drawing instrument and the ability to make a mark on a page do not develop until about age two. These first marks are randomly placed and are relatively disordered sweeps across the paper.

Random Scribbling

Random scribbles are records of kinesthetic actions and are intrinsically pleasing to the child. There is no connection between these marks on the paper and any specific object in the real environs.

Controlled Scribbling

Next, according to Lowenfeld, a child will move into the controlled scribbling stage which occurs *about six months after his first random scribbles.* These controlled scribbles are achieved as the child learns that there is a connection between his marks on the page and the movements which he has made. With this connection established, the child will repeat similar or same kinds of lines. One researcher (Kellogg, 1970) has identified 20 different basic scribbles which children make.

Named Scribbles

At around 3½ years, the child moves from thinking kinesthetically to thinking imaginatively. He names his marks. These marks appear little changed from other controlled scribbles he has made. Naming his

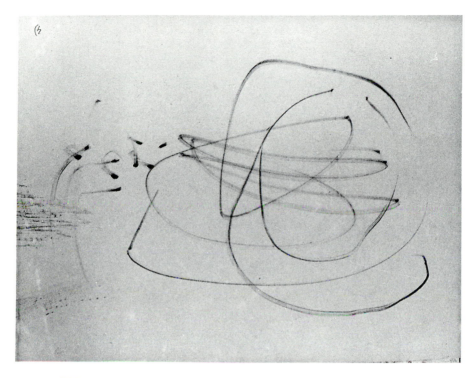

Figure 2.1. A scribble drawing done by a three-year-old boy. The repetition of several of the same lines and marks indicates that the child has gained some control over his drawing tool. This control was also evident during the creation of the drawing. The child watched what he was doing and did not go off the page with the marker. (*c.* 33 by 48 cm.)

scribbles means that the child is relating to the world outside of himself.

Art Skills

Some of the basic art skills that have been identified at this level include the child's ability to draw a circle at three years and a square at age four (Cratty, 1970). Color discrimination also begins at this developmental point, and by the time the child is four years old, he can correctly name five colors and two geometric shapes (Castrup & Scott, 1972).

Art content

Activities need to be chosen for their appeal to several senses, and part of the focus should be on discovery (Young, 1972). This does not mean a whole host of media is presented. It does mean that a careful selection and presentation of art activities that can assist in building the child's concepts of his environment should be utilized (Young, 1972; Harms, 1972).

TABLE 2.1
GROWING CHART/SCRIBBLING STAGE
(TYPICALLY 1.5-4 YEARS)

	Yes	*Sometimes*	*Not Yet*

Random Scribbles

1. Makes disordered marks
2. Copies a straight line
3. Pounds clay randomly

Controlled Scribbles

1. Repeats marks
   A. Horizontal
   B. Vertical
   C. Circular
2. Uses various methods of grasping, drawing, or painting
   instrument
3. Copies a circle
4. Makes coils and balls in clay

Named Scribbles

1. Gives names to scribbles and lumps of clay
2. Distinguishes one color from another
3. Names 5 colors
4. Names 2 geometric shapes
5. Matches shapes on the basis of color
6. Copies a square
7. Picks colors for painting randomly
8. Has increased attention span

Other

1. Follows cleanup procedures
2. Shares sometimes

Comments:

Preschematic Stage (*Four to Seven Years Typically*)

The child begins to relate more to his environment and less to his own body movements, and his created images reflect this. Thus, his drawings become a concrete record of these thought processes. One of the first graphic symbols (schema) to emerge is that of a person. This commonly consists of a head and extended lines for arms or legs and indicates the commencement of logical thought processes.

Schemata Emerge

At about five years the child starts to draw some representational symbols of objects other than the human figure. As he develops and refines his concepts of these items, the changes will be reflected in his drawing of them. Thus, many variations of a child's rendering of persons, houses, trees, or other items appear. The child experiments with his symbols for these objects until around age seven. Then the early symbols become fairly well-established schemata and the child moves into the next stage of artistic development called the schematic stage.

The child is also very much at the center of his world and is not fully ready to share and cooperate. He relates things and objects in the world mainly to his own body. This is reflected in his drawings where things may appear to float randomly in space. Beginning as early as four (and no later than age seven) the child can accurately judge right and left and visual space, using himself as the reference point (Cratty, 1970).

Link Between Art and Word Recognition and Counting Skills

According to Lowenfeld, word recognition and counting abilities develop during this period. Even though the child may be able to identify a word or count up to 10, the child does not really understand number concepts or what a particular word actually means. So while able to identify one or two words that are written, the child cannot yet read sentences. It is not until the child reaches the next stage of artistic development (schematic) that he is able to read sentences and paragraphs.

Artwork May Reflect Intellectual Functioning

Drawing also **may reflect** to some degree the child's level of intellectual functioning, his physical abilities, his emotional state or a perceptual problem. Thus, the child who is still scribbling, albeit in an ordered fashion, may not be as developed intellectually as the child who is drawing representational objects such as human figures or houses (Harris, 1963). While this is not a hard-and-fast conclusion, a child who is part of a typical class and who continues to scribble consistently while his age-mates are drawing objects that are recognizable to an adult, *may* be developmentally delayed or be having some perceptual, emotional or physical problem which warrants further investigation. The point is that given similar cultural backgrounds and school experiences, a normal five-year-old child should be drawing some recognizable images. Children whose drawings of objects are very

Figure 2.2. This crayon drawing is by a five-year-old boy. It shows his developing symbols for a man and for a house. The emerging mansymbol—head and feet and eye(s)—is drawn five times in the picture. The figures change each time so that one time the figure has no feet (*left*), another time it has arms and a hat and feet (*top*), or head, eyes, nose, and mouth (*right*). The large square near the center of the drawing is a television set. There is an orientation to the drawing in terms of top and bottom; however, there appears to be no meaningful visual relationship between the floating figures. These emerging symbols and floating placements suggest that the child is in the preschematic stage of artistic development. (*c.* 33 by 48 cm, from the collection of R. A. Salome.)

detailed may reflect their informational level about these items. Generally, children (beginning at around five years of age) who fail to include items from their surroundings, or who rather consistently draw stereotypic images, *may* have some degree of mental retardation or physical, emotional or cultural deprivation, or physical, sexual or emotional abuse (Lowenfeld and Brittain, 1987; Manning, 1987; Oster & Gould, 1987; Malchiodi, 1990).

Schemata and Color Variance

The drawings of the same object in the preschematic stage may vary greatly. By about six years of age, many children draw parts of items in meticulous detail even though these objects may be inaccurate in proportion. Color is usually chosen for its subjective appeal and not for its adherence to accurately matching colors that occur in the real world.

Social Interactions

Children in the four- to seven-year age range are generally inquisitive, enthusiastic and unafraid to try new tasks. These children are generally egocentric, and some may play side by side and fail to cooperate with one another.

Drawing becomes a means to help children figure out relationships and to understand items, concepts and their encounters with the world. Five-year-olds draw body parts with more accuracy than their ability to verbally identify these parts in other drawings or visuals. Therefore, the process of creating a drawing is more meaningful to the child than the process of looking at images.

Motivation

This stage of development is characterized by a period of accelerated perceptual growth. Most children need only the assistance of the adult to point out color differences in nature, or where a neck ends and a face begins. Once children have this greater awareness, these observations may be translated into details that are included in their artwork.

The most motivating situations will be those in which the child is directly involved and in which there is little time lapse between the experience and the art lesson. Topics for artwork should be directly relevant to the child. For example, the first symbols for persons the child draws are usually depictions of the child's own body or that of some family member. Motivational themes that are most potent will be related to the child's world and himself. In any motivation, care should be given to helping the child become aware of the details related to an art theme or topic. For example, having the children draw where they live will have more motivating power if some questions are asked about the child's dwelling place. The questions themselves become motivators. Questions might include: What color is your house (apartment)? Of what is the building made? How many rooms does it have?

Immediate, direct experience is one of the most powerful motivators for children. Field trips to a zoo or live experiences with pets in a classroom will be much more powerful learning experiences than just looking at pictures of these animals. Another example of a direct experience would be to have the children touch, taste (if feasible) or smell an object before drawing it. If vegetables are a topic of study, for example, it would be helpful to have vegetables in the room that children could examine. Or if the class is studying teeth, it might make sense to have the children taste or chew something before proceeding with a drawing or painting of someone chewing something. This experience would be a more powerful motivator than just talking about what foods were easy or hard to chew.

The materials of art can be motivating as well. The child is involved in a trip of exploration of his world. Paint, glue, nature objects, and other art media can be a part of that world. Clay is one of the most powerful, intrinsically motivating media because it engages several senses including the ability to see and to touch. Merely providing these various materials and having the child explore them does **not** constitute a total art program. An art program is much more than mere exploration.

Art Skills and Content

Some of the expected psychomotor skills (Castrup & Scott, 1972) are enumerated in the summary chart (Table 2.2) for this level. It is important for the teacher or adult who works with children at this or any other level to provide a supportive, encouraging atmosphere and an attitude of interest and flexibility. This supportive approach is better than a teacher who runs an authoritarian or laissez faire, totally permissive classroom. A program should provide sensory experiences and relate directly to the child and his world; suggesting topics such as "my family" or "my house" can help to motivate the child in his artwork.

An art program should focus on developing expressive skills, aesthetic awareness, and conceptual learning. Care should be taken to insure that the child goes beyond his discoveries of materials to the development of expressive skills using these materials. The child needs time and repeated experiences with the same media to develop in-depth artistic expression (Saunders, 1968). A great deal of the program will involve painting, drawing and cut-and-paste paper pictures.

The basic aim of the art program should be on the creative process—the doing, the creating, rather than the end product. Adults should be aware of this and not expect polished finished products. In fact, although some children are concerned with the finished art product, many at this level of development may not have any interest in the completed artwork (Lowenfeld & Brittain, 1975, 1987).

Schematic Stage (*Seven to Nine Years*)

During the preschematic stage the child experiments with his graphic symbols as he attempts to develop his own schemata. In the schematic stage, these schemata become specific personal symbols and are consistently drawn. (A schema is an individual's own unique visual concept of an object, such as a person, house, tree, or flower. A schema is consistently drawn unless

TABLE 2.2
GROWING CHART/PRESCHEMATIC STAGE
(TYPICALLY 4-7 YEARS)

	Yes	Sometimes	Not Yet

Two-Dimensional Work

1. Form for person emerges — is usually a representation of self or some family member
   a. Head, feet depicted (c. 5 years)
   b. Details of arms, face, and others included in figure drawings (c. 6 years)
   c. Body parts drawn with greater accuracy than ability to name or recognize them
   d. Names all parts of face and rest of body
2. **Schemata** for trees, persons, houses, etc.
   a. Constantly being altered as concepts are being built
3. Colors picked for their intrinsic, subjective appeal. Rarely relate to actual color of object in world
4. Spatial Representation
   a. Objects float in space
   b. Objects appear randomly placed
   c. Placement reflects egocentricity of child

Three-Dimensional Work

1. Can make a ball of clay
2. Can make a flat clay form
3. Can join 2 pieces of clay
4. Can make a construction that stands on its own

Art Skills Achieved (c. 5 years)

1. Correctly holds crayons
2. Correctly holds brush
3. Correctly holds scissors
4. Tears paper in straight line
5. Mixes 2 colors correctly
6. Glues objects but may
   a. have trouble using right amount
   b. have trouble applying even coat
   c. place glue on wrong side of object
7. Identifies most colors except
   a. grey
   b. bright and dull colors
8. Has trouble identifying smooth textures, thick/thin, and light lines

TABLE 2.2 (Continued)

	Yes	Sometimes	Not Yet

Other

1. Will work side by side and share art media but cannot really cooperate with other children
2. Can identify own work
3. Can follow directions in sequence
4. Can clean up without prodding
5. Can cut paper with scissors
6. Can cut some cloth with scissors

Comments:

specific instruction in a particular lesson alters this image or it is exaggerated due to the importance the creator may place on it.) Schemata are not stereotypes but are, rather, the child's own visual vocabulary; they reflect what he knows about an object represented.

Baseline and Skyline Appears

During the schematic stage, the child begins to order objects in his drawings along a baseline. By about eight years of age almost all children include a baseline. The child is representing only the flat (two-dimensional) aspects of objects. A strip of sky may appear at the top of the page. On occasion, the child may use two baselines in the same drawing. Sometimes this is the child's attempt to create the appearance of depth in a two-dimensional drawing. Objects on these baselines are often perpendicular to the baselines, even if the baseline is a curved one.

Spatial Representation

There are variations in the way the child represents space during this stage. He may use baselines, foldovers, and/or x-ray drawings. In a foldover (or foldup) picture, part of the drawing appears upside down or sideways to the viewer. If the picture were folded (up or over, depending on the placement of the objects), all items would appear right side up. In this way, the child may draw both sides of a street in the same picture. What really appears to be happening is that the child includes two parallel baselines with objects drawn perpendicular to them. Figures 2.3 to 2.6 illustrate these ways of representing space.

Figure 2.3. This crayon drawing, entitled "My Friends at Church," is by a seven-year-old girl. The repetition of the stick figures indicates that the artist's schema for figures has been established. Although the figures and cars seem to float in space, the child has used the edge of the paper as a baseline for the church. Although the girl has not actually drawn-in either a skyline or a baseline, she has shown an x-ray view of the interior of the church with all the chairs lined up. The work is an early schematic drawing. (*c.* 33 by 48 cm, International Collection of Child Art, Ewing Museum of Nations, Illinois State University, Normal, Illinois.)

Sometimes it is only a part of an object that is folded or tilted up. The child may do this because a particular object may have special significance and importance in a drawing. Or the child may be trying to attempt foreshortening. Thus, in a picture of the family eating Thanksgiving dinner, the tabletop may be tilted up so that the viewer gets a bird's eye view of it and all the dishes on it. This mixture of plane and elevation in the same picture may also be done to show several activities or to indicate several different time segments or several different points of view in a drawing. The child seems to desire being inclusive of one important event which may have several parts to it.

Additionally in this stage, children may draw x-ray pictures to depict both the inside and outside of an object. This x-ray depiction may in fact be cut away to show what is going on inside the object. These spatial representations follow a child's logic and what he knows about the subject rather than laws of perspective or representation from an adult point of view.

Figure 2.4. This painting, "Girl with Braids in the Spring," is by a five-year-old girl. The artist's work is typical of the schematic stage, and she may be artistically advanced. The child may be reflecting an early exposure to complex visual images via television which may accelerate development. A skyline is painted across the top of the picture. A schema for flowers is developed and repeated along the bottom. The exaggerated braids and bows illustrate how a child will enlarge those items which have a particular significance. This exaggeration, the skyline, and the flower schema are all typical of work in the schematic stage. (*c.* 48 by 64 cm, International Collection of Child Art, Ewing Museum of Nations, Illinois State University, Normal, Illinois.)

Variations in Schemata

The child may vary his developed schemata intentionally. He may emphasize and enlarge important parts. For example, if the child just went to the dentist and had a tooth filled, he might enlarge his mouth and his teeth in a drawing or painting of the experience. The child may omit seemingly unimportant parts of objects. Also, the child may ignore (deny) some parts for emotional and psychological reasons. For example, the child who is confined to a wheelchair may omit legs on his figure drawings. The child that wears a hearing aid may omit earphones on his depictions of human heads. The children may be omitting these details because they have not fully accepted their disability, or because feet and ears are unimportant to, or not used by them. These variations depend on the child's experiences and the significance which such experiences have for him. The proportions which a child may use in a picture, therefore, may shift from time to time.

Color Use

The child also develops a schemata for color. His concepts of colors of objects will depend on the particular experiences he has had with these

Figure 2.5. "Jumping Rope on the Playground" is by a seven-year-old boy. The artist has painted two views of these rope jumpers. The figures appear to be lying down on either side of an invisible centerline. If the painting were folded along this invisible line, the figures would be standing up. This means of depicting space is called a foldover and is typical of the schematic stage. (*c.* 48 by 64 cm, International Collection of Child Art, Ewing Museum of Nations, Illinois State University, Normal, Illinois.)

objects. For example, if the child's initial awareness of the color of shoes were blue, then all shoes might be generalized as being blue. The child's ability to generalize and develop schemata for colors or objects represent an important development in his ability to think abstractly. As the child generalizes from "this leaf is green" to "trees are green," his color schema for trees is being established. The development of correct object color choice and use indicate that the child has found that there is logic to the way things in the world are organized and is relating in a concrete way to this order.

Relationship of Art to Reading

According to Lowenfeld (Lowenfeld & Brittain, 1987), the child in this period moves from a predominately ego-centered perspective to a more other-centered perspective on the world. As the child perceives himself along with others in his environs, he becomes more of a social being and is able to cooperate with others. The inclusion of a baseline in pictures and the placement of other objects on it suggests that the child is ready to begin a full-fledged program of reading. Children view graphic symbols, letters, and words in a similar way (as opposed to viewing words as symbols for sounds). This similar way of viewing words, letters, and graphic symbols may be the basis behind the relationship between baselines occurring in

Figure 2.6. "My Friends at Play" is a crayon drawing by a seven-year-old girl. The figures here have less of the stick-like quality and are fuller than those in "My Friends at Church" (Fig. 2.3). The figures here are placed along two distinct baselines. This double baseline is a way of ordering space in the schematic stage. Note the developed schemata for girls, boys, and birds. Note also that the schema for girls is specifically changed in the rendering of the two larger figures in the middle of the picture. This kind of conscious alteration in schema does occur when a specific individual or object is depicted. (*c.* 33 by 48 cm, International Collection of Child Art, Ewing Museum of Nations, Illinois State University, Normal, Illinois.)

drawing and the development of reading readiness. Relationships between symbols are important in these drawings, and the relationships parallel word relationships in reading.

Stereotyped Schemata

According to Lowenfeld there is a danger of the child's schemata becoming rigid and stereotyped unless many varied experiences with the objects are provided. By offering these varied experiences, the teacher can help the child expand his concepts and alter his schemata from time to time. It is important to focus on expanding the child's personal awareness of aspects of his world rather than imposing information on him. This fostering of personal awareness of the environs can be enhanced by asking the child careful and discerning questions about his experiences and by relating these experiences to what the child records in paint and crayon or marker.

For example, a child may have a specific schema for a flower. During the spring the teacher may want to bring in several different kinds of flowers or take the class to a greenhouse. As they draw spring pictures for the field trip

Figure 2.7. This painting, entitled "Friends Walking in the Rain," is by an eight-year-old boy. Here, the figures are full, though flat and stiff, and facial details such as eyelashes are shown. The figures are placed along the paper edge as though on a baseline. Some details of the raincoat are shown. The space between the top and bottom, though filled with raindrops, does not have depth to it. The two-dimensional nature of the picture, the still figures, facial details, the placement on a "paper" baseline, and the outlining with a continuous contour of the figures are all characteristic of work in the later phases of the schematic stage. (c. 48 by 61 cm, International Collection of Child Art, Ewing Museum of Nations, Illinois State University, Normal, Illinois.)

experience, the teacher can show them the different colors and smells and shapes that each plant has. This will encourage a variety of drawn symbols for flowers.

Late Schematic Art

Toward the close of the schematic stage at around nine years of age, the child begins to draw more of what he sees of objects and relies less and less on what he knows of these objects. (Concepts and precepts begin to be reciprocal.) Therefore, more activities which have direct experiences and observations may encourage this development in the child.

Also, toward the end of the schematic stage the space between the sky and ground becomes important and there is a conscious effort to fill the entire page with items that are related to each other (see Figure 2.9). The child acquires an increasing interest in the world and a curiosity about both nature and man-made objects. These characteristics become more pronounced in the gang stage which is the next stage of artistic development.

Figure 2.8. The seven-year-old male artist of "My Mother Irons Clothes" has tilted up the ironing board because it is a particularly important part of the crayon drawing. In showing this view of the ironing board by drawing it from the top, the child can show all the important items on it. Tilting up a part of a drawing in this way to show two points of view in the same picture typically occurs during the schematic level of artistic development. Note that the child has begun to fill the space between the bottom and the top of the drawing, shown some action, and included a little intentional overlapping. This suggests more advanced work occurring late in the schematic stage. (*c.* 33 by 48 cm, International Collection of Child Art, Ewing Museum of Nations, Illinois State University, Normal, Illinois.)

Themes and Content of the Art Program

Themes from the child's dreams and fantasy world can be very motivating to the child as well as direct experience with the immediate environment. During this schematic stage children should be encouraged to further develop their basic cutting, gluing, and construction abilities. As the child uses three-dimensional media such as wood, clay, and cardboard, he begins to expand his spatial concepts. In working with clay, the additive or add-on method of constructing is still valid, and it is not important to have a finished, kiln-fired ceramic work. In fact, in the add-on approach, most clay work will not survive the firing. For the child in this level, the artistic/creative process is still of primary importance to him. There should be a good match between the art activity selected and the art media used to execute that activity. For example, clay has expressive properties that other art media lack. Paint has fluid qualities that other media such as markers or pencils lack. Alternatively, markers provide for a much more controlled expressive form.

The basic aim of an art program at this stage of development should be

Figure 2.9. In this crayon drawing, entitled, "My Town" by an eight-year-old girl, every part of the picture is organized and filled with objects. This filling of the page also occurs late in the schematic stage. The space, though ordered, remains flat and two-dimensional in spite of the child's attempt at showing depth by adding diagonal lines in the sidewalk. Two baselines have been used (one at the top of the picture with cars on it and one along the bottom of the buildings), yet the space between them is filled with numerous objects. An x-ray of one of the stores has also been used. The front of the department store on the right has been cut away to reveal all three of the interior floors (including clothing on the racks, a salesperson, a customer, and a woman buying shoes). A schema for cars has been used. This schema includes four wheels and indicates the artist has represented what she knows about automobiles, not what is actually seen. (*c.* 46 by 61 cm, International Collection of Child Art, Ewing Museum of Nations, Illinois State University, Normal, Illinois.)

"to develop a positive self-image, to encourage self-confidence in expression, and to provide the opportunity for constructive divergent thinking" (Lowenfeld and Brittain, 1987, p. 302).

Gang Age: The Dawning Realism (*Typically 9 to 12 Years*)

During this period children discover that they are a part of a larger world, a world that includes their peers. They learn that cooperation is a necessary skill to function successfully in the adult world. This is a period of group relationships and activities. Girls tend to prefer the company of other girls, and boys prefer all-male cliques. Each group develops some special interests that are reflected in their artwork.

In the past, such interests coincided somewhat with externally imposed role expectations. For example, boys had a great interest in cars and machines;

TABLE 2.3
GROWING CHART/SCHEMATIC STAGE
(TYPICALLY 7–9 YEARS)

	Yes	*Sometimes*	*Not Yet*

Human Schema (2-dimensional work)

1. Clearly identifiable
2. Includes body, arms, legs (or clothing)
   a. Head and facial parts
   b. Other details
3. Frontal or side view or combination but figures rarely seen directly interacting with each other
4. Human form depicted with ease in 3-dimensional as well as 2-dimensional media

Spatial Representation (2-dimensional work)

1. Objects set along a baseline
2. Sometimes 2 baselines in same picture
3. Objects are flat
4. Skyline appears
5. Fold-over or fold-up pictures
6. Several items form different points of view
7. Different events or time sequences in same picture
8. X-ray presentations

Color

1. Schema for colors develops
2. More accurate relationship of colors to objects

Schemata vary at times

1. Significant parts enlarged
2. Unimportant items omitted
3. Suppressed objects (ideas) also left out

Art Skills

1. Full ability to use correctly
   a. paint
   b. drawing items
   c. scissors
2. Can sculpt with clay using the additive method
3. Better able to share work
4. Can cooperate with others on group projects

Comments:

girls preferred animals, especially horses. With the current women's rights movement, these sexually stereotyped interests may be shifting to more idiosyncratic ones. We do still see that boys exhibit a greater interest in group sports activities, cars, space themes, gangs and hideouts, while girls have a greater interest in clothes, horses/unicorns, music, clubs (for girls only) and parties.

Schemata Becomes More Representational

In the child's two-dimensional work, he finds his schemata too limiting, and he may expand these to include more details. Instead of geometric shapes, a more representational rendering of shapes and forms is used to depict body parts, houses, trees, and other items. However, these drawings are not yet a totally representational view of the world as an adult would perceive it.

Also during this period there is less inclusion of movement and action in figures than might occur during the schematic stage. In fact, figures appear rather stiff. Folds in clothing usually are not included, and hemlines are usually drawn as straight lines. No longer do exaggeration and omissions of parts occur, nor foldover or x-ray pictures. Occasionally, there may be enlargements or distortions of one segment of a drawing.

Color Use

Color is freed now from its former strict adherence to objects, and subtler color differences are noted. The child is now aware that the green color of grass is a different green from the green of a leaf or a particular kind of plant. However, children still will not have developed their color perceptions enough to note the difference between colors in sunlight and in shade or the changes which distance and atmosphere have on colors, unless art instruction is provided to assist in this awareness of the subtleties of color.

Spatial Representation

While object placement in relationship to other objects and in relationship to the picture plane occurs during the late schematic stage, objects in the gang stage are even more carefully arranged on the page in a definite relationship to each other. This reflects the child's growing ability to handle several ideas at the same time. Objects are not now exclusively placed along the baseline. The space between the sky and the ground becomes more important, and this space (called the ground plane) is consciously filled by the child. The child begins to more consciously overlap objects in his drawings and paintings. There appears to be a link between the ability to draw and the ability to read a map at this stage of development. An 11-year-old will draw an event from one perspective or viewpoint. This one viewpoint is different from the multiple viewpoints typical of schematic age learners.

Figure 2.10. This painting, entitled "My Friends," is by a nine-year-old boy. The picture is typical of work executed early in the Gang Age. Several repeated figures are shown and some attempt at showing action is made, yet the figures remain stiff and frozen. The artist has overlapped several objects in the picture and placed the fence above and behind the figures to create more depth to the picture. This illusion of some depth to the picture is characteristic at this developmental level. The figures have been turned to present a profile view. Clothing details such as belt tabs and cuffs are shown. (*c.* 48 by 64 cm, International Collection of Child Art, Ewing Museum of Nations, Illinois State University, Normal, Illinois.)

Figure 2.11. During the Gang Age more attention is given to clothing details and patterns. In "The Carol Singers," the nine-year-old female artist has rendered the dresses with attention to the details. The "baseline" has disappeared and has been replaced with a shallow plane on which the three figures stand. A beginning awareness of perspective is indicated by the way the music books are drawn and in the rendering of the front view of the feet in the figures on the right and in the middle. (*c.* 61 by 46 cm, International Collection of Child Art, Ewing Museum of Nations, Illinois State University, Normal, Illinois.)

Figure 2.12. Both profile and frontal views of figures are included in this painting, entitled "Singing on the Corner," by a twelve-year-old girl. Although stiff, the figures are better proportioned in this work from the later phases of the Gang Age. Now, within the same drawing, changes appear from figure to figure in terms of clothing, size, placement, and position. The artist has considerable overlapping of figures and objects in the picture and has attempted one-point perspective in her rendering of the sidewalk which goes off the page at the right. The figures stand in a shallow plane in front of the building. (c. 48 by 64 cm, International Collection of Child Art, Ewing Museum of Nations, Illinois State University, Normal, Illinois.)

Subject Matter

The child becomes more aware of the world around him. While also characteristic of the late schematic stage, this awareness is keener during the gang age. There is an increased curiosity of the man-made and natural environs. Children become collectors of all sorts of treasures from their environment. This can be a potent motivating force in their art. Design principles can be studied by studying nature as a designer. Additionally now in rendering figures children focus more on decoration and attend to details such as pattern on clothing.

The nine-year-old develops a strong sense of right and wrong; this is part of his moral development. A child's inner world will be important subject matter during this stage of development. Artwork can reveal intense emotions. Wilson and Wilson (1977), in fact, have documented an out-of-school artistic style that occurs throughout the child's school years which is more intense, base and expressive than the work the child may do as part of a planned school art activity.

Children enjoy working on group (especially same-sex group) art projects

because of the greater awareness of peers and groups at this age. Cooperation as an overall theme will be important as this relates to community
participation. Examples of this would be topics such as helping with flood
victims or helping the homeless. The key is to gear the art activity to what
seems to be of greatest interest to the child.

ART PROGRAMS IN THE MIDDLE SCHOOL

As the learner leaves the elementary school and enters middle or junior
high school, there may be an end to his exposure to a regular art program.
In a study of art offerings only 30 states reported having visual arts available
in about half of their schools at these grade levels (Mills & Thompson, 1981).
More recent economic cutbacks have resulted in serious curtailments of art
programs and the elimination of trained art teachers to teach in them. The
years in secondary school are a time when the learner is attempting to
discover who he is, what his core values are, and what direction his life will
take.

Peer and Television Influence

Television and peers may well be some of the most powerful influences on
students in the middle school. By 15 years of age the average adolescent has
spent more time in front of the television set than in school (Swerdlow,
1981). The peer group becomes even more important and members serve as
mirrors, models and mentors for the learner. In a study of who adolescents
considered significant to them, more listed same-sex peers than any other
person (Blythe, Hill & Theil, 1982).

Two Types of Creative Mindedness—Haptic/Visual Types

Based on early work with the partially sighted, Lowenfeld (1939) found
that some individuals relied on what sight they had to explore their environment while others relied primarily on their tactile sense. Later work by
Lowenfeld (1945, 1966) showed that of eight subjects, 47 percent displayed
clear visual tendencies and 23 percent haptic. The remainder were somewhere in the middle. This tendency to be either haptic or visual occurred
around 12 years of age.

These divisions and descriptors of the ways students learn in art have
been refuted in other research (Rouse, 1965). Few art educators today refer to
haptic or visually oriented learners. In the 1990s there is an awareness that
students have different learning styles and that some rely more on kinesis
and active learning. Other students are primarily auditory learners and still
others are visual learners. Therefore, instruction should take into account
the ways students receive and process information, and all learning chan-

TABLE 2.4
GROWING CHART/GANG AGE: THE DAWNING REALISM
(TYPICALLY 9–12 YEARS)

	Yes	*Sometimes*	*Not Yet*

Human Schema (2-dimensional work)

1. Many more details appear
2. Fewer geometric shapes and more natural forms and shapes included for body parts
3. Many more details in the figure
4. Many more details in clothing (patterns, decoration)
5. Hemlines straight
6. Folds omitted
7. Figures stiff, little action portrayed
8. Schema appears in 3-dimensional media as well

Spatial Representation (2-dimensional work)

1. Space between sky and ground filled and ordered
2. Baseline disappears
3. Overlapping of objects
4. Still some exaggeration of objects due to emotional importance

Color

1. Less generalized schema
2. Variations in the object-color adherence

Topics differ for artwork by boys and girls

1. Girl's work tends to have
   a. more smiling people
   b. more clothing details
   c. more objects depicting the environs
   d. fewer sports themes
   e. music/parties
   f. horses
2. Boy's work tends to have
   a. cars
   b. sports themes
   c. space/rocket themes

Art Skills

1. Can mix own colors
2. Can use wood tools appropriately
3. Can work 3-dimensionally with paper
4. Still uses additive method in clay

Works well with others (in same-sex groupings)

Comments:

nels (auditory, visual, kinesthetic and tactile) should be utilized by art teachers and therapists in working with students.

Pseudo-Naturalistic Stage Age of Reasoning (*Typically 12 to 14 Years*)

This stage is characterized as the preadolescent period. Emotionally, learners are torn between moving into the peer culture with the attendant anxiety of this move and remaining loyal to the values of their families. They vacillate between acquiring mastery in relationships and moving toward peers or choosing an alternative path of withdrawal into a fantasy world which is often very solitary. Intellectually, the learner grasps abstractions. This period of middle or junior high school may be the last time many learners will encounter art in school.

In this stage, there is a change to an adult point of view in artistic rendering and expression. No longer do students draw what they know about objects; rather, they draw what they perceive in the natural world. There is an increased critical awareness of the outcomes (product) of their own work. The focus is now much more on the end product and how it is accepted by peers, adults and the creator himself.

Schemata Replaced by More Representational Renderings

Schemata for human figures and other objects disappear and are replaced by a more representational depiction. The student includes joints in his figure drawings, and human forms move and appear more active and less **stiff** than in the gang age of development.

Folds of clothing appear, and there is an awareness of the effect of light and shade on colors and form. This awareness is reflected in figure drawings. Facial characteristics and hairstyles, while depicted by learners operating in earlier stages, are now more often depicted in drawings. Also, some students depict figures in caricature and cartoon forms. Males especially enjoy cartooning.

Differing Interests of Girls and Boys

Girls are more interested in drawing the human figure. In figure drawings by both boys and girls, exaggerated sexual characteristics may be included. This exaggeration is typical at this age and reflects the learner's concerns about his own physical changes. Drawings that omit sexual characteristics may suggest the learner is afraid or is not accepting the physical changes occurring in his body. These figure drawings often occur in margins of notebooks or on paper scraps. The subjects are typical expressions appropriate to this stage of development. They are representations of what

Figure 2.13. "My Friends Are Marketing," by a thirteen-year-old boy, shows an awareness of linear perspectives in the rendering of the cans on the shelves, the counter, and the floor tiles. Compared with "Singing on the Corner" (Figure 2.12), this picture has greater depth, and the viewer is now actually looking into space. This depth and the more naturalistic proportioning and three-quarter view of the cashier are characteristic of the pseudo-naturalistic stage of artistic development. (*c.* 46 by 61 cm, International Collection of Child Art, Ewing Museum of Nations, Illinois State University, Normal, Illinois.)

Figure 2.14. In the painting entitled "First Baptist Church," the twelve-year-old male artist indicated depth by using linear perspective in his rendering of the church building and the sidewalk on the right which narrows. The attention to detail and pattern in the building, along with the depth in the picture and use of perspective, are typical of the pseudo-naturalistic level of development in art. (*c.* 48 by 61 cm, International Collection of Child Art, Ewing Museum of Nations, Illinois State University, Normal, Illinois.)

Wilson and Wilson (1977) identified as *out-of-school art.* Spatial representation is more sophisticated now. However, unless the student discovers for himself rules of perspective (or is specifically taught these rules), he will not make use of these artistic methods in his own work. The more kinesthetic learner will have little or no interest in learning perspective conventions.

There is still strong peer pressure to conform. Male interests include sports, computer hacking, and video games. Boys will tend to view art as an unmasculine activity—one for girls only. Strong motivation may be necessary to involve boys in the art room. Topics range from favorite sports or entertainment to aspects of school life. Materials choice and use should emerge out of the learner's own need to create and not be imposed by the teacher. More complex art media may be desirable. Crayons and tempera paint should be replaced by acrylic paint and oil pastels. As with all uses of art media, care should be taken to check for potentially dangerous health hazards that may come with the use of some art materials.

Content and Role of Art

Consideration should be given to the student as a future consumer and advocate of a well-designed environment. This is especially important since many students may never have another art class after junior high. Students should also be made aware of the vocational as well as avocational possibilities of the arts.

According to Lowenfeld and Brittain (1987), "the role of art at this stage of development is to support the youngster's individuality, to provide a socially acceptable release for emotions and tensions, and to ease the transition from the expression of a child to a type of expression typical of an adult" (Lowenfeld and Brittain, 1987, p. 395–396).

The role of art as articulated by Lowenfeld and Brittain (1987) may not be in keeping with current trends in art education toward a more discipline-based approach (Chapman, 1988, 1978; Duke, 1988, 1983). It is, however, quite compatible with goals that an art therapist might have for students who are between the ages of 12 and 14.

HIGH SCHOOL ART PROGRAMS

Adolescent Art: The Period of Decision (*14 to 17 Years of Age*)

Although one out of seven high school students choose to take art, only about half of the nation's high schools offer art as a subject. Lowenfeld and Brittain (1987) state that the purpose for a high school art program "should be to involve students more fully in the culture in which they find themselves;

Figure 2.15. In the pseudo-naturalistic stage, figures become more realistic. In this painting, entitled "My Friends," by a fourteen-year-old boy, features are rendered in a naturalistic way which includes shading and considerable attention to facial details. The central figure has more volume and is less stiff and flat than figures drawn by a child in any of the earlier developmental stages. The arm bends at the elbow, showing the artist's awareness of joints. (*c.* 47 by 61 cm, International Collection of Child Art, Ewing Museum of Nations, Illinois State University, Normal, Illinois.)

Figure 2.16. In the pseudo-naturalistic stage, the student sometimes is introspective and focuses on his own inner fantasy world. This painting, entitled "As I See Myself," by a thirteen-year-old female, reflects this introspectiveness. As the artist develops through this stage, she becomes more aware of the special effects that may be created with the medium. (*c.* 48 by 61 cm, International Collection of Child Art, Ewing Museum of Nations, Illinois State University, Normal, Illinois.)

TABLE 2.5
GROWING CHART/PSEUDO-NATURALISTIC STAGE:
THE AGE OF REASONING (TYPICALLY 12-14 YEARS)

	Yes	Sometimes	Not Yet

Human Figure (2-dimensional work)

1. Schema disappears
2. Joints indicated, figures active
3. Color changes indicated
4. Sexual characteristics sometimes exaggerated
5. Folds and wrinkles in clothes
6. Age factors included in figures
7. Cartoons/caricatures
8. The above reflected in 3-dimensional media as well

Spatial Representation (2-dimensional work)

1. Baseline disappears
2. Horizon line included
3. Discovery of perspective methods
   a. one point
   b. aerial (things smaller in distance)

Three-Dimensional Work

1. Interest in making functional clay work
2. Interest in making representational figures in clay, plaster, and wire

Other General Concerns

1. Focus on decorative qualities in work
2. Interest in fantasy topics
3. Concern for various artistic techniques
4. Concern for end product
5. Heightened criticism of own work

Comments:

it should provide a means of making tangible changes and the opportunity to face themselves and their own needs" (Lowenfeld and Brittain, 1987, p. 444).

During the adolescent period, artwork of these learners does not go through any major developmental transformation. The learners are concerned about how they fit into society. They are introspective, idealistic and

Figure 2.17. This drawing, entitled "SUE," by a seventeen-year-old girl, shows the artist's mastery of drawing techniques and sensitive use of line. This is an artistic statement by a high school student. (*c.* 46 by 61 cm, International Collection of Child Art, Ewing Museum of Nations, Illinois State University, Normal, Illinois.)

Figure 2.18. This untitled collage is by a seventeen-year-old female student. It is a commentary on the reality and fantasy of love. The subject and the way the artist has handled the materials reflect her own growing maturity and adult view of the world. (*c.* 31 by 46 cm, International Collection of Child Art, Ewing Museum of Nations, Illinois State University, Normal, Illinois.)

self-critical. They need chances for the expression of feelings and to feel their art has importance. High schoolers are ready for in-depth study of the fundamental methods, materials, and tools of the artist. The history of the world's artistic achievements and the aesthetic principles which have and do govern these achievements should also be a part of the art program. Learners should also be educated, informed consumers of art as it exists in everyday life. Rarely does the high school student end up becoming a professional artist (Lowenfeld & Brittain, 1987, 1975).

SOME OTHER DEVELOPMENTAL APPROACHES AND WAYS CHILDREN'S ART HAS BEEN STUDIED

The concluding section of this chapter briefly outlines Piaget's developmental approach and the approaches of some other scholars who have advocated a developmental perspective on children's artistic endeavors. Also, some recent findings in the field of developmental psychology are discussed which call into question Piaget's emphasis on universal developmental stages that transcend cultures. A chart that illustrates how the various developmental approaches parallel normal ages of children is included to give the reader a visual summary of these approaches.

Piaget

Piaget's developmental approach is noted briefly because Lansing (1969) based his theory of children's artistic development on Piaget's research. As the reader may know, Piaget (Piaget & Inhelder, 1956) identified three developmental stages relative to the child's emerging development of perception of spatial relationships and intelligence. Piaget noted that after the perception of images by a child occurs, then mental image development follows. These three Piagetian stages are: the sensorimotor period which runs from birth to 2 years, the concrete operations period which runs from age 2 to age 11, and the formal operations stage which runs from about 9 years to 11 years of age.

The concrete operations stage is subdivided into three parts: the preoperational or preparatory stage running from about age 2 to about age 4; the intuitive thought stage which runs from about age 4 to age 7; and the concrete operations stage which runs from around age 7 to age 11.

Lansing

As noted above, Lansing (1969) based his study of children's artistic development on the research of Piaget. Lansing identified three major stages of artistic development: the scribbling phase which runs from about 1.5 to 2 years, the figurative stage (with three parts; an early, middle and late

TABLE 2.6
ADOLESCENT ART: THE PERIOD OF DECISION
(14 TO 17 YEARS)

	Yes	*No*	*Not Yet*

Two-Dimensional Work

1. Drawings similar to 12-year-old work
2. Concern for acquiring art skills
3. Learner concerned about including details in work, including light and shadow or
4. Has much greater focus on subjective impressions of subject matter
5. Increased attention span
6. Mastery of a variety of art media

Spatial Representation (2-dimensional work)

1. Interest in learning one, two and three pt. and atmospheric perspective or
2. Will include subjective impressions based on mood. May distort representation to serve subjective purpose

Human Figure (2-dimensional work)

1. Some learners will attempt naturalistic representations including proportion and visual detail and action
2. Some will exaggerate details for specific purpose
3. Some learners will cartoon and caricature to make a point

Other:

Comments:

figurative stage) which runs from about 3 years to 12 years and the stage of artistic decision which begins at around 12 years of age. Lansing's stages, while different in name, are similar to those described by Lowenfeld and included earlier in this chapter. A chart (Table 2.7) has been included that summarizes the stages identified by Lowenfeld, Piaget, Lansing, and others. This chart shows how the varying developmental approaches relate to each other and to normal ages of children. In studying this chart the reader should keep in mind that while terms for stages may vary from researcher to

Figure 2.19. The careful rendering and execution of a sixteen-year-old high school student in the woodcut medium in "Old Man and His Dreams" indicate his concern for artistic skills and his successful mastery of them. He has gone beyond mastering skills to make an artistic interpretation of the subject. This kind of work may be expected from high school students who have had opportunities for an in-depth artistic study. (*c.* 43 by 38 cm, International Collection of Child Art, Ewing Museum of Nations, Illinois State University, Normal, Illinois.)

researcher, the general characteristics for art executed at specific ages detailed in the discussion of Lowenfeld will be similar, the "labels" will differ.

McFee

After extensive review of the research on how children develop in art (including the studies by Harris, 1963; Munro, Lark-Horovitz & Barnhart, 1942; Dennis, 1966a, 1966b; and Lowenfeld & Brittain, 1970), McFee (1970) concluded that Lowenfeld's stages of artistic development were too narrow and that there are only three major stages of development in art. These three stages are: scribbling, schematic and cultural realism. The age ranges for each of these stages overlap. Children in the scribbling stage start at around 2 years of age, and if children are left to their own efforts and there is no instruction, they can continue to scribble up to 5.5 years of age. The schematic stage can begin as early as 3 years of age and can run as long as 16

TABLE 2.7
**SUMMARY CHART OF CHILD ART DEVELOPMENT
ACCORDING TO: LOWENFELD, PIAGET, LANSING, MCFEE,
CHAPMAN, SALOME & MOORE, GARDNER**

LOWENFELD (1987)

AGE 0....1.5 yrs.....2 yrs.....4 yrs.....7 yrs.....9 yrs.....12 yrs.....14 yrs.

SCRIBBLING
(1.5.............................4 yrs)
  a. uncontrolled
    b. controlled
      c. named
        PRESCHEMATIC
          (4 ......7 yrs)
         SCHEMATIC
            (7 ......9 yrs)
              GANG
                (9 ......12 yrs)
                PSEUDONATURALISTIC
                  (12 ......14 yrs)
                HIGH SCHOOL-
                ADOLESCENT ART
                    (14 .....Adult)

PIAGET (1956)

AGE 0....2 yrs.....4 yrs.....7 yrs.....11 yrs.....12 yrs.....14 yrs.

SENSORIMOTOR
  (0 ...2 yrs)
CONCRETE OPERATIONS
    (2 ....11 yrs)
  Preoperational
    (2 ...... 4 yrs)
      Intuitive Thought
        (4 ......7 yrs)
          Concrete Operations
            (7 ......11 yrs)
              FORMAL OPERATIONS
              (12 yrs)

TABLE 2.7 (continued)

LANSING (1969)

AGE....1.5 yrs.....3 yrs.....6 yrs.....7 yrs.....9–10 yrs.....11 yrs.....12 yrs.

    SCRIBBLING
    (1.5 ......3 yrs)
    a. uncontrolled
      b. controlled
        c. named
    FIGURATIVE
          3 yrs................................11 yrs
      Early Figurative
          (3 ....7 yrs)
        Mid Figurative
            (6.................10 yrs)
          Late Figurative
              (9 ....11 yrs)
               ARTISTIC DECISION
                  (12 yrs)

MCFEE (1970)

AGE........2 yrs.....3 yrs.....5 yrs.....6.5 yrs............15–16 yrs.

    SCRIBBLING
      (2 ....5.5 yrs)
        SCHEMATIC
        (3.5.........................15 yrs on)
        CULTURAL REALISM
          (6.5 ....16 yrs on)

CHAPMAN (1978)

AGE....3 yrs.....5 yrs.....6 yrs.....8 yrs.....9 yrs.....11 yrs.....12 yrs. ....14 yrs.

    EARLY EXPLORATORY
      (3 ......5 yrs)
        EARLY EXPRESSIVE
        (6 ......8 yrs)
          PREADOLESCENT
          (9 ....11 yrs)
          ADOLESCENT
            (12 ....14 yrs)

TABLE 2.7 (continued)

SALOME & MOORE (1979a, 1979b)

```
AGE....2....3....4....5....6....7....9....10....11....12
        SCRIBBLING
        (2 ........4 yrs)
            PRESCHEMATIC
            (3 ................7 yrs)
                    SCHEMATIC
                    (6 ............10 yrs)
                        TRANSITIONAL
                        (9 ..............12 yrs)
                            REALISM
                            (11 ......on)
```

GARDNER (1990)

```
AGE....1 year........7 yrs.,8 yrs.........11 yrs.........14 yrs.
        SCRIBBLING
        (age not specified)
                CONVENTIONAL
                (7....8 yrs)
                        CULTURAL INFLUENCE
                        (9 years on .................)
                            ARTISTIC PROWESS
                            (Adolescence up)
                            (not all reach
                            this stage)
                                (13...on)
```

years or older. The final stage, cultural realism, can begin as early as 6½ years of age through adulthood, and some individuals never achieve it.

Salome and Moore

In 1979, Salome and Moore studied children's artistic development and concluded that there were five stages: scribbling (2 years to 4 years); preschematic (3 years to 7); schematic (6 years to 10 years); transitional (9 years to 12 years); and realism (from 11 years on). The major difference from Lowenfeld and McFee's theories in Salome and Moore's breakdown of stages comes in the 9- to 12-year period which they call transitional. Their characteristics of the transitional stage coincide with Lowenfeld's dawning realism/gang age stage. The realism stage of Salome and Moore coincides with Lowenfeld's pseudonaturalistic stage.

The chart in Table 2.7 summarizes the stages identified by Lowenfeld,

Piaget, Lansing, McFee and Gardner and shows how these all relate to one
another and to normal ages of children.

Some Explanations of Child Development in Art Production

Art as a Reflection of Personality

In a study in the late 1940s Altschuler and Hattwick (1969) tried to
relate the behavior characteristics of 150 nursery school children to their
paintings. Specifically, they concluded that children's color choice related
to their personalities. For example, children who chose warm colors were
more open and warm in their personalities, while children using cool
colors tended to be more aloof and controlled. Children who used mostly
black tended to be emotionally empty or flat. Altschuler and Hattwick
concluded that paintings of these children reflected traits similar to those
displayed by the same children in social situations. Lowenfeld and Brittain (1987) give some evidence that color choices made by young children may be more a function of where and in what order paints are
lined up on an easel. However, a child's art may reflect that child's emotional state (see the overview of art therapy with children by M. Rosal in
Chapter 3).

Art Based on Memory

Lowenfeld and Brittain (1987) look at children's drawings as a developmental continuum of stages and ages. Their research has relied primarily on
children's artwork drawn from memory and not on artwork produced as a
part of formal art instruction.

Art as an Index of Intelligence

Goodenough (1924) and Harris (1963) found that there was a positive
correlation between the number of details a child includes in his drawings
and his intelligence quotient. This relationship begins to drop off after
about 11 years of age. Harris was also aware that a child's culture impacts on
the number and types of details that child might include in a drawing.
Harris therefore concluded that scoring norms for drawings had to be
established and developed these criteria for each culture in which a child
under study was reared. Children in today's society come from an even more
diverse variety of subcultures than when Harris first realized the need for
different criteria for drawings by children from multicultural backgrounds.
Therefore, the child's specific subculture must be taken into account when
determining intelligence from the number of details that are included in a
drawing.

The Influence of Culture on Children's Art

Hess-Behrens (1973) conducted one of the most systematic and comprehensive cross-cultural studies of children's drawings (Anderson, 1979) and discovered that Piaget's theory of universal developmental stages was not supported (1973). Dennis (1966b) found that in children from cultures where human figure drawings were discouraged (had a negative value) those children's ability to draw the human figure disappeared the older they became. McFee (McFee & Degge, 1980), acknowledging these studies, concluded that no one theory can account for all the variables that impact on a child's development.

McFee (McFee & Degge, 1980) found that research did not support the conclusion that drawings of children could be fairly compared with other children's work—unless all had the same opportunities to learn and came from the same culture and subculture. McFee concludes that the following factors must be considered in studying children's artwork.

1. The way the culture has directed his or her attention.
2. Cognitive style in handling information: more analytic or global, more reflective or impulsive.
3. How he or she learned to relate to three-dimensional space.
4. Development of and dependence on the perceptual constancies.
5. How home and school environment encouraged the child to develop the creative traits of fluency, flexibility, originality, playful attitudes, and independence of conformity.
6. The learned concepts and how visual information is related to these concepts.
7. The precepts he or she is aware of, ability to manipulate forms in space, and analyze relationships.
8. The richness or dullness of visual environment. Whether there are drawings in his or her environment.
9. Past experiences in art, whether supportive, encouraging, defeating, or inhibiting.
10. Adaptation to the school environment as contrasted with the spatial environment at home.
11. Attitudes toward art activities compared to the kinds of art in his or her background culture. (McFee & Degge, 1980, p. 362)

McFee (McFee & Degge, 1980) came to the conclusion that the best approach to use in studying the artwork of children is to use the child's own prior artwork against which to make any comparisons.

Gardner

Like McFee, Gardner (1990) also acknowledged that there is a definite cultural influence on the way art is valued and the ways children depict objects in their artwork. Gardner cites research completed in the last decade that confirms McFee's earlier findings. Children coming from different cultures do have quite different cognitive styles and abilities. These differences are even greater when one takes into account the schooling factor. That is, there are greater differences between the development of children coming from cultures in which they attend formal schools and children coming from cultures in which there is no formal educational system. These conclusions run counter to Piaget's claim that children are more similar across all cultures than they are different.

Gardner, like McFee, does acknowledge that Western children generally do pass through a scribbling stage and then move into a transitional period in which simple crosses, dots and lines, and geometric forms are drawn. Next, human figures, animal forms, trees and suns, i.e., schemata, are developed and there is a schematic stage.

Then, according to Gardner, at seven or eight years of age children who are now in school become less idiosyncratic. They rely less on experimentation with forms, colors and pictoral composition and less on opportunistic subject matter, and their work becomes more uniform and conventional. These children begin to value an aesthetic in artwork that is more representational and relativistic. They become more critical of their own artwork, especially when it does not resemble the ways objects actually look in the real world. This third stage is similar to what McFee called cultural realism.

There is some disagreement as to reasons for this shift to a more realistic and representational rubric for art. Some researchers claim that this is the course of naturally developing events partly due to cultural influence. Other scholars agree the shift is a consequence of being in schools and is reflective of pressure on the student by teachers, fellow students or older schoolmates. This representational art occurs in the art room as a part of formal instruction. There is another type of art style that also begins to appear outside of the formal educational setting. Wilson and Wilson (1977) have documented an out-of-school artistic style which is more expressive, theatrical and base in its essence. These out-of-school artistic depictions occur in diaries, edges of notebook pages, on walls of public places such as subways and on sides of subway trains. There is at least one area of concurrence in the debate: children in Western culture, as they get older, tend to draw more infrequently.

With adolescence those who continue to be involved in art move to a different art style called "artistic prowess." This style is a mingling of a more personal expressiveness with increased artistic know-how and skill. When this synthesis is achieved the adolescent will continue his commitment and involvement in artistic endeavors.

After an examination of the research on development in art, Gardner concludes that artistic development appears to be more in the form of U-shaped curves rather than a gradual upward-moving line (Gardner, 1990).

Some New Findings from Developmental Psychology

Feldman (1987a, 1987b, 1980), citing recent research in developmental psychology, calls into question Piaget's universal tenet that everyone passes through growth stages.

According to Feldman, new findings in developmental psychological theory make distinctions between universals of development and human change that will happen in all children, and those components of development that will necessitate the ordered application of effort and resources in order for change to occur. That is, there are both universals and nonuniversals.

For nonuniversals to occur, conditions in the environment must be planned and specific and cultural. To learn specific art skills then there is a need for structured, sustained, and appropriate attempts for mastery within a specific culture context.

The universalist view in developmental psychology with respect to changes "is that children at different age levels tend to have quite differently organized minds and to go about their business in quite different ways; they are preoccupied with different issues and make sense of the world in dramatically different ways" (Feldman, 1987b, p. 249).

Feldman advocates the use of the universalist view of general developmental changes. This view should become a guide for expectations of what can work educationally with children at a set age or grade level. He does not stop with this universalist view but rather suggests a continuum of cognitive development in children that runs from universal to cultural to discipline-based to idiosyncratic to unique. Feldman's continuum "is to array developmental domains from those which are indeed universal in the usual sense of the word, i.e., which may be achieved initially by perhaps a single individual" (Feldman, 1987a, p. 20). His continuum is more than a taxonomy, there is movement from simpler levels of mastery to higher levels of mastery "of an invariant sequence of stages" (Feldman, 1987a, p. 20). In addition, "there are regular periods of major *qualitative transformation* brought about through a set of common transition mechanisms" (Feldman, 1987a, p. 20). For example, reading is considered a cultural domain, learning about medicine is a discipline-based domain while physical therapy is practiced by fewer cultures and is thus a part of the idiosyncratic domain. The invention of a computer that can understand the spoken word would fall into the unique domain and would be considered a developmental transformation of unique proportions.

According to Feldman (1987a), "art is inherently not a universal activity. In all its forms, encompassing appreciation as well as production, art is by its very nature a matter of acquiring cultural and disciplined knowledge. Indeed, at its frontiers, art is as far removed from the universal as one can imagine, a matter of unique expression under unique conditions" (p. 19).

CONCLUSION

It is important for both therapists and teachers to be aware of current trends in developmental psychology. Recent studies suggest that there may not be a universal developmental continuum in children's artistic development that transcends culture.

Indeed, Wilson and Wilson (1983)—recognized art education scholars— have concluded that developmental stages in art: (a) do not account for cultural, instructional, nor peer influences; (b) do not take into account that graphic development is markedly different today; (c) were based on norms that are over 50 years old; (d) do not account for artwork that is in transition; (e) tend to ignore emotional and aesthetic aspects of the artwork; and (f) have no real credence and have exceeded their usefulness.

> If the main tool on which we have relied to inform us about children's drawing development is found to seriously misinform, to be inaccurate and unreliable by almost any standard of reliability, to overlook many salient features of children's drawings, and to ignore at least half of the factors necessary for an adequate explanation of graphic development, then it is time to throw the old tool away and to search for a new one (Wilson & Wilson, 1983, p. 5).

Therefore, it may not be appropriate to compare the artwork of one child against some established universal developmental criterion. Also, it might not be appropriate to assume that children naturally progress from one artistic developmental stage to another without specific intentional instructional efforts and opportunities to practice and master art skills.

No matter what approach one selects to govern one's study of children's artwork, these recent studies have underscored the importance of cultural, educational and societal influences on how the child responds to art, executes art, and understands artistic endeavors. These scholars have highlighted the importance that subcultural influences (including the child's immediate family) play and the impact that schooling has on the child's ability to engage in artistic activity.

At the same time it still will be important to have some grasp of what children normally can be expected to create. One should still be aware of the universals of artistic development no matter whether one chooses to espouse a Piagetian, Lowenfeldian, or some other developmentalist's variation as a model for comparing the art of a particular child. It will be important to have **some** basic perspective and understanding against which individual artwork by a particular child can be reflected. Additionally, one needs to take into account cultural and subcultural issues, and mental, physical, emotional, and social strengths (and limitations) that each child may have. Therefore, one must be cautious in making comparisons between the artwork of one child and another. Probably the best course to pursue is to compare artwork of a child with *his own work* done at various times and in various situations.

Finally, while universal developmental artistic stages are being questioned, they still are useful in providing teachers (and therapists) with guidelines for the type of art media to use, the type of instruction that will be effective, the type of motivation and learning approach to implement, and the type of evaluation that will be used to assess teaching and counseling effectiveness.

It would seem to be important to understand a child's artwork from both a universal developmental perspective *as well as* from a culturally idiosyncratic and, at times, unique perspective.

REFERENCES

Altschuler, R., & Hattwick, L. (1969 reprinted). *Painting and personality.* Chicago: University of Chicago Press. 1947.

Blythe, D. A., Hill, J. P., & Theil, K. S. (1982). Early adolescents' significant others. Grade and gender differences in perceived relationships with familial and nonfamilial adults and young people. *Journal of Youth and Adolescence, 11*(6), 425–450.

Castrup, J. A. E., & Scott, B. (1972). Art skills of preschool children. *Studies in Art Education, 13*(3), 62–69.

Chapman, L. (1978). *Approaches to art in education.* New York: Harcourt, Brace, Jovanovich.

Cratty, B. J. (1970). *Perceptual and motor development in infants and children.* New York: Macmillan.

Dennis, W. (1966a). Goodenough scores, art education, and modernization. *Journal of Social Psychology, 51,* pp. 213–215.

Dennis, W. (1966b). The human figure drawings of Bedowins. *Journal of Social Psychology, 52,* pp. 209–219.

Duke, L. L. (1983). The Getty Center for Education in the Arts. *Art Education, 36*(5), 4–13.

Duke, L. L. (1988). The Getty Center for Education in the Arts and discipline-based art education. *Art Education, 41*(2), 7–12.

Feldman, D. H. (1980). *Beyond universals in cognitive development.* Norwood, NJ: Ablex Publishing Corp.

Feldman, D. H. (1987a). Developmental psychology and art education. *Art Education, 36*(2), 19–21.

Feldman, D. H. (1987b). Developmental psychology and art education; two fields at the crossroads. *Journal of Aesthetic Education, 21*(2), 243–254.

Gardner, H. (1990). *Art education and human development.* (Occasional Paper number 3). Los Angeles CA: The Getty Center for Education in the Arts.

Goodenough, F. (1924). *The intellectual factor in children's drawings.* Doctoral Dissertation. Stanford University.

Golomb, C. (1976). The child as image-maker: The invention of representational models, the effects of the medium. *Studies in Art Education, 17*(2), 19–27.

Harms, J. (1972). Presenting materials effectively. In H. P. Lewis (Ed.), *Art for the preprimary child.* Reston, VA: National Art Education Association.

Harris, D. B. (1963). *Children's drawings as measures of intellectual maturity.* New York: Harcourt Brace Jovanovich.

Hess-Behrens, N. N. (1973). The development of the concept of space as observed in children's drawings: A cross-nation/cross-cultural study. National Center for Educational Research and Development (H.E.W. R02-0611).

Kellogg, R. (1970). *Analyzing children's art.* Palo Alto, CA: National Press.

Lansing, K. (1969). *Art, artists and art education.* New York: McGraw-Hill.

Lindstrom, M. (1964). *Children's art.* Berkeley: University of California Press.

Lowenfeld, V. (1939). *The nature of creative activity.* London: Kegan, Paul, Trench, Trubner and Co.

Lowenfeld, V. (1945). Tests for visual and haptical aptitudes. *American Journal of Psychology, 58*(1), 100–111. Reprinted: In Eisner, E., & Ecker, D. (Eds), *Readings in art education* (pp. 97–104). Waltham, MA: Blaisdell, 1966.

Lowenfeld, V., & Brittain, L. (1970). *Creative and mental growth* (4th ed). New York: MacMillan Publishers.

Lowenfeld, V., & Brittain, L. (1975). *Creative and mental growth* (5th ed). New York: MacMillan Publishers.

Lowenfeld, V., & Brittain, L. (1987). *Creative and mental growth* (8th ed). New York: MacMillan Publishers.

Manning, T. (1987). Aggression depicted in abused children's drawings. *The Arts in Psychotherapy, 14,* 15–24.

Malchiodi, C. (1990). *Breaking the silence: Art therapy with children from violent homes.* New York: Brunner/Mazel.

McFee, J. (1970). *Preparation for art.* Belmont, CA: Wadsworth Publishing Co.

McFee, J. K., & Degge, R. (1980). *Art, culture, and environment: A catalyst for teaching.* Dubuque, IA: Kendall/Hunt Publishing.

Mills, E. A., & Thompson, D. R. (1981). State of the arts in the states. *Art Education, 34*(1), 40–44.

Munro, T., Lark-Horovitz, B., & Barnhart, E. N. (1942). Children's art abilities: Studies at the Cleveland Museum of Art. *Journal of Experimental Education, 11,* pp. 97–155.

Oster, G. D., & Gould, P. (1987). *Using drawings in assessment and therapy.* New York: Brunner/Mazel.

Piaget, J., & Inhelder, B. C. (1956). *The child's concept of space.* New York: Humanities Press, Inc.

Rouse, M. (1965). A new look at an old theory. *Studies in Art Education, 18*(4), 8–15.

Rubin, J. (1975). Art is for all human beings, especially the handicapped. *Art Education, 28*(8), 5–10.

Salome, R. A., & Moore, B. (1979). *Development of figure concepts in the graphic art work by children from different countries.* Chicago, IL: International Film Bureau, Inc.

Salome, R. A., & Moore, B. (1979). *Development of spatial relations in the graphic art work by children from different countries.* Chicago, IL: International Film Bureau, Inc.

Saunders, R. J. (1968). The levels of development in child art. Paper presented at the Institute for Teachers of Trainable Children. Southern Connecticut State College.

Smith, R. A. (Ed). (1987). Special issue: Discipline-based art education. *The Journal of Aesthetic Education, 21*(2).

Swerdlow, J. A. (1981). A question of impact. *Wilson Quarterly, 5*(1), 86–99.

Uhlin, D., & DeChira, E. (1984). *Art for exceptional children* (3rd ed). Dubuque, IA: William C. Brown Publisher.

Wilson, B., & Wilson, M. (1977). *Teaching children to draw.* Worcester, MA: Davis Publishers.

Wilson, B., & Wilson, M. (1983). The use and uselessness of developmental stages. *Art Education, 36*(2), 4–5.

Young, E. (1972). Art in children's learning. In H. P. Lewis (Ed.), *Art for the preprimary child.* Reston, VA: The National Art Education Association.

Chapter 3

APPROACHES TO ART THERAPY WITH CHILDREN

Marcia Rosal

C hildren are natural artists. Often, visual expression is the preferred channel of communication for children. At times, expression with a pencil, brush or marker is easier for children than verbal means. Therapists find the art of children to be helpful in psychotherapy, counseling or treatment. Art making for children is as spontaneous as being involved in play. Art therapists have written on the similarity between play and art and the overlap between the two (Aach, 1984; Kramer, 1977, 1979; Roth, 1978; Rubin, 1978). Art therapy and play therapy as treatment modalities have developed and become the treatments of choice for children.

There are many different ways art therapists approach working with children who are experiencing emotional, behavioral, physical or cognitive deficits. The development of these approaches is similar to the development of other theoretical models in psychology and education. The theoretical approaches explored in this chapter are: psychoanalytic, developmental, adaptive and cognitive-behavioral. These are by no means the only approaches used with children in art therapy. However, these approaches were selected for inclusion here because they are the ones that have been discussed in the art therapy literature or at art therapy conferences.

There has been uneven coverage of these four approaches both in terms of conference presentations and in terms of articles in the art therapy journals. For example, the psychoanalytic approach is quite well documented, but the cognitive-behavioral approach is only beginning to have some exposure in the literature of the art therapy field. Thus, the psychoanalytic, developmental, adaptive and cognitive-behavioral approaches will be discussed in terms of each approach's theory, general principles, the type of children with whom the treatment approach has been successful, the art therapist's role and evidence of the treatment's effectiveness. These approaches are shared by several art therapists, each of whom has a unique perspective within the broader category or descriptor. Thus, each art therapy author will be included in our discussions. Overall, each approach that is discussed, as well as each author's specific contribution or unique orientation within an approach category, has new information to add to our understanding of how art can be

142

useful to children and how the helping professionals can use art to relieve the pains of children or to encourage the growth of children.

PSYCHOANALYTIC APPROACHES

The origins of art therapy, as with most other forms of psychotherapy, began in the psychoanalytic tradition. The two earliest writers in art therapy were both schooled in the psychoanalytic approach. Naumburg (1950) and Kramer (1958, 1971, 1979) brought various psychoanalytic principles to their work with children who were experiencing behavior problems. Later art therapists such as Rubin (1978), Landgarten (1981), Roth (1982), Levick (1983), and Wilson (1977, 1985a, 1985b, 1987) contributed more specific ideas for the treatment of children using psychoanalytic principles. Their contributions are outlined in Table 3.1.

The information written by the psychoanalytic art therapists working with children shows that this approach can be characterized by three main concepts: (a) the creative process taps the unconscious; (b) art aids in the development of defenses and socially acceptable forms of expression for sexual and aggressive drives or conflicts; and (c) the role of the art therapist is to provide the opportunity for the creative process to take place in a neutral and safe environment.

The creative process is the most important factor in psychoanalytic art therapy. The creative process allows for the emergence of difficult unconscious conflicts, wishes, concerns, and drives. Naumburg, Rubin, and Landgarten all agreed that unconscious material is evident in the art productions and that the art provides the child psychological distance from the conflictual material. Because the unconscious material is in a symbolic form, it is not as threatening as expression in a verbal form.

The use of art to develop appropriate defense mechanisms and to identify a child's particular defensive structure is the second concept of psychoanalytic art therapy. Kramer, Roth, and Wilson stated that art and the creative process aid in the development of civilized behavior. Roth and Levick agreed and added that other defense mechanisms can be identified in art productions and that art can aid in the development of age-appropriate defense mechanisms.

Finally, the role of the art therapist is one of being a neutral and supportive partner to the release of a child's unconscious symbolic material. Because the art therapist is neutral, the relationship that develops between the art therapist and the child is laden with symbolic meaning as it would be in any transference relationship.

The psychoanalytic approach to art therapy has been successful with children who have behavior problems and emotional disturbances. It has

TABLE 3.1
PSYCHOANALYTIC ART THERAPY

Author	*General Theoretical Stance*	*Type of Children or Disorder*
Naumburg (1950)	Dynamically Oriented Art Therapy	Hospitalized behavior problem children adolescents
General Principles	*Role of the Art Therapist*	*Evidence of Effect*
(1) Art and free spontaneous creative expression can aid in the release of unconscious, repressed emotions and conflicts	(1) To remain neutral	(1) Spontaneity is a healthy response
(2) Through art, children project material too threatening to discuss	(2) To aid in the growth of spontaneous expression	(2) Child's art progress from stereotypy to originality
(3) Through art, children express fantasies		(3) Child discriminates between fantasy and reality
(4) Art helps in the diagnosis of children because children are less able to express verbally		(4) Child readjusts to situation
(5) Children gain control of mastery through art		
(6) Art is an expression of the transference relationship		
Kramer (1958, 1971, 1979)	Psychoanalytic	Children with behavior problems in a school setting
General Principles	*Role of the Art Therapist*	*Evidence of Effect*
(1) The art process is a means of sublimation	(1) To provide conditions for the creative process	Child moves from stereotype to formal expression
(2) Art is a means of catharsis	(2) To respond to both covert and overt messages in art	
(3) Art making is equated with ego building	(3) To act as a model for ego functioning	
	(4) To help children produce art which is expressive and formed	

TABLE 3.1 (continued)

Author	General Theoretical Stance	Type of Children or Disorder
Rubin (1978)	Psychoanalytic-symbolic interpretation	Emotionally disturbed children in outpatient clinics and physically, visually, and hearing impaired in school settings

General Principles	*Role of the Art Therapist*	*Evidence of Effect*
(1) Through art children fulfill symbolically both positive and negative wishes and impulses	(1) To provide a framework for freedom	(1) Child increases in spontaneity with art materials
(2) Art helps children as a means of sending messages on many levels	(2) To facilitate the creative process	(2) Child increased form and form of expression indicates control and mastery
(3) Symbolized communication occurs in making art		
(4) Interaction with art materials can aid in diagnosis		
(5) The therapeutic relationship has symbolic meaning		

Author	General Theoretical Stance	Type of Children or Disorder
Landgarten (1981)	Neo-Freudian	Children with emotional problems, children with poor impulse control, and children with medical problems

General Principles	*Role of the Art Therapist*	*Evidence of Effect*
(1) Art increases distance between child and threatening material	(1) To be flexible and supportive	Art serves as a record of developmental changes
(2) Art can aid in sublimation of poor impulse control	(2) To use educational techniques to aid children	
(3) Art can be used to gain insight		
(4) Art can be used as a basis for interpretation		
(5) Art can reveal unconscious secrets of feelings		
(6) Art is a means of self-expression		

TABLE 3.1 (continued)

Author	General Theoretical Stance	Type of Children or Disorder
Roth (1982)	Ego development psychology	Disturbed, retarded children

General Principles	Role of the Art Therapist	Evidence of Effect
(1) Art activities promote ego development and decrease disturbed behavior	(1) To understand ego functions and ego disturbances	Decrease of disturbed behavior is observed
(2) A healthy child has adaptive ego functions	(2) To understand the importance of the transference relationship	
(3) Art therapy offers an appropriate outlet for unacceptable impulses		
(4) Art therapy can help children control drives and postpone gratification		
(5) Art therapy promotes autonomous ego functions by expanding sensory, perceptual motor and intellectual experiences		
(6) Art therapy provides reality testing in terms of body image and spatial relationships		
(7) Art therapy can aid in healthy object relationships		
(8) Art therapy provides opportunities to develop useful defense mechanisms and self-image impulses		
(9) Art therapy can promote synthetic ego functions or help child become more organized		
(10) Retarded children are capable of symbolic processes		

TABLE 3.1 (continued)

Author	General Theoretical Stance	Type of Children or Disorder
Levick (1983)	Defense mechanisms of the ego	Emotionally disturbed children

General Principles	Role of the Art Therapist	Evidence of Effect
(1) Defense mechanisms can be identified in the graphic productions of children	(1) To identify the defense structures of the child	Art can chronicle the development of healthy defense mechanisms
(2) The identification of defense mechanisms can aid in diagnosis	(2) To help the child gain age-appropriate defense mechanisms	

Author	General Theoretical Stance	Type of Children or Disorder
Wilson (1985a, 1985b, 1987)	Psychoanalytic ego psychology	Emotionally disturbed and learning disabled children

General Principles	Role of the Art Therapist	Evidence of Effect
(1) Art therapy promotes ego functioning	(1) Is child dependent	(1) Changes in therapeutic relationship and in artwork
(2) Growth may occur through identification with clinician and by art therapist acting as auxiliary ego	(2) To see strengths	(2) Developmental changes occur
(3) Symbols serve as the connection between reality and human thought and fantasy	(3) Help child view his world through art	(3) Behavior at home and school is changed
(4) Through making visual images the capacity to symbolize is developed	(4) Represent adult world which is tolerant	
(5) The ability to symbolize may be a link to other complex mental representations (images, fantasies, thoughts, concepts, or dreams)	(5) Is an appreciative audience	
(6) Ability to symbolize is vital to functioning and further development	(6) Liaison w/treatment team	
	(7) Help child make best art he can	
	(8) Offer technical assistance when needed	
	(9) To read symbols to help understand the unconscious conflict of the child	

also been successful with children who have learning problems and mental retardation. This approach has been useful with children who need help in adjusting to a particular situation such as medically ill children and children who need help in adjusting to physical, visual, or hearing impairments.

Case Example

Jeanne's course of art therapy serves as an example of how art therapists work within a psychoanalytic framework. Jeanne, age 12, was brought to art therapy by her father, a widower who had recently remarried. Jeanne's mother died three years prior to the onset of treatment. He stated that Jeanne's academic performance had decreased, that she had withdrawn from the family, and that she had few friends at school.

Jeanne admitted to liking art, but said little else during her first art therapy session. She sat quietly and drew a pumpkin on a fence (see Figure 3.1). It was October and so the drawing was seasonal. However, it depicts a shell of an object, insides removed, looking scared and helpless. The drawing was typical of Jeanne's productions over the next several months: stereotypic, constricted, emotionally distant and defensive, and produced with resistive media (i.e., crayons and colored pencils) (see Figure 3.2). The nature of Jeanne's interactions with the therapist was also restrictive and reserved. Jeanne seemed to be pouring her anger into rigid designs and motifs. Any attempt by the therapist to encourage spontaneity or change of medium was met with silence. Nonetheless, Jeanne attended the sessions faithfully.

After six months, Jeanne stated that she wished to try other materials and chose finger paints. At first, Jeanne used only her fingertip to dip into the paint jar and to make fingerprints and squiggles on the slippery paper. Over the next four sessions, Jeanne became increasingly bold with her use of the finger paints. Next, she made handprints. Finally, she used both hands to scribble and swirl the paint. Her verbal interactions increased with the accompanying looseness with the medium.

During the last of the four sessions, Jeanne produced a piece which she said reminded her of flowers at her mother's funeral (see Figure 3.3). The flower image stimulated Jeanne to talk nonstop about her mother: how she had cancer, how she died, the day the death occurred, that Jeanne did not cry, etc. Then Jeanne decided to make her mother's tombstone. She smoothed the paint until she got it just right and with her fingertip wrote her mother's name on the tombstone (see Figure 3.4). She stated that her mother and she shared the same name, and therefore it had been frightening for her to see the original tombstone. Jeanne made several tombstones for her mother. She admitted that part of her died when her mother passed away. In addition, Jeanne stated that she was having difficulty accepting a stepmother.

From that point in therapy, Jeanne was more animated. She discussed problems at school, troubles with friends, and more about her feelings. During a session close to termination, Jeanne produced a collage about how she saw herself (see Figure 3.5).

Figure 3.1. Jeanne's first themes in art therapy were stereotypic. In her first drawing, the client drew a seasonal picture.

Jeanne's art productions over the nine-month course of treatment went from rigid, stereotypic symbols to regressed, yet healing, images of trauma, to a more personal expression as is typical of adolescent art. It was hypothesized that the controlled symbols gave Jeanne the opportunity to express anger and grief in a safe manner. Only after a safety threshold was reached on an unconscious level was she able to spontaneously express painful feelings.

This case illustrates several aspects of the psychoanalytic approach. First, Jeanne's drawings during the first months of treatment were examples of what Kramer labels compulsive defenses. In addition, the symbolic content of Jeanne's art was understood on many levels. The art therapist was able to understand the symbolic nature of the therapeutic relationship for Jeanne. Finally, the art therapist was able to remain neutral, yet be supportive, and was able to encourage spontaneous expressions once Jeanne was able.

Figure 3.2. Jeanne used colored pencils to draw constricted motifs and designs.

DEVELOPMENTAL APPROACHES

While Naumburg and Kramer were developing models of art therapy from their experience within the psychoanalytic tradition, many educators and psychologists were using art as a tool to gauge cognitive and emotional growth.

One of the most prominent of these writers was Lowenfeld (1947) who studied the graphic development of children's drawings. As an art educator, he encouraged art teachers to use developmental information for curriculum development and for information to assess the level of the students in order to best serve their needs.

Lowenfeld coined the term "art education therapy" in 1957 to discuss how to use art as a therapeutic modality in art education for children who had disabilities. The purpose of art education therapy was to help disabled children grow and develop both cognitively and creatively—just like their nondisabled peers. By starting on the developmental level of the disabled child, art education therapy is then utilized to broaden the child's "frame of

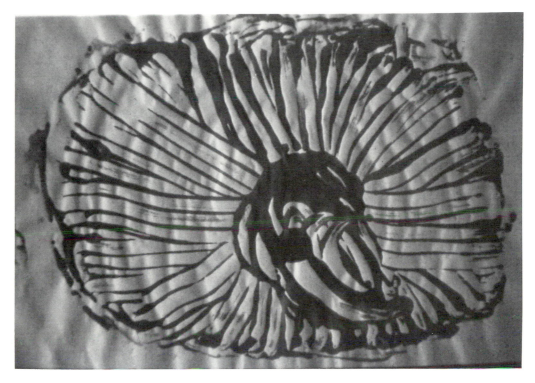

Figure 3.3. Jeanne used fingerpaints to make flower prints. This image reminded Jeanne of her mother's funeral.

reference until the individual accepts himself, and with it, his own handicap" (Lowenfeld, 1957, p. 436).

Lowenfeld's approach to art education for the disabled child utilized psychoeducational philosophies and techniques. For example, Lowenfeld stated that creative activities in education should provide an emotional release in order to promote positive adjustment. He also advocated the use of creative art to develop "independence and flexibility of thinking . . . for group dynamics and social interaction" (1957, p. 431). These themes permeate psychoeducational ideals today.

Another developmental psychologist who influenced the work of art therapists was Piaget. Piaget (1962) studied the cognitive growth of children and discussed how play and other symbolic interactions with the environment could be used to chart and to encourage cognitive growth. In fact, Lowenfeld's work in graphic development was based on several of Piaget's concepts.

Many art therapists, particularly those working in special schools or developmental centers, have used graphic and cognitive development and

Figure 3.4. Fingerpaints were used by Jeanne to make a tombstone for her mother who had her same name.

psychoeducational approaches as theoretical bases for their work with children. The earliest writers using the term, "developmental art therapy," were Williams and Wood (1977). Their approach will be discussed in this section as well as the developmental approaches of Uhlin (1972), Musick (1978), Silver (1978, 1987), Aach-Feldman and Kunkle-Miller (1987), and Kunkle-Miller and Aach-Feldman (1983) (see Table 3.2).

Throughout the literature on the developmental approach to art therapy, three basic principles seem to apply to all the theories: (a) that creativity can aid in cognitive and emotional development; (b) that there are stages or phases which are evident in the art, in the treatment of children, and in a child's behavior with art materials; and (c) that the role of the art therapist must be flexible in order to be at times directed and action-oriented, and at other times spontaneous and allow for freedom of expression.

The main premise for the developmental approach to art therapy with children is that the process of making art somehow stimulates growth. Lowenfeld theorized that interaction with the materials inspired development and change. Uhlin added that by providing particular materials and having

Figure 3.5. During termination, Jeanne produced a collage of how she was herself. The themes are typical for adolescents and emphasized her love of roller skating.

clear objectives, the art therapist can assist a child to develop in specific ways. Musick built onto this principle by hypothesizing that the art stimulates the right hemisphere of the brain and thus makes a direct link between art and development. Silver echoed Musick's idea concerning the use of art to develop right hemispheric thinking. In addition, Silver thought that art could be used as a second language in order to effectively assess the cognitive abilities of disabled children. Aach-Feldman and Kunkle-Miller surmised that if art can help children grow once they are at a level to interact with art materials in a symbolic way, preart experiences may aid development toward the beginning of symbolization.

The charting and observation of growth through the delineation of stages is the second common feature of developmental art therapy. Uhlin, Musick, and Aach-Feldman and Kunkle-Miller use stages of pregraphic and graphic growth to assess and plan treatment. Silver developed drawing tests in order to evaluate development. Williams and Wood suggest stages in treatment as a means to develop objectives for art therapy.

The role of the art therapist in developmental art therapy is most often

TABLE 3.2
DEVELOPMENTAL ART THERAPY

Author	General Theoretical Stance	Type of Children or Disorder
Uhlin (1972)	Developmental and Psychoeducational approaches	Disabled children with mental retardation, physical disabilities, minimal brain damage, emotion disturbance/disability

General Principles	Role of the Art Therapist	Evidence of Effect
(1) Understanding growth and development in the art of normal children is a base for understanding children with disabilities	(1) To understand developmental issues in the art	Children grow or develop at different rates, but still grow similarly to normal children. Therefore, advances in in graphic development can help in assessment of treatment
(2) Art is helpful in the assessment and development of body image and sense of self	(2) To be aware of the needs of each individual child	
(3) Art materials can be used to stimulate sensory modalities	(3) To help children reach their potential	
(4) Arrests in development can be overcome through interaction with art materials		
(5) Art can enrich and expand experiences		

	Developmental therapy Psychoeducational curriculum	Children 2–14 yrs. emotionally disturbed, and disabled
Williams & Wood (1977)		

General Principles	Role of the Art Therapist	Evidence of Effect
Four stages in developmental therapy approach:		Child is able to move from one stage of the treatment model to the next, and the child is able to meet objectives able to meet objectives
(1) Stage 1 Children need stimulating material and need to be enticed	(1) Stage 1 To be directive and make short observational statements	
(2) Stage 2 Art issued for enrichment, personal expression and to increase: (a) self-esteem (b) ability to manipulate (c) conceptual skill	(2) Stage 2 To insure success and to: (a) redirect (b) reassure (c) restructure	

TABLE 3.2 (continued)

Author	General Theoretical Stance	Type of Children or Disorder
Williams & Wood (*continued*)		
(3) Stage 3 Children respond to limitations and expectations. Emphasis is on group needs and successful peer interactions	(3) Stage 3 To provide motivating suggestions and to manage behavior	
(4) Stage 4 Emphasis is on individualization and on the emergence of each child's personality. Preparations are made for return to regular home and/or school environment	(4) Stage 4 To provide support and set limits	
Musick (1978)	Developmental	Disabled children and mentally retarded children
General Principles (1) Creativity is vital to developmental achievement (2) Both directed and and spontaneous art experiences help children achieve and move up the developmental ladder	*Role of the Art Therapist* (1) To understand stages of development in creativity (2) To use both directed and spontaneous art experiences (3) To help the child use all senses	*Evidence of Effect* Progress is evident from lower developmental stage to higher stage
Silver (1978, 1983a, 1983b, 1987)	Art as a means to develop cognitively	Learning disabled, communication disorders, hearing impairments
General Principles (1) Art therapy can be used to develop, identify, and evaluate cognitive skills (2) Art can be a second language and can be used to express concepts	*Role of the Art Therapist* (1) To relinquish their thoughts of low expectations for disabled children (2) To look for abilities in disabled children	*Evidence of Effect* Testing procedures are used which measure concept learning and creative thinking

TABLE 3.2 (continued)

Author	General Theoretical Stance	Type of Children or Disorder
Silver (*continued*)		
(3) Therapeutic and educational goals can be met effectively through art	(3) To widen communication possibilities	
(4) A child's drawings reflect her thinking process	(4) To invite exploratory learning	
(5) Art stimulates the right hemisphere of the brain	(5) To provide tasks which are self-rewarding	
(6) Children who have left hemisphere damage learn more easily through art	(6) To reinforce emotional balance	
(7) Art can be useful in learning cognitive skills, assessment, adjustment, and creative and problem-solving		
Aach-Feldman, Kunkle-Miller (1983, 1987)	Developmental and cognitive growth	Mentally retarded, developmentally delayed, emotionally disturbed, visually impaired, multi-disabled
General Principles	*Role of the Art Therapist*	*Evidence of Effect*
(1) Focus is on three stages of representational development: (a) prerepresentational (b) simple representational (c) complex representational	(1) To establish contact through active involvement	Child progresses from one developmental level to a higher level
(2) Piaget's cognitive developmental stages are used: (a) sensorimotor (b) preoperational (c) operational	(2) To use direct intervention	
(3) Art therapy is process oriented	(3) To feel comfortable exploring and stimulating in the play process	

TABLE 3.2 (continued)

Author	General Theoretical Stance	Type of Children or Disorder
Aach-Feldman, Kunkle-Miller (*continued*)		
(4) Art therapy is affective and emphasizes sensory methods	(4) To use pre-art materials	
(5) Presymbolic expression is when child does not have skill to conceptualize		
(6) Representational involvement with materials precedes symbolic use of materials		
(7) Imitation has vital role to make link from presymbolic to symbolic representation		

active. Art therapists direct, redirect, assess, reassess, model, use stimulating materials, and set behavioral limits. Developmental art therapists are willing to be directive in one session and allow for spontaneous expression in the next.

The developmental art therapy approach has been successful with children suffering from a wide range of physical and emotional disorders. Due to the developmental base of this approach, it can be used with children of all ages including those who are very young or severely delayed. This approach is adaptable to both clinical and educational settings due to its psychoeducational base. Developmental art therapy principles can aid in both assessment and treatment.

Case Example

The developmental approach can be illustrated through the case of Naomi. Naomi, a biracial, four-year-old female, was referred to art therapy for angry outbursts and a short attention span. Due to the natural mother's chemical dependency, Naomi was in foster care.

When Naomi first entered the art room, she was tentative, cautious, and anxious. Naomi experimented with several materials in a play-like manner. Her first crayon drawing (see Figure 3.6) revealed that Naomi was in the controlled scribbling stage of graphic development (Lowenfeld, 1957). It was evident through the drawing and through her excitement with all the choices of art materials that Naomi's development was delayed and that her background had been deprived of normal sensory experiences. In addition,

Naomi's verbal communications were limited and her speech garbled. She did not know the names of basic colors. Therefore, the approach to treatment was developmental in nature.

Figure 3.6. A controlled scribble by Naomi, age 4, is indicative of her developmental delays.

Naomi was given many opportunities to play and to manipulate clay, plasticene, blocks, etc. She was able to explore her body through mirror exercises and through art experiences such as making handprints (see Figure 3.7). She was asked many questions during art making to encourage speech.

At the end of four months of weekly art therapy sessions, Naomi had entered the preschematic stage of graphic development as she began to draw human figures (see Figure 3.8). In addition, she was able to use the total space of the paper as can be illustrated through her drawing of a landscape

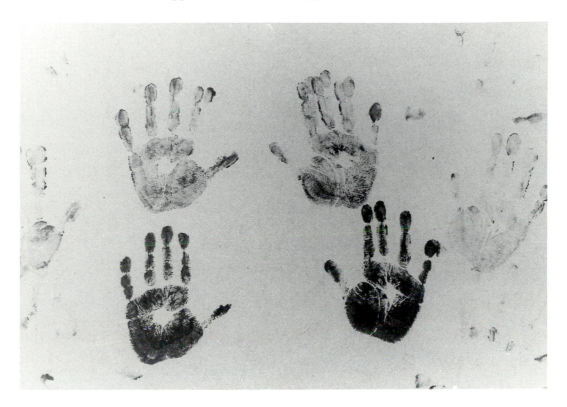

Figure 3.7. Naomi explored her body image through play and manipulation of art materials. Here, Naomi produced handprints.

(see Figure 3.9). This drawing shows evidence of a baseline, and she used longitudinal scribbles to fill in the sky. In addition, Naomi's behavior at preschool had improved dramatically. She no longer hit or bit the other children. At the foster home, Naomi was easier to manage and her spells of yelling and crying had decreased.

Art therapy with Naomi reflected four principles of the developmental approach with children. First, Naomi was given many sensory experiences based on her needs and her developmental level. Secondly, she was encouraged to talk about her work as she was creating. Thirdly, the art therapist was active in creating experiences to enhance Naomi's sensory awareness. Finally, the art therapist used graphic development as a means of charting Naomi's growth and development.

ADAPTIVE APPROACHES

A revolution was occurring in the field of special education during the 1970s. The revolution focused on children who had various disabilities and

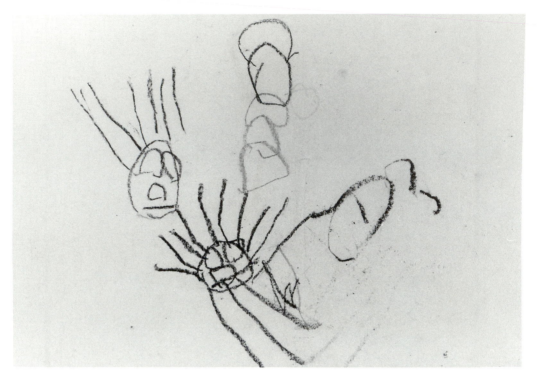

Figure 3.8. After four months of art therapy, Naomi's drawing level was age appropriate and was in the preschematic stage of graphic development.

was based on the concept of normalization. Normalization is the belief that all disabled individuals should have opportunities to lead as "normal" an existence as possible. The effect of normalization theory on special education was profound. It forced parents and teachers of disabled children into thinking about what was really the best education for their children.

At the same time, research on the effectiveness of separate special education classrooms and schools pointed to the fact that separate classes and schools were not effective in teaching disabled children how to survive in the world. Also, special education classes were often an exclusionary means for isolating minority children and children who exhibited behavior problems in the regular classroom.

The combination of normalization and the lack of evidence supporting special and separate classes for disabled children mobilized parents and educators who put pressure on state and federal governments to change the laws of education for children with special needs. In 1975, the federal government adopted the Education for All Handicapped Children Act which mandated that **all** children be entitled to a free, public education in

Figure 3.9. In a spontaneous drawing, Naomi described a landscape with a ground line and blue longitudinal scribbles to represent the sky.

the least restrictive environment (PL 94-142). By mandating education in the least restrictive environment, the federal government adopted the concept of normalization for its special children, meaning that many special children could be placed in the regular classroom.

Placing special children in the regular classroom (mainstreaming) meant that children and teachers would need the services of various support personnel in order for mainstreaming to be effective. Art therapy was targeted as one of the special services available to students.

Therefore, parents could demand that their child be seen by an art therapist. In addition, many disabled children were mainstreamed into regular art classes; therefore, the art teacher could receive support from art therapists who (a) had skills in working with children who had special needs and (b) who could consult with the regular teacher about a special needs child. Thus, the revolution in special education thrust upon the field of art therapy the responsibility for developing theories about programs for **all** children with special needs.

Art therapists who had backgrounds in education and art education effectively took on this task. The authors who wrote about their theoretical principles of adaptive art therapy and discussed their ideas for programming were Anderson (1978, 1982), Jungels (1977, 1978), Mayhew (1979), Gonick-Barris (1976), and Clements and Clements (1984) (see Table 3.3).

In the theory of adaptive art therapy, three principles seem to apply: (a) that art experiences can provide normalizing influences over the disabled child, (b) that all art experiences can be adapted to meet the unique needs of the disabled child, and (c) that art therapists should be astute observers in order to solve the problems of adaptation and to investigate art experiences which best meet the needs of the child.

The first and most prominent principle of adaptive art therapy is that of normalization. Art is a means of helping disabled children participate in life as nondisabled children experience it. The normalization experience can help the child with special needs to interact more fully with their environment. Mayhew and Clements and Clements viewed art as a powerful normalizer in the realm of peer relations. Mayhew also observed that art can help disabled children normalize their feelings about themselves by aiding in the acceptance of the disabling condition.

The second common principle of adaptive art therapy is that art experiences can be adapted for all children so that they can participate, learn, and enjoy art. Adapting art experiences may also mean that structure may be imposed to maximize the benefit to the child. Learning from art experiences may be strengthened, if the planning includes sequenced activities.

The role of the adaptive art therapist is to be a person dedicated to the observation of each child with whom she works. Observation is vital at all stages of the therapeutic process: (a) at the initial assessment, (b) in adapting ideas and materials, (c) during the art experience, and (d) in analysis of the outcome. Observation is vital because the art therapist's role is to attend to the emotional, physical, and educational needs of the child.

Adaptive art therapy techniques have been effective within educational settings with a variety of children who have disabilities. Those who have benefited from this form of art therapy include children with: (a) physical and neurological impairments, (b) hearing and visual impairments, (c) communication, learning, and behavior problems, (d) mental retardation, (e) emotional difficulties, and (f) multiple disabilities.

Case Example

Art therapy with Charles, an autistic ten-year-old, serves as a solid example of an adaptive art therapy approach. Charles, a very active, nonverbal child with receptive language and the ability to use some sign language, had

TABLE 3.3
ADAPTIVE ART THERAPY APPROACHES

Author	General Theoretical Stance	Type of Children or Disorder
Anderson (1978, 1982)	Normalization Adaptation	Children with various disabilities

General Principles	Role of the Art Therapist	Evidence of Effect
(1) All children should be involved in art experiences	(1) To also work with art materials	Evidence is seen through analysis of behavioral objectives
(2) Art experiences greatly benefit children	(2) To be able to problem-solve in order to adapt art experiences	
(3) Art aids in the learning process	(3) To be able to assess the needs of the child	
(4) All art experiences can be adapted to meet the child's unique needs	(4) To be able to analyze tasks	
(5) Art should be designed to meet emotional, physical, and educational needs		
(6) Art experiences can be sequential to maximize learning concepts		
(7) Children should learn about the content and process of making art		

Author	General Theoretical Stance	Type of Children or Disorder
Jungels (1977, 1978)	Normalization Adaptation	Children with various disabilities— physical, learning, emotional

General Principles	Role of the Art Therapist	Evidence of Effect
(1) Art experiences should be expanded to include all students	(1) To use problem-solving in order to expand art experiences	Evidence is successful integration of child into art programming
(2) Art should aid in the process of problem-solving	(2) To expand art experiences to include all children	
(3) Art exercises should stimulate all the senses	(3) To be a careful observer of the child's needs	
(4) Art experiences should be success-oriented		

TABLE 3.3 (continued)

Author	General Theoretical Stance	Type of Children or Disorder
Jungels (*continued*) (5) Emphasis should be placed on the process rather than the product		
Mayhew (1979)	Normalization Adaptation	Children with various disabilities—physical, learning, behavioral communication
General Principles (1) Art aids in minimizing deprivation/ isolation caused by disabilities (2) Art can provide opportunity to release feelings (3) Kinetic release is socially acceptable (4) Art promotes social interaction and interpersonal relationships (5) Art provides sensory-motor development (6) Art improves perceptual skills (7) Art aids in helping children accept disabilities	*Role of the Art Therapist* (1) To be flexible (2) To be able to meet individual needs (3) To attend to emotional, social, and educational needs of the child	*Evidence of Effect* Evidence is inclusion of all children into art experiences
Gonick-Barris (1976)	Normalization Adaptation	Children with minimal brain damage (MBD), neurological impairments
General Principles (1) Art experiences need to be structured, planned, and adapted to meet specific needs of the child (2) MBD children need the experience of exploring, creating, and playing in a structured environment	*Role of the Art Therapist* (1) To understand the child's disability (2) To plan art experiences to meet specific needs	*Evidence of Effect* Evidence is successful inclusion of MBD child into art classes

TABLE 3.3 (continued)

Author	General Theoretical Stance	Type of Children or Disorder
Gonick-Barris (*continued*) (3) Art provides an alternate mode of expression		
Clements & Clements (1984)	Normalization Adaptation	Children with various disabilities
General Principles (1) Art is a means of keeping disabled children involved with their nondisabled peers (2) Art helps children relate to the world in healthy ways	*Role of the Art Therapist* (1) To adapt art expressions to specific needs (2) To direct art experiences which will increase interaction between children — especially between disabled and non-disabled classmates	*Evidence of Effect* Evidence is successful interactions between peers

a very short attention span. Charles was referred to art therapy for frequent inappropriate touching, aggressive grabbing, and hugging of adults. The art therapist's goal for Charles was to help set boundaries, particularly body boundary consolidation.

Charles had several strengths, including a love of puzzles, a love of snacks, and great energy for scribbling. In order to meet the treatment goal, the art therapist carefully assessed Charles's strengths and weaknesses in the use of art materials. The art therapist realized that simple lines on paper were not as sufficiently powerful as a symbol of boundaries. Consequently, the art therapist used cardboard shapes and cardboard tubes as cues for the boundaries in such activities as painting and cutting. With the use of heavy cardboard, the art therapist helped Charles to cut out and paint pieces for simple toys (see Figure 3.10).

Charles responded positively to his achievements; therefore, the art therapist had Charles make simple shape and color puzzles in a similar manner (see Figure 3.11). Since Charles loved food, the art therapist encouraged him to make a puzzle with the shapes of his favorite snacks (see Figure 3.12). The therapist's work with Charles culminated with the production of a large play box (see Figure 3.13). The box incorporated all the skills of the toy and puzzle work, plus it was large enough for Charles to climb into and to play inside.

Photograph of Ring Stack: rings, centers, and tubes

Figure 3.10. Due to Charles's love of puzzles, the art therapist assisted him in making his own. This is a puzzle of rings and tubes.

This short case exemplifies several aspects of the adaptive art therapy approach. At the beginning of treatment, the art therapist evaluated the child's strengths. By using his love of toys and puzzles, the art therapist developed several creative ideas to help resolve Charles's problem with bodily boundaries. The use of cardboard also illustrates the use of an adapted media approach to complete art therapy exercises. In addition, through the course of treatment, Charles was able to receive positive acclamation from his teachers and peers for his work. This positive reinforcement aided in the normalization of Charles's life.

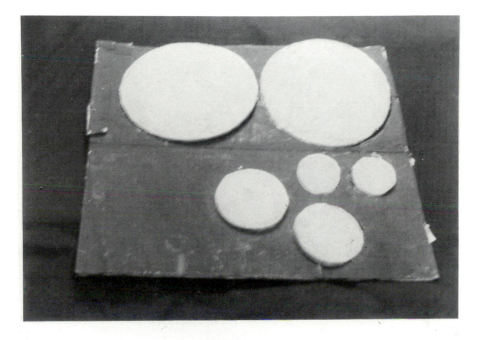

Photograph of Pre-Puzzle, with circles inserted

Figure 3.11. Charles made puzzles of shapes and colors.

COGNITIVE-BEHAVIORAL APPROACHES

Art therapy had its roots in the psychoanalytic tradition, and therefore, art therapists have been concerned about the trends in behavioral psychology. Sobol (1985) wrote about the "alarm" and "distaste" (p. 35) most art therapists have towards behavioral treatment. However, Sobol admitted that in some cases, such as with antisocial or conduct-disordered children, the behavioral aspects of treatment should not be ignored by art therapists.

Many art therapists do not realize that the recent cognitive-behavioral therapies are a product of social learning theory which is a marriage of the two major psychological traditions—psychoanalytic and behaviorism. Social learning theory bridged the gap between the inner mental processes of psychoanalytic theories and the overt behavior of the behavioral and learning theories. The emphasis of social learning theory is the effect of higher mental processes such as imagery, language, thinking, and affect on overt behavior. Therefore, to help a person change, an investigation of higher mental processes can provide a direct link with changing problematic overt

Photograph of Puzzle #2, with removal of inner rings demonstrated

Figure 3.12. Charles loved to eat; therefore, the art therapist suggested food as a theme for a puzzle.

behavior (Bandura, 1969; Miller & Dollard, 1941; Rotter, 1954). Miller and Dollard (1941) wrote that "the words and sentences that a person thinks to himself can have a strong motivating effect" (p. 106) and acknowledged the importance of changing clients' ineffective cognitions and of aiding in problem-solving abilities. This laid the foundation for cognitive therapies.

Mahoney and Arnkoff (1978) identified three major forms of cognitive-behavioral treatments: (a) cognitive restructuring therapies which include therapies developed by Ellis (1962), Luria (1961), and Beck (1976); (b) coping skills therapies which include therapies such as stress inoculation (Meichenbaum, 1975), covert modeling (Kazdin, 1974), and modified desensitization (Goldfried, 1971); and (c) problem-solving therapies which include therapies designed by Spivack and Shure (1974), D'Zurilla and Goldfried (1971), and Mahoney (1977). Cognitive therapy techniques have helped children who are impulsive (Meichenbaum & Goodman, 1971) and have behavior disorders (DiGiuseppe, 1981; Kanfer & Zich, 1974; Spivack & Shure, 1974).

Three major principles of the cognitive therapies were defined by Mahoney and Arnkoff (1978):

Figure 3.13. Combining all the skills of puzzle-making, Charles made a large play box. Charles was able to climb inside and play.

(1) Humans develop adaptive and maladaptive behavior and affective patterns through cognitive processes;

(2) These cognitive processes are functionally activated by procedures that are generally isomorphic with those of the human learning laboratory;

(3) The resultant task of the therapist is that of a diagnostician-educator who assesses maladaptive cognitive processes and subsequently arranges learning experiences that will alter cognitions and behavior and affect patterns with which they correlate. (p. 692)

Recently, psychotherapists in the field are discovering that mental processes, particularly mental images, are powerful tools for changing problem behaviors—especially in the area of self-control. Singer and Pope (1978) proposed that imagery could be used constructively for adaptive escapism, self-awareness, self-regulation and biofeedback, and for creativity and aesthetic experiences. In addition, Bandura (1977) hypothesized that mental images are self-reinforcing. Thus, they can be used for helping people to maintain behavioral changes.

Although the use of the cognitive-behavioral therapies in art therapy is limited, a few art therapists have been exploring the possibility of using those techniques in their work with children: Packard (1977), Roth (1978, 1987), DeFrancisco (1983), and Rosal (1985a, 1985b, 1986, 1987) (see Table 3.4).

The four major characteristics of cognitive-behavioral approaches with children include: (a) that art is a cognitive activity, (b) that art can help to change cognitive distortions, (c) that mental images can be used therapeutically to affect behavioral changes, and (d) that art can be used to help children gain self-control.

Packard (1977) discussed the power of art making as a cognitive activity. For Packard, art making could induce the retrieval of mental information, could promote the rearrangement of ideas and mental layouts, and could aid in the production of new thought patterns.

Roth used art to change distorted or unclear concepts. Her reality-shaping technique helped a child concretize the distorted concepts into concepts which were clear and had distinct boundaries. DeFrancisco used drawings to help the child produce distorted concepts caused by anxiety and fear. The drawings were then used as a means of evaluating the progressive decrease in distortion. Rosal found that art could change distorted self-images and negative self-messages.

Mental images can be used in art therapy. The mental image can be used (a) as a preliminary activity to drawing and (b) as a means of changing distorted visual images. Imagery can also be used to plan and develop treatments. In addition, changes in mental imagery can be produced in art therapy treatment and can lead to behavior changes.

Throughout the cognitive-behavioral art therapy approaches reviewed, the main goal for the child is to gain self-control. Behavioral self-control is evident in Packard's attempt to understand the power of art therapy with learning disabled children. Packard found learning disabled children could be given more power over their confused thought patterns through the use of art therapy. Roth used reality shaping to give disturbed retarded children control over vague and emotion-laden concepts. DeFrancisco used mental and visual imagery to help children control fears of specific situations. Rosal (1985a, 1987) used cognitive techniques to help children control acting-out behaviors, to control their ability to stay on task, and to problem solve.

Cognitive-behavioral art therapy approaches have been successful in the treatment of children with learning disabilities and behavioral difficulties, including children who are emotionally disturbed, mentally retarded, phobic, and hyperactive.

TABLE 3.4
COGNITIVE ART THERAPY APPROACHES

Author	General Theoretical Stance	Type of Children or Disorder
Packard (1977)	Cognitive Mapping Theory	Learning disabled children

General Principles	Role of the Art Therapist	Evidence of Effect
(1) Art activity involves cognitive processes	(1) To evaluate through art processes and art products	The child has increased ability to plan art experiences and exhibits increased problem-solving abilities increased problem-solving abilities
(2) In producing art, mental layouts are retrieved	(2) To look for cognitive mapping in drawings and art experiences	
(3) Mental layouts are combined in new ways through art therapy	(3) To aid in problem-solving through the art experiences provided	
(4) Creative cognition theory promotes mental fitness		

Author	General Theoretical Stance	Type of Children or Disorder
Roth (1978, 1987)	Behavioral Approach	Children with emotional disturbance, mental retardation

General Principles	Role of the Art Therapist	Evidence of Effect
(1) Aberrant behavior is learned	(1) To take a history of the complaint	Target behavior is achieved or goal is met
(2) The goal of therapy is to help client learn new behavior	(2) To develop treatment goals	
(3) Treatment is developed to change a specific complaint or problem behavior	(3) To gather frequency data	
(4) Treatment goals are clearly stated	(4) To use: (a) reinforcements (b) prompts (c) modeling	
(5) Reality shaping is a specific form of behavior and art therapy	(5) To evaluate the child for follow-up to ascertain the maintenance of the learned behavior	
(6) In reality shaping, a specific concept is targeted for change		

TABLE 3.4 (continued)

Author	General Theoretical Stance	Type of Children or Disorder
Roth (*continued*)		

(7) In reality shaping, the child expresses disturbing concepts and thereby may make developmental gains

(8) Art therapy helps to bring vague, disturbing concepts to concrete form

(9) The learning in art therapy should generalize to other situations

	Implosive Art Therapy (I.A.T.)	Phobic disorders in childhood
DeFrancisco (1983)		

General Principles	Role of the Art Therapist	Evidence of Effect
(1) Maladaptive behavior is learned and is a result of stimulus-response mechanisms	(1) To gather information surrounding the fear or problem situation	There is reduced or no anxiety when phobic object or situation is either imagined or encountered in vivo (in the real world)
(2) Maladaptive behavior, particularly avoidance, is a learned form of protection from anxiety	(2) To teach the child relaxation techniques	
(3) Problem behaviors can be decreased through the use of imagery and art	(3) To help uncover original cause of anxiety	
(4) Through relaxation and imagery, a child can come closer to the feared object or situation	(4) To understand both learning theory and psychoanalytic principles	
(5) I.A.T. has 6 steps: (a) diagnostic interview, (b) neutral art and imagery, (c) implosive art sessions, (d) hypothesized approximations (e) homework, (f) duration of treatment.	(5) To obtain appropriate training in implosive therapy	

TABLE 3.4 (continued)

Author	*General Theoretical Stance*	*Type of Children or Disorder*
Rosal (1985b, 1986)	Personal construct psychology	Learning or behavior problem children

General Principles	*Role of the Art Therapist*	*Evidence of Effect*
(1) This approach is based on Kelly's personal construct psychology	(1) To assess the child and her constructs	(1) Child sees self as more positive in relationship to peers/adults
(2) Constructs are assumptions or hypotheses about one's world	(2) To support the child in the discovery of constructs	(2) Personal construct drawings/repertory goods can evaluate therapeutic effectiveness
(3) Constructs are bipolar	(3) To teach about bipolar nature of ideas and constructs	
(4) Clients can use constructs to understand their behavior		
(5) Constructs can be used as a means for children to role play		
(6) Repertory grids can help adults understand a child's world		
(7) Personal constructs can aid in improving self-image		
(8) Personal constructs can be drawn or provided in art therapy		

		Children with learning problems and children with
Rosal (1985a, 1987)	Cognitive Approaches	poor self-control

General Principles	*Role of the Art Therapist*	*Evidence of Effect*
(1) Higher mental processes can be used as a direct link to overt behavior	(1) To understand how higher mental processes affect behavior	(1) The problem behavior is solved
(2) Mental imagery as a cognitive process can be tapped and altered	(2) To assess the cognitive component of a child's behavior	(2) The child gains control over anxious or angry feelings

TABLE 3.4 (continued)

Author	*General Theoretical Stance*	*Type of Children or Disorder*
Rosal (*continued*)		
(3) Both mental messages and mental imagery affect a child's sense of self and self-control	(3) To use mental messages and images as a key to behavior change	(3) Mental messages become more positive
(4) Relaxation helps child produce images and improve self-control	(4) To teach relaxation techniques	(4) New behaviors and coping skills are evident in the class-room or at home
(5) Images can prompt relaxed states	(5) To use reinforce-ments, prompts and modeling	
(6) Concrete images can alter mental images and mental images can alter concrete images		

Case Example

Scott, age 12, was able to better control his conduct disorder and antisocial personality problems after 20 sessions of art therapy based on cognitive-behavioral principles. Scott was referred to art therapy by his teacher because of Scott's behavior problems in the classroom. In addition, Scott held delinquent status due to numerous incidents of thefts in the neighborhood.

Scott's lack of impulse control was assessed through a drawing, "someone being bad at school" (see Figure 3.14). Scott stated that the boy "is sitting on the other one so he can't move . . . he probably will hit him."

In treatment, Scott was taught relaxation techniques, and mental imagery was tapped to acquaint Scott with his mental messages. The mental images first were simple and concrete: "get a picture of the school in your head." Scott's visual image of his mental picture is primitive and disorganized (see Figure 3.15). The lack of impulse control and the lack of organization in his thinking and visualizing processes led the therapist to believe that this may be a factor in Scott's out-of-control behavior.

Relaxation and mental imagery work continued with Scott and his ability to concentrate and visualize improved dramatically. For example, Scott was taken on a guided imagery into a cave to meet a dragon and retrieve a treasure. Figure 3.16 shows Scott's depiction of his entrance into the cave. In

Figure 3.14. Scott completed this personal construct drawing during assessment. Scott's aggressiveness towards peers as well as his lack of impulse control were noted in this drawing.

this painting, Scott revealed his need for power as in Figure 3-14, but the power needs are more controlled and the energy is directed in a more positive direction than in previous drawings.

In the final session, Scott was asked to image something which he learned about himself in art therapy. His drawing portrays a happy face and Scott stated that he never had felt happy before and now he knows he can feel that way (see Figure 3.17).

Scott's increased attention to inner messages and images helped him to increase impulse control and attention span in the classroom. His classroom behavior difficulties decreased. In addition, Scott admitted that he had never had any friends before and that he had made some friends during the treatment period.

The therapist's work with Scott utilized several principles of cognitive-behavioral therapy. First, the therapist utilized Scott's mental images as a tool in treatment. Stress inoculation (a means of helping children cope with increasingly greater amounts of stress) and modified desensitization was used while Scott was relaxed and imaging stressful classroom situations. In addition, the sessions were planned in a building block manner—one idea was built upon another in order to help Scott gain the most from art therapy.

Figure 3.15. After a guided imagery of going to school, Scott, age 12, painted his image of school.

CONCLUSION

For the purpose of understanding the different approaches to art therapy with children, theoretical material which has been discussed through publication and at conferences has been organized into four major categories. Each approach has a set of principles which guides art therapists in: (a) developing treatment goals, (b) session planning, (c) understanding the role of the art therapist, and (d) defining avenues of assessment and evaluation of treatment.

It is evident from the four theoretical approaches described that the use of art therapy with children is complex. Each of the four theories offers a rich, divergent view of human nature and how children fit into a particular theoretical framework. Art therapy has then been introduced into that framework as a means of remediating the emotional and behavioral problems that can occur. It is also evident that the approaches overlap in significant ways.

The psychoanalytic approach is an approach that demands profound

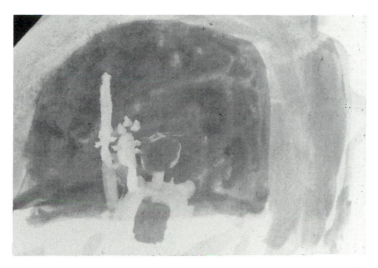

Figure 3.16. Scott painted himself in front of a cave with a sword held high and with a backpack. This painting was completed after a guided imagery of going into a cave for treasure.

understanding of symbolic content and meaning in art process and product. This approach also requires the therapist to accept the therapeutic relationship as one which is meaningful (on a symbolic level) for the child.

Thorough understanding of child development is necessary for art therapists who utilize the developmental approach to art therapy. The therapist must be able to accurately assess the level of development of a particular child and, based on that assessment, create a treatment plan to offer the child developmental tasks necessary to encourage growth.

The art therapist who works within the realm of the adaptive approach targets the unique strengths of each child as a touchstone for their work. These art therapists devise a program to minimize deficits and to maximize normalization experiences.

To work within the cognitive-behavioral approach, understanding of higher mental processes is necessary. The art therapist investigates the child's mental messages and images and uses imagery, both mental and concrete visual, to intervene in mental processes which have been detrimental to the child.

Although each approach has definite and unique principles, common themes apply to all approaches: (a) art therapists have, as a basis of their work, a strong theoretical stance, (b) art therapists have a solid understanding of art media, (c) art therapists assess the children prior to developing treatment goals and plans, (d) art therapists carefully observe changes in both the art and the behavior of their clients, (e) the art therapist respects the integrity of the art of each child, and (f) art therapists are advocates for their child client's well-being and growth.

Figure 3.17. This was Scott's final drawing in art therapy. Scott was surprised to discover that he could feel happy.

The most significant way the approaches overlap in working with children is that children are developing naturally. Therefore, all art therapists must take into account developmental issues. It is Wilson who realizes this issue among the psychoanalytic theorists. Her work with mentally retarded and learning disabled children employs developmental principles. Among the adaptive theorists, Anderson readily recognizes that art therapists must keep graphic development principles in mind when evaluating and working with children. Packard, Roth and Rosal note the need to evaluate progress through behavioral and developmental changes. Art therapy affects brain development (Musick), ego development (Wilson), graphic development (Uhlin and Anderson), cognitive development (Aach-Feldman and Kunckle-Miller, Silver), and behavioral development (Packard, Roth, Rosal).

The role of the art therapist is one of the common aspects important to each of the approaches to art therapy with children discussed in this overview. There are many consistencies between the theoretical approaches concerning how the therapist interacts with the child. For example, art therapists provide art materials of interest for the child. Also, art therapists provide an open and safe environment for each child. The art therapist is always supportive and yet challenges the child. The art therapists respects the integrity of the work of each child.

After studying each theory and approach with a critical eye, what seems most important is that art therapists have a theoretical basis for their work. One theory is not necessarily more effective than another. However, each art therapist who works with children should be a careful theoretician as well as a careful clinician.

REFERENCES

Aach, S. R. (1984). The play process in art therapy. In A. E. DiMaria, E. S. Kramer, & I. Rosner (Eds.), *Proceedings of the Twelfth Annual Conference of the American Art Therapy Association* (p. 38). Baltimore, MD: AATA.

Aach-Feldman, S., & Kunkle-Miller, C. (1987). A developmental approach to art therapy. In J. A. Rubin (Ed.), *Approaches to art therapy: Theory and technique* (pp. 251–274). New York: Brunner/Mazel, Inc.

Anderson, F. E. (1978). *Art for all the children: A creative sourcebook for the impaired child.* Springfield, IL: Charles C Thomas.

Anderson, F. E. (1982). Some issues in considering the role of art therapists in public school settings. In L. Gantt & A. Evans (Eds.), *Proceedings of the Tenth Annual Conference of the American Art Therapy Association* (pp. 86–89). Falls Church, VA: AATA.

Bandura, A. (1969). *Principles of behavior modification.* New York: Holt, Rinehart, and Winston.

Bandura, A. (1977). *Social learning theory.* Englewood Cliffs, NJ: Prentice-Hall.

Beck, A. T. (1976). *Cognitive therapy and the emotional disorders.* New York: International Universities Press.

Clements, C. B., & Clements, R. D. (1984). *Art and mainstreaming: Art instruction for exceptional children in regular school classes.* Springfield, IL: Charles C Thomas.

De Francisco, J. (1983). Implosive art therapy: A learning-theory based, psychodynamic approach. In L. Gantt & S. Whitman (Eds.), *Proceedings of the Eleventh Annual Conference of the American Art Therapy Association* (pp. 74–79). Baltimore, MD: AATA.

DiGuiseppe, R. A. (1981). Cognitive therapy with children. In G. Emery, S. D. Hollon, & R. D. Bedrosian (Eds.), *New directions in cognitive therapy: A casebook* (pp. 50–67). New York: The Guilford Press.

D'Zurilla, T. J., & Goldfried, M. R. (1971). Problem solving and behavior modification. *Journal of Abnormal Psychology, 78,* 107–126.

Ellis, A. (1962). *Reason and emotion in psychotherapy.* New York: Lyle Stuart.

Goldfried, M. R. (1971). Systematic desensitization as training in self-control. *Journal of Consulting and Clinical Psychology, 37,* 228–234.

Gonick-Barris, S. E. (1976). Art for children with minimal brain dysfunction. *American Journal of Art Therapy, 15,* 67–73.

Jungels, G. (1977). Expanding art experiences in schools to include all children. In R. H. Shoemaker & S. E. Gonick-Barris (Eds.), *Proceedings of the Seventh Annual Conference of the American Art Therapy Association* (pp. 31–32.) Baltimore, MD: AATA.

Jungels, G. (1978). Expanding art experiences in schools to include all children. *The NYSATA Bulletin, 28*(3), 15.

Kanfer, F. H., & Zich, J. (1974). Self-control training: The effects of external control on children's resistance to temptation. *Developmental Psychology, 10*(1), 108–115.

Kazdin, A. E. (1974). Effects of covert modeling and modeling reinforcement on assertive behavior. *Journal of Abnormal Psychology, 82,* 240–252.

Kramer, E. (1958). *Art therapy in a children's community.* Springfield, IL: Charles C Thomas.

Kramer, E. (1971). *Art as therapy with children.* New York: Schocken Books.

Kramer, E. (1977). Art therapy and play. *American Journal of Art Therapy, 17*(1), 3–11.

Kramer, E. (1979). *Childhood and art therapy: Notes on theory and application.* New York: Schocken Books.

Kunkle-Miller, C., & Aach, S. (1983). Presymbolic levels of expression—their relation to the theory and practice of art therapy. In L. Gantt & S. Whitman (Eds.), *Proceedings of the Eleventh Annual Conference of the American Art Therapy Association* (pp. 55–60). Baltimore, MD: AATA.

Landgarten, H. B. (1981). *Clinical art therapy: A comprehensive guide.* New York: Brunner/Mazel.

Levick, M. F. (1983). *They could not talk and so they drew: Children's styles of coping and thinking.* Springfield, IL: Charles C Thomas.

Lowenfeld, V. (1947). *Creative and mental growth* (1st ed.). New York: Macmillan.

Lowenfeld, V. (1957). *Creative and mental growth* (3rd ed.). New York: Macmillan.

Lowenfeld, V., & Brittain, L. (1975). *Creative and mental growth* (6th ed.) New York: MacMillan.

Luria, A. R. (1961). *The role of speech in the regulation of normal and abnormal behavior.* New York: Liveright.

Mahoney, M. J. (1977). Personal science: A cognitive learning therapy. In A. Ellis & R. Grieger (Eds.), *Handbook of rational psychotherapy.* New York: Springer.

Mahoney, M. J., & Arnkoff, D. (1978). Cognitive and self-control therapies. In S. L. Garfield & A. E. Bergin (Eds.), *Handbook of psychotherapy and behavior change* (2nd ed.) (pp. 689–722). New York: John Wiley & Sons.

Mayhew, N. (1979). The practice of art therapy in a special education setting. In L. Gantt, G. Forrest, D. Siverman, & R. J. H. Shoemaker (Eds.), *Proceedings of the Ninth Annual Conference of the American Art Therapy Association* (pp. 22–25). Baltimore, MD: AATA.

Meichenbaum, D. (1975). A self-instructional approach to stress management: A proposal for stress inoculation training. In I. Sarason & C. D. Spielberger (Eds.), *Stress and anxiety: Vol. 2* (pp. 227–263). New York: John Wiley & Sons.

Meichenbaum, D., & Goodman, J. (1971). Training impulsive children to talk to themselves: A means of developing self-control. *Journal of Abnormal Psychology, 77*(2), 115–126.

Miller, N. E., & Dollard, J. (1941). *Social learning and imitation.* New Haven, CT: Yale University Press.

Musick, P. L. (1978). Special child—special growth: Developmental creativity. In B. K. Mandel, R. H. Shoemaker, & R. E. Hays (Eds.), *Proceedings of the Eighth Annual Conference of the American Art Therapy Association* (pp. 63–65). Baltimore, MD: AATA.

Naumburg, M. (1950). *An introduction to art therapy: Studies of the "free" art expression of behavior problem children and adolescents as a means of diagnosis and therapy.* New York: Teachers College Press.

Packard, S. (1977). Learning disabilities: Identification and remediation through creative art activity. In R. H. Shoemaker & S. E. Gonick-Barris (Eds.), *Proceedings of the Seventh Annual Conference of the American Art Therapy Association* (pp. 57–61). Baltimore, MD: AATA.

Piaget, J. (1962). *Play, dreams, and imitation in childhood.* New York: W. W. Norton.

Public Law 94-142. 1975.

Rosal, M. L. (1985a). *The use of art therapy to modify the focus of control and adaptive behavior of behavior disordered students.* Unpublished doctoral dissertation, University of Queensland, Brisbane, Australia.

Rosal, M. L. (1985b). *The use of personal construct drawings as an art therapeutic outcome measure.* Paper presented at the Annual Conference of the American Art Therapy Association, New Orleans, LA.

Rosal, M. L. (1986). *The rating of personal construct drawings to measure behavior change.* Paper presented at the Annual Conference of American Art Therapy Association, Los Angeles, CA.

Rosal, M. L. (1987). *Cognitive approaches in art therapy with children.* Paper presented at the Annual Conference of the American Art Therapy Association, Miami, FL.

Roth, E. A. (1978). Art therapy with emotionally disturbed-mentally retarded children: A technique of reality shaping. In B. K. Mandel, R. H. Shoemaker, & R. E. Hays (Eds.), *Proceedings of the Eighth Annual Conference of the American Art Therapy Association* (pp. 168–172). Baltimore, MD: AATA.

Roth, E. A. (1982). Symbolic expression in art therapy and play therapy with a disturbed child. In L. Gantt & A. Evans (Eds.), *Proceedings of the Tenth Annual Conference of the American Art Therapy Association* (pp. 23–26). Falls Church, VA: AATA.

Roth, E. A. (1987). A behavioral approach to art therapy. In J. A. Rubin (Ed.), *Approaches to art therapy: Theory and technique* (pp. 213–232). New York: Brunner/Mazel, Inc.

Rotter, J. B. (1954). *Social learning and clinical psychology.* Englewood Cliffs, NJ: Prentice-Hall.

Rubin, J. A. (1978). *Child art therapy: Understanding and helping children grow through art.* New York: Van Nostrand Reinhold.

Segal, E. (1976). *Language, representation, and the control of behavior* (pp. 25–26). Palo Alto, CA: Stanford University.

Silver, R. A. (1978). *Developing cognitive and creative skills through art: Programs for children with communication disorders or learning disabilities.* Baltimore, MD: University Park Press.

Silver, R. A. (1983a). Developing cognitive skills through art: Report of a 1980 National Institute of Education Project. In L. Gantt & S. Whitman (Eds.), *Proceedings of the Eleventh Annual Conference of the American Art Therapy Association* (p. 41). Falls Church, VA: AATA.

Silver, R. A. (1983b). *Silver drawing test of cognitive and creative skills.* Seattle, WA: Special Child Publications.

Silver, R. A. (1987). A cognitive approach to art therapy. In J. A. Rubin (Ed.), *Approaches to art therapy: Theory and technique* (pp. 233–250). New York: Brunner/Mazel.

Singer, J. L., & Pope, K. S. (1978). *The power of human imagination: New methods in psychotherapy.* New York: Plenum Press.

Sobol, B. (1985). Art therapy, behavior modification, and conduct disorder. *American Journal of Art Therapy, 24,* 35–43.

Spivack, G., & Shure, M. B. (1974). *Social adjustment of young children: A cognitive approach to solving real-life problems.* San Francisco, CA: Jossey-Bass.

Uhlin, D. M. (1972). *Art for exceptional children.* Dubuque, IA: Wm. C. Brown.

Williams, G. H., & Wood, M. M. (1977). *Developmental art therapy.* Baltimore, MD: University Park Press.

Wilson, L. (1977). Theory and practice of art therapy with the mentally retarded. *American Journal of Art Therapy, 16*(3), 89–97.

Wilson, L. (1982). Art therapy with the mentally retarded. In L. Gantt & A. Evans (Eds.), *Proceedings of the Tenth Annual Conference of the American Art Therapy Association* (p. 31). Falls Church, VA: AATA.

Wilson, L. (1985a). Symbolism and art therapy: I. Symbolism's role in the development of ego functions. *American Journal of Art Therapy, 23,* 79–88.

Wilson, L. (1985b). Symbolism and art therapy: II. Symbolism's relationship to basic psychic functioning. *American Journal of Art Therapy, 23,* 129–133.

Wilson, L. (1987). Symbolism and art therapy: Theory and clinical practice. In J. A. Rubin (Ed.), *Approaches to art therapy: Theory and technique* (pp. 44–62). New York: Brunner/Mazel.

Chapter 4

ART AND
THE INDIVIDUALIZED EDUCATION PROGRAM

In 1775, Public Law 94-142, the Education for All Handicapped Children Act, became Law. In 1990 this law was reauthorized as the Individuals with Disabilities Education Act (IDEA), (PL 101-476). These laws and Section 504 regulations of the Vocational Rehabilitation Act Amendments of 1973 (PL 93-112) mandate that children with Disabilities are to participate in the "regular education program, 'to the maximum extent appropriate'" (*NAEA Advisory,* 1989). Children with disabilities must be availed of the least restrictive educational alternative. The term "mainstreaming" has been derived from this mandate to insure that children with disabilities be placed whenever feasible into regular school classrooms.

Placements of children with disabilities (either in regular classrooms or in special education classrooms) are determined as a part of the child's annual Individualized Education Program (IEP). Public Law 94-142 (now IDEA) requires that each child who is to receive special education must have an IEP developed on an annual basis. In developing an IEP for a child, he is evaluated on his current skills and abilities in each of the following areas: academic/cognitive, communication status, motor and perceptual skills, self-help skills, social/emotional status, and prevocational/vocational. Once these assessments are completed, a staffing is held, and parents or guardians and a representative from the school district or instructional unit who is administratively responsible for supervision of the delivery of services in special education are present. All teachers who instruct the child and the child himself (when possible or feasible) should also be present.

At this staffing an IEP is developed for the child and annual goals are established, and decisions are made as to what educational services and which regular education classes are appropriate for the child. Specifically, the following six parts are included in an IEP:

1. the current level of performance of the learner
2. annual goals
3. short-term instructional objectives
4. the educational services and experiences that will be provided, as well as

the dates that these begin and the period of time that these experiences and services will be provided.

5. the nature of the child's participation in regular education programs
6. schedules, procedures and objective criteria for annual evaluation (Morreau & Anderson, 1984).

The IDEA added a seventh part, a transition plan that is required only for students 14 years and older (PL 101-476, 1990).

While art is not one of the specific subjects in which IEPs are written, there are several ways art can be included in an IEP. A regular art class can be one of the specified placements for the child. Art can be included as a related service for the child. Finally, art can be used in the best sense to remediate some problem identified in one or more of the six major areas in which the child is assessed and in which annual goals are written.

Mainstreaming Children into Regular Art Classes

Once annual goals and short-term objectives based on an assessment of the learner's performance are established, decisions will be made relative to the placement of the learner in either regular education or self-contained classrooms. As noted above, the mandates of PL 94-142 (1975) (now IDEA, 1990) stress that learners with disabilities should be educated whenever possible along with their "normal" peers. Children's placements depend on their physical skill levels, social skill levels, and their needs. Often, learners are placed in regular art classes without a complete understanding of the physical, social, and cognitive skills needed for those learners to be comfortable or to succeed in the placement. This situation occurs because decisions to place children with disabilities in an art class are often made without the art teacher being present at the staffing at which the decision was made. This fact was borne out in a study (Anderson, 1980) in which over 140 art teachers were surveyed as to the extent to which they had mainstreamed students and the extent to which they were involved in the IEP planning process. While about one-third of the teachers surveyed reported having disabled students mainstreamed into their regular art classes, only four reported being involved in the staffings at which these placement decisions were made. In 1989 and 1990, straw polls at conferences for art therapists and art teachers in the states of Michigan and Florida confirmed that this practice continues.

Also, special learners often end up in regular art classes that have too many students for the art teacher to adequately accommodate those with special needs. The art teacher may not have the training or preparation to instruct children with disabilities who are mainstreamed in their regular art classes (Anderson, Colchado & McAnally, 1979; Anderson, 1980). Also, art teachers may not have access to school records and may be prevented from gaining access to this information even though they do have a right to information that may impact on their instructional approaches with children who are disabled (Thorne, 1990).

Art as a Related Service

Every IEP must include not only short-term behavioral objectives but also a description of the specific educational services and experiences that are to be provided, as well as the time frame for their provision. This section of the IEP may include related services such as special adaptive art or art therapy. A lobbying effort on the national level resulted in art therapy being listed specifically as a related service which can be requested in an IEP PL 94-142, now IDEA. Art therapists in Michigan also have been successful in lobbying efforts to have art therapy specified as a related service in the state guidelines for IEPs. Parents and teachers (especially art teachers) should be aware that these related services can be requested and will be provided (and funded) if requested in many states.

Art for Remediation

There is a growing body of research that supports (with hard data) the fact that the arts can be used in the best sense to teach other academic concepts, to motivate students and to remediate learning problems (Anderson, Ash, & Gambach, 1981; Anderson, 1983; Anderson, 1988; Anderson, 1991). It is unfortunate that art, music, and dance or related arts are not required in most of the university preservice special education curricula and are often not elected because of extreme limitations on electives in the special education required course of study.

The result of inadequate training in the arts means that special education teachers may not be aware of the power that art has in remediating problems that children with disabilities have. This fact was borne out in a study of IEPs in the state of Illinois. A review of 210 IEPs revealed that **not one** included art in any long-term or short-term goal statement (Morreau & Anderson, 1984).

We must try to inform special educators that art can be used in the best sense to remediate problems listed in **all** of the six major areas of performance that are included specifically on an IEP. This use of art for remediation is a growing trend and will continue to grow as parents, special and art educators, and public school administrators become more aware of the ways that art can be used to facilitate the total development of children with disabilities. This writer predicts (if the economy is healthy) that more and more art therapists will be utilized in public school settings around the country in compliance with the mandates of PL 94-142 (now IDEA).

The trend will grow also because not only are many art teachers unprepared to handle special education children in mainstreamed and in self-contained situations, but there are other pressures on the art teacher. These pressures include the growing trend toward Discipline Based Art Education (Duke, 1983) and the trend toward required art competencies that many states are now mandating. These demands will further press art teachers to attend to a more content-oriented art education which may not be appropriate for some mainstreamed students whose needs are not "beyond creating"—who have more basic needs for expression and skill development in art production and for therapeutic art interventions.

Art Therapists in the Public Schools

Already in at least three parts of the country, art therapy and art therapists are being utilized in public schools. In the Milwaukee, Wisconsin public schools, art therapy is being included in the education of special needs students. This is being accomplished by a few teachers who hold a special art and special education certificate. These teachers have training in art education, special education, and art therapy. They must have teacher certification before they can work in the public schools. Efforts to have the job title "art therapist" included on the special certificate in Wisconsin are continuous but have not as yet been successful.

The Dade County Public Schools in Miami, Florida have had an infusion of art therapists since 1979. These art therapists, who are also certified art teachers, provide individual art therapy for students with severe emotional disturbances. Students in the Dade County Public Schools receive special art therapy when it is written into their Individualized Therapeutic and Education Program which is similar to the Individualized Education Program but includes emotional as well as academic goals. This program, funded with local monies through the Dade County Public School's Division of Exceptional Student Education, will be discussed in more detail later.

Additionally, in the Washington, D.C. area, at least two art therapists are providing therapeutic interventions for public school children with disabilities. Audrey Di Maria has been involved in providing therapeutic art interventions in public schools for over a decade. One segment of this chapter includes a model example of an IEP written by Di Maria to demonstrate how art can be included in all six components of a child's IEP.

We begin our discussion of writing IEPs in art with a segment written by

Betty Jo Troeger. This segment includes examples of art assessment tools which were used to incorporate art into the IEPs of disabled children in a special school for children with health impairments and orthopedic disabilities in Washington, D.C. This model (Troeger-Clifford, 1981) has been used in a variety of special education situations since its development.

An Example of the Development and Implementation of Individualized Education Programs in Art for Three Learners With Physical and Multiple Disabilities

Betty Jo Troeger

In 1981, five components that need to be considered in the development of an IEP that includes art were established and field-tested (Troeger-Clifford, 1981). These components are:

Identify	Predict	Decide	Implement	Evaluate
• art development	• goals	• learning activity	• concept development	• developmental growth
• art skills	• objectives	• media needed	• awareness experiences	• learning environment
• previous school record	• skills that are compatible with development	• task analysis	• observation of learner	• learning behavior
• disability as it might affect learning		• adaptation		• media preference
				• time/task art product

Assessment: A Key Factor

Assessment is the key factor that links art learning to prior learning. Assessment is also essential to enable the matching of development capacities to art skills and concepts. When assessing individuals, it is important to keep in mind that a student can only be measured, appraised, or assessed within the context of his own learning and maturation (Maier, 1969). A class of special education students has varying levels of growth. Each student is unique and thus each art assessment is unique (Troeger, 1985).

Identify

Observing the child as he makes art will be an *essential* part of the assessment process. Additionally, it will be important to review prior data in the child's records.

If the learner appears to be developmentally delayed or demonstrates early developmental patterns, the artwork that one would observe the child making might include the following tasks:

1. a scribble drawing
2. a tempera painting
3. a clay experience
4. an activity involving cutting and pasting paper

Additionally, the adult should record any verbalizations the child makes during these four art activities.

Using a developmental approach, if the learner appears to be operating in the early schematic or schematic level of development (McFee, 1970; Eisner, 1976; Chapman, 1978, 1985), the art tasks might include the following:

1. a drawing of a person
2. a drawing of a simple geometric form
3. a painting accompanied by a written or dictated story about the picture by the artist
4. a clay sculpture
5. a cut paper design collage

Art Skill Sheet

To record the learners' competencies in manipulating art materials and in developing symbolic representations, the following art skill sheet was developed. This skill sheet was based in part on an inventory developed by Brigance (1978) which focused on the early development of fine motor skills and behaviors. In Brigance's inventory, skills were listed in a developmental sequence that ran from six months to six years. Brigance's starting points for drawing, painting, cut paper, and clay were also the starting points for the Art Skill Sheet that follows (Troeger-Clifford, 1981).

ART SKILL SHEET

Name: _____   *Date:* _____ *Age:* _____ *Sex:* _____

Drawing

____ establish hand/eye contact with marker
____ manipulate large marker on flat surface
____ draw a circle
____ draw a triangle
____ draw a square
____ draw a face
____ draw a person
____ draw a person with head, arms, legs
____ draw a person with head, body, arms, legs
____ draw a person beyond schematic level
____ draw objects in front of or behind others
____ utilize variation of shapes and details
____ utilize different kinds of lines (continuous, short, thin, wide) to convey contours or texture

Painting

____ control handling of brush
____ paint freely on paper with large brush
____ paint areas of color
____ paint horizontal lines
____ paint vertical lines
____ recognize and choose colors:
    ____ red   ____ green   ____ black
    ____ yellow ____ purple ____ brown
    ____ blue   ____ orange ____ white
____ mix colors to create new colors
____ paint representational symbols
    ____ house ____ person ____ car
    ____ tree   ____ animal ____ others
____ paint shapes, lines, and colors as designs
____ utilize language to describe painting

Cut Paper

____ hold scissors
____ open and close scissors
____ cut on a straight line
____ cut out a circle
____ cut out numerous shapes
____ place paste on back of shape
____ attach shape to design surface
____ experiment with a few shapes, cutting and pasting at random
____ combine shapes in simple patterns
____ use papers varied in texture, color, and shape to make complex designs
____ construct three-dimensional forms by folding, fitting, and fastening

Clay

____ grasp clay
____ break clay into pieces
____ change shape of clay (patting, poking, kneading)
____ roll clay into a ball
____ roll clay into a coil
____ pinch or pull shape from lump of clay
____ roll clay into slab with rolling pin
____ join two or more shapes by smoothing, scoring, and use of slip
____ add appropriate amount of water to keep clay in good working condition
____ construct familiar objects (animals, people, cars, pots) with uniform thickness
____ use simple tools to create texture

Other Helpful Data

Learners' cumulative records can provide information as to age, medical diagnoses, physical involvement, or restrictions. These records may also include developmental measures noted by the psychologist, education specialists, or placement officials. As the reader may be aware, many special needs students may have a chronological age that is different from their developmental age. Medical records and diagnosis of the specific disabilities are also important information sources, especially because they may include factors about the learners' expressive and receptive language capacities. With an accurate diagnosis of both medical and physical limitations of the learners, one can expand the awareness of the teacher and therapist as to what might be affecting how the learner perceives the learning environment. Particularly with learners who have neurological problems, it is essential to understand how this particular learner perceives and responds to information that is presented.

The focus in records will be on the diagnosis of learning problems and physical modifications that would require special education placements.

The following seven pre-staffing directives have been included for their usefulness to the teacher or therapist in preparing for an IEP conference.

1. Review all existing educational records: vision, speech, language and hearing screenings, health, and formal and informal assessment.
2. Administer formal diagnostic assessments in various skill areas.
3. Document attendance patterns, suspensions or expulsions, and any disciplinary problems in the classroom.
4. Document how the student relates to peers and authority figures.
5. Note discrepancies between test performance and actual classroom performance.
6. Collect student's work samples.
7. Note student's interests, likes, and dislikes (*Individualized Education Program,* 1989).

It may be helpful to record information obtained from school placement records, as well as existing medical, physical, or occupational therapy units in a systematic format like the following one.

Name: _____ *Date:* _____ *Age:* _____ *Sex:* _____

ASSESSMENT DATA

disability: _____

degree of involvement: _____ mild _____ moderate _____ severe _____

adaptive devices: _____

medication: _____

limitations: _____ gross motor _____ fine motor _____ perception

developmental levels:

_____ art _____ Language _____ auditory _____ reading

living environment: _____ mother _____ father _____ sisters

_____ brothers _____ other

art therapy: _____ preventive _____ adjustment _____ special problem

notes:

Key: + above grade level
  × grade level
  — below grade level

Predict

After the assessment data are analyzed and recorded, art annual goals and art short-term objectives can be formulated for each student. The IEP team consisting of parents, guardians, administrator, teacher, student, and specialist agree upon these goals and objectives. Predicted goals, objectives, and learning activities should be compatible with each student's development. Individual school districts and systems have different forms for IEPs. However, the information that is included is generally very similar.

Public Law 94-142 (now IDEA) requires annual goal statements for each student. Vague and unrealistic accomplishments are eliminated from programming because goals must be supported by assessment data and should describe a specific behavior expected in a particular time frame. Goals are usually annual ones which are then broken down into short-term objectives that are measurable, behavioral, and observable. Goals and objectives are designed to meet each learner's unique instructional situation. When incorporating art experiences into annual goals and short-term objectives, these experiences should be compatible with the child's developmental capacities.

The Teacher Observation Progress Sheet (TOPS)

A Teacher Observation Progress Sheet (TOPS) was designed for students at the District of Columbia's public school for physically disabled and health-impaired students. With this form, there is some flexibility in determining and recording the learner's artistic developmental levels of early exploratory (ca. 0–3 years), preschematic (ca. 4–7 years), schematic (ca. 7–9), and cultural realism (9 and older) depending on the individual learner's assessments (McFee, 1964).

The TOPS sheet is used during the *implementation* of the IEP and is completed as an evaluation at the end of the year or the semester depending on the length of time prescribed by the IEP team. Beginning and ending dates are designated for the art intervention. Depending on the assessment outcomes, artistic developmental levels of early exploratory, preschematic, schematic and cultural realism are indicated.

An annual goal is developed and short-term objectives are designated to initiate art experiences and/or behavioral changes. Multiple learning activities are listed to reinforce each objective. Repetition of related experiences is an important factor in educational programming of many students with special needs.

The evaluation of artwork on the TOPS sheet utilizes the following broad categories: *creative, satisfactory, with help,* and *unsatisfactory. Creative* indicates work that reflects imaginative use of symbols and fantasy themes. It also indicates fluency and flexibility in using media in a variety of ways. A **creative** response to art generates many ideas around a subject or theme and also reflects shifts from one subject or media to another. Original or unique work is often described as **creative.**

Satisfactory work indicates that the student has met the goals, objectives, and learning activities prescribed for him. The term also means the artwork met the criteria but was not particularly unique, imaginative, or generative of other ideas and activities.

The term *with help* is an indication of the continual need for adult assistance. This need may be based on severe motor limitations or on low developmental levels. It may also be indicative of using an art media that does not work for that particular child, i.e., modeling clay, or clay that is not very soft or very malleable being used by a child with muscular dystrophy.

Unsatisfactory is an evaluation term that indicates the goal, objectives, and learning activities could not be accomplished. The IEP team would need to examine those goals, objectives, or learning activities that were rated as **unsatisfactory** and make modifications in planning further programs.

The category *learning environment* on the TOPS sheet implies that artistic expression occurs consistently and most freely in one of the three settings: a one-to-one situation, a small group, or a large group setting. Some children need continual adult support, while others may be very uncomfortable in an intimate setting. This is particularly true of children who spend little time with adults, those from institutional settings, or single family homes where a parent works several jobs. This environment may also be one in which an older sibling is often in charge.

The next evaluation component, *learning behavior,* should reflect the patterns the student exhibits during the implementation of the art therapy program. Some children are self-motivated. These children choose a media, initiate their own art, and express ideas and behaviors related to their goal and objectives.

Other children are motivated by their peers' actions. These children are more on task in a group setting where other persons' ideas influence their desire for expression.

Many students with special needs require adult guidance for art expression and behavioral choices. The category *adult directed* reflects this situation.

The category *learning style* can be evaluated through an observation of the art therapy process. While most students will utilize all sensory systems (seeing, moving, listening, touching, smelling, talking, and reading) to comprehend their environment, other children use only one sensory system or a combination of several. This limitation to only one or a few, but not all, sensory systems is often a reflection of a specific disability or a reflection of the way information has been presented to the child.

The next component, *media preference,* is also an observational evaluation which helps the art therapist determine future goals to present to the IEP team. Giving a choice of materials to the student to use during art expression provides the child with important independence-building choices and makes it possible for the child (if he chooses) to develop in-depth art skills in one media.

The last category on the TOPS sheet is *time/task relationship.* Some students work very rapidly. This rapid work pace may be indicative of a young child or student with an attention deficit disorder. Other students work on art activities at a time rate compatible with normal grade or developmental level expectations. Individuals with severe gross and fine motor limitations take much longer than the average person to complete many art activities. In observing the **time/task relationship,** particular attention should be given to those students who fall outside of the normal work pace (i.e., those who work very slowly or very rapidly on an art task).

Three Case Studies

Three cases are presented to illustrate how these three assessment forms (the Art Skill Sheet, the Assessment Data Sheet, and the Teacher Observation Progress Sheet) can be used.

The Case of Betty

Betty (not her real name) reflected a complex history during the *identifying* phase. She was a ten-year-old girl with spina bifida. Betty had a shunt, experienced diminished sensation in her lower body, and was diagnosed as mildly retarded. Her home environment was very unstable. She wore glasses and stuttered, and her school records indicated she was at a preprimer level in reading and math. Betty exhibited disruptive behavior in her classroom and in the lunchroom, but appeared to enjoy art.

Betty's art skill sheet reflected an early exploratory stage of development in painting, clay, and cut paper activities. She was at a preschematic stage of development in drawing.

In the *predicting* component a goal was designed for Betty with an art therapy focus, developing acceptable classroom behavior that involved making art and receiving positive reinforcement for her constructive activity. The objectives designed to help the student meet this goal were (a) the student will make choices concerning the use of materials and experiences to produce art at an exploratory stage of development, (b) the student will describe colors and shapes in her drawings and paintings, and (c) the student will receive positive verbal reinforcement for appropriate behavior in the art area and for meaningful art expressions.

The *deciding* component included learning activities related to the student's preference toward drawing and painting. Those activities were planned to culminate in positive outcomes. The student will (a) select drawing or painting as an art activity, (b) choose colors of markers or tempera paint to use on paper, (c) produce a drawing or painting, (d) talk about artwork, (e) place art on the bulletin board, and (f) receive positive responses from the art instructor. No special adaptation of the environment was necessary for Betty to make art.

The *implementing* period of five months revealed that Betty worked most productively in a one-on-one individualized setting. She was, however, able to stay on task using appropriate behaviors when placed in a group setting of older students. She did not interact with them but remained attentive to her art production. Betty's learning style appeared to be multisensory with the exception of reading instruction, which was beyond her developmental capacities.

Evaluating Betty included both the behavioral and artistic aspects of her goal and objectives. Her artwork was rated satisfactory (it met the objective), although it reflected few significant growth indicators. This lack of significant growth indicators is typical of children with developmental delays. Betty appeared to have better control of areas of color with less accidental blending and more deliberate layering of colors on top of or next to dry areas of color. In her drawings she named people and told what they were doing or where they were. Extra time was given to these verbal descriptions so that Betty could pronounce her words in a relaxed setting. Her time/task relationships were average duration for her chronological age. The art activities lasted about 55 minutes, and she was able to stay on task for that time. Because she had no fine motor limitations, drawing and painting processes occurred with an average time expectation.

Betty's behavior showed significant improvement both in the art room and in her regular classroom setting. Betty generally began to transfer staying under control to places other than the art room. There were a few remissions, but they were not met with severe restrictions such as not being permitted to have art during the day. These remissions were used as opportunities to discuss the importance of making better choices of behaviors. Strong praise seemed to be the most effective means of changing her disruptive behavior. Art activities were concrete experiences that Betty could use to gain praise for productive actions.

Name: __Betty_____ Date: _____ Age: __10__ Sex: __F____

ASSESSMENT DATA

*disability: __Spina bifida with shunt, seizure disorder_____

degree of involvement: _____ mild __×__ moderate _____ severe _____

adaptive devices: __glasses_____

medication: _____

limitations: __−__ gross motor __×__ fine motor __×__ perception

developmental levels:

__×__ art __−__ language __+__ auditory __−__ reading

living environment: __×__ mother _____ father __×__ sisters

_____ brothers _____ other

art therapy: _____ preventive __×__ adjustment _____ special problem

notes: * disability produced diminished sensations in lower body
       * stutters
       does not separate imaginary events from reality
       time reference problems
       relates best to younger children
       stealing problem
       physically destructive in classroom/lunchroom

Key: + above grade level
     × grade level
     − below grade level

ART SKILL SHEET

Name: Betty_____   *Date:* __1/79__ *Age:* __10__ *Sex:* __F__

Drawing

__×__ establish hand/eye contact with marker
__×__ manipulate large marker on flat surface
__×__ draw a circle
__×__ draw a triangle
__×__ draw a square
__×__ draw a face
__×__ draw a person
__×__ draw a person with head, arms, legs
__×__ draw a person with head, body, arms, legs
____ draw a person beyond schematic level
____ draw objects in front of or behind others
____ utilize variation of shapes and details
____ utilize different kinds of lines (continuous, short, thin, wide) to convey contours or texture

Painting

__×__ control handling of brush
__×__ paint freely on paper with large brush
__×__ paint areas of color
__×__ paint horizontal lines
__×__ paint vertical lines
__×__ recognize and choose colors:

    __×__ red   __×__ green   ____ black
    __×__ yellow   ____ purple   ____ brown
    ____ blue   __×__ orange   ____ white

____ mix colors to create new colors
____ paint representational symbols

    ____ house   ____ person   ____ car
    ____ tree   ____ animal   ____ others

____ paint shapes, lines, and colors as designs
____ utilize language to describe painting

Cut Paper

__×__ hold scissors
__×__ open and close scissors
__×__ cut on a straight line
__×__ cut out a circle
____ cut out numerous shapes
____ place paste on back of shape
____ attach shape to design surface
____ experiment with a few shapes, cutting and pasting at random
____ combine shapes in simple patterns
____ use papers varied in texture, color, and shape to make complex designs
____ construct three-dimensional forms by folding, fitting, and fastening

Clay

__×__ grasp clay
__×__ break clay into pieces
__×__ change shape of clay (patting, poking, kneading)
__×__ roll clay into a ball
__×__ roll clay into a coil
____ pinch or pull shape from lump of clay
____ roll clay into slab with rolling pin
____ join two or more shapes by smoothing, scoring, and use of slip
____ add appropriate amount of water to keep clay in good working condition
____ construct familiar objects (animals, people, cars, pots) with uniform thickness
____ use simple tools to create texture

Figure 4.1. Betty, age 10, organizes space by painting areas of color and controlling color blending.

The Case of Chris

Chris (not his real name) was a ten-year-old boy who had muscular dystrophy (Duchenne's). He and his mother had recently moved to the United States from Trinidad. This major change coincided with ambulatory problems that were associated with Chris's muscular dystrophy, i.e., falling without any provocation. He appeared shy and apprehensive on admission to the school.

During the *identifying* period the assessment information revealed a preprimer level of development in academic subjects. Chris spoke infrequently in his classroom setting and responded in a similar manner in physical therapy. His mother said he was experiencing anxiety over approaching surgery.

TABLE 4.1

TEACHER OBSERVATION PROGRESS SHEET FOR SPECIAL POPULATIONS

STUDENT Betty
Growth Indicator ⟶

Dates			Early Exploratory	Schematic	Cultural Realism
1/79-6/79	Annual Goal		Given opportunities to participate in bi-weekly art experiences the student will develop acceptable classroom behavior and will be positively reinforced through the pleasure of making art and through verbal support by the art therapist.		
	Short Term Objectives		The student will: 1. make choices concerning use of materials and experiences to produce art at an exploratory stage of development, 2. describe colors and shapes in her drawings and paintings, 3. receive positive verbal reinforcement for appropriate behavior in the art area and for meaningful art expressions.		
	Learning Activities		The student will: 1. select drawing or painting as an art activity, 2. choose colors of markers or paint to use on paper, 3. produce a drawing or painting, 4. tell about art work, 4. place art on bulletin board, 5. receive positive responses from the art instructor.		
Learner Evaluation (Art work)	Creative				
	Satisfactory	✓			
	With help				
	Unsatisfactory				
Learning Environ- ment	Individual	✓			
	Small group				
	Large Group				
Learning Behavior	Self-directed	✓			
	Peer-directed				
	Teacher dir.				
Learning Style	Multisensory				
	Auditory	✓			
	Visual	✓			
	Verbal	✓			
	Written				
	Gestural	✓			
Media Prefer- ence	Drawing	✓			
	Painting				
	Cut paper				
	Clay				
	Other				
Time/Task Relation- ship	Rapid				
	Average	✓			
	Delayed				

In completing activities on the art skill sheet, Chris had great difficulty cutting and manipulating clay. His drawings, however, indicated he was entering the schematic level of art expression. There was evidence of imagination and knowledge of the world about him.

The *predicting* component in his artwork focused on experiences which would develop communication both verbally and visually. Small group art therapy sessions were designed to encourage verbal expression of Chris's visual images. The objectives stated that Chris would (a) paint a special person and share information about the painting with one other child and (b) draw events either real or imaginary and dictate a sentence for each visual expression.

Deciding components were learning activities which stated that Chris would (a) paint an outer space person and tell who he or she is, (b) paint a sportsperson and tell what sport he or she plays, (c) paint a superhero and tell what he or she can do, (d) draw his family and tell who is in the picture, and (e) draw a story about a hero and dictate a sentence about the drawing.

Chris participated in an art therapy group during the five-month *implementing* period. He began painting with a small group of three boys in the weekly session. These boys also had muscular dystrophy and they were very verbal.

At first, Chris appeared to be observing the other boys and the therapist. The boys usually painted or drew during the major portion of the session, and at the ten-minute closure time each child would dictate a paragraph or a sentence or a word to the instructor to describe elements or action in his art. These sentences usually concerned monsters, space creatures, or superheroes, very typical of this age level.

Chris's first painting was simply large areas of color. He was asked if he would like to name these (areas) shapes at the end of the session. Chris did, but speaking very softly. His shapes were robots and monsters, just like the other boys who had used the same labels for shapes in their work. Chris did not choose to share with the group. As the weeks passed, he painted people and rocket ships, and drew Superman at a schematic level of artistic representation. He had these drawing and painting skills when he came into the group, but he had waited to use them. As the other boys exclaimed how good Chris could draw, he drew better—better than any of them. Chris's artwork was prolific. He slowly began to verbalize more often; but he still had great control over the group, for they had decided Chris was the best artist, and they waited patiently for him to talk when he felt like it.

In *evaluating* Chris's artwork, it was apparent that creativity was an integral part of his work. He appeared to enjoy working with a small group of students, but he needed direction from the therapist before and after his working time to communicate successfully. Drawing was Chris's favorite media. His time/task relationship fell within an average range.

Figure 4.2. Chris, age 10, draws at a schematic level figures of Batman and Robin on skateboards.

Name: Chris _____ *Date:* _____ *Age:* 10 *Sex:* M

ASSESSMENT DATA

disability: Muscular Dystrophy (Duchenne's)

degree of involvement: _____ mild __×__ moderate _____ severe _____

adaptive devices: walker/braces

medications: _____

limitations: __—__ gross motor __+__ fine motor _____ perception

developmental levels:

__+__ art __—__ language __+__ auditory __—__ reading

living environment: __×__ mother _____ father _____ sisters

_____ brothers _____ other

art therapy: _____ preventive __×__ adjustment _____ special problem

notes: associate language with visual symbols, prefers drawing and painting

Key: + above grade level
   × grade level
   — below grade level

ART SKILL SHEET

Name: __Chris__   *Date:* __1/79__   *Age:* __10__   *Sex:* __M__

Drawing

- _×_ establish hand/eye contact with marker
- _×_ manipulate large marker on flat surface
- _×_ draw a circle
- _×_ draw a triangle
- _×_ draw a square
- _×_ draw a face
- _×_ draw a person
- _×_ draw a person with head, arms, legs
- ____ draw a person with head, body, arms, legs
- ____ draw a person beyond schematic level
- ____ draw objects in front of or behind others
- ____ utilize variation of shapes and details
- ____ utilize different kinds of lines (continuous, short, thin, wide) to convey contours or texture

Painting

- _×_ control handling of brush
- _×_ paint freely on paper with large brush
- _×_ paint areas of color
- _×_ paint horizontal lines
- _×_ paint vertical lines
- _×_ recognize and choose colors:
  - _×_ red   _×_ green   _×_ black
  - _×_ yellow   _×_ purple   _×_ brown
  - _×_ blue   _×_ orange   _×_ white
- _×_ mix colors to create new colors
- _×_ paint representational symbols
  - _×_ house   _×_ person   _×_ car
  - ____ tree   ____ animal   ____ others
- ____ paint shapes, lines, and colors as designs
- ____ utilize language to describe painting

Cut Paper (with difficulty)

- _×_ hold scissors
- _×_ open and close scissors
- _×_ cut on a straight line
- _×_ cut out a circle
- ____ cut out numerous shapes
- ____ place paste on back of shape
- ____ attach shape to design surface
- ____ experiment with a few shapes, cutting and pasting at random
- ____ combine shapes in simple patterns
- ____ use papers varied in texture, color, and shape to make complex designs
- ____ construct three-dimensional forms by folding, fitting, and fastening

Clay (with difficulty)

- _×_ grasp clay
- _×_ break clay into pieces
- _×_ change shape of clay (patting, poking, kneading)
- _×_ roll clay into a ball
- _×_ roll clay into a coil
- ____ pinch or pull shape from lump of clay
- ____ roll clay into slab with rolling pin
- ____ join two or more shapes by smoothing, scoring, and use of slip
- ____ add appropriate amount of water to keep clay in good working condition
- ____ construct familiar objects (animals, people, cars, pots) with uniform thickness
- ____ use simple tools to create texture

The Case of Don

Don (not his real name) was an eleven-year-old boy with a spinal cord injury that paralyzed his lower body. He had been confined to a wheelchair since age three. Following his accident, Don stayed at a residential hospital for several years. Don was living with his father and grandmother at the time his assessment was made.

The *identifying* phase revealed that Don's reading and math scores were on a third grade level, but his art expression was not developmentally delayed. Don had a very high energy level. The art skill sheet indicated that Don was at a schematic level of art development. He had a vivid imagination.

During the *predicting* component in planning, an art goal was written to develop specific skills. This goal was: Given opportunities for developing skills in three-dimensional art expression, the student will create images in response to his environment and his imagination. The objectives focused on exploring techniques in clay and constructing three-dimensional forms.

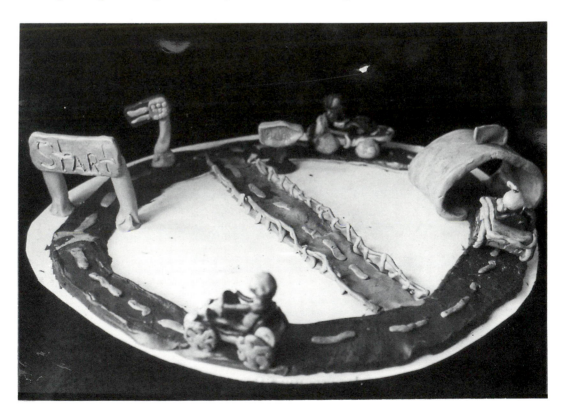

Figure 4.3. Don, age 11, constructs a racetrack including cars, drivers, starting lines, flags and architectural structures in modeling clay.

TABLE 4.2

TEACHER OBSERVATION PROGRESS SHEET FOR SPECIAL POPULATIONS

STUDENT CHRIS
Growth Indicator ⟶

Dates	IEP Information	Early Exploratory	Schematic	Cultural Realism
1/79–6/79	Annual Goal		Given biweekly opportunities for individualized and small group art therapy sessions designed to encourage verbal expression, the student will increase verbal communication of his visual images.	
	Short Term Objectives		The student will: 1. paint a special person and share information about the painting with one other child, 2. draw events either real or imaginary and dictate a sentence for each visual expression.	
	Learning Activities		The student will: 1. paint an outer space person and tell who he is, 2. paint a sports person and tell what sport he plays, 3. paint a superhero and tell what he can do, 4. draw his family and tell who is in the picture, 5. draw a story about a hero and dictate a sentence.	
Learner Evalua-tion (Art work)	Creative		✓	
	Satisfactory			
	With help			
	Unsatisfactory			
Learning Environ-ment	Individual			
	Small group		✓	
	Large Group			
Learning Behavior	Self-directed			
	Peer-directed			
	Teacher dir.		✓	
Learning Style	Multisensory		✓	
	Auditory		✓	
	Visual		✓	
	Verbal			
	Written			
	Gestural		✓	
Media Prefer-ence	Drawing		✓	
	Painting			
	Cut paper			
	Clay			
	Other			
Time/Task Relation-ship	Rapid			
	Average		✓	
	Delayed			

The student will (a) explore techniques in earth clay and modeling clay and (b) construct action figures, modes of transportation, and environments using either earth clay or modeling clay.

Deciding on art learning activities took into account that Don seemed to prefer three-dimensional expression. His drawings were folded or cut out, and he stated a preference to work with clay. These activities included: (a) form and support clay shapes to form a whole work, (b) construct a human figure performing an action, (c) construct a space vehicle by the same methods, and (d) create an environment with people, machines, or both performing an action.

Throughout the *implementing* period Don's artwork was highly creative. He worked best in an individual learning environment, much like a studio artist. He processed information by looking at artists' work in galleries, peers' artwork, and art reproductions. He listened to and watched the art therapist's demonstration of art processes, and he manipulated and experimented with art materials.

Evaluating Don's art experiences included both assessing the imaginative objects he created and the expressive intent of the art. His energy level was apparent in his choice of subjects. Don's time/task relationship was in an average range. His power of concentration was excellent in that he was not easily distracted from his art making. He appeared focused and seemed to direct his energy toward constructive art production. Don's imagination soared as he dictated stories about the figures he created. These improvised stories described a variety of characters and story lines.

Name: __Don__   Date: __1/79__ Age: __11__ Sex: __M__

ASSESSMENT DATA

disability: __spinal cord injury__

degree of involvement: _____ mild __×__ moderate _____ severe _____

adaptive devices: __wheelchair, braces__

medication: _____

limitations: __−__ gross motor _____ fine motor _____ perception

developmental levels:

__+__ art __+__ language __+__ auditory __−__ reading

living environment: _____ mother __×__ father _____ sisters

_____ brothers __×__ other (grandmother)

art therapy: _____ preventive __×__ adjustment _____ special problem

notes: vivid imagination, high energy level, prefers clay

Key: + above grade level
     × grade level
     − below grade level

ART SKILL SHEET

Name: __Don__   *Date:* __1/79__ *Age:* __12__ *Sex:* __M__

Drawing

- _×_ establish hand/eye contact with marker
- _×_ manipulate large marker on flat surface
- _×_ draw a circle
- _×_ draw a triangle
- _×_ draw a square
- _×_ draw a face
- _×_ draw a person
- _×_ draw a person with head, arms, legs
- _×_ draw a person with head, body, arms, legs
- ___ draw a person beyond schematic level
- ___ draw objects in front of or behind others
- _×_ utilize variation of shapes and details
- _×_ utilize different kinds of lines (continuous, short, thin, wide) to convey contours or texture

Painting

- _×_ control handling of brush
- _×_ paint freely on paper with large brush
- _×_ paint areas of color
- _×_ paint horizontal lines
- _×_ paint vertical lines
- _×_ recognize and choose colors:
  - _×_ red _×_ green _×_ black
  - _×_ yellow _×_ purple _×_ brown
  - _×_ blue _×_ orange _×_ white
- _×_ mix colors to create new colors
- ___ paint representational symbols
  - ___ house _×_ person ___ car
  - ___ tree ___ animal ___ others
- _×_ paint shapes, lines, and colors as designs
- _×_ utilize language to describe painting

Cut Paper

- _×_ hold scissors
- _×_ open and close scissors
- _×_ cut on a straight line
- _×_ cut out a circle
- _×_ cut out numerous shapes
- _×_ place paste on back of shape
- _×_ attach shape to design surface
- _×_ experiment with a few shapes, cutting and pasting at random
- _×_ combine shapes in simple patterns
- _×_ use papers varied in texture, color, and shape to make complex designs
- _×_ construct three-dimensional forms by folding, fitting, and fastening

Clay

- _×_ grasp clay
- _×_ break clay into pieces
- _×_ change shape of clay (patting, poking, kneading)
- _×_ roll clay into a ball
- _×_ roll clay into a coil
- _×_ pinch or pull shape from lump of clay
- _×_ roll clay into slab with rolling pin
- _×_ join two or more shapes by smoothing, scoring, and use of slip
- _×_ add appropriate amount of water to keep clay in good working condition
- _×_ construct familiar objects (animals, people, cars, pots) with uniform thickness
- _×_ use simple tools to create texture

TABLE 4.3

TEACHER OBSERVATION PROGRESS SHEET FOR SPECIAL POPULATIONS

STUDENT ___DON___

Growth Indicator ____→

Dates	IEP Information	Early Exploratory	Schematic	Cultural Realism
1/79-6/79	Annual Goal		Given opportunities for developing skills in three dimensional art expression during biweekly art classes, the student will create images in response to his environment and his imagination.	
	Short Term Objectives		The student will: 1. explore techniques in earth clay and modeling clay, 2. construct action figures, modes and transportation and environments using either earth clay or modeling clay.	
	Learning Activities		The student will: 1. join and support clay shapes to form a whole work, 2. construct a human figure performing in action using the above techniques, 3. construct a space vehicle by the same methods, 4. create an environment with people or machines or both performing an action.	

Learner Evaluation (Art work)				
Creative			✓	
Satisfactory				
With help				
Unsatisfactory				

Learning Environment				
Individual			✓	
Small group			✓	
Large Group				

Learning Behavior				
Self directed				
Peer directed				
Teacher dir.				

Learning Style				
Multisensory			✓	
Auditory				
Visual				
Verbal				
Written				
Gestural				

Media Preference				
Drawing				
Painting				
Cut paper				
Clay			✓	
Other				

Time/Task Relationship				
Rapid				
Average			✓	
Delayed				

Summary

As these cases indicate, art learning is highly individualized through the development of IEP goals and objectives. The one aspect common to these IEPs was their compatibility with the sequential development of each child's visual images. Children develop a visual vocabulary of symbols much like that of a verbal vocabulary of words. In these cases, whether the students were delayed or not, their visual symbols reflected the children's perception of people, objects, and events in their environment or from their own imagination.

As the child gains awareness of meaning in his imagery, communication skills evolve that associate visual images with the spoken or written word. A child's ideas begin to form sequences of thoughts, and he can participate in art learning activities that develop a sense of time, space, and the use of the basic art elements and principles in creative expression.

As demonstrated in these three cases, the five-point model of *identifying, predicting, deciding, implementing,* and *evaluating* learning for special students can be used in developing individualized (art) programs for them. *Identifying the learner* as the initial phase in planning experiences, as well as *implementing goals and objectives* and *evaluating the outcomes,* are essential components in working with any person who has unique needs.

AN ILLUSTRATION OF HOW ART CAN BE WRITTEN INTO EVERY COMPONENT OF AN IEP

As noted earlier, there are three ways in which art can be a part of the Individualized Education Program (IEP) of a special learner. First, art can be requested as a related service; second, it can be recommended that the child be placed in special adaptive art classes or mainstreamed into regular art classes; and third, art can be used to remediate other problem areas. The segment in this chapter by Di Maria (1982) presents the hypothetical case of a child who had problems in each of the six major areas for which IEP goals are typically written. Di Maria demonstrates ways in which art can be utilized in all six areas of an IEP to remediate this child's "problems." No child would really have as many problems or deficits as the child presented in the case that follows.

The Di Maria example is included in hopes that readers will become more aware of the capacity that the visual arts have to modify inappropriate behaviors, to facilitate academic learning, and to remediate specific learning problems. This information has been included to illustrate the many ways that art can be central to the development and education of special needs children (Anderson, Ash & Gambach, 1982; Anderson, 1983; Anderson, 1988; Anderson, 1991).

ART AND THE IEP
(INDIVIDUALIZED EDUCATION PROGRAM)

Audrey Di Maria

Art therapy may qualify, under PL 92-142 (now IDEA), as a related service in the education of handicapped children and thus be mandated by law. The vehicle for this, the Individualized Education Program, has been underutilized by art therapists. Art therapy may be beneficial in addressing children's needs in all six areas of performance enumerated on the IEP:

- Academic/Cognitive
- Communicative Status
- Motor and Perceptual Skills
- Prevocational/Vocational Skills
- Self-Help Skills, as well as the area most familiar to art therapists
- Social/Emotional Status

Although procedures for completing IEP forms—and even the forms themselves—vary from school district to school district, common to all is the need to formulate prioritized annual goals and to design short-term objectives that include the following five components:

A. Audience
B. Behavior
C. Condition
D. Degree
E. Evaluation

The sample IEP form that follows uses a hypothetical case (concerning a child named Mark) to illustrate not only the kind of needs a child may present but also the variety of ways in which those needs may be addressed through art therapy.

Note: A modified version of this article was first published in A.E. Di Maria, E. Kramer, and I. Rosner (Eds.) (1982). *Proceedings of the Twelfth Annual Conference of the American Art Therapy Association* (Falls Church, VA: American Art Therapy Association). Reprinted by permission. This article was written by Audrey Di Maria in her private capacity. No official support or endorsement by the District of Columbia government or the District of Columbia Public School System is intended or should be inferred.

INDIVIDUALIZED EDUCATION PROGRAM (IEP)

Agency: _____ Date of Report: _____

1. Identifying Information

Name of Student: _____ Birth Date: _____ Age: _____

School: _____ Teacher: _____

Name of Parent/Guardian: _____ Phone Number: _____

Address: _____

2. Special Notations

a. **Health Status, Visual and Hearing Acuity:** _____

_____

_____

_____

b. **Observed Learning Style:** _Mark learns most effectively through a combination of visual_
   and kinesthetic methods (e.g., a multisensory approach). _____

c. **Other** _____

_____

_____

3. Period, Plan

From June, 1991 To June, 1992

Interim/Annual Review and Recommendations and Revisions	**Dates**
Interim Review:	December, 1991
Annual Review:	June, 1992

4. Present Level(s) of Educational Performance

Academic/Cognitive Levels: (include reading, math, and general abilities)

Reading/reading readiness skills: Mark has difficulty in identifying and naming colors, shapes, and objects. (Counteract environmental deprivation by providing sensory stimulation and opportunities to explore wide variety of media.)

Math skills: Mark has trouble in sorting, classifying, categorizing, selecting, combining, matching, and sequencing. (Encourage selecting, grouping, and using art materials).

General skills: Mark has difficulty in deriving relationships of time, space, and number, and in determining cause-and-effect relationships. (Promote abstract reasoning and ability to conceptualize through use of picture/storytelling, cartoon strips, TV story pads, and paper collages. Demonstrate cause and effect in social relationships through discussing what makes children angry, happy, or frightened and what responses these situations arouse.)

Communicative Status: (include speech, language and writing skills)

Expressive language: Mark is almost nonverbal (or he is excessively verbal or overly intellectual). (Encourage observation, exploration, and inventive behavior; stimulate imagination and foster school communication skills through storytelling about pictures while respecting the displacement they afford.)

Receptive language: Mark appears to be inattentive, with a short attention span. He needs help in following directions. His receptive language is extremely limited by his underdeveloped vocabulary (or by a foreign language barrier). (Encourage dialogues.)

Written language: Mark enjoys writing, but his work is not always legible. (Create an illustrated autobiography.)

Motor and Perceptual Skills: (include fine and gross motor, visual and auditory perception)

Fine motor skills: Mark has difficulty in grasping and in manipulating objects. (Offer opportunities for modeling clay, cutting and pasting, coloring, sorting and stringing beads, stenciling, using tools.)

Gross motor skills: Mark stumbles a lot and shows a lack of coordination; he may be accident prone. (Employ movement exercises as warm-up to drawing; use of mural paper, large brushes, introduce body image work.)

Auditory perception: Mark is easily distracted by extraneous classroom noises. He has difficulty in discriminating among auditory stimuli. (Provide individual work within nonstimulating environment; use simple, concrete language; make expectations clear.)

Sensory motor integration: Mark has trouble with hand/eye coordination, directionality, laterality. (Provide opportunities for handling manipulative objects, and engaging in drawing exercises.)

Visual perception: Mark has trouble with sequencing, closure, discriminating differences, distinguishing figure/ground relationships, spatial relationships. (Utilize cut paper collages, modeling clay, printing materials.)

Social/Emotional Status: (include interaction in school, home and neighborhood with adults and peers)

Mark has a short attention span and is easily distracted from a task. (Provide art activities of short duration, structured tasks, opportunity for immediate feedback.)

Mark exhibits a low level of frustration tolerance. He is often unable to control his impulses and is frequently aggressive toward peers and adults. (Afford opportunities for sublimation of aggressive impulses and for verbalization of feelings through artwork, puppetry, role play, dramatic play, and direct discussion.)

Mark portrays himself as having a poor self-concept. (Arrange opportunities to experience success and develop confidence through pride in personal achievement. Affirm ego through emphasis on individuality and uniqueness, e.g., making self-portraits.)

Mark seems to have a poor body image. (Body tracing to address this concern, or to address need for integration of body parts and boundaries.)

Mark seems to be extremely fearful. (Furnish nonthreatening environment and safe avenues for self-expression and the elaboration of concerns.)

Mark makes excessive use of fantasy. (Engage in reality testing exercises and still-life drawings. Provide clear, dependable structure.)

Mark is withdrawn and isolates himself from others. (Supply indirect form of communication with environment, providing for both involvement and detachment.)

Attach additional sheets as needed

_____

_____

_____

_____

Prevocational/Vocational Skills: (include in the relevant area abilities in that area)
Mark has trouble in following directions, in adjusting to a work situation, and in completing tasks. He has an awareness of time, but he does not seem to be able to budget time or material effectively. He demonstrates an ability to invest himself in his task, but has difficulty in leaving his project when his time is finished and in returning to it to reinvest himself in the task. (Provide oportunities to test concepts, strengths, and skills. Document development with regard to behavior, activities, completed works. Foster independent function through opportunities to set one's own goals, to challenge oneself, and to master tools, processes. Promote problem-solving ability through the discovery and discussion of alternatives.)

Self-Help Skills: (include the degree of independence in daily living skills, study habits, etc.)
Mark has trouble in sustaining himself at work without a great deal of verbal reinforcement. In the classroom, he seems to feel that he can learn only through imitation, although he demonstrates leadership skills with peers in the neighborhood. (Fosters ability to originate, communicate, and appreciate ideas.)

Other: (include any pertinent information not stated above)

5. **Prioritized Annual Goals:**

Area		Goal
Social/	1.	Mark will be able to structure himself and to make responsible choices.
Emotional	2.	Mark will exhibit decreased destructive behavior and increased productive behavior.
Status	3.	Mark will respect the property of others and will demonstrate an
Motor and		improved ability to interact with peers, adults, and family members.
Perceptual	4.	Mark will exhibit significant growth in the areas of visual discrimination
Skills		and visual memory.

6. **Short-Term Objectives (include evaluative procedures and criteria)**	7. **Special Education Services and Resources**	8. **Projected Dates for Initiation of Services and Anticipated Duration of Services**

(Letters A, B, C, D, and E below refer to the five components of short-term objectives described earlier.)

1.1 Given art therapy (C), Mark (A) will develop an ability to make appropriate decisions in choosing and in using art materials (e.g., through learning painting skills and clay-modeling techniques) (B) 80% of the time (D), as measured by art therapist's observations (E).	Art therapy (individual sessions 2x week)	June, 1991–June, 1992
1.2 Given responsibility for choosing an activity, Mark	Art therapy (individual sessions, 2x week)	June, 1991–June, 1992

will focus his attention on the activity and will carry it through to completion 75% of the time, as measured by art therapist's observations.

2.1 Given task orientation and increased ability to focus, Mark will make wise use of materials, will improve his level of performance, and will exhibit increased pride in his art products 80% of the time, as measured by art therapist's observations.

Art therapy (individual sessions, 2x week)

June, 1991–June, 1992

3.1 Given the opportunity to see artwork made by other children, Mark will be able to look at it and talk about it, without touching it, 90% of the time, as measured by art therapist's observations.

Art therapy (group sessions, 1x week)

June, 1991–June, 1992e

3.2 Through use of art materials, puppet play, and role play, Mark will learn to verbally identify facial expressions, recognize and identify his feelings as they occur, and use more appropriate behavior in relating to his peers and to adults (e.g., discussing angry feelings with the person involved as soon as possible using nonaggressive words rather than physical action or aggressive words) 80% of the time, as measured by art therapist's observations.

Art therapy (group sessions, 1x week)

June, 1991–June, 1992

4. Given art therapy, Mark will be able to do the following with mastery:
   (a) group objects according to size, shape, and color
   (b) focus upon a given object or task for an increased period of time
   (c) describe previous visual experiences within the environment to give evidence of delayed

Art therapy (individual sessions, 2x week)

June, 1991–June, 1992

recall 85% of the time,
as measured by art
therapist's observations.

9. a. **Description of proposed instructional services:**

_____

_____

_____

 b. **Comments and suggestions to facilitate instructional programming:** One-to-one
    relationships facilitate Mark's learning process. Mark participates in group activities
    only with specialized individual assistance. Art Therapy recommended, individual
    and group sessions.

10. **Hours/days per week in regular education** _____

 Hours/days per week in physical education _____

11. **Schedule for determining whether short term objectives are being achieved:**
    a. **Annual Review Date(s)** June, 1992
    b. **Interim Review Date(s)** December, 1991

12. **IEP Meeting(s)**
    Participants:
    Name (print or type)   **Signature**

 _____   _____ **Parent**

 _____   _____ **Special Education**

 Teacher

 _____   _____ **Educational Technician**

 _____   _____ **Art Therapist**

 _____   _____ **Social Worker**

 _____   _____ **Psychologist**

 _____   _____ **Psychiatrist**

REFERENCES

Cohen, E.P. & Gainer, R.S. (1976). *Art another language for learning.* New York:
    Citation Press.
Jones, N.T. (1979). *Art and the handicapped child.* Virginia Department of Education.
Smith, S.L. (1979). *No easy answers.* Teaching the learning disabled child. Cambridge,
    MA: Winthrop Publishers, Inc.

ART THERAPY IN A LARGE URBAN SCHOOL DISTRICT:
THE MIAMI, FLORIDA–DADE COUNTY
PUBLIC SCHOOL EXPERIENCE

As noted earlier, in 1979 Janet Bush initiated a pilot art therapy program in the Dade County Public Schools of Miami, Florida. Her initial task was the challenge offered by Ms. Jackie Hinchey, Art Supervisor, to take one year and set up a program in art therapy. Initially, art therapists also taught art education and helped in schools where there were children with a variety of disabilities. Many of these were children who could not function in a typical mainstreamed situation.

By 1985 there were eight art therapists working in a variety of school settings in the Dade County Public Schools. Funding for the art therapists came from local sources. At this time the art therapy program which had been under the administrative umbrella of the Art Education Division moved to the Division of Exceptional Student Education. This move was made partly because of the increasing number of students diagnosed as severely emotionally disturbed and was made partly because there were enriched funds to serve this population. From that time on, art therapy services have been provided primarily to students with severe emotional disturbances or to students who were dually diagnosed (with severe emotional disturbance being one of the disabling conditions).

Shortly after the move of the art therapy program to the Division of Exceptional Student Education, the Dade County Public Schools began contracting with outside agencies to serve its ever-growing number of students with severe emotional disturbance. (In 1990, approximately 600 students had been identified as having severe emotional disturbance.) Several outside agencies provide these services including a private foundation, the Bertha Abess Children's Center, and the Metro-Dade County Department of Youth and Family Development. Services include specially trained teachers, school psychologists and support staff. The art therapists are not part of the outside contracts for services but continue to be funded by local monies through the Division of Exceptional Student Education. According to Bush,

> In the Dade County Public Schools, Art Therapy is both diagnostic and therapeutic. It creates a conduit through which trained art therapists help individuals talk about their private demons. Students with special needs are provided opportunities to work through obstacles that may be impeding their

---

In 1990, Penny Dachinger, one of the art therapists working in the Miami, Florida Dade County School Art Therapy Program, died unexpectedly. This segment of the book is dedicated to her memory.

educational success. They are helped to expand their understanding, to grow, and to improve their lives. (Bush, 1990)

In 1991 there were 15 art therapists working with learners with severe emotional disturbance (J. Bush, personal communication, June 17, 1991). Each art therapist served two schools or placements and split her time between these two facilities on a half-weekly basis. For example, at Palmetto Elementary School there is a special unit for children with severe emotional disturbance. One art therapist spends two-and-one-half days at this facility. She works individually or in small groups with elementary aged severely emotionally disturbed children. Her case load is about 15 students. The sessions last about 30 minutes, and students are seen on a weekly basis. At the beginning of the school year or when a child is placed in this unit, an assessment is done. The assessment is a series of measures to determine the child's emotional and academic level of functioning.

The art therapists in the Dade County Public Schools use a special assessment tool, the Levick Emotional and Cognitive Art Therapy Assessment (LECATA) (Levick, 1989). The LECATA takes about one hour to complete. The student is asked to complete six drawings, including:

1. a free art task and story about the completed image
2. a drawing of self
3. a scribble with one color
4. a picture created from the scribble
5. a place you would like to be (3–5 years)
   a place that is important to you (5–13 years)
6. a family (Levick, 1989)

The LECATA was developed to "measure normal emotional and cognitive development of children between the ages of three and thirteen years. Emotional indicators are identified by defense mechanisms of the ego" (Levick, 1989, p. 3). The assessment through scoring will indicate the extent to which a learner deviates (either above or below) from the normal range.

Once an art therapy assessment is complete a recommendation is made as to the appropriateness of art therapy for the learner. Before the learner is placed in a program, a staffing is held and an Individualized Emotional and Educational Program is developed for that student. At the Palmetto Elementary School if the learner is assigned to art therapy, then she most likely does not receive the individual services of a psychologist. If the learner is not to receive art therapy, then she probably does receive the individual services of the psychologist. The art therapist works very closely with the psychologist and other staff so all are kept informed as to a particular learner's progress. Often, there are weekly case reviews with the staff and there are always monthly reviews. All students with severe emotional disturbance also receive regular art and music instruction in self-contained classes. In fact, *all* students with or without disabilities in the Dade County Public Schools receive regular art and music instruction from an arts education specialist.

The Specialized Development Center is another site at which art therapy is being utilized as a primary treatment for learners with severe emotional disturbance. This setting is a day treatment program and serves elementary and secondary students. (The Dade County Public Schools must serve all students from 3 to 21 years of age.) At the Specialized Development Center the learners have severe emotional disturbance and some other disability (are dually diagnosed). As at the other sites, all students are seen once by the art therapist for an assessment utilizing the LECATA. An Individualized Education Program (IEP) is developed for the student prior to being placed in a setting that serves students with severe emotional disturbance. At these staffings, based on the recommendation of the art therapist, those students who can best benefit from art therapy are identified. After students are placed, another staffing occurs at which an Individualized Emotional and Educational Program is developed.

At the Specialized Development Center the art therapy program serves about 17 students on an individual basis and in groups of two. This center generally has learners who are functioning at a level typical of students with some mental retardation. The art therapy program is a functional one. Sessions last about one-half hour and students are seen weekly. The art therapist works closely with other staff and with the regular art teacher. Each session is documented by the art therapist and case records are updated on a monthly basis. All students are on a behavior modification system and earn points for appropriate behaviors.

The art therapist spends two-and-one-half days at the Specialized Development Center, and the rest of her week she works in a hospital setting assisting with the diagnosis of children whose severe emotional disturbance has caused them to be hospitalized. Generally, the children spend about two months in the hospital. Once these children are diagnosed, then the staff work to find an appropriate school placement somewhere in the school district.

It is a tribute to the pioneering efforts of Janet Bush that art therapy is firmly established in the Miami's Dade County Public Schools. From a modest beginning in 1979, the program has grown to include (in 1991) a staff of 15 art therapists who serve over 26 schools and agencies. Thus, at the time of this report the Dade County Public Schools Division of Exceptional Student Education was the largest employer of art therapists in the country. The success of this program is due in large part to the ongoing efforts of its founder, Janet Bush. Another aspect of the success of the program is its commitment to ongoing education. Since 1979 there has been an average of 10 in-service workshops for both art therapists, other teachers, and administrators. This large educational effort has been a key element in the acceptance of art therapy as a viable treatment modality in the Dade County Public Schools. Additionally, there has been a monthly article on some aspect of art therapy included in the newsletter of the local office of the Florida Diagnostic and Learning Resources System which covers a three-county area.

Another key ingredient in the establishment and ongoing support of the art therapy program is the commitment of administrative staff. It is the strong support of school principals (who often have the final say as to whether an art therapist works in a school) and key administrators in the Division of Exceptional Student Education that have made the art therapy program a strong and viable one. Credit must go to many—but most importantly to Ms. Jackie Hinchey who had the vision to start an art therapy program and to Ms. Terri Kanov, Executive Director of the Division of Exceptional Student Education, who continues to strongly support the art therapy program.

The future of this unique art therapy program looks very bright. There are still many children with severe emotional disturbance who are waiting to be served in the Miami Florida-Dade County School District. As funding becomes available, more art therapists will most likely be hired. Most importantly, the Miami, Florida-Dade County School District Art Therapy Program is a model that can be replicated in many places around Florida and across the country. One key ingredient is a strong network of broad-based support for an art therapy program that includes support from local school boards, principals and school district special education administrators (J. Bush, personal interview, May 23, 1991).

Excerpts from the Florida Diagnostic and Learning Resource System/South Newsletter

The following articles were written by art therapists from the Miami, Florida-Dade County School District Art Therapy Program. They have been included to provide a better understanding of how art therapists work in this public school setting. The Florida Diagnostic and Learning Resource System (FDLRS) is a statewide resource network of special education professionals that provide a variety of services to special needs students and their teachers. The *FDLRS/South Newsletter* is published on a monthly or bimonthly basis and has a circulation of about four thousand. It serves a tri-county region. There is a regular column in this newsletter that is written by art therapists from the Miami, Florida-Dade County School District Art Therapy Program.

Art and Therapy—A Successful Partnership
Penny Dachinger

Art and therapy are a successful partnership in working with children in emotional distress in our schools. The art therapist is able to use painting, drawing, and sculpture as tools with which to engage the student in self-expression and personal and cognitive growth. Making art gives children the opportunity to portray their feelings, conflicts and wishes in concrete form.

Often the children with whom we work are guarded about sharing their lives with adults, since adults have often been the source of most of the pain in their lives. Problems started for most of these children very early, perhaps even before they had language with which to express their rage, fear, or pain.

Instead, they found a way to protect themselves. While this may have been adaptive at first, the behavior is repeated for its safety and comfort and later becomes restrictive, or maladaptive, and the child ceases to grow. It may be only through the use of art materials and the opportunity for symbolic speech that the child is able to describe the problem and the feelings. Instead of being locked in behaviors inappropriate for the age, the child may learn to express feelings in ways that will free him from the maladaptive behaviors, giving the opportunity to learn new, more appropriate and adaptive ways of functioning in the world.

Art and art materials are very seductive in the best sense of the word. They give the child a way to express himself to himself—and to others—when he cannot find the words to release frustration, aggression, fear, or confusions. Once expressed, the feelings can be explored and the child can learn to gain control over them. The child can get involved with materials and with himself in art therapy in ways that are not possible in verbal therapies. And in addition to learning by himself, there is a relationship with the therapist who has provided this millieu for self-expression and personal growth.

Art therapists have an advantage over those using traditional verbal therapies: children are generally *eager* to use art materials. The younger children have not yet learned to be expressive verbally about a range of feelings and so can use the art that they make to deal with problems in symbolic ways. They can therefore reveal and resolve conflicts through their art, even before they have developed the verbal skills to express them.

As the children grow, some of them develop verbal fencing skills which

From Penny Dachinger, "Art and Therapy—A Successful Partnership." Reprinted by permission from the *Florida Diagnostic and Learning Resources System-South Newsletter*, December 1988–January 1989.

have enabled them to avoid facing their real problems. Using art materials forces them to lower the walls which have prevented them from expressing their needs to others.

They can drop their defensive postures—those menacing physical poses—which keep them safe from relating to others on a personal level, begin to develop relationships and, even later on, some sense of intimacy with others.

It is true that the development of intimacy is a far-reaching goal, but it is the loss of intimacy and the inability to achieve it after damaging early experiences which has sent these children into the kinds of problems for which they have been referred for treatment.

If the first intimacy that they can achieve is with themselves through the art that they make, then we have started them on the path to other achievements in their lives.

We do not cure these children, we treat their problems. Even better, we help them to help themselves. The task is great; the achievement even greater.

The Art Therapist as Part of a Clinical Team
Enid Shayna Garber

Art therapy doesn't stop at the art therapist's door. In programs for severely emotionally disturbed students, art therapists work as part of clinical teams. The teams can include classroom teachers, a psychologist, diagnostician, counselor, and visiting psychiatrist.

Art therapy assessments completed on each student at the onset of the school year begin to open many doors for communication between the art therapist and the clinical team. The diagnostic information gleaned from each assessment is presented at weekly case conferences, where different students are reviewed. Many times the art therapy assessment reveals underlying issues and conflicts that are not always manifested in observable behaviors and psychological tests. Information gathered early in the school year assists the team in developing individualized therapeutic goals and objectives that best meet the unique needs of each child.

The art therapist assists the team when a child is in a crisis and is unable to communicate and ventilate verbally about the provoking situation. In this case, art therapy can be an immediate outlet for overwhelming feelings and concerns. Through a sometimes nonverbal means of communication, the student is able to have his needs for support and nurturance met. This information helps provide the team with insight on how to best approach the child and be of support through the remainder of the school day.

A post art therapy assessment completed at the close of the school year provides feedback regarding a student's growth and areas of continued vulnerability. This assists the team in placement decisions.

From Enid Shayna Garber, "The Art Therapist as Part of a Clinical Team." Reprinted by permission from the *Florida Diagnostic and Learning Resources System-South Newsletter,* September 1988.

The art therapist as part of the clinical team can make dramatic differences in a child's life by communicating vital information which fosters the understanding of student needs and support, thereby facilitating educational and personal growth for students.

Puppets Have Feelings, Too!
Enid Shayna Garber

Puppetry, like many media, transmits information. What makes puppetry special is the way in which it transmits information. Unlike print, it does not necessitate sophisticated understanding of symbols. Instead, most puppetry has a direct biological analogy, in that it represents familiar life forms. It also lends itself to theatrics, and thus to metaphor. But it lends itself to a *special* kind of theater—the theater of fantasy.

Simply put, puppetry is a special medium which is uniquely adapted to communicate illusion. In art therapy, this provides another language in which to work with severely emotionally disturbed students.

Clinical art therapists utilize puppets to provide a safe distance for thoughts and feelings the severely emotionally disturbed child may find too difficult and frightening. Puppets often provide the resistant, overly guarded, insecure, and nonverbal child with permission to speak. This permission comes from the child's projection of thoughts, feelings, and behaviors onto the puppet—those that are often too threatening for the child to accept about himself or herself. Puppetry lends itself to the imaginative play which young children are drawn to and are able to control and feel confident with. A child can, therefore, pretend that the puppet is experiencing what the child knows is true but is not ready to accept.

When a child uses puppets to create a spontaneous, individual production, a constructive emotional outlet is provided. The child can express inner conflicts, problems, desires and fantasies without having to immediately take direct responsibility for them and without being physically exposed. Puppetry provides a socially acceptable way to release pent-up frustrations and anxieties.

Many art therapists have found puppets useful because of their adaptability to role playing and the way in which a child can freely disappear behind the personality of the puppet. When the child uses puppets in role playing, the child's problems can be acted out and possible solutions can be tried.

There is also therapeutic value in having a child see a puppet show performed by others in which a puppet works through a problem. In this approach, the puppets themselves present a problem and then ask the children to work out a solution. The show can be stopped and group discussions held.

From Enid Shayna Garber, "Puppets Have Feelings Too!". Reprinted by permission from the *Florida Diagnostic and Learning Resources System-South Newsletter*, May–June 1989.

A positive group experience can be created by having children produce a puppet show together. In order for the children to make a good show, they have to cooperate with each other. An excellent opportunity is provided to discuss and stress constructive criticism. The actual performance of the show provides a special kind of group experience for all children.

Additionally, a therapeutic aspect of puppetry occurs before using the puppet. The manipulation of the puppet is made directly by the child's hands when s/he designs and forms the puppet. Children are vulnerable and view themselves as being manipulated by the adults in their lives who have often not been a source of protection. A puppet can be a symbolic version of a child—it provides an opportunity for the child to be the manipulator. This can be a time for the powerless child to experience control and power.

Speaking directly through a puppet character provides an opportunity to tell a personal story. The severely emotionally disturbed students I work with experience many conflicting situations and emotions. Puppet play allows these students to play out their inner feelings which they perceive as unacceptable. With puppets, children can reveal and work on identifying parts of themselves, such as the good, the bad, the slow learner, the angry, the victim, and the baby.

Children often project roles as well as feelings onto puppets. The puppet can become mother, father, sibling, stepparent, teacher, and friends with whom the child is trying to develop understanding and form trusting relationships. A puppet can also take on roles the child sees him or herself as performing or wishes s/he could perform.

What do puppets offer that justifies wide application and appeal? Basically, it is their unique ability to stimulate and enhance imagination. Everyday life situations can be transformed into new and exciting areas to explore, for both performers and viewers alike.

Art Therapy—A Vehicle Towards Communication
Linda Jo Stellato-Pfeiffer

One of the most common art therapy referrals are children whose communication deficits render them unable to verbally communicate their thoughts, feelings and ideas. Whether the dysfunction originates from a neurological disorder or an emotional dysfunction, their handicapping condition makes them isolated from a world that they neither participate in nor comprehend. Art therapy affords these children an alternative means of communication through the symbolic language of visual imagery. It offers them the possibility of translating their ideas and feelings into readable imagery and receiving immediate feedback from the art therapist. Once trust is established and

From Linda Jo Stellato-Pfeiffer, "Art Therapy—A Vehicle Towards Communication. Reprinted by permission from the *Florida Diagnostic and Learning Resources System-South Newsletter,* February 1988.

a working relationship is developed, the art therapist and child begin a dialogue which provides an avenue for increased communication and the acquisition of concepts which have eluded the child thus far. An example wherein art therapy is used as a facilitator for communication is illustrated in the following case.

Tim, a depressed nine-year-old Hispanic youth, was referred to art therapy due to severe withdrawal and a reluctance to interact verbally with both adults and children. Initially, Tim came to the art therapy sessions unable to make eye contact or participate in conversation. To posed questions, Tim would either shrug his shoulders and look away or mumble "I don't know." Tim was a nonverbal child in need of finding a means to relate to others in a meaningful manner. He had experienced a great deal of failure in the academic realm of school activities and in the physical arena of sports. Tim was in need of finding an area of success—not only to raise his self-esteem but to reintroduce him to his environment.

As is natural with most children, Tim enjoyed drawing and painting. He felt successful in art and became more and more willing to invest his energies in producing "visual stories." Tim was encouraged to talk about what he had made after each art therapy experience. Questions such as "What is this person doing?" prompted Tim to converse verbally. By directing the focal point of each session away from him and onto what he had created, Tim began to relax and feel less threatened. It allowed him to suspend his well-established defenses for a time, and converse about his artwork in relationship to himself and his own personal history.

After three months in art therapy, Tim readily adds a verbal description to his completed artwork. His story telling in pictures is slowly progressing towards verbalizing his thoughts and feelings. His eye contact has improved. His shuffling gait and dropped head stance are no longer as pronounced as they had been. Most encouraging of all, Tim came to his last session before Christmas break with something to share. For the first time, Tim initiated a conversation. He smiled as he told all about his latest possessions and shared the intimacy of having a "friend." It was the first spontaneous smile seen from Tim. Although he has a long way to go, Tim has begun to reach out to others and become a participant in the world around him.

A Student's Point of View
Linda Jo Stellato-Pfeiffer

Getting a student's perspective of the art therapy experience is oftentimes both insightful and rewarding. Students who are familiar with art therapy will give varied responses to the question, "What is art therapy?" It is

From Linda Jo Stellato-Pfeiffer, "A Student's Point of View." Reprinted by permission from the *Florida Diagnostic and Learning Resources System-South Newsletter,* February 1990.

surprising to find that even elementary-aged students have a fairly good grasp of the therapeutic benefit inherent in a directed art therapy experience. The following paragraph was submitted in response to a free-writing assignment given by the teacher of an elementary-aged student in a program for the severely emotionally disturbed.

> Art therapy is great and art therapy is fun. I like art therapy the best because we talk about our feelings. (The art therapist) makes me feel good about myself and she is nice. I go with (another student) and he shares his feelings. He makes me feel like sharing my feelings too. I am getting better at sharing my feelings and I am getting better.

There are many benefits derived from art therapy. Happily, this student was able to pinpoint that aspect of the experience which was most important to him. In a dyad format, he felt support from both the other student and the therapist. The student who wrote this paragraph initially presented himself as a depressed, withdrawn, fairly nonverbal child. He exhibited poor eye contact, low motivation and poor self-esteem.

As seen through this spontaneous paragraph about art therapy, he no longer resembles that earlier student. He is now more confident and more sure of himself. He is able to express his feelings and derive pleasure from this newfound ability. Both his affect and attitude have changed.

Art therapy has made a difference. It has helped him gain some of the personal strengths needed to venture from childhood to adolescence. This student's perspective of how art therapy has helped him reveals an optimism always sought after, and in his case achieved.

Coming to Terms Through Art Therapy
Penny Dachinger

Daniel came to art therapy suspicious of how making art could be valuable to him even though he liked to draw. He was an unusual child among his peers. He was of mixed black/white heritage, light skinned, red haired and obese. He had slightly above average intelligence and an appreciation of classical music (especially that of Mozart). He had an aggressive self-defensive stance in the world, a reading level five years below his chronological age of 14, and a long history of referrals to principals and legal authorities for his aggressive and antisocial behaviors. In some ways he seemed to fit in with his peer group, where many of the youngsters came from a chaotic home life.

We were able to form a rapport almost immediately when he chose to listen to the classical music station while he worked and we talked about our mutual love for *Amadeus,* the movie (him) and the show (me). He had some

From Penny Dachinger, "Coming to Terms Through Art Therapy." Reprinted by permission from the *Florida Diagnostic and Learning Resources System—South Newsletter,* November 1989.

difficulty sharing his feelings, because it was difficult for him to trust anyone new. When I brought him photographs of his sixth grade prom, given to me by the teacher's aide from his former school, he began to open up about his feelings of neglect and lack of caring by his mother who had left him in the care of her aunt who was his champion in the world. The sudden death of this woman provoked a severe depression in this already depressed child. He returned to his mother's home where he slept on a couch in the living room. He began to be plagued by even more doubts about his worth, as his mother continued to neglect him while spoiling his younger twin brothers. He reported that his mother told him that he was a total loss and that she was not going to "mess up" with the twins the way she had with him.

At this time his physical appearance deteriorated: he often dressed in the same clothing for days on end, or wore clothing that had become threadbare or no longer fitted him. At this point, he drew dark, foreboding pictures of stormy weather and precarious situations which continued almost unabated for nearly a year. Intermittently, he would draw bright cheery landscapes with children flying kites, the sun shining with a smile on its face—the drawings of a child developmentally younger than those of his depressive side. Sometimes these drawings were in reaction to some good interactions with his mother, but they would be short-lived as she reverted to her usual behavior with him. The developmental difference may also be seen as his attempt to undo his feeling of worthlessness and an attempt to present a pleasant view of his life. His lack of experience in feeling this way may have provoked a desire to show his pleasure and to hide his pain, but his ability to do so lay underdeveloped. The fictional competition between Mozart and Salleri served as an underlying topic, possibly paralleling his sense of real competition with the twins for recognition and (in his case) caring and affection.

His mother had many schemes for making money and would talk to him at length about them. He would come to art therapy to try to reality test her ideas, often deciding that she was a dreamer and really could not be trusted. This trust was even further diminished when she promised him a room of his own when they moved into a new apartment. This promise never came to fruition because an aunt and uncle moved into this space "temporarily" and he found himself once again on the couch. He started staying out late at night, spending his time with people seriously involved with drugs and petty crimes. A deeply religious boy, he found his actions contrary to his beliefs and described his life as being "on the edge." He drew pictures of himself straddling an abyss with drugs, money, and guns on one side, and home, church, and family on the other. For the topic of giving someone a second chance, he drew a picture of Lazarus rising from the grave. He said that he hoped his faith would give him strength in the war he was waging internally. His drawings got darker and darker, stormier, and more dangerous.

He continued to talk about the "narrow edge" he was living on, as his poverty (both fiscal and emotional) took its toll on his body and social life. Selling drugs started to seem to be a viable option. Fast, easy money seemed attractive to him when no other alternatives seemed to be open to him.

He had a major fight with his uncle over a minor issue, some months after the "temporary" housing situation seemed to become permanent. A dispute about a television show escalated to the point that his uncle insisted that his mother take Daniel to Jackson Memorial Hospital, or the uncle would call the police and press assault charges. She agreed to take Daniel to the clinic at Jackson Memorial Hospital, where she herself was in psychiatric treatment. This turned out to be a fortunate move. Daniel was assigned to a counselor with whom he was able to develop rapport almost immediately. He began to see her twice weekly, as well as in therapy with his mother. It was decided that he would change schools so that he could have a fresh start as he continued therapy with his counselor who had her office close to his new school. He was to be seen twice a week with her in addition to seeing a counselor at the school.

Daniel was able to use art therapy to explore the duality of his feelings and choices, to talk about his conflicts and to face them in a very concrete manner. He was able to learn to trust adults to a greater degree, and he learned to ask for help when the situation he was in became unbearable. His depression pervaded all areas in his life, making it difficult for him to develop any self-esteem. His ability to draw and to express himself seems to have been a motivator for change in the face of dire consequences, and his work in art therapy important in helping him to grow.

REFERENCES

Anderson, F. E. (1980). *The effects of mainstreaming on secondary art education in Illinois.* Unpublished paper, Illinois State University, Normal, IL.

Anderson, F. E. (1983). A critical analysis of *A Review of the Published Research Literature on Arts with the Handicapped, 1971-1981,* with special attention to the visual arts. *Art Therapy, 1*(1), 26–35.

Anderson, F. E. (1991). *A review of the published research literature on arts with children with disabilities.* Unpublished manuscript, Illinois State University, Normal, IL.

Anderson, F. E. (1988). *A review of the published research literature on arts with children with disabilities.* Unpublished manuscript, Illinois State University, Normal, IL.

Anderson, F. E., Ash, L., and Gambach, J. (1982). *A review of the published research literature on arts with the handicapped, 1971-1981.* Washington, DC: National Committee, Arts with the Handicapped.

Anderson, F. E., Colchado, J., and McAnally, P. (1991). *Art for the handicapped.* Normal, IL: Illinois State University.

Brigance, A. (1978). *Brigance diagnostic inventory of early development.* Woburn, MA: Curriculum Associates Incorporated.

Bush, J. (1990). *Art therapy has healing power.* (Publicity packet.) (Available from

Dade County Public Schools Art Therapy Program, Division of Exceptional Student Education, Miami, FL.)

Chapman, L. (1978). *Approaches to art in education.* Englewood Cliffs, NJ: Prentice-Hall.

Chapman, L. (1985). *Discover art, 1–6.* Worcester, MA: Davis.

Di Maria, A. E., Kramer, E., and Rosner, I. (Eds.). (1982). *Proceedings of the Twelfth Annual Conference of the American Art Therapy Association.* Falls Church, VA: American Art Therapy Association.

Duke, L. L. (1983). The Getty Center for Education in the Arts. *Art Education, 36*(5), 4–13.

Eisner, E. (1976). *The arts, human development and education.* Berkely, CA: McCutchan.

Individual Education Program/IEP. (1989). Tallahassee, FL: State of Florida, Department of Education, Division of Public Schools, Bureau of Education for Exceptional Students.

Levick, M. (1989). *The Levick Emotional and Cognitive Art Therapy Assessment.* (Available from Myra Levick, 21710 Palm Circle, Boca Raton, FL 33433.)

Maier, (1969). *Three theories of child development.* New York: Harper and Row.

McFee, J. (1964). *Preparation for art.* Belmont, CA: Wadsworth.

Morreau, L., & Anderson, F. E. (1984). Art and the individualized education program: Benefit or burden? *Art Education, 32*(6), 10–14.

NAEA Advisory. (1989). Least restrictive environment. Reston, VA: The National Art Education Association.

Public Law 94-142, 1975.

Public Law 93-112, 1973.

Public Law 101-476, 1990.

Thorne, J. H. (1990). Mainstreaming procedures: Support services and training. *NAEA Advisory.* Reston, VA: National Art Education Association.

Troeger-Clifford, B. (1981). *The development of a model to include art in the individualized education program for physically handicapped and health impaired students.* Unpublished doctoral dissertation, North Texas State University, Denton, TX.

Troeger, B. (1985). Art education includes special populations: An issue and applications. *Viewpoints: Dialogue in Art Education.* Fall, 9–12.

Chapter 5

ART THERAPY WITH A PUBLIC SCHOOL CHILD

Doris Arrington

I n 1917 Margaret Naumburg wrote:

> We have spent much of our time training children to think and act properly
> by themselves. But we have done this without being aware of the funda-
> mental basis of thought and action. The new psychology (analytic) has uncov-
> ered the true nature of primitive thought and has shown that it still lives on
> in the unconscious mental being of the adult as well as of the child. Most of
> our thinking is in this primitive or "fantasy" form; and only a minor part of
> our mental life occurs as directed thought . . . we know that most of such
> behavior, common to all children in and out of school, is significant not so
> much in itself, but rather as a symptom of deeper and more intricate states in
> the unconscious life . . . we are now able to regard such actions as symptomatic
> and to trace them back, step by step, to their source. Up to the present time
> education has missed the real significance of the child's behavior by treating
> surface actions as isolated conditions. Having failed to recognize the true
> sources of behavior, it has been unable effectively to correct and guide the
> impulses of human growth. (Frank, Detre, Kniazzeh, Robinson, Rubin &
> Ulman, 1983, p. 113)

In 1986, almost 70 years after Naumburg wrote these thoughts, the state of
California passed Assembly Bill 3632/882. This law affected all children
with disabilities. Assembly Bill 3632/882 required a number of state and
local public agencies (Departments of Education, Health Services, Social
Services, and Rehabilitation) to not only provide various services necessary
to assist children with exceptional needs so that they could benefit from
their special education program but to coordinate and share resources
(human and fiscal) which are necessary to provide such children with a free,
appropriate public education (FAPE). California labels these services as
Designated Instruction and Services (DIS).

Assembly Bill 3632/882, as a state law, is consistent with the federal law
(PL 94-142 now IDEA) and extends, rather than reduces or narrows, the
current rights for services of children with disabilities or their parents.
These services include physical therapy, occupational therapy, mental health
counseling, residential placement, a home health aide, and rehabilitation.

The comment to PL 94-142 (now IDEA) regulations states:

> The list of related services is not exhaustive and may include other developmental, corrective, or supportive services (such as artistic and cultural programs, and art, music, and dance therapy), if they are required to assist a handicapped child to benefit from special education. (Community Alliance for Special Education, p. 53).

In each state, the Department of Education is responsible for ensuring that programs administered by other public agencies comply with PL 94-142 (now IDEA). In California this responsibility includes administering AB 3632/882. The local education agency is responsible for the actual provision of these services. Assembly Bill 3632/882 does not set out any eligibility requirements, but the emergency regulations do list the criteria when a referral by the local educational agency to county mental health would be appropriate. These criteria include the following:

> (a) the behavioral characteristics of the pupil adversely affect the pupil's educational performance; (b) the behavioral characteristics of the pupil cannot be defined solely as a behavior disorder or a temporary adjustment problem, or cannot be resolved with short-term counseling; (c) the age of onset was from 30 months to 21 years and has been observed for at least six months; (d) the behavioral characteristics of the pupil are present in several settings, including the school, the community, and the home; and (e) the adverse behavioral characteristics of the pupil are severe, as indicated by their rate of occurrence and intensity. (Community Alliance for Special Education, 1988, p. 97)

This chapter will discuss a case treated under AB 3632.

SYSTEMATICALLY-ORIENTED ART THERAPY— A THEORETICAL PERSPECTIVE

As an art psychotherapist, when I work with two or more in a family, I use an integrative systemically oriented art therapy approach from historical, interactional and existential perspectives (Arrington, 1991; Nichols & Everett, 1986). I review historical situations and data that create the emotional milieu that helps "connect the current context of the family with its living history" (Nichols & Everett, 1986, p. 83). I assess the interaction of the art process (Kramer, 1987) as well as the historical material represented in graphically expressed images (Fairbairn, 1954; Freud, 1915; Jung, 1934/1974, 1964; Naumburg, 1966). I observe and monitor the client/family's current emotional state (Bowen, 1976). I assess the family's developmental state (Duval, 1957) (see Appendix A) and each individual's developmental level of graphic expression (Lowenfeld, 1957). In addition, I monitor and adjust my reactions and responses to the client/family and to the treatment process. My approach is both neutral and empathic (Emerson, 1989).

Freud (1915) as reported by Wilcoxen (1987) "emphasized the importance of the gratification of biological needs at crucial stages of personality development" (p. 2); particularly important in determining if these individual needs are satisfactorily met is the mother-child relationship. "This time," quoting Fairbairn, Wilcoxon (1987) continues, "the child internalizes familial interactions, both satisfactory and unsatisfactory, as psychological representations of early life experiences . . . these retained experiences . . . influence the child's cognitive and affective functioning, as well as the child's perception of self and others" (Wilcoxen, 1987, p. 3).

Whereas Freud (1900/1955) emphasized the language of the unconscious in dreams and symbols, and Jung (1934/1974) recognized the importance of visual imagery and universal symbols in human personality development, it was Naumburg (1966) who explored the inner personal meaning of symbols. Wilson (1987), supporting Naumburg (1966) and Beres (1965), says that images (and schematic symbols) develop in a "hierarchy of perceptual experiences" (1987, p. 46) along with personality development and serve both "adaptation and communication" (1987, p. 57).

CASE STUDY

Sandy was a shy five-year-old who had been referred by her psychiatrist of six months. There was a two-year discrepancy between Sandy's age and behavior. Using the DSM–III–R (APA, 1987), Sandy had been identified as an avoidant personality. She clung to her mother, avoided looking at anyone in public, but chattered "like a magpie" when she was with the family or with someone she trusted.

When I first saw Sandy in the playroom she was a slender and attractive child, carefully dressed from her big bow that matched her pink and lavender sweater and slacks to her lace anklets and colored shoelaces. Sandy told me she helped her dad clean house after school and played with her brother. Sometimes she didn't like her Mom, and most of the time she did not like anything at school. Her records indicated that she whined, talked baby talk and had few friends. She had been known to be argumentative and verbally abusive to children at school and in her neighborhood.

Permission was obtained from the family to discuss only their daughter's case and her artwork in this chapter.

Presenting Problem

Sandy and her brother, Ronald, age 6, had originally been referred by the school as children who possibly qualified for AB 3632 because of poor classroom behavior, peer relationships and academic performance. Ronald had begun to see a woman therapist and Sandy a male therapist. Sandy repeatedly asked her therapist why she was being punished and not allowed to see a woman. After a complete assessment, Sandy was identified as meeting AB 3632 guidelines; Ronald was not.

Methodology

I worked with Sandy for two years and seven months. During the first year, I saw her at least once a week; after that I saw her twice a month. When Sandy needed to see me more often she would tell her mother and her mother would call for an appointment. Although Ronald did not qualify for AB 3632, he continued in treatment. His therapist and I worked conjointly with the family at the beginning of treatment. Later, because of a scheduling conflict, his therapist continued with the parents alone until the father refused to continue and then the therapist saw the mother in a women's group. The therapist and I consulted regularly, and I consulted with Mom each week as she picked up Sandy. I consulted with the special educational teacher as needed.

Historical/Interactional Perspectives
(*Information Gathering and Art Assessment*)

Treatment was begun by gathering historical information. Ronald's therapist and I met with the parents to make a genogram which is a three-generational family tree (Guerin and Pendagast, 1976), and with the entire family to gather information in a family art assessment. Consistent with every case, the primary concern at the beginning of treatment was to assess whether crisis intervention was indicated.

Genogram

Mom, 33, and Dad, 44, had been married 11 years. Dad had been married once before.

1. Mom had an older sister and brother. Her father had died when she was very young. Her mother had remarried and had ten more children. Mom was a caretaker who wanted the best for her children and her pets. In addition, she worked as a supervisor in a highly respected local manufacturing firm. She was a hard worker and had a difficult time saying no.

2. Dad, a large, overweight man, was an only child. His father, a rancher, had died when he was a child, leaving a comfortable living for him and his mother. His mother had remarried late in life. She continued to supplement her son's income so that, although he led fishing and hunting trips for money, he had never developed a traditional work ethic; therefore, he had never supported himself or his family. He had married early and had three sons. The marriage had ended bitterly. Dad had been reluctant to have a second family.

Family Art Assessment

Because of the universality of art and its accessibility (Bruscia, 1988), I chose two art tasks from Kwiatkowska's (1978) Family Art Evaluation and one from Rubin's (1984) Family Evaluation to assess the organization of the family. I asked each member of the family to complete each task. The first art task (1978) was a *Free Picture*. Used as an icebreaker, it allowed freedom and flexibility of choice. Kwiatkowska (1978) noted that the first drawing is often an introduction of the self, or may present the family problem. The second art task (1978) was a *Family Portrait*. The Family Portrait illicits reactions and insights not as likely to occur in other therapeutic situations. The third art task (Rubin, 1984) was a *Joint Family Mural* which allowed for direct observation of how the family worked together.

1. FIRST ART TASK: *A Free Picture.* Draw what you would like.

Sandy drew an orange box and filled it in with blue chalk, and orange, green, brown and black markers. Drawing at a three- to early four-year-old level of graphic development, she drew four brown circles for heads and filled in eyes, noses and mouths. Identifying with her mother's picture, she drew three sets of markings that she called birds and then she named her picture "The Rainbow House."

Mom used chalks and primitively drew a rainbow over a blue sky which was over a small black sailboat sailing to the left in blue water. There were brown lines indicating land. On the left bank there was a small green Christmas tree. Above the rainbow, Mom drew seven black birds. She called her picture "Fishing Under the Rainbow."

Dad carefully drew two large mountains with a rough stream running between them. A small wooden fence stretched across the picture. Seven small Christmas trees sat on the left hill in front of the fence. He called his picture "The Hills."

Ronald, using a black marker, drew a box with four sharp triangle mountains and colored three mountains blue and one black. Two blue clouds hovered over the mountains. Single blades of green grass bordered the bottom of the picture like a picket fence. Ronald identified with his dad and called his picture "The Mountein Plase" (Mountain Place).

Figure 5.1. The Rainbow House. A free picture, the first task by a 5-year-old girl in a Family Art-Based Assessment.

2. SECOND ART TASK: *Family Portrait.* Draw the family doing something together.

Sandy's picture contained four purple circle heads with eyes, noses, mouths and whisker-like arms or legs, and a pink flower on a single pink stem. She overlaid the picture with pink and blue chalk. On the top of the page she wrote "JT" in blue, her name in pink, and "ey" over her name. She covered "ey" in black chalk and then wrote her brother's name also in black chalk.

Mom, using a green marker, drew the outline of a two-story house with smoke coming out of the chimney. Upstairs she drew stick figures of Sandy and Ronald in boxes for chairs. Downstairs she drew Dad and herself in chairs watching TV. A fire was in the fireplace. Drawn in black marker on the left side of the house was a smaller house and two dogs, one on each side of a red flower. On the right side of the house, she drew two red flowers on wavy, green lines.

Dad drew four realistic heads in colored markers. They graduated in size from left to right. Mom was drawn first in brown. Next, he drew Sandy (looking older than her five years) with a ponytail in navy blue, followed by Ronald drawn in green with no eyeballs, and then himself in black, with a black beard (which he had) and red ears.

Ronald's picture was drawn with a brown marker. He drew Sandy first.

Figure 5.2. Fishing under the Rainbow. A free picture, the first task by the 33-year-old mom in a Family Art-Based Assessment.

She was large and dressed in slacks and a shirt. She had a smile on her face, striped feet and circle hands with six fingers on each hand. Next, he drew himself as a stick figure, with a face half as large as Sandy's. Ronald's arm overlapped with Dad's arm. Dad was drawn twice as large as Sandy and three times as large as Ronald. He had a big circle in his stomach, no face and a square crotch area colored in solid. Mother was excluded.

3. THIRD ART TASK: *Family mural.* Draw a mural together and name it.

Sandy used a blue marker and drew two concentric circles with large circles inside and a strange-smiling face at the bottom. On the right side she drew an 18-inch, large phallic shape. On the left side she drew a large and overwhelming colored waterfall, falling over the hood of one of Ronald's cars.

Mom, on Sandy's right, drew a woman's face with two eyes, eyebrows, eyelashes, a nose, two cheeks and a mouth. She drew light brown hair and underneath the face she drew three circles inserted by two triangles. On the right she put in blue clouds with a green tornado on the bottom.

Dad drew a box in three-dimensional perspective, a triangle, and two rectangles in purple, blue, orange and green markers. Ronald, on the end, drew two strange-looking cars and an orange boat that he overlapped onto Sandy's picture.

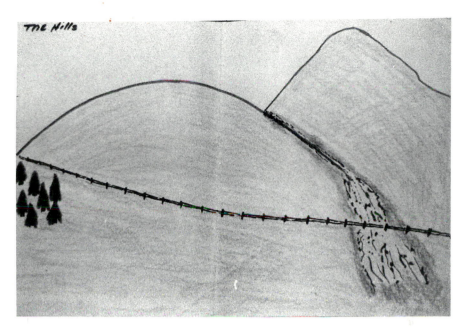

Figure 5.3. The Hills. A free picture, the first task by the 44-year-old dad in a Family Art-Based Assessment.

Integrating the Interactional Perspective

1. FAMILY STRUCTURE. While I directed the art assessment, the cotherapist observed and took notes on the family behavior. Structurally, the family hierarchy was out of balance. The family was divided into two subsystems: the females and the males, with the children competing for attention from their same-sex parent.

2. INTERACTION. The children played out the family dynamics. Ronald was concerned that Sandy was copying him when she drew a frame around her picture. Dad gave directions to Ronald, whereas Mom gave directions to Sandy. Ronald was critical of everyone's artwork, but particularly Dad's work. Mom encouraged everyone, but particularly Dad, saying that he was better in art than she was. When the family was asked to draw a Family Mural, no one said a thing; each member just started drawing in his/her own corner. Mom began with the face and then looked up. She appeared surprised when she observed what other family members were doing and she changed her drawings to shapes that were less personal than the revealing face she had drawn. Dad never said a word while he drew his geometric shapes. The children argued back and forth over their space. When the family had finished the mural, I asked them if they would name it. Mom

Figure 5.4. The "Mountein Plase." A free picture, the first task by the 6-year-old brother in a Family Art-Based Assessment.

picked up a marker and wrote "The (Family's last name) Creations" as she commented to the family, "How is that? That pretty well says it."

Existential Perspective

1. FEELINGS. Both parents were cordial and cooperative. The therapists felt the parents were interested in the children and in maintaining a family. The children, however, were small and the parents were large. Both therapists felt the size of Dad was enough to intimidate both children. If he were threatening, he would overwhelm them. If he physically punished them, he could be abusive. Throughout the session, the two children bickered and tested their parents with minimal correction. The therapists could feel the suffering of each member in the chaotic family, but particularly the children, who were having difficulty making the adjustments between home and school. Both children indicated a protective device from a hostile environment (Ulhin, 1972) in the frames they put around their pictures. In addition, Mom's transparent house in her family portrait was a cause for concern (Drachnik, 1983) as was Ronald's family picture that omitted Mom and colored in Dad's crotch area (Wench, 1980).

2. HYPOTHESIS. The cotherapists hypothesized that because there was a weak spousal subsystem, the children acted as they did in order to get

Figure 5.5. Family Portrait. The second task by a 5-year-old girl in a Family Art-Based Assessment.

the parenting they needed. The therapists also hypothesized that the children had not been prepared for the structured school environment. The family needed education in supporting their children to act age-appropriately.

3. REFRAMING. Reframing is a family therapy term that is used to provide positive feedback to clients. Mom and Dad were reframed as good parents who needed help in assisting their children to meet public school expectations. They were also reframed as parents who had become so involved with the children that they had forgotten how to take care of themselves and each other.

4. NEUTRALITY. The cotherapists maintained a neutral position with all members of the family, trying to help the family see that there was not one bad member or one good member. All members equally contributed to the positive or negative attitude and behavior in the family. Although the actual work of the children was kept confidential, the therapists were able to be open and supportive with the parents.

5. EMPATHETIC RESPONSE. In addition to the neutral position, the therapists were empathetic to the family's psychic suffering. Truax and Carkhuff,

Figure 5.6. Family Portrait. The second task by the 33-year-old mother in a Family Art-Based Assessment.

as described in Emerson (1989), "conducted a long term study on the effectiveness of psychotherapy for adults":

> Much to their surprise they found that the effectiveness of therapy depended not on types of therapy, but on the degree to which therapists were empathic, compassionate, and directional with their clients. The most vital of the therapeutic qualities was empathy. (Truax & Carkhuff, cited by Emerson, 1989, p. 191)

In addition, Emerson (1989) in his own work with infants and children found:

> Empathy to be an imperative concomitant of the therapy, in inverse relation to age. In older children, empathy was essential, and techniques were seldom successful without it. But with younger children and infants, empathy was mandatory. (Emerson, 1989, p. 191)

6. RECOMMENDATIONS. The cotherapists recommended couples therapy sessions to provide parenting support which would include parenting education. The parents were given a homework assignment to spend time together, away from the children. Ronald was recommended to continue in therapy, and Sandy was recommended for art and play therapy.

Figure 5.7. Family Portrait. The second task by the 44-year-old dad in a Family Art-Based Assessment.

Clinical Illness Described

In school, Sandy often suffered acute distress and isolation. She had trouble understanding assignments and making friends. She would often be listless and sad because of her many perceived problems. At home, Sandy was jealous of her brother and angry toward what she perceived as a lack of support from both her Mom and her Dad: her Mom for leaving her, and her Dad for not understanding and supporting her need to be a child. In and out of school, she appeared to be fearful of both children and adults.

Treatment Plans

Sandy's individual treatment plan focused on assessing the source of her unhappiness as quickly as possible. Treatment goals included building trust and raising self-esteem using art and play therapy while continuing with family and school consultations.

1. ART THERAPY. Art therapy, because of its universal appeal and accessibility, is often the treatment of choice for children. With any age, it often

Figure 5.8. Family Portrait. The second task by the 6-year-old brother in a Family Art-Based Assessment.

becomes a second language for describing the clients' psychological view of their inner world and the environment in which they grew and live (Arrington, 1986). Ulman (1975), summarizing Naumburg's words, cites advantages to using art in therapy:

> First, it permits direct expression of dreams, fantasies and other inner experiences that occur as pictures instead of words. Second, the pictured projections of unconscious material escape censorship more easily than do verbal expressions so that the therapeutic process is speeded up. Third, the productions are durable and unchanging: their content cannot be erased by forgetting, and their authorship is hard to deny. Fourth, the resolution of transference is made easier. (Ulman, 1975, p. 5)

Rubin (1978) encourages art therapists to accept and value all that is said and done that is truly individualistic and unique. She promotes a "framework for freedom" which encourages dormant creative expression. She says the therapist "must provide a physical and psychological setting which makes it possible for each person to become him/herself" (p. 31). Sometimes this may necessitate including intermodal activities like music,

Figure 5.9. The (Family name) Creation. A family mural. The third task in a Family Art-Based Assessment completed by a 5-year-old girl, a 6-year-old boy and Mother and Father.

drama and poetry. Rubin believes that risk-taking in therapy is often a precursor to growth.

2. PLAY THERAPY

> Modern play therapy is based on the observation that a child made insecure by a secret hate against or fear of the natural protectors of his play in family and neighborhood seems able to use the protective sanction of an understanding adult to regain some play peace. (Erikson, 1950, p. 222)

Oaklander (1976) notes that play is the child's form of improvisional dramatics. Playing is how the young child tries out her world; therefore, it is essential to healthy development. Play acting also acts as a second language and becomes a child's form of self-therapy through which confusions, anxieties, and conflicts can be formulated and assimilated.

Establishing Trust

When I first saw Sandy I knew that she had an auditory learning deficit, behavior problems and low self-esteem. I followed her lead as she walked around in the playroom looking at her play possibilities. Occasionally, I would bring something to her attention. After Sandy's first visit, I hypothesized that Sandy, a curious and engaging child, had emotional problems that plagued her interactions with other people. The problems, whatever they were, helped to maintain her lack of trust which in turn contributed to her low self-esteem and interfered with her entering into her own growth and development. I began Sandy's treatment focusing on establishing trust, raising her self-esteem and building Sandy's sense of self. My initial interaction with Sandy was as an accepting guide into a world of art and play.

Sandy touched the dollhouse and the sand in the sand tray. She looked at the sand play toys and wrote her name (letters backwards) on the chalkboard. I showed her the paints and the puppets. She returned to the sand and pulled out the toys. She began by saying, "I can make a house."

The toy house came in two parts and Sandy could not put the parts together, so she put the pieces back in the box, pulled out three little houses, placed them in the sand and said, "Look, I can make a castle house and I can put a fence around it. See, I can pull the fence apart so that I have enough fence to go all around my castle and no one can get inside." She added a variety of gates, big ones and small ones. She continued, "It doesn't matter if they are high or low gates, no one can get in. There are lots of gates, but no one can get in ever, ever, ever, only my friends."

She picked up a rock and two marbles. "Gates get broken at my house so I need some things to protect me if anyone tries to hurt me," she said. She picked up a large rubber seagull and in a baby voice continued, "I could hide and my seagull would protect me so that no one could hurt me. He knows me and likes me. I need cars and trucks." She proceeded to fill the sand tray with cars, trucks, buses, airplanes, a racing car, a train, a motorcycle, a boat and a four-wheel truck. She said simply, "I get every single truck and my bumpy jump, an Indian man who takes care of me. I have a dragon and all my friends." She threw more airplanes and cars and a rubber alligator in the tray. She continued picking up sand play figures while talking to herself and out loud for my benefit. "I have a little boat for my baby, and my friendly alligator never hurts me and my friends. I have all kinds of things at my place. Now, I need some people for the cars." She picked up a man in shorts and said, "My friendly man, and he's magic. Here are his two little birds, and this woman is my friend. She is a ghost, but she can do anything. Here is my little girl, my daughter and my fairy. That's enough. No, I need a snowman and a king and a judge." She selected the Chewbacca and said, "Everyone can take care of me and kill the whole wide world."

Ego States and Regression

In Jungian terms, Sandy appeared to be in Steward's (1981) Early Childhood II Play Age, and Neumann's (1976) Magic and Warlike Ego state. However, immediately upon taking the initiative of building a sand picture (Kalff, 1971) and verbalizing her inner feelings, "Everyone can take care of me and kill the whole wide world," she regressed (Erikson, 1950). She picked up the baby bottle she had seen earlier and sucked on it. She asked if she could put water in it. Then she walked around sucking on the water in the bottle, looking for a doll she liked. She picked out a baby doll and gave the bottle to the doll. I said, "Sometimes it feels good to be a baby and be taken care of."

Before she left, I asked Sandy to draw a picture of her family (Figure 5.10). Using art as a second language, Sandy identified her feelings of isolation in the family (Burns & Kaufman, 1972). Ronald is in a box at the top of the page. Sandy and her parents are in separate boxes on the bottom. Only the heads and eyes are drawn and then quickly and haphazardly colored.

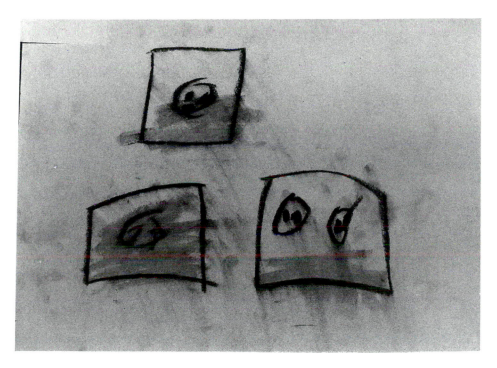

Figure 5.10. A 6-year-old girl's drawing of "My family." The brother is in the top box. The girl is in the left box. The parents are in the right box.

Reducing Confusion

In the next session, Sandy started by beating on the large Wham-it (a plastic toy with air at the top and sand in the bottom to keep it upright). She whacked it again and again. She gave it a real beating. She was angry. She turned around and said, "I think my brother broke my Cabbage Patch doll."

I questioned Sandy if she knew why she was coming to see me. She answered, "Yes, because my Dad says bad words and my Mom does too and so does my brother and I've done bad things." I said, "Sandy, I help people feel better and I know you don't feel too good right now." She moved to the playhouse on the bookcase. Following her lead, I asked her if she would like me to get it down and she said, "Yes, and then I can play in the house." She used the little girl in the playhouse family telling her, "You have to go to the doctor. Your ears hurt and your heart hurts."

Puppets

The rubber hand puppets include a mother, father, daughter, son, male doctor (white coat), a wolf and a baby dolphin. In early months of treatment, Sandy used the hand puppets to communicate that the lady doctor would get her well. This was a check-in communication tool she used at the beginning of every session. It was not a play experience. When she used the soft, fluffy hand puppets, she would tell me what part I was to play. I played different puppets on different days. Sometimes it was the puppet at which she would yell and fuss, saying how dumb and stupid the puppet was. As the puppet, I would cry and tell her my feelings were hurt. Sometimes I was a puppet she caressed and nurtured. Again, as the puppet I would purr, snuggle or respond in kind. Sometimes she wanted an audience and would tell me where to sit. Then she would throw the soft puppets in every direction, laughing and having a wild time.

Mom as a Relief

In the beginning of treatment, Mom was often invited in at the end of the session as both a relief and for Sandy to show Mom what she could do in the playroom. Sandy would set up the puppet theater and proceed with the soft puppet show. Screaming and yelling at the puppets, she would be outrageous. At the end, she would laugh and throw puppets all over the play room.

Art Materials

One session, the rubber hand puppet doctor and the mother and girl were missing. Sandy looked and looked; when she didn't find them she threw everything around—the soft puppets deliberately, and other toys, subtly. I thought this might be a good opportunity to work on emotions. I asked her to put on a smock and then I introduced Sandy to finger paints (Figure 5.11). Sandy participated first by smearing and making mud and then by scratching the paper and smearing the paint. She got paint all over her hands and the smock. When she was no longer involved, she became impatient with the mess she had made. She tore the painting and did another one with a brush (Figure 5.12). As we cleaned up, I commented that sometimes we get upset when things don't go as we think they should.

Figure 5.11. Six-year-old Sandy's first finger painting.

Sandy's work in art and play therapy followed the serial drawing stages identified by Jungian school counselor, John Allan (1988). The serial drawing approach is a method whereby the therapist meets on a regular basis with the child and "simply asks the child to draw-a-picture" (Allan, 1988, p. 20). Allan concludes that "over time a relationship forms, problems are expressed symbolically in the drawings, and healing and resolution of inner conflicts occurs" (p. 20). Since Naumburg (1966) and Kramer (1958) first started seeing clients and drawing pictures, clients of art therapists have been producing serial drawings. But until Allan (1988), no one had identified so clearly the organization of the reparative symbolic themes and stages that occur in the process.

Allan's Serial Drawing Stages

Allan identifies three stages: the initial stage, the middle stage, and the termination stage. Pictures in Allan's initial stage appear to "(a) give a view of the child's internal world, (b) reflect the feelings of hopelessness, (c) represent a vehicle for establishing the initial contact with the helper" (Allan, 1988, pp. 32–33). In Sandy's Initial Stage, her view of her internal world was one of confusion and trauma (as seen in the overcrowded sand tray), loss of internal control and hopelessness (as seen in her regression and need to be cared for and protected) and isolation (as seen in her artwork). In addition, the art and play therapy provided her with a vehicle for establishing the initial rapport with her therapist. Sandy incorporated her therapist (the female puppet doctor) into her actual symbolic language.

When Sandy came in for the session after the puppets had disappeared, she ignored me and went to the blackboard where she printed her name. I said, "Sandy, do you know who is back?" She turned, looked me in the eye, and with a big grin she answered, "The mummy puppet, the doctor and the baby." That day she began the first of her "having a baby" themes.

Bagarozzi and Anderson (1989) note, "Unresolved developmental conflicts become the major source of themes in one's personal mythology" (p. 24). These themes are expressed in specific affects, behaviors and cognitions (i.e., internal dialogues, self-statements, belief systems, and expectations).

The following sequence of Sandy playing all parts is an example of Sandy's personal mythology: Sandy, as the mother puppet, with the help of the doctor puppet, had a baby boy, then a baby girl, and then twins. Sandy, as the doctor puppet, gave them their shots. Then Sandy as the mother puppet gave birth again and again and again. The mother puppet let the good daddy puppet hold the babies and then the mother died. Sandy verbalized that she didn't like that, so she brought the mother back to life to marry the doctor. Sandy holding both mother and doctor had them kiss and kiss. Sandy began to feel guilty, so acting as Daddy she said, "You're not taking my wife away," and with that Sandy as the doctor killed Dad. Next, Sandy said, "Now mother and doctor can get married." Sandy asked me to help set up for the wedding, with chairs and a puppet audience. She began singing "My Country 'Tis of Thee"; as in the role of the bride, she went down the aisle. Next, Sandy picked up the mother puppet and said to the doctor puppet, "Do you want to kiss?" and to me she said, "They are going to sleep together naked. They make sex after they get married. I want to stay, but I can't. My baby is coming."

Anxiety and change of subject

The process had been more than five-year-old Sandy could understand. She turned to me and said, "I don't want to play anymore." But Sandy's feelings of not being OK continued. She said, "I hate the way my teacher wants me to write." She printed her name on the blackboard six different times. Then she purposely regressed. First, she put on a smock, opened the paints and painted red circles. She stopped and made dots along the edge saying, "I like to make poops." I stated, "Sandy, you like this room because you can do anything." Sandy without looking up answered, "Yes, anything" (Figure 5.12).

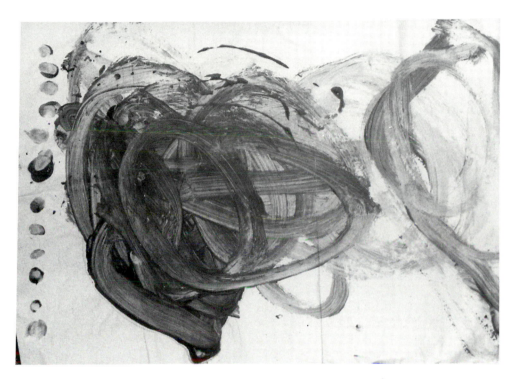

Figure 5.12. "I like to make poops." Six-year-old Sandy exploring in the playroom.

Themes continued

In the early part of treatment, Sandy talked in two voices: her normal voice and her baby voice. In addition, her confusion between the good and the bad parts of herself pervaded most of her work. Her themes included:

1. *Black rainbows* (Figure 5.13) *and Rainbow Houses* (Figure 5.14). She painted these pictures with almost no comment. Cirlot (1962) sees rainbows as "bridges representing change or the desire for change" (p. 33). He sees black as "guilt, origin, a symbol of the soul in its original condition and primal material" (p. 6).

2. *Badness.* "Brother is bad, he hits, hurts and lies. Daddy is bad, he lies just like brother. He makes me clean my room. He's mean. School is bad. The teacher is mean. The children are bad. They don't do their homework. They lie about me. The rubber hand puppet little girl is bad. The five-year-

Figure 5.13. "Black rainbow." Typical themes by Sandy, a six-year-old girl in the initial stage of treatment.

old baby lives at the bad school where the bad mother and father sent her."

3. *Her brother.* She both loved and hated her brother. "He is a good brother, sometimes I punch him and he likes me anyway. He's losing weight. He made the football team. He pees like my daddy. The girl is sad because her brother is dead. Someone kidnapped and killed him and the girl liked him because he played with her. See, he is clapping because the sister plays with him. The sister has pretty, long hair. The little boy is happy because Dad hugs him every morning. This girl is crying because brother tied her hat too tight and she is choking. This girl is happy because she gets candy and coke from her brother."

4. *Illness.* "The little girl is ill and sad (Figure 5.15). The dolphin is ill. Mommie is ill. The lady doctor can make us better. Dad is sick and he dies. I need to put something over his grave to say that his wife loved him."

5. *Babies and sexuality.* Sandy often played out her internal view of babies and sexuality. "Mother and daddy hand puppets are having a baby. Women have babies in their bellies. Her husband gave her a real baby for a present. She is happy. Playhouse toys are having babies, sand play figures are having babies, lots of them." She demonstrated the play couples on top of each other. Afterwards, she crawled into the old squashed refrigerator box and

Figure 5.14. "Rainbow house." Typical themes by Sandy, a six-year-old girl in the initial stage of treatment.

birthed herself again and again, allowing me to assist and hold her. She said, "I like being a baby and being held and carried." Sandy appeared to be starting over, healing her own birth and bonding traumas (Emerson, 1989).

6. *Weddings.* She loved to dress up. The playroom had several women's dresses and she would put my scarf on her head and become the bride. "This woman is happy because her husband is a policemen and can save her."

7. *Death and the devil.* "The devil lives down in that hole. I'll put this over it so he can't get through. He is green with red eyes. I saw a devil movie. My brother closed his eyes, but I didn't. This is medicine. You pour it in someone's mouth and they get sick and die. I don't want to die. I don't want to go to the devil. I get to live longer if I don't get married and have a baby. My Dad is going to get old and die."

As seen in the themes, Sandy had moved into Allan's (1988) Middle Stage in the serial drawing series. She was able to: (a) "express an emotion in its true form" (p. 34) while struggling with opposites of good versus bad. (b) She had "struggled with ambivalent feelings" (p. 34), and (c) "established

Figure 5.15. "The little girl is ill." Drawn by Sandy, a six-year-old in the initial stage of treatment.

a deeper relationship with her therapist" (p. 36). Sandy's psyche was now in a position to "disclose painful issues or a deep secret" (p. 32).

A Degenerate Clinical State

Sandy's teacher called to report that for several days Sandy had been rubbing her genitals in class. I asked her to ask Sandy if she wanted to come talk to me. When Sandy came into the playroom, we went to the chalkboard where I drew a little paper doll type figure with a bathing suit and I asked Sandy if anyone had ever touched her under her bathing suit, pointing to the picture I had drawn on the board. She answered quickly and not in her baby voice, "Yes, Uncle George had." I went into an inquiry to find out who Uncle George was, how serious the touching was, and if this touching was still occurring or how recently it had occurred. Sandy had established trust which allowed her to be open and clear in her responses. Uncle George was the husband of the baby-sitter that the family had used when the children were smaller. They no longer used a baby-sitter. Sandy also clearly stated that she had told her Mom and Dad when the incidents were first occurring, but that they had not believed her. I told her I believed her and perhaps if she told her parents again they would believe her. I also told her that Uncle George must be reported to the police for touching her body in private parts. She said, "I told him to stop but he wouldn't do it."

Although it was 5:30 P.M. on Wednesday before Thanksgiving, I notified Child Protective Services (CPS). I was told that since Sandy was not in immediate danger I could proceed with the reporting on Friday after Thanksgiving. When Mother came to pick up Sandy, we made an appointment for Friday morning. Friday morning, Mom met me and I told her what Sandy had told me. Mom reacted with both sadness and confusion. She explained that Uncle George was the husband of a former baby-sitter. Mom had been supportive of the family when another child had accused Uncle George of touching her inappropriately. The couple had been investigated and, although no charges had been filed, the woman had lost her day-care license. During the investigative process Uncle George, a man in his sixties, had suffered a heart attack. Mom admitted Sandy had told her what was happening, but she and Dad thought three-year-old Sandy was copying her friend.

We discussed how Mom and Dad could support Sandy during the investigation that would begin immediately with both a social worker and a policewoman. Mom was concerned that Sandy would be put on the witness stand or that the school and her friends would know. I explained that we would work very hard to insure that would not happen. I knew that Sandy's reaction could make or break the case. She had an avoidant personality and I did not know how she would react with total strangers. Sandy resolved our concerns by asking if I would be present when she talked to the police. I also accompanied Sandy and her Mom to the District Attorney's office prior to criminal charges being filed against Uncle George.

Pieces of the puzzle now began to fit together, i.e., Sandy's regressed cognitive abilities, lack of trust, anger, and low-self esteem. Sandy would need support. She would need to know her parents believed her. She would need to know they were sorry for what had happened and that they had not protected her. Sandy's family would also need information and support in the weeks and months ahead.

When I saw her on Monday, I had her tell me her experience with Uncle George and draw how she felt (Figure 5.16). She drew these feelings for weeks (Figures 5.17). At three to four years of age, Sandy had not liked her body being violated. As she got older, the memory of the experience faded but the memory of the feelings were even more distasteful. It was important that she have a chance to talk, draw, and play out every memory or fantasy. She needed to know in her very being that she was not bad because someone had been bad to her. She needed to be able to trust adult men and women.

She needed to know that she wasn't dumb or ugly because of what had happened to her. Sandy also needed to know that people believed her.

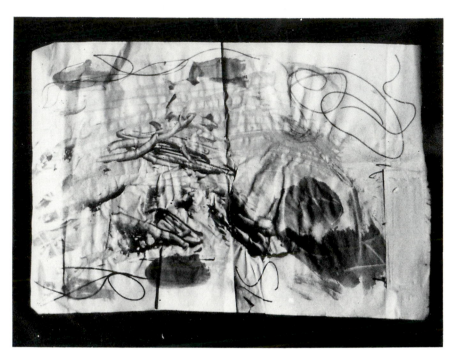

Figure 5.16. "My experience with Uncle George." Drawn by Sandy, a six-year-old in the middle stages of treatment.

Body Image

Sandy's body concept at age six was regressed with a distorted concept of a four-year-old. "A child must have a concept before she can draw representationally" (Anderson, 1978, p. 26). A child that has a distorted and confused concept will draw distorted and confused pictures. Sandy was betrayed by a friend of the family—someone that took care of her. When she told her parents they did not believe her. The molestation had gone on for many months and Sandy's preverbal reality had become menacing. Sandy had found it much safer to retreat into a world of her own than to live in a world that was as unsavory as hers had become.

Torras De Bea (1987), as reported by Schneider, Ostroff and Legow (1990), believes that "the child partly receives its body schema (ideal body image) from the mother and father and from the sensorimotor experiences with all their relational and affective components" (p. 135). With the molestation occurring between two and three years of age, Sandy had not as yet estab-

Figure 5.17. "YUK! My experience with Uncle George." Drawn by Sandy, a six-year-old in the middle stages of treatment.

lished an ego. She had never developed a positive sense of self. Her body image expressed in her art represented the emotional maturity of a three-year-old (Figure 5.18) with emotional disturbance (Figures 5.19 and 5.20).

Establishing a Sense of Self

The milieu of family and school became less important for the time being as therapy became more important and directive. Following Sandy's lead, we worked to help Sandy develop a sense of self and mastery.

"Once the deeper feelings and pain have been expressed symbolically and shared verbally there tends to be a rapid movement toward a resolution" (Allan, 1988, p. 39) characterized by: "images of mastery and self-control, and worth; the emergence of positive imagery: (i.e., an absence of war, violence, and damage); a central self symbol, humorous scenes and pictures reflecting a detachment from the therapist" (Allan, 1988, p. 26).

Sandy now moved into Allan's Termination Stage. She lost interest in the symbology of the puppets and incorporated the symbology of her school classroom. She stood on a chair in front of the chalkboard and in a firm voice directed me in numbers, spelling and writing lessons. She would show me and then she would ask me to show her. When mine was different (correct), she would erase it and then try hers, first wrong and then correctly.

Figure 5.18. Sandy's emerging self. A six-year-old's red painting in the middle stage of treatment.

I quickly learned to encourage Sandy's desire for mastery by providing her with choices. Choices provided Sandy with more chances of succeeding on her own.

First she practiced writing SANDY, again and again. Then she moved out of her ego-centered perspective to another perspective where she practiced writing my name. It was Dors (Figure 5.21) for many weeks. I used art tasks that moved progressively in a more difficult continuum, but I continued to use Sandy's perception of her body image to assess her progress. We traced hands and feet and bodies. I drew her and she tried to draw me (Figure 5.22). We looked in magazines at body parts of people standing and moving. We practiced folding and cutting. I drew shapes on the blackboard that she could copy. She drew shapes that I could copy. We drew on white and colored paper. Sandy was anxious to explore. But nothing came easy. Sandy

Figure 5.19. Sandy's first self-image. A six-year-old's drawing in the middle stage of treatment.

Figure 5.20. Sandy's self-image in the middle stage of treatment.

had lost confidence in her ability to do and to be. As noted by Rubin (1978), Sandy's creativity had become dormant. Each failure was a reminder of previous failures (Figure 5.23). My job was to provide Sandy with not only an environment where she could begin to be in charge of her own learning processes but provide her opportunities of emotional safety and success. Sandy was still a child with many of the same issues, but now they had a different importance. In Sandy's mind the family hierarchy had been reestablished. Adults were protecting Sandy.

Her themes became less intense and more quickly released. At one session Sandy started off talking baby talk. She wanted to play with clay. She said, "My brother gets to play in clay. Why can't I?" I said, "Sandy, you don't like to get your hands dirty." She took the clay and made "poops," then she moved to the chalkboard, told me to sit in the audience and she told me I didn't know my lessons. Then she used colored playdough to make hot chocolate and graham crackers. She invited me to a tea party where she began to talk about school activities and school outings. I was impressed with her knowledge and memory of trips to the zoo and the aquarium, as well as with subjects discussed by classroom visitors, i.e., planets, the tides, and police dogs.

Figure 5.21. "Doris." Sandy, a six-year-old girl, had connected to the therapist and was practicing skills in the middle stage of treatment.

Separation — Termination

After eight months, Sandy came in with her own agenda. She drew Mom and Sandy (Figure 5.24). She drew brother and Sandy (Figure 5.25). She and Dad had a fight and she drew the fight (Figure 5.26). She no longer talked of Uncle George. I would bring him up and ask Sandy to once again draw how she felt when Uncle George had touched her. She would paint blobs and messes, saying "yuk" and "gross" (Figure 5.27) and then she would return to discussing school or problems with friends or family. I knew the molestation

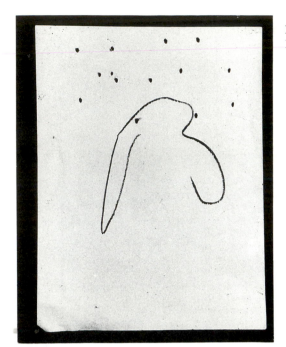

Figure 5.22. "Doris." Sandy's attempt at a portrait of Doris drawn during the middle stage of treatment.

Figure 5.23. "The rainbow house." Sandy, a six-year-old girl, had a bad day at school. Each failure was a reminder of previous failures.

Figure 5.24. Mom and Sandy. Drawn by Sandy, a seven-year-old girl establishing a self-image.

was not resolved, but I concluded that Sandy had decided it was time to move on. She was using her therapy to help her with age-appropriate problems and hurts.

Sandy's treatment plans now included things like:

1. Saying hello to the receptionist as she came into the center, rather than curling up in her nook.

2. Joining a Girl Scout group, rather than going home alone after school. (This was not an easy task, in that Sandy now had to learn some social skills so she would not be excluded.) In fact, this task took two trials because one group asked that she not return due to her immature behavior.

3. Taking ballet or a body-oriented sport so that she could learn to use her body effectively and gracefully. In addition, we played "Follow the Leader" (Gayle, 1987) using a 12-inch roll of paper. I started, and then after rolling the paper or wrapping it around something, I would write instructions for her to follow: i.e., sign your name. Draw a purple people eater. Change colors. Make a happy face. Make a star. Give the paper a big red kiss. Move back three spaces and write Doris. She particularly liked the game when she was the leader and wrote instructions for me to follow. Because her spelling was generally phonetic, occasionally I had to ask her, "What am I going to do now?"

Figure 5.25. Brother and Sandy. Drawn by Sandy, a seven-year-old girl establishing a self-image.

We made cards of Mother's Day and Father's Day. We made our own puppets out of lunch bags and socks and we made lots of playdough goodies to eat with our play tea while Sandy told me about school. Sandy was still having problems accepting the drawings she made of herself (Figure 5.28).

At the end of Sandy's second year of treatment, she had a friend at school, was speaking to the receptionist, had been active in Girl Scouts, but dropped out because of other interests. In addition, she had participated in a swim team during the summer.

Dad was taking Ronald to play Pop Warner football and Sandy, now eight, liked to go with them. The team had a pep squad of 20 eight- to ten-year-old girls who had uniforms and cheered for the team. Sandy, who had recently turned eight, decided on her own that she wanted to be in the pep squad. She tried out and made the squad.

Figure 5.26. A fight with Dad. A picture of Sandy's experience of a fight with her Dad. Drawn by Sandy, a seven-year-old girl establishing a self-image in the terminating stage of treatment.

I knew we had completed our work the day Sandy walked in, asked for paper and crayolas and drew an age-appropriate picture of herself, complete with labeled ribbon, pocket, blouse, skirt and shoes (Figure 5.29). Sandy had moved from the kinesthetic to the symbolic in her artwork (Lusebrink, 1990). The girl in the picture had her tongue sticking out. A symbol Drachnik (1983) identifies as indicative of sexually abused youngsters. When Sandy first started therapy she did not like to leave. She would pull out new toys right at the end. She would whine or cry or ask Mom to come and see what she had done. Later, she understood her therapeutic time and used it to meet her needs. She had learned to ask for what she wanted and to set her own limits.

Sandy had learned that therapy was a place she could trust her efforts to explore her feelings. She learned to risk and to play. More importantly, she discovered her creativity and learned to appreciate her abilities and her self-worth (Rubin, 1984). It was a joy and a luxury to work with a client to this stage.

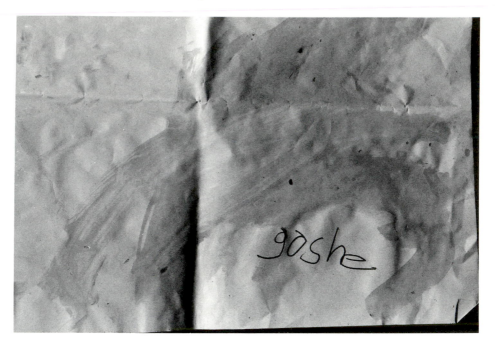

Figure 5.27. "Goshe." Sandy's gross feelings of her experience with Uncle George. Sandy is a seven-year-old girl in the terminating stage of treatment.

Epilogue

As releases were obtained from the family to print Sandy's experiences, Mom and Sandy came in to see me. Sandy, at 11, was wearing braces. She was tall, slender and quite elegant with her straight, shiny blond hair and bright blue eyes. Sandy had been moved into a regular class the year before. She no longer qualified for placement in the learning disabled special education program. She no longer had a cognitive deficit. Although Sandy tried regular classes, at her own request the school let her stay with her special class until she completed elementary school. She had talked Mom and Dad into letting her enroll in a modeling class and she hoped to do some modeling.

Sandy may have additional memories of her early molestation, particularly at transitional points in her life, but she has developed a trust in herself and in others. In addition, she developed self-esteem through counseling, her own maturation and support from her environmental systems.

Figure 5.28. "Sandy." A seven-year-old girl's ambivalent feelings about her self-concept in the terminal stage of treatment.

Figure 5.29. "Let me draw you a picture." Eight-year-old Sandy's self-image in the terminal stage of treatment.

REFERENCES

Allan, J. (1988). *Inscapes of the child's world.* Dallas: Spring.

American Psychiatric Association. (1987). *Diagnostic and statistical manual of mental disorders* (3rd ed.). Washington, DC: Author.

Anderson, F. (1978). *Art for all the children.* Springfield, IL: Charles C Thomas.

Arrington, D. (1986). A Jungian based study of selected visual constructs preferred by women. Dissertation, University of San Francisco. *University Microfilm International,* Ann Arbor, MI. No. 87-13, 271.

Arrington, D. (in press). Thinking systems: Seeing systems. Systemically oriented art therapy: An integrative model. *Arts in Psychotherapy.*

Bagarozzi, D. A., & Anderson, S. (1989). *Personal, marital, and family myths.* New York: W. W. Norton.

Beres, D. (1965). *Symbol & object. Bulletin of the Menninger Clinic, 29,* 3–23.

Bowen, M. (1978). *Family therapy in clinical practice.* New York: Jason Aronson.

Bruscia, K. (1988). Standards for clinical assessment in the arts therapies. *Arts in Psychotherapy, 15,* 5–10.

Burns, R., & Kaufman, H. S. (1972). *Actions, styles and symbols in kinetic family drawings (K-F-D).* New York: Brunner/Mazel.

Cirlot, J. E. (1962). *A dictionary of symbols.* New York: Philosophical Library.

Community Alliance for Special Education (CASE). (1988). *Special education rights and responsibilities.* San Francisco: Community Alliance for Special Education.

Drachnik, C. (1983). *Manual: Symbols of psychopathology: Children.* Unpublished manual.

Duval, E. (1957). *Family development.* New York: Harper & Row.

Emerson, W. R. (1989). Psychotherapy with infants and children. *Peri-Natal Psychology, 3*(3), 190–217.

Erikson, E. (1950). *Childhood and society.* New York: W. W. Norton.

Fairbairn, W. R. (1954). *An object relations theory of the personality.* New York: Basic Books.

Frank, T., Detre, K., Kniazzeh, C.R., Robinson, M., Rubin, J., & Ulman, E. (1983). Roots of art therapy; Margaret Naumburg (1890–1983) and Florence Cane (1882–1952)—A family portrait. *Art Therapy, 22*(4), 113.

Freud, S. (1900/1955). *The interpretation of dreams.* (Standard ed. Vols. 4–5). London: Hogarth Press.

Freud, S. (1915). *General introduction to psychoanalysis.* New York: Liveright.

Freud, S. (1919/1955). *From the history of an infantile neurosis.* (Standard ed. Vol 17). London: Hogarth Press.

Gayle, T. (1987). Unpublished presentation. College of Notre Dame, Belmont, Ca.

Guerin, P. & Pendagast, E. (1976). Evaluation of the family system and the genogram. In P. Guerin (Ed.), *Family Therapy: Theory & practice.* NY: Gardner Press.

Haley, J. (1963). Marriage therapy. In J. Haley (Ed.), *Strategies of psychotherapy.* New York: Grune & Stratton.

Jung, C. (1934/1974). *The development of the personality.* (R.F.C. Hull, Trans.). Princeton: Princeton University Press.

Jung, C. (1964). Approaching the unconscious. In J. Freeman (Ed.), *Man and his symbols.* (pp. 18–103). Garden City: Doubleday.

Kalff, D. M. (1971). *Sandplay: Mirror of a child's psyche.* SF: Brouser Press. (Republished 1980 as *Sandplay: A psychotherapeutic approach to the psyche.* Santa Monica: Sigo Press.)

Kramer, E. (1958). *Art therapy in a children's community.* Springfield, IL: Charles C Thomas.

Kramer, E. (1987). Sublimation and art therapy. In J. Rubin (Ed.), *Approaches to art therapy: Theory and technique* (pp. 26–43). New York: Brunner/Mazel.

Kwiatkowska, H. (1978). *Family therapy and evaluation through art.* Springfield, IL: Charles C Thomas.

Levick, M. (1983). *They could not talk and so they drew: Children's styles of coping and thinking.* Springfield, IL: Charles C Thomas.

Lowenfeld, V. (1957). *Creative and mental growth* (3rd Ed.). New York: MacMillan.

Lusebrink, V. (1990). *Imagery and visual expression in therapy.* New York: Plenum.

Mahler, M., Pine, F., & Bergman, A. (1975). *The psychological birth of the human infant: Symbiosis and individuation.* New York: Basic Books.

Minuchin, S. (1974). *Families and family therapy.* Cambridge, MA: Harvard University Press.

Naumburg, M. (1917). Unpublished paper. Cited in "Roots of Art Therapy." *The American Journal of Art Therapy, 22.*

Naumburg, M. (1966). *Dynamically oriented art therapy: Its principles and practice.* New York: Grune & Stratton.

Neumann, E. (1976). *The child.* New York: Harper Colophon.

Nichols, W. C., & Everett, C. (1986). *Systematic family therapy: An integrative approach.* New York: Guildford Press.

Public Law 94-142, 1975.

Oaklander, V. (1976). *Windows to our children.* Moab, UT: Peoples Press.

Rubin, J. (1978). *Child art therapy: Understanding and helping children grow through art.* New York: Van Nostrand Reinhold.

Rubin, J. (1984). *The art of art therapy.* New York: Brunner/Mazel.

Rubin, J. (1987). Freudian psychoanalytic theory: Emphasis on uncovering insight in art therapy. In Rubin, J. (Ed.), *Approaches to Art Therapy. Theory & Technique* (pp. 7–25). New York: Brunner/Mazel.

Schneider, S., Ostroff, S., & Legrow, N. (1990). Enhancement of body-image: A structured art therapy group with adolescents. *Art Therapy, 7*(3), 134–138.

Steward, C. T. (1981). The developmental psychology of sandplay. In Hill, Alpert, Bel, Bradway, Henderson, McClintock, Stewart (Eds.), *Sandplay Studies: Origins, theory and practice* (pp. 35–42). San Francisco: C. G. Jung Institute of San Francisco.

Uhlin, D. (1972). *Art for exceptional children* (2nd ed.). Dubuque, IA: Wm. C. Brown.

Ulman, E. (1974). Innovation and aberration. *American Journal of Art Therapy, 14*(1), 14.

Ulman, E. (1975). Art therapy: Problems of definition. In Ulman & Dachinger (Eds.), *Art Therapy* (pp. 3–13). New York: Schocken.

Wadeson, H. (1980). *Art psychotherapy.* New York: John Wiley.

Wench, L. S. (1980). *House-Tree-Person: An illustrated diagnostic handbook.* Los Angeles: Western Psychological Services.

Wilcoxon, S. (1987). Perspective in Intergenerational Concepts. *Families of origin therapy.* Rockville, MD: Aspen.

Wilson, L. (1987). Symbolism and art therapy. In J. Rubin (Ed.), *Approaches to art therapy* (pp. 44–62). New York: Brunner/Mazel.

Chapter 6

ADAPTING ART FOR
CHILDREN WITH DISABILITIES

ADAPTATIONS ARE THE KEY CONCEPT

Often in bewilderment parents, teachers, and therapists have stated that they are frantically searching for new art ideas and that they can find nothing written for a particular disability. In reality, these persons may be searching for a recipe or cookbook for art. There is no such thing!

There are many books that have been written on art and art education, and an ever-increasing number of books are becoming available in art therapy. There are also a few titles on art for children with disabilities. These books are not all inclusive, nor should they be. In fact, it would be a sad state of affairs if the definitive book had been written on art. It is not possible in one short book or in one course to cover the topic of art for children with disabilities. Moreover, more than one book or one source would be needed simply because the teacher, therapist, or parent eventually would end up repeating the same series of art experiences (which is not always undesirable—some repetition can be most appropriate).

In many ways, teaching and working therapeutically with children who have disabilities is the most challenging and taxing of one's creative abilities. Being able to solve the daily problems that occur in designing art adaptations for children with disabilities is the most rewarding and intellectually stimulating of endeavors. It also is one of the most exciting challenges to one's own creativity. Being able to creatively design individualized adaptations is the key to planning appropriate art experiences for the disabled child. To do so, the adult must know both the child and all his *abilities* (as well as disabilities), and the adult must also be very familiar with the art materials and processes that will be utilized.

FOUR CATEGORIES OF ADAPTATIONS

Art adaptations may be broken down into three major categories: adaptations in the physical environment, adaptations in the art media and tools,

The author wishes to acknowledge Larry S. Barnfield as the source for this concept.

and adaptations in the instructional sequence. There is a fourth category which we will term *technological adaptations*. We shall discuss each of these categories and present examples. The chapter concludes with a discussion of health and safety issues because they can also be considered adaptations.

Adaptations in the Physical Environment

Physical space can affect behavior. Have you ever entered a huge auditorium or gymnasium that was empty? The space can give one an expansive feeling—or can make one feel very small and insignificant. Space in an art room or classroom can have profound effects on children. If children are working in a very large space, it can influence their behavior, and they may become less controlled. Conversely, children who are working in a small space may be better behaved. The adult must be sensitive to providing the best match between actual room size and the size of the group that is to work in the space. Space can also be very intimate and cozy, depending on how it is ordered and decorated (Susi, 1989).

The adult must seriously consider the nature of the space in which the art sessions will occur, and the nature of the child or children who will be working in that space (Susi, 1989). For example, if the child has a learning disability and is easily distracted, then a space that has walls that are relatively free of distractions may be optimal. Also, a child who has problems with short attention span may work better in an area in which there are only a few art materials present (fewer distracting items).

A blind child needs to have a work space that has consistent placement and storage of art materials and supplies. In this way the child can quickly learn where everything "lives" and can find what he needs without having to rely on an adult to provide these items. This will promote a sense of independence and mobility.

A child with physical disabilities may need to work at a specific height, and a wheelchair may not fit under the worktable. If such a child cannot be moved from his wheelchair for medical reasons, then the adult may have to create a work surface that can be attached to the wheelchair. This can be accomplished by using a drawing board or a "board" cut from heavy cardboard (Figure 6.1). The board must be secured to the arms of the wheelchair. This can be done by using C-clamps if the board is made from wood, or by using masking tape or duct tape if the board is made from heavy cardboard (Anderson, 1979).

Sometimes children with physical disabilities work best lying down (Figure 6.3). If the child can be moved from his wheelchair (the school nurse or the classroom teacher will know if it is medically permissible to take the child

Figure 6.1. If a wheelchair cannot fit under the art table and the child cannot be moved from his chair, then a board can be placed on the arms of the wheelchair and secured with strong tape. The board should not be too heavy and often thick cardboard can be used. Note that the paper on which the child is drawing has been secured to the work surface with masking tape. Illustration credit: V. Foster and R. Mechtly.

from the wheelchair), then the adult can discuss with the child what might be the best workplace—either in a regular chair or lying on the floor. **In fact, in developing adaptations, a team effort between the teacher, parent or therapist, and the child will be an optimal way of working.** Often, it will be a trial-and-error affair with the child being the major source of information about what will be the best working position or angle of a chair or other adaptations. Be sure that you include the child in the adaptation planning, and do not be afraid to ask the child what seems to work best.

Often if a child has movement in only one direction, then the child or the work space may need to be rotated at intervals so that the child can reach the empty spaces in his work. Figure 6.4 and Figure 6.5 illustrate how a child may need to be positioned for executing a drawing activity.

At times, specially selected music can facilitate an art session. For example, children with hyperactivity may be calmed by a slow classical music background. Conversely, children who are hypoactive may be energized by a faster-paced music selection. If music is utilized, it can be a subtle background factor or it can be incorporated directly into the planned art experiences (such as discussing how the music makes one feel and then painting this feeling).

Figure 6.2. This illustrates how a child with physical disabilities can work at a table easel. This easel may be preferable for the child who must sit and work. The paper is placed against a strong piece of cardboard and then taped to the easel. For added security, the easel can be anchored from behind with a sandbag.

Some children have a tendency to copy each other's work. This copying may be due to a child not fully understanding what he is supposed to do in an art activity. At other times it may indicate a very insecure child who is afraid to do any art that is different from that being done by other children. Mentally retarded and hearing-impaired children tend to copy more frequently than children with other disabling conditions. This copying behavior is partly due to the teaching methods used with the mentally retarded child and to the reliance on visual examples for instructing the hearing-impaired learner. One adaptation that may be helpful in preventing the tendency for a child to copy is to only show the child a partially completed example of the artwork which the child is to do—or to provide several different completed examples that are removed from the child's sight during the work period. Another adaptation that is helpful is to tell the children that what they are making is a secret and that no one is to see what others are doing until the end of the art session. To reinforce this secret

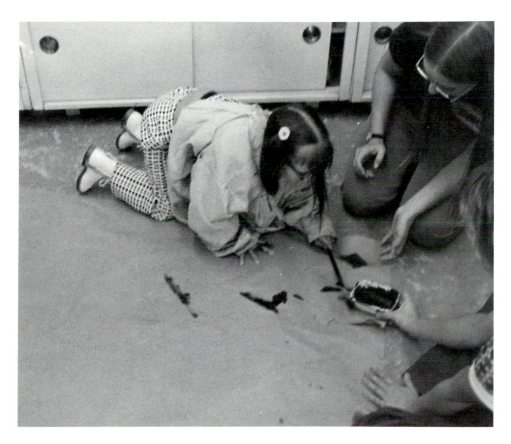

Figure 6.3. If it is medically permissible, sometimes it is easier for a child to work on the floor. Here, a child with visual impairments and physical handicaps who is six years old begins painting with tempera.

approach, the children can be separated from one another by putting them in individual carrels or simply by placing large pieces of cardboard between the children so that no one can see what the others are doing (Figure 6.6). One should always be careful when isolating a child because (especially children with hearing impairments) isolation can be a punishment. If the children are to be separated, the adult should be sure that children understand why they are being separated during their working time (i.e., that this will make it easier to keep each one's work a secret). It also will be important to bring all the children together at the close of the session to share what everyone has made (Anderson, 1979).

There are a number of adaptations that fall under a subcategory called "nailing things down." These are also adaptations in the physical environment. Often the paper on which a child is working must be secured by taping it down to the worktable. Water containers may need to be weighted to prevent

Figure 6.4. Finding the best working conditions takes time, patience, and teamwork. Often just asking the child what is best for her will provide the answer. The teacher and the therapist should consider themselves part of a team working in cooperation with the child to find the best working conditions and adaptations. Here, a ten-year-old child with cerebral palsy is drawing with markers, a medium which she prefers because she has more control with markers than with more fluid media such as paint. She has decided on her own working position. Sometimes (as in this case) when the child cannot easily move, the paper must be rotated.

spilling. Figure 6.7 illustrates how a water container can be weighted by adding gravel to it. Similarly, paint containers may need to be weighted down. This also can be done by adding pebbles to them or by having a special paintboard with velcro where the containers are placed. C-clamps are very helpful in holding down pieces of wood. Sandbags also can be used to hold sculptures or other types of artwork in place while they are being painted (Anderson, 1979). Finally, an adaptation that falls literally in the "nailing things down" category is to use a pair of plyers to hold a nail that is being hammered into hold pieces of wood together (Figure 6.8).

Adaptations in the Art Tools and Media

Perhaps the largest group of adaptations fall into this category. Often, long-handled paintbrushes may need to be shortened so that the child can more easily hold them. Other times children may need long-handled brushes. Again, the overriding rule is to adapt for each *individual* child.

Figure 6.5. Here is the completed drawing by the ten-year-old girl. She has depicted a girl playing ball outside. In spite of her physical disability her work shows exceptional control—especially in view of her cerebral palsy which limits good control of the lines she makes.

Some children cannot easily select a brush or drawing tool if it is placed in a can. To enable these art tools to be easily selected a special holder can be made from a block of wood. Three- to five-inch-deep holes are drilled into the wood block so that handles of brushes and drawing tools can be placed into these holes. Then the child can more easily select his brush, marker or pencil on his own and also replace it without assistance.

In some instances it is difficult for children to grasp and hold drawing tools and brushes that have narrow shafts. In these cases, these handles can be thickened. This can be accomplished by taping or rubberbanding pieces of foam rubber or sponge to the handle. Sometimes the drawing or painting instrument will work best if it is taped directly to the child's hand.

Often, a specially designed adaptation is necessary. Orthoplast is a special plastic material that can be molded when warm. It is used by physical therapists in hospitals mostly to make splints for individuals who need added orthopedic support for their limbs. It can be heated in warm water or an oven. If heated in an oven (to 250° F), it should be wrapped in wax paper. When heated, it has maximum malleability. When cooled it has great strength. What is most exciting about this material is that it can be molded to fit a handle or a hand (Figure 6.9, 6.10) and thus enable a child who never had the opportunity to hold a brush or a pencil the thrill of doing this. Also,

Figure 6.6. If children are easily distracted or tend to copy one another's art ideas, then they can be separated during the working part of the art session. When isolating children, care should be taken that they understand that this is not a punishment. One way to insure that the child does not think working in an individual carrel is punishment is to encourage each child to keep her work a secret (as is being done here) until it is completed and it is time to show everyone what has been created. Illustration credit: V. Foster and R. Mechtly.

it enables that child to have the experience of being able to create his very own expressions (Callan, 1987).

Velcro wriststrips can be adapted by adding two rubber bands, so that a drawing tool can be held (Figure 6.11) (Callan, 1987).

A head pointer can be adapted to hold a drawing tool for students who cannot use their hands. It has several adjustments and comes only with a pointer attached to come out at the forehead level. With some ingenuity, a drawing tool, brush, or marker can be attached (Figure 6.12) (Callan, 1987).

If the head pointer does not work or is not available, a special adaptation can be made so that the child can hold a pencil or brush in his mouth. Before deciding to use a mouth tube, be sure to check the child's medical records and, with medical staff, determine if the child can use a mouth tube and that this will not interfere with dental work or breathing. Plastic tubing that has a diameter wide enough to hold a brush or drawing tool can be purchased at a pharmacy. The tubing can be cut to the optimal length and the brush inserted until the proper length is determined. Further trimming

Figure 6.7. Paint and water containers can be anchored by adding gravel to them. Also, velcro can be added to a board and to bottoms of containers to prevent them from spilling. Illustration credit: V. Foster and R. Mechtly.

may be done until the proper length is determined through a trial-and-error process. Once there is a good fit, this mouthpiece and brush and/or drawing instrument should be stored in a sanitary container or plastic bag and ONLY used by that one student (Anderson, 1979). If the child cannot steady the brush or pencil in his mouth using the tubing, a rubber spatula can be used. In this instance the spatula's handle is cut off leaving only about two inches to which the brush or pencil is attached using duct tape. The child then holds the spatula in his mouth by biting the rubber end (Ludens-Katz, 1985).

Some children cannot use their hands but have full use of their legs and feet. These students can learn to paint and draw holding the brush and/or pencil in the toes. Some older students have even been able to do stitchery using their toes. In Europe there is a special society of artists who paint with their feet or their toes (Association of Mouth and Foot Painting Artists Worldwide, 9490 Vadwz, Landstrasse 3b, Switzerland).

Sometimes children simply cannot hold a paint brush but can manipulate larger objects. Some students can apply paint much more easily by using a

Figure 6.8. To avoid hitting fingers when nailing things together a pair of pliers can be used to hold the nail. In this way if the hammer misses its mark, only the pliers will be hit. Illustration credit: V. Foster and R. Mechtly.

sponge instead of a brush. A variation on this idea is to use a stamp moistener that has a sponge tip. This item can be filled with paint and used like a brush. Recycled plastic squeeze-bottles like the ones that mustard or ketchup come in can be filled with paint. Empty salt and pepper shakers can be filled with dry tempera paint. These paint shakers can then be used to sprinkle tempera onto a wet surface (Callan, 1987).

Some students may have limited mobility and need a means for making large marks or strokes. A one-inch dowel rod can be adapted to hold a brush or a pencil. A hole is drilled in the center of the dowel that is large enough to fit the handle of the drawing or painting tool. The length of the dowel will depend on the individual student's needs and will be determined in a trial-and-error manner (Figure 6.13). The student who cannot grasp the dowel can be accommodated by stapling velcro to the dowel and also attaching velcro to the palm of a glove (Figure 6.14). The student then can grasp the dowel with greater ease with the added help of the velcro glove (Callan, 1987).

Sometimes a student can only make a fist and needs a fist-type grip for a drawing tool or paintbrush. This can be accomplished by using handles cut from plastic milk cartons or soap or bleach bottles. In cutting out the handle, enough space should be left so that holes are big enough so that the

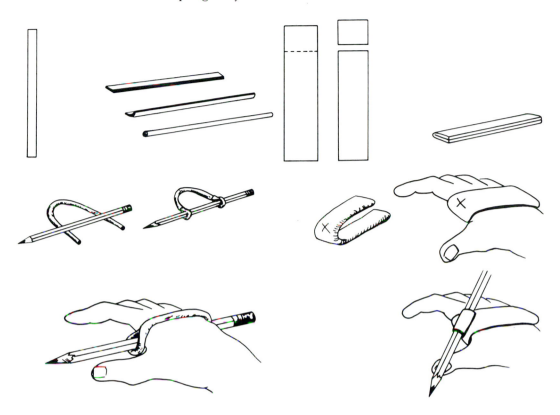

Figures 6.9 and 6.10. These are two illustrations of ways that orthoplast can be manipulated to enable a learner with physical disabilities to easily grasp a drawing or painting tool. Adapted from Callan (1987) by permission. Illustration credit: R. Mechtly.

pencil or brush handle can be punched into the plastic. For added security, the pencil or brush may need to be taped to the handle. In this way, the child will have a fist-type handle for drawing or painting tools (Figure 6.15) (Callan, 1987).

For students who have difficulty holding crayons or chalk lengthwise as would be necessary to make texture rubbings (Chapter 7 has a discussion of texture activities), there are two adaptations that will help. The first is to place a crayon into a large bulldog clip; the clip handle is much easier to grasp than the crayon (Figure 6.16) (Barnfield cited by Anderson, 1979). Another adaptation would be to melt crayon bits and broken pieces in a round 6½-ounce can. When the crayon is cooled and removed, the result is a large disk that can be easily held by the children (Callan, 1987).

Some students just cannot hold drawing and painting tools. If these children are old enough, it may be best to think about other types of art media or processes that may not require fine motor ability. One such

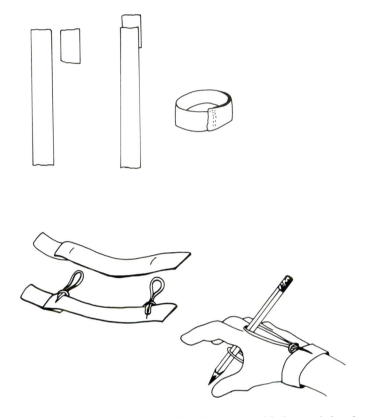

Figure 6.11. This illustration shows how rubber bands can be added to wristbands that have velcro fasteners. The rubber bands are attached by slipping them through slits made in the wristbands. The result is a springy tension that helps both hold and manipulate the drawing tool. Adapted from Callan (1987) by permission. Illustration credit: R. Mechtly.

medium is photography. In using photography, the child is still making design decisions. The camera is merely the means of recording those decisions. In Figure 6.17, there is a detailed illustration of an adaptation for using a small autofocus camera with persons with physical disabilities. The adaptation enables a physically disabled child to take pictures with minimal use of one finger. With the advances in autofocus cameras on the market, photography is an even more accessible art medium than in the past.

Application of Glue

Often children who have difficulty in holding drawing or painting tools also have difficulty applying glue. Some of the same adaptations already discussed for use in applying paint can be modified to assist the child in applying glue. White glue can be sponged on or brushed on. Be sure that

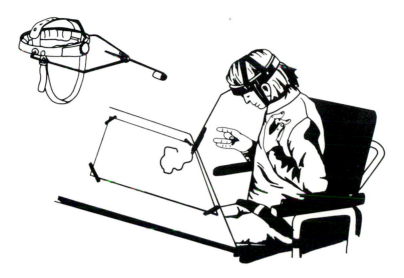

Figure 6.12. A head pointer can be adapted to hold a drawing or painting tool so that a learner with no use of his hands can make marks by moving his head. Illustration credit: R. Mechtly.

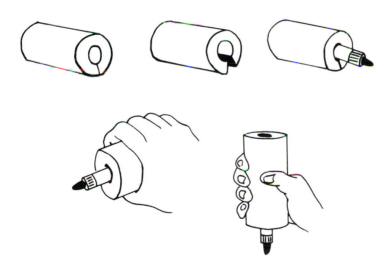

Figure 6.13. Another way of thickening a handle of a brush or marker is to drill a hole in a one-inch diameter dowel rod (*lower center*). Another way of thickening the marker is to cut a hole in a thick piece of synthetic foam (*upper center*). Illustration credit: R. Mechtly.

the sponge or brush is washed thoroughly in water immediately after use so that the glue does not dry and ruin these items.

Using a roll-on glue bottle, a glue stick, or a brayer to apply glue may be

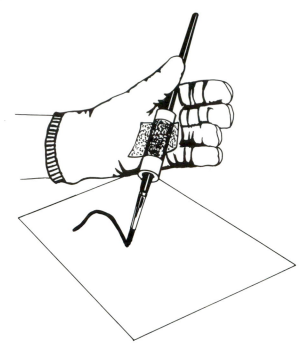

Figure 6.14. A student who has difficulty grasping the dowel may be more successful if velcro is stapled to the dowel and glued to the palm of a discarded glove. The velcro then provides the added grasping power for the child. Illustration credit: R. Mechtly.

easier and less messy than using a brush or sponge. Again, the overriding principle is to see which method works best for an individual child. Sometimes a child does not have the patience to wait for glue to dry. This is a typical occurrence in construction of wood sculpture. To help the child wait the appropriate amount of time, one could have the child count to 30 before going on to glue another object. This can be presented in a game format and the adult and the child can count out loud together (Anderson, 1979).

Prepreparation

Prepreparation of art media and tools is sometimes necessary. Examples of prepreparation would be precutting geometric shapes for a child to use in making a cut paper design. Another example would be to preprepare clay in balls for children who lack the motor skills to do this (Anderson, 1979). The adult could also preglue a surface and the items to be attached to that surface. This pregluing can be done using either a spray-on rubber cement used in mounting photographs or bottled rubber cement. Rubber cement is a toxic substance and must be handled very carefully and used in a *well-ventilated* area. It should not be used with children who would put the glued

TOP VIEW

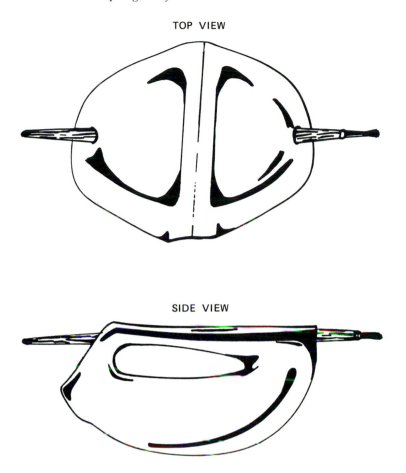

SIDE VIEW

Figure 6.15. If a child can only make a fist, a fist-type grip can be made by using a handle cut from a gallon plastic bottle. In cutting out the handle, enough space should be left so that holes are large enough for the brush or pencil handle to be punched into the plastic. Note that there are two ways of punching the handles of the art tools into the plastic. For added security the art tool should be taped to the plastic handle. Adapted from Callan (1987) by permission. Illustration credit: R. Mechtly.

items into their mouths. Pregluing using rubber cement should be done away from the children in a well-ventilated area (Callan, 1987).

Contact paper can also be used instead of glue. Clear contact paper is taped to a work surface so that the sticky side faces up. Relatively flat items such as cut paper shapes or buttons can then be added. Finally, the contact paper is turned over onto a piece of colored cardboard and pressed down (Callan, 1987). A variation of this use of the contact paper would be to mount it sticky side up onto colored cardboard before having the child add items to it. When the child finishes his design, another sheet of clear contact paper can be placed on top of the artwork to insure all of the items in the design

Figure 6.16. Sometimes children have difficulty holding crayons sideways when making texture rubbing. To help in holding a crayon on its side, put the peeled crayon sideways into a large bulldog clip. The child then can grasp the clip and easily create large areas of rubbed color on the paper. Illustration credit: V. Foster and R. Mechtly.

are securely attached to the cardboard. The result is a cut paper design that is more easily perceived (Anderson, 1979).

The use of contact paper has been very helpful for children who are tactually defensive (afraid to touch sticky or messy surfaces). They can gradually get over their defensiveness just by touching the sticky surface. An added benefit is that by just touching the paper and then removing one's finger, a nifty sound results that most children enjoy (Callan, 1987).

Sometimes rather than using glue, it is easier for a child to staple items together for an art project. Care should be taken to instruct the child in the appropriate ways of using a stapler. Unless it is stressed that the child should *slowly press* down on the stapler head, the stapler will jam. One also must be careful to check on medical issues related to each child before introducing the use of the stapler. One can make it easier for children to use the stapler by placing a piece of wood that is about four inches by six inches by one-half-inch thick on top of the stapler head (Figure 6.18). The child then can stand up and place his hands on the board and slowly lean on it. The result is a slow pressure that insures the staple enters the paper and the stapler is not jammed. Some children lack the strength to use a stapler and others can hurt themselves in exerting the pressure needed to make the stapler work. Children with hearing impairments also have trouble using staplers because they cannot hear the "click" sounds that the stapler makes when it is working properly. These sounds are important cues that tell the user that the stapler is working correctly.

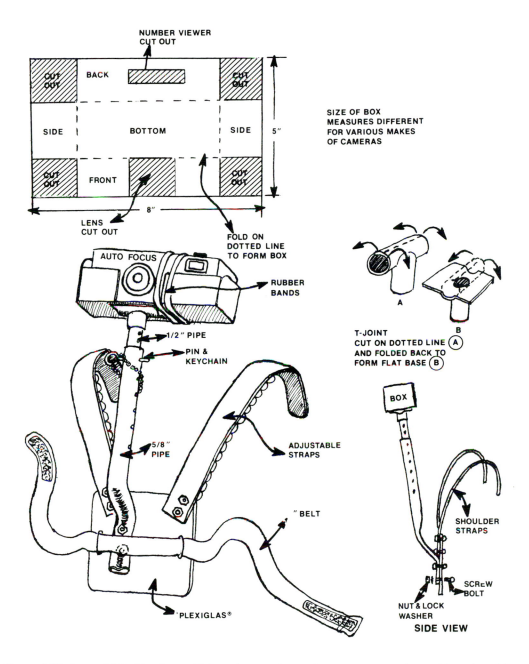

Figure 6.17. A special holder into which an instamatic autofocus camera can be positioned enables a child with limited use of his hands to take pictures. Design decisions are still being made by the child. The camera has eliminated the need for fine motor skills that would be necessary in painting and drawing activities.

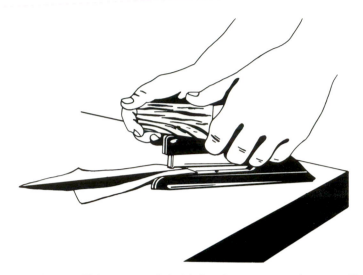

Figure 6.18. A child with insufficient strength in his hands to use a stapler can still staple. All that is needed is for a board that is about 6 by 8 inches to be placed on top of the stapler head. The child then stands up and while holding the board leans on to it. This is a gentle way of stapling something and it is unlikely that the stapler will jam if it is used in this way. Illustration credit: R. Mechtly.

Adaptations for Cutting

One of the most frequently cited skills that children with disabilities lack (with which they have problems) is the ability to use scissors appropriately (Anderson, Colchado & McAnally, 1979). There are several adaptations that can alleviate this problem. Two types of commercially available scissors can be most helpful. Double-handled scissors permit the adult to put his hand over the child's hand who is holding the scissors (Figure 6.19). The two outer holes are for the adult's fingers. By using this hand-over-hand method, the child begins to understand how to use scissors correctly.

Easy-grip scissors also help in showing the child how to use scissors. These scissors automatically remain open between cuts and help the child learn how to open and close the scissors between cuts. They also are very easy to use and cut with much less effort than conventional scissors (Figure 6.19).

Other variations on scissors are the grip scissors and board-mounted scissors. The grip scissors are constructed by welding a second pair of scissors' holes to another pair of scissors so that a child can hold the scissors in a fist grip (Figure 6.19). The board-mounted scissors enables one to cut using only one hand (Figure 6.20).

It may be necessary to do a task analysis of cutting with scissors to understand just what steps are causing problems for the child. Task analysis

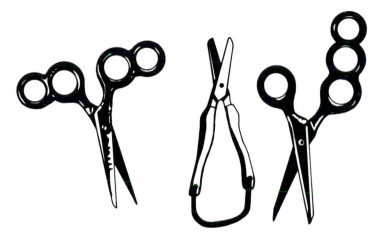

Figure 6.19. Three types of scissors are illustrated here. On the left are double-handled scissors. These are used by having the child place his fingers in the inner two holes and an adult places his fingers in the outer two holes. Then the adult shows the child the proper way to hold the hand and wrist by demonstrating cutting. The scissors in the center are Easy Grip scissors. These scissors enable the child to make a cut with very little effort. They also are already opened to the proper place and always go back automatically to this same place. The scissors on the right (the fist grip scissors) have been adapted for a particular child whose hand is continually in a semi-fist configuration. The thumb goes into the side with only one hole and the other three fingers fit into the side with the three holes. Illustration credit: R. Mechtly.

is discussed in the following adaptations section dealing with adaptations in the instructional sequence.

For older students, electric scissors can help. The electric scissors are mounted permanently on a nontipping board. Then the student can manipulate the scissors much more easily. Additionally, it may make sense to team up students for cutting, being sure that one child in each team has the motor abilities to cut successfully and safely.

For students who cannot hold or manipulate scissors at all, it may be necessary to precut items for them or to have them tear the art media. If the child is tearing paper, a guide will help. A guide can be a straight edge of a ruler or a large board. The child can lean on the board with one hand and pull the paper along the edge with the other. Pairing up students in teams so that they can combine their strengths may be helpful in this situation.

Children can also tear cloth. If one uses this method, be sure that all the material and cloth scraps that are in the scrap box can be easily torn. (Some types of material just do not tear easily. One example is jersey.) The material to be torn must have a small cut made in it before the child begins to tear.

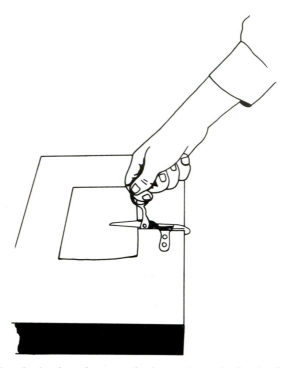

Figure 6.20. This illustration depicts board-mounted scissors. A standard pair of scissors is mounted on a board so that half of the pair is stationary and the other half can be moved. This enables a child to make a cut with just one hand. The paper needs to be moved after each downward cutting stroke. Illustration credit: V. Foster and R. Mechtly.

Adaptations in Art Tools and Media for Children with Visual Impairments

While it may surprise some readers, the children who are visually impaired can benefit a great deal from art experiences. As noted earlier, visually impaired children need to have a consistently organized workspace. It also will help to have a reference point for these artists. A reference point can be made in several ways. The child can work in a tray with shallow raised edges. The edges help to provide a reference point on all sides so the child knows where the paper stops. Using a tray with raised edges also can be helpful and useful for artists with physical disabilities and for children who have problems with control, limit setting, and perseveration problems (Figure 6.21).

A reference point can be as simple an item as a piece of masking tape put in the lower right-hand corner of the paper, or one corner torn off the paper. The child with visual impairments should be verbally oriented to the reference point. This is accomplished simply by telling the child, "There is a piece of masking tape on the lower right-hand corner of your paper. Can you locate this?"

Figure 6.21. Working in a tray with raised edges can provide a child with visual impairment a point of reference for the parameters of his work. Working in a tray with raised edges can also assist children with physical and other disabilities who have difficulty in controlling the application of paint or tend to have problems with boundaries. Illustration credit: R. Mechtly.

Raised or textured surfaces can also be reference points for the child with visual impairments. Like many children who are multi-disabled, the visually impaired child is often tactile defensive. Having a board with different types of textured items secured to it can help the child get over his fear of touching things (Callan, 1987). The board can be used in a game format.

One can make a simple texture drawing board for the child with visual impairments by cutting a piece of screen standard paper size (9 inches by 12 inches, or 18 inches by 12 inches). After taping the rough edges of the screen, tape it to a piece of cardboard that is about 11 inches by 14 inches in size. Add a frame of 1 3/4-inch thick cardboard to provide a parameter for the paper. Secure a piece of drawing paper on top of the screen. The child then draws on the paper with crayons. The marks made by the child will be slightly textured and raised. After the drawing is completed, the paper is removed from the screen and the marks can be "read" by touching them.

Raised surfaces can also be made by using a glue bottle that leaves a trail. When the glue is dried, a raised trail of glue remains that can be read by touching it. Another way of creating a trail is by having the learner with visual impairments use a tracing wheel (Rodriguez, 1984). A tracing wheel is a tool used in sewing and is available at commercial sewing departments in dry goods stores. The wheel makes a depression on the paper and when the drawing is complete the page can be reversed so that the line made by the tracing wheel is raised. Most shapes can be made with the tracing wheel. Circles are the one exception and are hard to create with the tracing wheel.

Scent can also be utilized to help orient children with visual impairments and help them associate smells to colors. For example, the red smells like cherry, the yellow smells like lemon, and the orange smells like an orange. Scented markers can be ordered through most commercial school materials suppliers.

Scented markers are appropriate for use with any child. They can provide additional sensory experiences and added motivation. Children with short attention spans stay on task longer when using scented markers. This increased attention to task behavior is partly due to the added stimulus of smell and the novelty of the markers.

Adaptations in the Instructional Sequence

Additional Challenges

There are three major types of adaptations in the instructional sequence category: additional challenges, correlations with other academic subjects, and task analysis. Adaptations in terms of additional challenges within the art activity itself can take several forms. No group of children all work at the same pace or level. Some will finish more quickly than others. Some will only complete the most basic parts of an activity. Some children will be gifted and want these added challenges in their art sessions. (Also, as we all know, a bored child is potentially a child who will cause problems in a group.) For example, a group of children may be working on a puppetry activity. All will be encouraged to complete the basic parts to a sock puppet which involves completing a head and face. The additional challenge (always as an option) would be to have the children add arms to the puppet. A further challenge might be to create arms that can move.

In a printmaking project, the children's basic task would be to complete a one-color print. The added challenge would be to make a print that had two or three colors in it.

Correlation with Other Subjects

Adaptations in the instructional sequence may be ones that integrate and correlate educational material and information being taught in a child's regular classroom. For example, an art experience focusing on construction of three-dimensional sculpture from cardboard boxes can be much more motivating and powerful an experience if it is related to what is being studied in the child's social studies class—in this case, neighborhoods.

Doing an art experience that involves crayon wax paper laminations has a much stronger appeal to students if, in addition to doing the activity, the children are graphically shown what happens when heat is applied to crayons. In this way the science concept of *melt* (which may be concurrently covered in the child's science study) is also reinforced.

Task Analysis

Task analysis or instructional sequencing may be relatively unfamiliar to the art therapist or art teacher or parent; however, task analysis may be a requisite for the instruction of a child with disabilities (Morreau, 1975), and it is a standard methodology in special education.

In a task analysis, all the steps necessary for achieving a particular behavioral objective are isolated, described, and sequenced. Task analysis enables the teacher or therapist to quickly pinpoint any specific skill with which a specific child is having difficulty. Consequently, a high success factor is built into the instruction of children with disabilities because complex operations are broken down into their simplest units. Additionally, a task analysis focuses on **the behavior or activity to be mastered and NOT on the disability of the child as a barrier to task completion.**

A task analysis requires several steps. First, the activity to be undertaken is stated as a behavioral objective. For example, the art activity might be making a valentine card from magazine photos and precut construction paper hearts. Restated as a behavioral objective, this experience would be:

> Given precut heart shapes and theme appropriate magazine pictures, the learner will arrange and paste up to five heart shapes and up to three cutout magazine picture items onto a larger piece of paper so that there is no excessive paste oozing out or showing on the larger background paper.

The instruction involved with this activity would include:

1. The identification of the particular steps the student needed to gain mastery over completing the card.
2. The determination of what related skills the activity required—such as counting, cutting, and pasting skills.
3. The determination of which of these steps in number two the student has already acquired.
4. The provision of the instruction in a one-step-at-a-time approach to give the student mastery over all the requisite skills he lacks to complete the activity.
5. The provision of opportunities for the student to try each step, to be given feedback as to how close the student is to mastering each step, and to have time to practice each step.

In a task analysis, *all* of the steps necessary for meeting a particular behavioral objective are recorded in terms of *observed* behavior and in terms of the most logical sequential order in which these steps can be placed. It is crucial that each task is completed by the teacher or therapist as well as by someone else who can be closely observed by the teacher or therapist as he is accomplishing the task.

There are two other essential parts to a task analysis. It is essential that each substep of a task analysis is placed in its most logical sequential order. Each and every observed step must be recorded. At times this may seem redundant, but it is essential for reliable instruction.

In summary then, a task analysis for a specific behavioral objective includes five procedures:

1. The behavioral sequence to be task analyzed must be observed and performed.
2. All of the behaviors (broken down into their smallest substep) that occurred are recorded in observable, measurable terms.
3. Check the behaviors that have been recorded to be sure they are placed in their most logical sequence.
4. Field test the task analysis with one student.
5. Make changes in the sequence or substeps as necessary.

For example, the behavioral objective, "Given paper, brush, and three colors of tempera paint, the child will paint a picture of one identifiable objective as indicated by teacher/peer review" would include these subskills necessary for painting with a brush:

1. Picks up brush with thumb and forefinger.
2. Holds brush two to four inches above bristles.
3. Puts brush into container of paint.
4. Covers bristles with paint.
5. Lifts brush one inch above paintline inside paint container.
6. Strokes side of paint container upward two inches with paint-covered bristles.
7. Repeats step six.
8. Moves brush up and out of container.
9. Moves brush three to six inches in the air over to paper.
10. Lowers brush until bristles with paint color touch page.
11. Moves brush across page, left to right, top to bottom, or circularly to make lines and shapes.
12. Lifts brush and repeats steps 10 and 11 until paint no longer flows off the brush.
13. Lifts brush from paper.
14. Repeats steps 3 through 12, if same color is selected.
15. Selects a different color.
16. Puts brush into clean water container.
17. Lowers brush into water so all bristles and any other paint-covered part of brush are covered with water.
18. Moves brush back and forth in water approximately five times.
19. Lifts brush out of water one inch.
20. Strokes side of water container upwards two inches.
21. Lowers brush in air two inches and repeats step 18.
22. Repeats step 21 four times.
23. Removes brush from water container completely.

24. Dabs bristles three times on pile of three paper towels.
25. Repeats steps 3 through 22 as needed to complete picture.

Task analysis is an important part of any art program that has as part of its goals the development of basic fine and gross motor art skills or other observable art abilities. Unless the child acquires these basic skills, he is also handicapped in the ability to express himself. Once these skills are mastered, the child can go beyond to the creating and expressing of fully developed artwork in clay, paint, or other media.

Technological Adaptations

Technological adaptations is the fourth major area of adaptations that needs to be discussed. In this area are included the numerous types of high technological equipment that are being developed. The most obvious are those that have developed through the use of the personal computer.

There are several advantages in using a computer.

1. The computer is less threatening as an instructional tool. Students with histories of failure can be placed in an individualized situation with many opportunities to practice in a private situation (Kirk, 1989).
2. The computer has an engaging quality that can hold the interest of even the most easily distractible student. Thus, the computer can have the capacity to be intrinsically motivating (Canter, 1989).
3. The computer is a neutral instructor that is not judgmental about errors children make. Students with histories of failures are placed in an individualized situation with many opportunities to practice in private.
4. The computer has an almost infinite amount of patience. There is immediate reinforcement and feedback to the student from the computer.
5. Many computer programs are cast in a game format which is very motivating.
6. Students can work at their own pace and according to their own strengths.
7. The computer can provide a sense of mastery and control to individuals whose physical disabilities give them little control over most of the events in their daily worlds. Using a computer can help build independence in children with disabilities.
8. Those persons who have little use of their hands can let the computer do the graphic designing for them. These individuals still are engaged in making aesthetic judgments without the frustrations inherent in attempting to use more traditional drawing and painting media.
9. Instruction can be geared for individualized learning based on student need.

10. Learners with histories of failures can be placed in an individualized situation with a personal computer that can provide many opportunities to practice in a private, tailored-to-fit situation.
11. If programmed well, computers can encourage skills in problem solving and discovery learning (Kirk & Galligher, 1989).
12. The computer does not rely on hearing ability for its use. In fact, the primary visual mode of learning that the computer represents is especially helpful to students with hearing impairments.
13. Research has shown that children who have short attention spans can benefit from the systematic structure that a computer can provide (Kirk & Galligher, 1989).

Computer graphics programs are becoming more and more available for use with all levels of students (*Art Education,* 1983; White, 1985; Ettinger & Roland, 1986; Greh, 1986).

The literature in art therapy is also reporting the use of personal computers as therapeutic tools. Johnson (1987) reported successful use of a microcomputer and a graphic tablet (Kaola Padd, 1983 cited by Johnson, 1987) to establish rapport with an overly dependent ten-year-old boy. The author felt that the computer was a non-threatening way to connect with the client and to have the client communicate. Canter (1987, 1989) used two graphics programs and one music program in conducting an art therapy pilot program for boys with learning disabilities and behavioral disorders. She concluded:

> Providing these tools gives clients with behavioral and emotional problems a sense of self-satisfaction while allowing them to participate in a unique, stimulating, and creative learning process. Creative and developmental growth in eye-hand coordination, visual motor skills, logical reasoning processes, creative decision making, and interpersonal relationships can all be enhanced through the use of the Macintosh.
>
> Continual use of computers and creativity software by children and adolescents with learning disabilities produced positive changes in their behavior. The results included increased attention span and development of visual expression, music expression, self-confidence, creativity, and communicative skills. (1989, p. 314)

The computer can provide a detailed record of the evolvement of images and of the movements that compose these same images. This has implications both for rehabilitation as well as for understanding the therapeutic aspects of image making for an individual (Weinberg, 1985).

OTHER SUGGESTED ADAPTATIONS

A summary table developed by Brown (Cain & Evans, 1990) follows that includes suggestions for adaptations for children with physical, intellectual and social differences.

Six Guidelines for Art Programming for Persons with Severe Disabilities

In 1988 Blandy, Pancosdar and Mockensturm detailed six guidelines to assist art teachers in planning art experiences for students with severe and profound disabilities. While many art teachers and therapists already adhere to these guidelines, some may not be aware of these signposts and they will be summarized here.

1. Use materials that are age-appropriate. As severely disabled learners grow in chronological age, the tendency for teachers to want to continue to use mental age-appropriate art media may persist. For example, using finger paint with a learner who is chronologically a teenager but has a mental age of six years is demeaning to that learner and not in keeping with educational goals that foster independence and maturity. Media such as finger paint (or painting with pudding) can be adapted to more age-appropriate materials such as paper pulp.

2. Use the partial participation principle. This principle is similar in some ways to task analysis. If a student with severe disabilities cannot complete an art task even with individual help, then practical/partial participation may be beneficial. There are several steps involved in implementing the partial participation strategy.
   a. assess the performance of the nondisabled learner on the same art activity.
   b. determine exactly what the learner with severe disabilities can and cannot master in doing this art activity.
   c. decide what skills the learner with disabilities can now do, and can probably learn (from b above), and tap into the specific learner's prior experience by checking with other teachers and parents or significant others and by discussing the task with the student.
   d. decide the skills which the disabled student most likely cannot master from a study of b above.
   e. make hypotheses as to ways adaptations might be made so that the learner with disabilities might acquire the skills to complete the art task in question.
   f. determine the skills needed in the adaptation and test these out with a nondisabled peer.

TABLE 6.1
ADAPTATIONS FOR CHILDREN WITH PHYSICAL DIFFERENCES

Disability	Physical Environment	Materials Modification	Methods Modification	Content Modification	Evaluation
Visual Impairment	Materials kept in predictable place Students seated near activity Sighted guide to aid in giving directions Well-lighted work area	Large-print or Braille reading materials Taped lessons Sighted tutor to read directions or guide movements Training with equipment prior to use Braile writer, slate and stylus, Braille typewriter, or large-print typewriter	Hands-on activities— use of other senses to observe More verbal description and use of touch Contact with real objects	None	More verbal evaluation or large-print materials Aid in writing responses Assistance with manipulation of materials
Hearing Impairment	Students seated near activity so they can hear better and lip-read if necessary Students seated away from distracting noises	Captioned films, filmstrips Visual text to accompany tapes Model or repetition of directions	Hands-on experience to develop concept Visual aids to accompany lectures List of new vocabulary before verbal presentation Eye contact before speaking Clear enunciation Contact with real objects Repetition of instructions and verbal presentation as necessary	None	None

TABLE 6.1 (continued)

Disability	Physical Environment	Materials Modification	Methods Modification	Content Modification	Evaluation
Health Impairment	Removal of things that could aggravate health condition (e.g., no sugar for diabetics; no plant pollen or animals for allergic child)	None	None	None	None
Physical Impairment	Adequate space for movement Desk and table height adjusted for wheelchairs Seats near exits whenever possible for safety Barrier-free access	Training with equipment prior to use Peer to help with manipulation of materials Mechanical aids for manipulation of materials as necessary	Contact with real objects	None	Assistance manipulation of materials Aid in writing responses

Contributed by Susan Brown, Ph.D.

    g. determine what adaptation might be most successful based on information from c, d and e above.

    h. determine which skills can be acquired by the learner with disabilities with the appropriate adaptation.

Table 6.4 explains how these steps can be used in an art activity using an instamatic camera.

3. A cue hierarchy is developed. A cue hierarchy is presented in Table 6.5. The final outcome of this process is for the learner to learn a new task

TABLE 6.2
ADAPTATIONS FOR CHILDREN WITH INTELLECTUAL DIFFERENCES

Disability	Physical Environment	Materials Modification	Methods Modification	Content Modification	Evaluation
Gifted	None	More advanced reading material	Less repetition More emphasis on problem solving	More advanced concepts, such as universals and abstractions Emphasis on processes and synthesis and evaluation levels	More emphasis on organization and application of information
Learning Disabilities	Students seated away from distracting noises	Concrete, relevant materials	Immediate feedback Short activities Cueing of relevant details Social praise Pairing of an object and its symbol Eye contact and priority seating for discussion Multisensory activities	None	Oral tests or modified reading level Aid in writing responses Structure and frequent progress checks on projects
Mental Retardation (and slow learners)	Students seated away from distracting noises	Low-reading-level materials Training with equipment prior to use Concrete, relevant, tangible materials	Social praise Eye contact and priority seating for discussions Short activities Repetition Active involvement Practice in a variety of settings	Emphasis on knowledge of specifics Emphasis on concrete and relevant experiences relevant experiences	Structure and frequent checks on projects Oral tests or modified reading-level materials Aid in writing responses More objective format

TABLE 6.2 (continued)

Disability	*Physical Environment*	*Materials Modification*	*Methods Modification*	*Content Modification*	*Evaluation*
			Contact with real objects		
			Immediate feedback		
			Pairing of an object with its symbol		
			Adaptations of reading material		
			Cueing of relevant details		
			Mastery learning		
			Cooperative learning		

Contributed by Susan Brown, Ph.D.

and to perform this task using naturally occurring cues in an independent working mode. This means the more independent the disabled learner can be (the less reliance on another adult or nondisabled peer), the better. Several cue patterns may be needed. Each cue pattern is individualized for each learner based on his history of learning.

4. Present and future environments are analyzed. Those art experiences that are intrinsically motivating and can be provided out of the art room will be the most successful. Parents, siblings and peers can provide this information. Leisure activities that can be undertaken with a maximum of independence are in great demand by families and service providers for learners with severe disabilities. Certain types of art activities fulfill these criteria. Photography is one such activity. Others include visits to local art centers, galleries and festivals, and engaging in painting, drawing, fiber and ceramic art, and looking at picture books.

5. Art experiences should include multicultural dimensions. Learners with severe disabilities may have fewer opportunities to experience ethnic, generational, religious, racial, occupational and regional differences in their community and hence have a greater need to be aware of these

differences. Art experiences can provide many opportunities for the development of multicultural awareness.

6. Encourage learners to be active participants in the larger art community. This can be accomplished by having learners with disabilities join art interest groups, attend art openings and art museums. Blandy also urges art specialists to lobby for accessible art facilities and accessible art exhibitions (ones that can be touched and viewed from the level of someone seated in a wheelchair).

Blandy concludes:

> We are opposed to the "us" and "them" attitude which often characterizes the art education of students experiencing significant mental/physical challenges. This characterization has resulted in special art curricula, segregated class-rooms and/or schools, and a widely held belief that only art teachers with specialized training can successfully work with people experiencing challenges. People with significant mental/physical challenges do not constitute a group outside of the community, but are individuals who can exercise their rights as citizens within the community at large. (Blandy, Pancosdar & Mockensturm, 1988, p. 65)

HEALTH HAZARDS OF ART MATERIALS
FOR CHILDREN WITH DISABILITIES

We cannot end this discussion of art adaptations without addressing the issues of health and safety in art. These issues also need to be considered in planning an art program and in designing art adaptations for children with disabilities.

In 1987 the Center for Safety in the Arts published a set of guidelines for art therapists and teachers to consider in working with children with disabilities (McCann, 1987). These guidelines will be summarized here. High-risk factors include the following: children with hearing impairments who work in wood shops and other situations where there is a lot of noise; children with epilepsy who may become exposed to paint thinners, lacquer thinners and turpentine; children with mental retardation and other problems that limit their ability to read, understand and follow safety directions and labels with warnings; children with physical and neurological disabilities that have problems and difficulty in running machinery that is hazardous; children with respiratory problems including asthmatics who may be exposed to molds, dusts and spray mists; and finally children who are on medications that may interact with solvents or that may impair judgment relative to operating hazardous equipment.

TABLE 6.3
ADAPTATIONS FOR CHILDREN WITH SOCIAL DIFFERENCES

Disability	Physical Environment	Materials Modification	Methods Modification	Content Modification	Evaluation
Behavior Disorders	Students seated away from distracting noises	Training with equipment prior to use	Motivation Immediate reinforcement Cueing of relevant details Short activities Eye contact and priority seating for Social praise	None	None
Cultural Differences	None	Concrete, relevant materials	Contact with real objects Cooperative learning	None	None
Limited English Proficiency	None	Modified reading material	Cooperative learning Concrete activities	None	Oral tests or modified for language

Contributed by Susan Brown, Ph.D. Reprinted from Cain, S. & Evans, J. M. (1990), *Sciencing: An involvement approach to elementary science methods* (Columbus, OH: Charles Merrill). Reproduced by permission of the publisher.

Chemical Hazards

Exposure over a long time to organic solvents (turpentine, paint thinners, lacquer thinners), asbestos, silica, cadmium and lead may cause immediate or long-term illness. This exposure can happen through ingestion, inhalation or skin contact and absorption. Chemical hazards can affect the skin, eyes, lungs, heart, nervous system, liver, kidneys and the reproductive system.

Physical Hazards

Included in the category of physical hazards are: noise, infrared and ultraviolet radiation, vibration and heat stress. For example, noise exposure has resulted in many wood designers and woodworking teachers (and sometimes students) developing hearing loss. Children with hearing impairments

TABLE 6.4

PLANNING USING PARTIAL PARTICIPATION (ADAPTED FROM BAUMGART ET AL., 1982)

Description of Activity:
Use of a Polaroid 600 Series Camera

I. Non-disabled Person Inventory	II. Significantly Mentally/ Physically Challenged Person Inventory	III. Skills Student Can Acquire	IV. Skills Student Cannot Acquire	V. Hypothesis or Hypotheses	VI. Skills Associated with Hypothesis	VII. Adaptation	VIII. Skills that can be acquired through Adaptation
1. Choose subject	1. Chose subject						
2. Grasp camera with 2 hands using a palmar grasp, lens should face subject.	2. Grasped camera with 2 hands using a palmar grasp, lens should face subject.						
3. Raise camera to eye level	3. Raised camera to eye level.						
4. Look through viewfinder at subject	4. Looked at subject through viewfinder.						

5. Using index finger apply pressure to shutter release button 6. Push button until completely depressed 7. Wait for photograph 8. Remove photograph	5. Index finger was not strong enough to apply pressure to shutter release button 6. Could not apply enough pressure 7. Waited for photograph 8. Removed photograph	5. and 6. The student could could squeeze trigger mechanism with one hand to activate the shutter release	5. and 6. Due to physical challenges it is likely that it would take this student an inordinate amount of time to strengthen her index finger to the point of being able to release the shutter.	5. and 6. It is possible that this student use the pistol grip shutter release available from SNAP	5. and 6. One hand palmar squeeze of the shutter release trigger	5. and 6. Purchase Polaroid Sun 600 with pistol grip from SNAP	5. and 6. Student will have the ability to release shutter.

Note. From "Guidelines for teaching Art to Children and Youth" by D. Blandy, E. Pancosfar, and T. Mochenstrum, *Art Education, 41*(1), p. 63. Copyright 1988 by the National Art Education Association. Reprinted by permission.

TABLE 6.5
SAMPLE CUE HIERARCHIES FOR OPERATING
A PISTOL GRIP SHUTTER RELEASE ON A POLOROID SUN 600 SERIES CAMERA

I. Example 1	
Nonspecific verbal cue	"What do you do next?"
Followed by:	
Specific verbal cue and a gesture	"Put your right hand here and squeeze" (as teacher gestures toward pistol grip).
Followed by:	"Put your right hand here and squeeze" (as
Specific verbal cue and a model	squeeze" (as teacher models skill). "Now, you do it."
II. Example 2	
Picture cue	Photograph of a person placing her right hand on pistol grip shutter release attached to a Polaroid 600 Sun Camera
Followed by:	
Specific verbal cue and picture cue	"Put your right hand here and squeeze (points to pistol grip) like the person in the picture."
III. Example 3	
Specific verbal cue	"Put your right hand on the pistol grip and squeeze."
Followed by:	"Put your right hand on the pistol grip and
Specific verbal cue and gesture	squeeze" (pointing to grip and making a squeeze gesture).
Followed by:	
Specific verbal cue and physical guidance	"Put your right hand on the pistol grip and squeeze like this" (as teacher guides student's hand to grip).

Note. From "Guidelines for Teaching Art to Children and Youth Experiencing Significant Mental/Physical Challenges" by D. Blandy, E. Pancosfar, and T. Mochenstrum, *Art Education, 41*(1), p. 63. Copyright 1988 by the National Art Education Association. Reprinted by permission.

can have added damage to their ears and hearing when exposed to high noise levels.

Safety Hazards

Safety hazards include working with unsafe hand and power tools and unsafe electrical equipment. Burns can result from exposure to hot surfaces and equipment. Excessive repetitive motions can result in damage to musculoskeletal and neuromuscular systems in the body.

Biological Hazards

Biological hazards include a wide variety of viral (including AIDS), bacterial, fungal, and mold and mildew infections and allergies. These infections can result from unsterilized tools held in the mouth (or failure to sterilize art tools that children put into their mouths), mold-contaminated clay or acrylic paints that have been diluted. These biological agents, if inhaled, ingested or absorbed via skin cuts, can result in allergies and infections.

Risks that Children with Specific Disabilities may Encounter

CHILDREN WITH MENTAL RETARDATION. Due to short attention spans, poor motor control and problems in grasping some concepts associated with chemical hazards and the tendency to put tools and hands and fingers in the mouth, these children are at risk for a variety of safety and health hazards in the art room. It is recommended that only art materials that are nontoxic for children be used. Sharp tools and machinery that could cause burns and cuts should not be used by these children, or used only under close adult supervision. Children need to be evaluated on a case-by-case basis to insure they have learned the proper use of art tools and machinery. Additionally, there is a greater tendency for children with mental retardation to carry the Hepatitus B virus. This virus can be transmitted via moist or wet art materials such as tempera paint and clay. Children should be checked to insure they are not carrying the virus. If they are, then they should not use wet art materials. Finally, therapists and teachers should know what medications children are taking to prevent hazards that may occur due to side effects of medications and risk factors that increase under the influence of medications.

CHILDREN WITH LEARNING DISABILITIES. Children may have poor coordination which can result in injuries as the result of handling art tools (especially sharp tools). These children may have difficulty understanding specific steps in written or spoken directions. Directions need to be repeated using as many communication channels as possible. To insure children understand directions, they should both repeat the directions and demonstrate the steps in a mock run-through. Children should be monitored to be sure they understand directions.

CHILDREN WITH BEHAVIOR DISORDERS AND EMOTIONAL DISTURBANCES. Children who have the potential to act out, be aggressive and violent both to themselves and to others can be at risk for causing hazards in the art room. Some of these children may totally reject rules and regulations on the proper use of tools, chemicals, and dangerous machinery. Inhalant abuse, commonly called glue sniffing and huffing, is a potential area of danger. Inhaling Liquid Paper and rubber cement are examples of materials that contain substances that can cause nerve and brain damage (and addiction). Many children with behavior disorders and emotional disturbances are on psychotropic drugs and medications that can impair judgment. Medications can also interact with inhaled substances and cause serious side effects. Art teachers and art therapists should know exactly what medications their students are taking and should know the side effects of taking these medications. Art therapists and art teachers should also know the substances in art media that can cause serious hazardous interactions with these medications. Organic solvents are especially potentially hazardous to children who are taking tranquilizers and similar medications. Close supervision of children is recommended around machinery and sharp tools. Children may need to be evaluated on a case-by-case basis to determine suitability and safety (to them and to other children) of placements in classes where there are dangerous machinery and tools.

Children With Neurological Impairments. Central nervous system impairments can result in some of the following symptoms: spasticity, loss or diminished motor control and balance, weakness, and fatigue. Peripheral nervous system damage may result in paralysis, numbness, pain, loss of reflexes and fine motor control. The resulting problems include motor difficulties (lessened muscular strength and endurance and/or spasticity, sensory difficulties, coordination, difficulty with eye-hand coordination, inaccurate sense of position), balance and behavior problems (emotional swings, alertness, judgment, hyperactivity). Organic solvents, lead, manganese, mercury and toxic art media can seriously damage already damaged nervous systems. Children should not be exposed to organic solvents and neurotoxins (except in small amounts in well-ventilated areas that include ventilation hoods). Use volunteers or physically able students to operate machinery or tools. Monitor students with impaired sense of touch to insure they do not burn or cut themselves. Monitor children with weak muscles and limited muscular endurance to insure their physical limitations are not exceeded (be particularly sensitive to the weight of art tools and dangers of repeated motions). Also, be sensitive to children who tire easily and provide limits to prevent fatigue. Check to insure children are not on medications that can impair judgment or can have dangerous interactions with art materials.

Children With Physical Disabilities. These children have difficulty in mobility, motor coordination and control, and problems in balance. They may have problems using tools safely and operating machinery. Falls and spills while handling art materials may occur. Nonbreakable containers should be substituted for glass containers. Medications may also affect perception. Ease of accessibility to art material and tools for children in wheelchairs and in braces is recommended. Dangerous tools and machinery need to be inaccessible. Aides and volunteers can provide additional margins of safety. Children who use their feet or mouths to manipulate art media may be at risk for ingesting or absorbing art media, so care needs to be taken to use nontoxic media. Also, art tools that are used in the mouth need to be washed and sterilized between use.

CHILDREN WITH HEARING IMPAIRMENTS. Contrary to some myths, it is inadvisable to expose children with hearing impairments to excessive noise because additional damage to hearing may result. Deafness can be a serious hazard because audible signals are one way of warning people about danger. Children should be tested by specialists to determine if further exposure to noise could cause further damage. Protective gear including earmuffs and earplugs may need to be worn around noisy equipment. Ear molds and hearing aids with vented earpieces that are not fitted properly can transmit additional noise, so the fit of these devices should be checked periodically. Visual warning signals may need to be utilized in addition to auditory signals to alert children with hearing impairments of danger including fire alarms. Safety procedures and safety precautions must be clearly articulated, verbally explained and written so that learners with hearing impairments understand all safety regulations.

CHILDREN WITH VISUAL IMPAIRMENTS. Special precautions need to be taken to protect the children's eyes from chemical splashes, flying objects and infrared and ultraviolet radiation. Moreover, because some learners with residual vision may work at exceptionally close distances to art media and materials, there is greater danger that toxic substances can be absorbed and inhaled. Some solvents and art materials can cause further damage to eyes. If learners work at very close proximity to art media, fatigue may result and then they may be less alert to other potential dangers and more prone to accidents. Teaming volunteers and learners with no vision problems with children who have visual impairments may be a good way of preventing possible hazards. Protective eye gear is strongly recommended (not only for students with visual impairments but for all students). Prescription lens goggles can be made. Good ventilation will be a priority for students with visual impairments who must work at very close range to potentially hazardous art materials.

Other General Guidelines

1. Students should not be allowed to use potentially dangerous machinery or tools if they are taking medications that affect the central nervous system, causing symptoms such as drowsiness, loss of coordination, dizziness, and slow reaction times.
2. Students taking pain medications should be monitored to insure that the medication is not masking warning signals.
3. Students taking medications known to interact with the central nervous system should not be exposed to organic solvents, unless the solvents are used in a local exhaust hood. For example, oil painting and use of per-

manent markers or rubber cement in the open room could be particularly hazardous.

4. Students taking medications which might interact with alcohol or other chemicals or cause photosensitization should have their art program evaluated to ensure that they will not be at excess risk for injury or illness.

5. Students taking any medication should be closely monitored by medical personnel to see if chemicals found in art materials might be causing an adverse reaction with the medication. (McCann, 1987, p. 5)

Other Precautions to Insure Safety in the Art Room and a Hazard-Free Environment and Art Program

For children under the age of 12 years, only nontoxic art materials should be used. A list of these materials can be obtained by writing the Center for Safety in the Arts (New York City, New York 10038). The list does not account in every case for long-term effects but only immediate hazards. The Arts and Crafts Materials Institute (715 Boylston St., Boston, MA 02116) does provide a list of chronic hazards for products. A form called the Material Safety Data Sheet (MSDS) can be requested from manufacturers of art materials. The MSDS should provide a list of ingredients, their industrial standards, data on health hazards, fire hazard information and "common chemicals with which it may react dangerously, and more" (Peltz and Rossol, 1984). Children with mental retardation who are chronologically older than 12 years should also use only nontoxic art materials.

Good ventilation is essential for any art room. Special ventilation is required when glazes are used and when a kiln is installed in a school or agency.

A plan for handling emergency medical situations should be in place. This plan should be updated on a regular basis.

If hazardous art materials are purchased and used in grades K–6, there may be cause for litigation (Fanning & Neville, n.d.). Additionally, if the art room is poorly ventilated and has other potentially hazardous situations such as tables that are not the right height for wheelchairs, space that inhibits mobility, etc., there also may be cause for litigation (Qualley, 1986). These factors may provide important justification for the teacher's school or the therapist's agency to provide a hazard-free art room, art materials and machinery (Fanning & Neville, n.d.).

THE AMERICANS WITH DISABILITIES ACT AND ADAPTATIONS

On July 26, 1990 Congress passed the Americans with Disabilities Act (ADA) which prohibits discrimination against individuals with disabilities.

The long term implications of this law are as yet unknown, but they will be significant for both public schools and society. The ADA has a provision for the "acquisition or modification of equipment or devices" (PL 101-336, 1990, U.S.C. 12102). Thus adaptative equipment is mandated in this law.

REFERENCES

Anderson, F. E. (1979). *Art Adaptations: A slide tape instructional program.* (slide tape). Normal, IL: Illinois State University.

Anderson, F.E. (1980). *The effects of mainstreaming on secondary art education in Illinois.* Unpublished paper. Illinois State University: Normal, IL.

Anderson, F.E., Colchado, J., & McAnally, P. (1979). *Art for the handicapped.* Normal, IL: Illinois State University.

Art Education. (1983). Mini Issue: Computers. *36*(3).

Binney and Smith. (1987). *Selection, testing and specifications guide. Criteria for purchasing school art supplies.* Easton, PA: Binney and Smith International.

Blandy, D., Pancosdar, E., & Mockensturm, T. (1988). Guidelines for teaching art to children and youth experiencing significant mental/physical challenges. *Art Education, 41*(1), 60–66.

Cain, S., & Evans, J. M. (1990). *Sciencing: An involvement approach to elementary science methods.* Columbus, OH: Charles Merrill.

Callan, E. (1987). Art adaptations. Presentation at the National Art Education Association Conference, Boston, MA.

Canter, D. S. (1987). The therapeutic effects of combining Apple Macintosh computers and creativity software in art therapy sessions. *Art Therapy, 4*(1), 17–26.

Canter, D. S. (1989). Art therapy and computers. In Wadeson, H. (Ed.), *Advances in Art therapy,* pp. 296–315.

Ettinger, L., & Roland, C. (1986). Using microcomputers in the art curriculum. *Art Education, 39*(1), 48–51.

Fanning, D. M., & Neville, M.J. (n.d.). *Does the new art material labeling law affect you?* Boston, MA. The Art and Craft Materials Institute, Inc.

Fukurai, S. (1971). *How can I make what I cannot see?* New York: Van Nostrand Reinhold.

Greh, D. (1986). *Using computers in secondary education, Art Education, 29*(6), 4–9.

Johnson, R. G. (1987). Using computer art in counseling children. *Elementary School Guidance and Counseling, 21*(4), 262–265.

Kirk, S., & Galligher, J. (1989). *Educating exceptional children.* Boston: Houghton Mifflin.

Ludins-Katz, F., & Katz, E. (1987). *Freedom to create.* Richmond, CA: Institute of Art and Disabilities.

McCann, M. (1987). *Teaching art safely to the disabled.* New York, NY: Center for Safety in the Arts.

Morreau, L. (1975). Objective-based task analysis. In J. Maestas & Y. Moores (Eds.),

Proceedings of the Minnesota special study institute on education of the deaf: Some practical considerations. Special Education Programs, Psychoeducational Studies. Minneapolis: University of Minnesota.

Morreau, L., & Anderson, F. E. (1986). Task analysis in art: Building skills and success for handicapped learners. *Art Education, 39*(1), 52–54.

Peltz, P., & Rossol, M. (1984). *Children's art supplies can be toxic.* New York, NY: Center for Occupational Hazards.

Qually, C. A. (1986). *Safety in the artroom.* Worcester, MA: Davis Publications.

Rodriguez, S. (1984). *The special artist's handbook.* Palo Alto, CA: Dale Seymour Publications.

Susi, F. G. (1989). The physical environment of art classrooms: A basis for effective discipline. *Art Education, 42*(4), 37–43.

Weinberg, D. J. (1985). The potential of rehabilitative computer art therapy for the quadriplegic, cerebral vascular accident and brain trauma client. *Art Therapy, 2*(2), 66–72.

White, D. (1985). Mini-Issue: A microcomputer in every art room? *Art Education, 38*(2), 4–27.

Chapter 7

DEVELOPING A SENSE OF SELF THROUGH ART

A developed body concept is one of the most basic needs of the child with disabilities. Normal children usually acquire this concept without special focus or learning. Such is not the case for children with disabilities. They simply do not have the usual opportunities for the development of this concept, and it usually takes a good deal longer to be refined. This is especially true with children who have physical disabilities. Additionally, many disabled children have some distorted concepts of themselves, both physically and emotionally. Developing a sense of self through art is a most appropriate beginning place in any discussion of art programming for special children.

In a discussion of the ways one's self-image is developed, Larose (1987) concluded:

> We tend to treat people of certain physical attributes and psychological temperaments in certain ways. Thus a person's self-image is sculpted by his interactions with others. Our desires, conflicts, compensations and social attitudes are somatically entrenched and influence self-projection through drawing the human figure as well as through ways of relating to others and the environment.
>
> The creative process can serve as a means for going beyond the blockages of a learned self-image. In tapping the source of creativity one can simultaneously become in touch with the true self and at least briefly have an expanded ideal of what is its potential. (Larose, 1987, p. 100)

This chapter is organized and written to assist the classroom teacher, the art teacher, and the art therapist who may not have full knowledge of and/or experience with children who have disabilities. The art teacher will probably focus on the way the sequence of activities builds to more and more complex learning and experiences. The classroom teacher will probably center more on the procedures, rationale, and motivation section of the art activities discussed. The art therapist may focus more on the expressive qualities revealed through each part of the art experiences. Attitudes that children have about their bodies, the ways they respond to the experiences, and the related information volunteered by the children will help the art therapist understand how the child perceives her body and how realistic her body concept is (Steinhardt, 1985).

313

A SENSE OF SELF

Body image and self-image are intimately related. The child's concept of *self* (psychologically, socially, emotionally) is developed and fostered by means of an awareness and understanding of the body (Wylie, 1974; Hamacheck, 1971). Art has an important and valuable role to play in developing the child's body concept. Through art, the child will learn general body parts and how these relate and are integrated to form a total concept, i.e., a boy, a girl, a man, a woman.

Moreover, by engaging in the following activities, the artistic process itself will in turn be self-affirming. With the development of body awareness and positive attitudes toward the body via art experiences, the children transfer these affirmative feelings to their concept of self. As children grow in their esteem of their body through art, so will they grow in their positive esteem of their self-concept.

The literature in both art therapy and art education affirms these points. In fact, concern for the enhancement of self-esteem through art goes back at least to the work of Lowenfeld (1957) and Mattil (1972). Rubin (1978) felt that there were intrinsic outcomes to involvement in art which contributed to enhancing self-esteem. Kramer (1971) also believed that art helped to build the ego and thus contributed to the development of the child's sense of self.

Art therapists have noted that the art product also enhances self-esteem and builds a real sense of worth (Ulman, 1977; Rubin, 1978). Erickson (1979) and Omizo and Omizo (1988) noted that the art product reflects most favorably back to the creator a sense of mastery and competency which in turn builds self-esteem. Williams and Wood (1977) further noted the importance of successful experiences in the form of appropriately developmentally sequenced art activities to enhancing the self-esteem of children.

These conclusions have been further documented through hard data research. In 1979, Colchado did a review of the research literature and noted three experimental studies in art that documented the significant positive relationship between art experiences and the self-concept of elementary and high school disadvantaged students and typical elementary students (Colchado, 1979). In an experimental study, Colchado (1979) found that elementary-aged Mexican-American students who had a specially designed art program including body awareness had significantly increased scores on two standard measures of self-concept (the Piers Harris Children's Self-Concept Scale [Piers & Harris, 1969] and the Tennessee Self-Concept Scale, [Fitts, 1971]). Also, after the special art program, these children had a significantly more positive body image!

Similar findings were noted in other reviews of the research literature

(Deske, 1987; Perez, 1989). Deske identified nine experimental studies of the effect of art or art therapy programming on the self-concept of normal, disadvantaged, and behavior disordered/emotionally disturbed children. The majority of these studies also used the same standard measures of self-concept cited above. In each study there was a significant relationship between art experiences and enhanced self-concepts of the children or young adults assigned to the specially designed art programs.

These research studies buttress what those of us in art have known intuitively for a long time. Art experiences can provide successful experiences for a child, and if they are focused on body awareness, there is carryover into an enhancement of both positive self-concept and positive body image.

PLEASE NOTE: The reader is asked to examine the photographs before reading further. Some of these photographs were taken over a five-year period and include several pictures of the same children at different ages.

Figure 7.1. A starter sheet can help a child get started in an art activity. It can also take the threat out of a drawing activity and out of confronting a blank page. A starter sheet that has the entire body missing so that the child is to draw the missing body may also help assess a child's schema for a person. A twelve-year-old girl with moderate mental retardation completed this starter sheet.

Figure 7.2. This completed starter sheet is by a fourteen-year-old boy with moderate mental retardation. He related the activity to bowling. After completing the figure, he added a bowling ball, then the bowling pins, and a second figure which was also a picture of himself about to throw a bowling ball.

Figure 7.3. Starter sheets can also be made with only the head missing. It is easier to complete such a figure, but the drawing of a head does not provide as much information about the child's artistic developmental level. This starter sheet was completed by an eleven-year-old girl with moderate mental retardation.

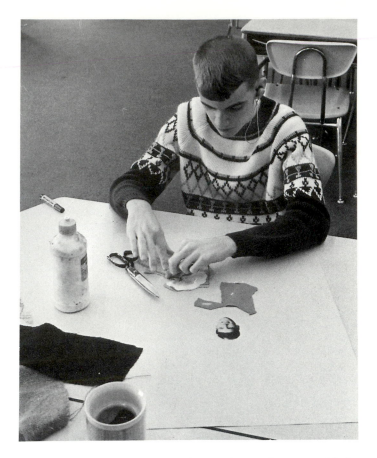

Figure 7.4. After doing a series of starter sheets using markers and crayons, this fourteen-year-old boy with severe mental retardation tries his hand at "dressing" his figure using paper and cloth.

Figure 7.5. In this variation, an eleven-year-old boy with learning disabilities was given a sheet with only the four triangles drawn on it. He finished the drawing by turning the triangles into kites and adding two people to fly them.

Figure 7.6. This teenager with a hearing impairment and severe mental retardation learns about printing and his hands at the same time.

Figure 7.7. A group of primary children with hearing impairments try some foot printing. This activity makes the child more aware of his feet and walking patterns.

Figure 7.8. A nine-year-old child with moderate mental retardation makes textures in her clay medallion using only her fingers.

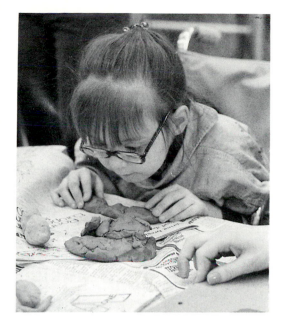

Figure 7.9. A five-year-old child with visual impairment examines the marks she is making in her clay with her fingers. This activity increases the child's awareness of textures and her fingers.

Figure 7.10. After the finger-textured medallion has been bisque fired, the artist covers it with glaze. After glaze firing it will become a part of a wind chime of medallions made by other children in the group.

Figure 7.11. A thirteen-year-old girl with cerebral palsy holds up one of the clay medallions she is stringing with leather for a mobile. Another clay medallion is on the table in front of her. She made these by flattening balls of water-based (earth) clay and texturing them with her fingers. The clay pieces were fired in a kiln and glazed by her before this final stringing and hanging operation.

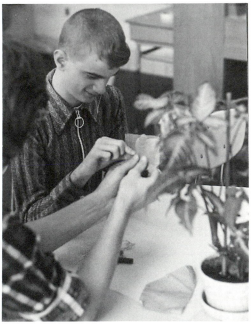

7.12   7.13

Figures 7.12 and 7.13. A teenager with severe mental retardation and a hearing impairment explores texture with his fingers and then makes a rubbing.

Figure 7.14. A seven-year-old girl with physical disabilities makes a face with seeds. This activity helps reinforce what the child knows about facial parts.

Figure 7.15. A sixteen-year-old wears his sack mask. This student with moderate mental retardation has been learning about facial and body parts, and the sack mask is one of a series of art activities to help him gain a greater sense of himself.

Figure 7.16. An eight-year-old child with a hearing impairment has her paper plate mask tied on. She has made a crown to go with her mask and has stepped into the regal realm.

Figure 7.17. A ten-year-old boy with cerebral palsy wears his space mask. He has transformed an ice cream carton by using paint and adding small cans.

Figure 7.18. A ten-year-old girl with moderate mental retardation dresses her life-size portrait by gluing cloth that has been cut to fit the outline. Notice that the portrait has been given braids just like those that the girl has.

Figure 7.19. If a child with physical disabilities cannot use scissors, she can **tear.** Here, a ten-year-old girl with cerebral palsy tears cloth for her life-size figures.

Figure 7.20. She then tears out the completed portrait, using a tearing board for a guide.

7.21

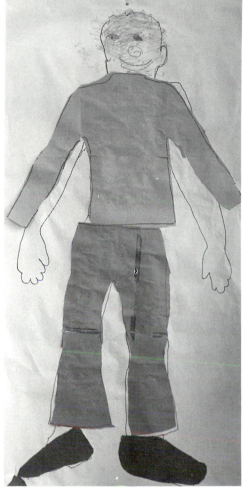

7.22

Figure 7.21. The artist has finished her self-portrait and stands beside it. She now has some concrete idea of how tall she is. Figure 7.22. These are three variations of the life-size figure. A teenager with severe mental retardation made his figure using crayons and construction paper.

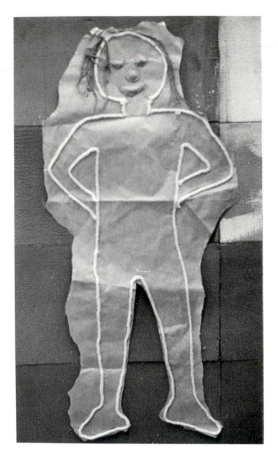

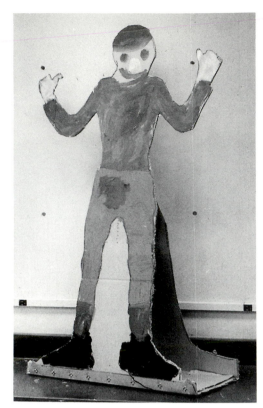

7.24

7.23

Figure 7.23. A thirteen-year-old boy who is blind used yarn and followed a "line of glue" that had been "traced" around him. Figure 7.24. The cardboard free-standing figure was made by an eight-year-old boy with a hearing impairment. He worked on a discarded bicycle box. An aide cut around it for him. Extra cardboard left at the bottom was later scored and folded up in back to support the figure.

THE GENESIS OR BEGINNING *HOW AND WHERE DO I START? WITH A STARTER SHEET.*

Purpose/Rationale

Sometimes it is hard to get started in an art activity. Sometimes a starting place can help, and a starter sheet can provide such a beginning point. By providing a hint (via a head), threat is taken out of the drawing situation and

The author wishes to acknowledge Larry S. Barnfield as the source for this concept.

Metric equivalents are indicated in parentheses in this and all subsequent materials sections.

it is easier to initiate responses to tasks. It is important that the head be of the same sex and ethnic origin as the child to ensure a healthy identification with the drawing. The focus is on the particular child's development of her own body concept. Starter sheets can also be *one* means of assessing the child's schema of a person.

Materials

Heads of boys, girls, men, and women from magazines or old pattern books
Newsprint or white drawing paper, 12 by 18 inches (*c.* 30 by 45 cm)
Water-color markers or crayons
White glue

It is crucial that all art materials be nontoxic. Chapter 6 includes a discussion of art materials and how to determine their toxicity. Most art materials will have information related to contents and toxicity printed on their labels. If there is no such statement, check with the manufacturer.

Outdated pattern books can be obtained from local fabric or sewing stores. The heads should be large and the same sex as the child who is to complete the picture. The heads should have no visible distracting elements such as cigarettes. One head per sheet is glued down. Other starter sheets can be made using bodies and omitting the heads.

Motivation

Hold up several of the starter sheets and ask the children what is missing. Discuss the missing parts and name them or point them out to the children, using their own bodies as a reference. If the aim is to find out how much the children know about their bodies, then give them one starter sheet at a time to complete. (These starter sheets should include some in which the head is missing and some in which only the head is included.)

Procedure

When the children know that they are to finish the picture, provide them with drawing tools. Give the children a choice of using watercolor markers or crayons. As they finish their pictures, point out the various body parts and ask the children to name them. To enlarge vocabulary, list the names of body parts and clothing on the chalkboard. The children can point out and name these parts on their completed pictures.

If a child omits a part such as the hands, touch or point to her hands and ask what they are. Or ask the child where the hands are in the picture.

Depending on the child's ability level and attention span, indicate (using her as the model) details such as fingernails and eyelashes. Whether this approach is used depends on the teacher's or therapist's assessment of the child's abilities.

The school year's art activity can begin with several starter sheet exercises (some with only the heads missing and others with only the bodies missing). The child completes these without any specific instruction on body parts. These then may become important benchmarks of where the child began in the learning of body parts and her artistic schema for a person. Depending on the length of presentation, it will probably only take two or three minutes to complete one starter sheet.

Adaptations

CHILDREN WITH MENTAL RETARDATION. Encourage the children to do their own work and not to copy. Suggest that they keep their pictures a secret until everyone has finished and then share what they have done. For the child with severe retardation, it is best to begin with starter sheets that have only the head missing. When the procedure is understood, have the child go on to the sheets that have the body missing. Another variation would be to have photographs of each child made into starter sheets. This may assist the child in relating and identifying with the activity.

CHILDREN WITH LEARNING DISABILITIES. The hyperactive child will probably complete one in a very short amount of time (a matter of seconds), so several starter sheets will be needed. Stress some naming of body parts, and also ask which part is up, down, left, and right. Other materials can be used to complete the project, such as construction paper and glue, scrap materials, textured paper, or cloth. This depends on the child. For some, too many choices will be frustrating. Some materials such as construction paper and glue can slow the hyperactive child because it takes longer to dress the figures with clothing cut from paper. Drawing materials can encourage swift completion of the project. Choose art materials that insure a sense of completion and little frustration.

CHILDREN WITH BEHAVIOR DISORDERS/EMOTIONAL DISTURBANCE. If the child appears reluctant, do not force her into doing any art activity. It may just be that the child might need to watch for awhile before becoming involved. Children can be given the option of watching others engaged in the activity. Children appreciate the security provided by the structure in this type of activity. Finally, some children will be bewildered if they are given too many materials choices.

CHILDREN WITH PHYSICAL DISABILITIES. These children may prefer using felt-tipped markers. Whatever the choice of drawing material, the tool may need thickening by taping sponge rubber around it or providing a thickened handle by putting the marker into a dowel rod holder. (See Chapter 6 for details on how to make a dowel rod holder.) The starter sheet should be taped down to the work surface. If the children cannot hold drawing tools, they may be able to use their teeth, helmets with a pencil attached, or their feet. If the child is too involved (very severely disabled), a starter sheet with the body parts ready to assemble can be used. The child indicates when the parts are in the right place. Or this involved child can work in a team with a more able classmate.

CHILDREN WITH HEARING IMPAIRMENTS. Do not show completed examples at all. These children have a tendency to copy. Begin by explaining what they are to do and then demonstrate by partially completing the picture. Or, try the "secret method" discussed in the adaptations for children with mental retardation.

CHILDREN WITH VISUAL IMPAIRMENTS. Begin with a sheet that has outlines of the head or body. To do this, use an outline of yarn or string or a "trail" of white glue that has dried. The child can complete this using either a glue outline or masking tape or some other substance that produces a raised surface. The sheet can also be placed on a window screen (see Chapter 6) in a frame and taped down. The child then can draw using a crayon and can feel where she has drawn. The child may also cut or tear the parts to be added from construction paper and either glue or tape them down.

OTHER ADAPTATIONS. Starter sheets can also be used in the following manner. First, heads of several persons or a combination of a head and part of some everyday item (a car, for example) can be placed on the page. Half of a face may be used, and the child must finish the other half. A long mural can be made with several items from magazines pasted down to get the children started.

Other parts of the curriculum can be tied in by using a house starter sheet (windows only or doors only) or a nature starter sheet (leaves only or a mountain or clouds). The children can make starter sheets for each other from magazines. Finally, the same idea may be used by just tearing or cutting shapes from construction paper and gluing them down for the children to complete.

A simple pencil line on a page may also become a starter sheet. Try a straight line on one page, a circle on another, or a diagonal line on another. Using ink or paint blots as the starting stimulus can be another variation.

Getting started has many, many types of beginnings and endings. However, do not try the variations until it is established that the child understands the basic idea that a picture is to be completed. Try these variations after the child has worked through the series of art activities geared to foster body concept.

Evaluation

POTENTIAL OUTCOMES. The child has completed one (or more) starter sheets using drawing materials. She has included appropriate body parts with making few (less than three) mistakes in placement and naming of these parts.

CLOSURE. Display the finished drawing. Students can make starter sheets for fellow classmates. Classmates may then check one another's work for accuracy. For reinforcement, play a game with each child's finished drawing by covering one body part and having someone tell what is missing.

FEET AND HANDS, FINGERS AND TOES

Purpose/Rationale

This is a continuation of art activities designed to foster body awareness. Through these activities, the children become more aware of their extremities and identify them as their own. This includes learning names of these parts. The aim is for the children to delight in the discovery that feet and hands and fingers and toes are marvelous to have and can do many exciting, wondrous things. A child's own response and the teacher's evaluation of her capacities will determine how much of this sequence will be accomplished.

FOOTPRINTS, HANDPRINTS, FINGERPRINTS

Materials

Aluminum pie tins larger than the items to be printed
Brown wrapping paper or butcher paper in long sheets
Drawing paper and newsprint about 12 × 12 inches (*c.* 30 by 45 cm)
Masking tape to hold paper
Old newspapers

Paint shirts or smocks
Paper towels
Soap
Sponge
Tempera paint
Tub of water

Motivation

Bring in handprints of someone whose hand is much bigger or smaller than those of the children in the class. Play a detective game. Have each child place a hand on the print. None will match. Suggest that they make their own prints.

Or display some fingerprints and handprints. Point out that each child has her own unique print, one that is as unique as her own signature. If the class is at an intermediate level and they understand the concepts, police and detectives can be discussed. Then have children make their own prints.

For younger children, just explain that they are going to make pictures using their hands and not anything else. Another alternative would be to tell them that the "brush thief stole all the paint brushes, so we will have to use our hands." Talk about prints and define them. Define print as a mark made by an object, a piece of type, a sponge, spool, or other found object that has been coated with ink or paint and is pressed on a surface. Demonstrate the process as part of the definition.

Procedure

Handprints

Take the hand and dip it into a shallow pan or tray of tempera paint that is not too thick. Press the hand several times in several places on the page. Have the children try several patterns or rows of handprints. Some math reinforcement can also be included by having the children print their hands a specific number of times. This can be done for both the left and right hands.

Another approach would be to start by having the children wiggle their fingers and play a game. Ask the class, for example, to "Show me your thumb," or "Show me your little finger." Then demonstrate how to make a print, and start with fingerprints first. Next, make handprints and have the children locate all of their thumbs, little fingers, etc., on their hands and then on the page. The child lifts a hand and presses, lifts, and presses, as opposed to using the paint like finger paint. Or begin the entire activity by finger painting and by showing how to make fingerprints and handprints. Variations such as "The Ten Little Handprint" song (similar to "The Ten Little Indian" song) can also be tried. This should take about one-half hour. Ample time should be provided for cleanup.

Footprints

Have the children take off their shoes and socks. Then have everyone wiggle their toes and count them. Roll up pant legs. Have a roll of brown paper laid out in the room or on the playground. Secure the paper to the ground or floor with masking tape. The playground may be the best place to do this activity, as the rain can do the cleaning up. Obtain permission to go out.

Have the children line up, step into the pan of tempera paint, and *walk* across the paper. Tell the children to walk slowly and to take care not to slip. Be prepared to "catch" any child who does start to slip. Label each row of footprints as the child finishes. Be sure to have a big tub of water to wash the children's feet when they are through. This activity should take about 45 minutes for the children to do, allowing lots of time for cleanup.

It is suggested that only a few children at a time do the footprints and that classroom rules and procedures are carefully worked out before doing this. (Otherwise, footprints may end up in the wrong places—the halls, the walls, the bathrooms!)

Adaptations

CHILDREN WITH MENTAL RETARDATION. A step-by-step method will probably be best. For example, tell the child to (a) dip a hand into the paint, (b) press once on the paper, and (c) if there is enough paint left, press on another *clean place* on the paper. Be sure that the child understands that she is to press rather than smear the paint, or the whole process becomes another finger-painting exercise. Remember, however, that finger painting can be one of the goals for this activity. This activity can be a good opportunity to teach some vocabulary. Key words might be *thumb, finger, hand, press, lift, right, left.*

CHILDREN WITH LEARNING DISABILITIES. The left and right foot and hand can be color coded. Have the child use the same color exclusively for the right hand and right foot. Before footprinting, have the children practice small steps and giant steps. Have some of the more coordinated children try this on the paper, but watch out for possible slips and falls. Later as a closure activity, cut out the feet and make them into a personalized hopscotch game by taping them on the ground or floor. The children can learn about fingernails and toenails by drawing them in on their own prints.

CHILDREN WITH BEHAVIOR DISORDERS/EMOTIONAL DISTURBANCE. In addition to the above, limit the activity to only one or two children per session. Have the rest of the class help by holding the paper. A whole mural of handprints or footprints may be made for the room. When the completed prints are put up, be sure each child's name appears underneath her prints so that the child identifies with them.

CHILDREN WITH PHYSICAL DISABILITIES. Be sure that the paper is taped down for the prints. The tempera should be of cream consistency. Test the tempera before proceeding. Emphasize that getting paint on the hands is a very necessary part of the activity. For the footprints, a large roll of paper should be taped to the floor. Those children in wheelchairs who cannot make footprints can print in their chairs by rolling through some paint and then crossing the paper. Make the most of the activity, and encourage the children to move their fingers and toes before beginning.

CHILDREN WITH HEARING IMPAIRMENTS. The language involved in the whole process should be stressed. Think through the steps and the key action words. In addition to words such as *hand, thumb, finger, right,* and *left,* there are *foot, big toe, walk, hop, jump, lift,* and *press.* These are all key words which the child will learn from these printing activities. It may help to use the step-by-step method described above.

CHILDREN WITH VISUAL IMPAIRMENTS. Tempera paint that has some texture added, such as fine sand, can be used. By doing so, the child is able to feel the print where it dries. Emphasize that part of the activity is getting paint on the hands. For some children, the footprints may have little meaning. In this case it may be best to do the clay activity described in the following sections.

Evaluation

POTENTIAL OUTCOMES. The child has made at least one foot-, thumb-, or handprint with the art materials. She has shown knowledge of the printing process by lifting and pressing (and by not smearing the paint). She has named body parts accurately, making less than three errors.

CLOSURE. When finished, the prints can be displayed. Help the child cut the prints out and use them for comparison or for identification. Prints can be used, for example, as arrows to direct children to some part of the room or building. Have the children make up stories about who made the hand- and footprints. The prints may be used as wallpaper in the room or a class can choose one or two prints and draw a picture to go with them.

It is important that learning body parts is emphasized and that the child gets satisfaction in making prints using her hands and her feet. With older children and thinner paint, fingerprints and patterns may be made. Enlarge these prints using an opaque projector, and discuss the whorls and lines found in them. The children can go on to create imaginary fingerprints and footprints and make stories to go with them.

Build on class knowledge of printing, and do other printing activities using found objects, spools, sponges, etc. The finished prints may be used as folder covers; handprints and footprints made on cloth using textile paint instead of tempera can become gift items (for example, a handprinted hand towel).

AWARENESS THROUGH CLAY: FINGER AND FOOT STAMPING

Purpose/Rationale

This activity is a continuation of the body awareness activities, with specific attention given to the fingers and toes and how they can create textures in clay. It is especially planned for those children who need hand and finger exercise. This would probably be a good logical follow-up of the printing activity and can be a lead into a series of activities based on texture. Texture is one of the elements of design and is a part of every artistic work.

Materials

For the first activity:
Oil-base clay (or earth water-base
   clay)
Old cookie sheet with sides
Paint shirt or smock
Stick of wood with smooth side
Willing fingers

For the second activity:
Canvas squares approximately
   16 by 24 inches (*c.* 40 by 60 cm)
Old newspapers
Paint shirts or smocks
Paper towels
Water
Water-based clay
Willing fingers

Salt and flour clay may be substituted for oil-base clay. The formula is equal parts of salt and flour, plus enough water to adhere and mix the dry ingredients, and a few drops of disinfectant. Remember that only water-base (earth) clay will make a sound, so it should be used for the wind chimes. Other heavy cloth scraps can be substituted for the canvas.

Motivation

The medium will probably be motivation in itself. Demonstrate and challenge the children to see how many different kinds of marks they can make with their fingers in the clay. The word *texture,* which can be defined as the way something feels, can also be emphasized. For older children, suggest that this activity leads into making a wind chime or trivet out of clay.

Procedure

Have an old four-sided tray half-filled with oil-based clay or water-based (earth) clay. However, remember that water-based (earth) clay will dry out. The clay will either have to be kept moist and covered with plastic between sessions or the clay replaced with fresh, moist clay for each session. Be sure it is smooth. Start by referring to the handprinting activity and the way this process was done. (The children did this by pressing their paint-covered fingers onto the paper.) Challenge the children to try and make as many different marks as they can in the clay with their fingers. Ask for a volunteer to show her clay marks. Talk about pattern, or count the marks. If the child does not like a mark, it can be erased with the straight edge of a piece of wood. This will be a brief, 10-minute activity.

With older children, the same idea can be used with water-based (earth) clay. The students can mix it themselves in large garbage bags, following directions on the package. If clay is going to be mixed in the classroom, allow one 45-minute period for this. While having the students mix their own clay can provide a better understanding of the whole ceramics process, mixing is time consuming and dry clay is a very fine dust which can cause problems if the room is not well-ventilated. It may make more sense to use premixed, moist clay. A compromise would be to dry out some clay, crush it and then have the students remix it so they understand the entire clay-mixing process.

Start with a ball of moist clay. Have the children flatten the ball and then experiment with the various kinds of marks that their hands and fingers can make.

The next step for both processes is to start with another ball of moist clay, flatten it, and repeat some of the marks the child liked the most from the experimentation. Make a hole in the top about 1/4 to 1/8 inch in diameter. The hole should not be less than one inch from any outer edge of the clay pancake. This hole will be used to hang the completed work. Set aside the clay to dry and fire. It then can be glazed (if there is a kiln available). The children will probably want to make several. If the clay wind chime parts are painted with tempera paint, the paint covering causes the clay to absorb sound. Thus, the painted wind chimes will not make any sounds.

These clay pieces can then become wind chimes, wall hangings, or trivets. If the students do not have the attention span to make several clay pieces individually, they can add theirs to make one group wind chime or wall hanging. Making the wind chimes will take one half-hour session. If there is high interest, a second period can also be spent in this activity.

Adaptations

CHILDREN WITH MENTAL RETARDATION. Depending on the child's ability level, the clay tray may be as involved or as simple as the teacher desires. Words such as *press, smooth, rough,* and *lift* should be reinforced. Math skills can be incorporated by counting how many marks the child makes in the tray. Also, writing skills can be reinforced by having the child make letters in the clay tray. The older children and some of the brighter ones may be quite capable of doing the wall hanging, wind chimes, or jewelry out of the water-based (earth) clay.

CHILDREN WITH LEARNING DISABILITIES. Not only making textures but also letters and words in the clay tray can help the child to identify and learn these figures. It may also help the child to separate figures from the background. Some textures and letters can already be made beforehand in clay or on paper. The child then matches some of these by creating them in her own tray. This can become a game. Each child may create one texture and have a teammate try to match it. Part of the activity should be set aside for exploration and for the child to make unique textures.

CHILDREN WITH BEHAVIOR DISORDERS/EMOTIONAL DISTURBANCE. Be sure that a supportive atmosphere is established so that the child understands that a part of the activity is getting her hands in the clay. As with all art activities, if the child does not want to participate, do not force her. Provide an alternative for those children who are hesitant about putting their hands in messy art materials. Many will just wish to explore the clay by pounding it and poking it. This may be the primary goal. If the class is interested, have them do the wind chimes and encourage them to contribute to a class wind chime. Another alternative would be to decorate a whole wall with clay tiles. Each child can create a clay tile, and these can become part of the larger group project.

CHILDREN WITH PHYSICAL DISABILITIES. Follow the same basic procedure. Be prepared to let the children use their feet and toes instead of their hands. Tape down canvas pieces (on the floor, if this is appropriate) and work on top of them. Let the child determine the best work posture for herself. Be sure that the clay is soft enough for stamping.

It may be beneficial for the children to understand how clay is mixed. Some children may need this type of physical activity and experience, so let them mix their own clay. Such an experience also builds cooperation because the children will probably do this in groups. Having the children do as much of their own work as possible builds a greater sense of independence and accomplishment. This includes mixing *some* of their own clay. (It is unrealistic to have the children mix all the clay. Also, it is more convenient to order clay premixed. At the same time, it will help the children understand more about the entire ceramics process to mix a bit of clay "from scratch.") Put the clay powder and the right amount of water (following directions on the package) into a large garbage bag. The children should work in pairs, and mix by kneading the bag. Leave the bag loosely closed overnight if the clay is still a little wet. Roll the clay into balls for use or have one of the less involved children help do this.

CHILDREN WITH HEARING IMPAIRMENTS. For older children, it may be best to talk about making a wall hanging or a hot plate (trivet). The children can also make smaller medallions. These can become necklaces, bracelets, or other kinds of jewelry (body adornment). Math concepts may be included by suggesting that the children put 10 to 15 marks on their clay pieces.

CHILDREN WITH VISUAL IMPAIRMENTS. These children will want an established work area. Have the children work in a large tray that has shallow sides and is secured to the work surface with C-clamps. This sets boundaries. Work on top of cloth taped to the tray so the clay will not stick. Set several clay balls to the right of the tray. Tell the child where these are. Place one ball in the tray for the child. She may need help in making the hole for the string. If the child is older and can grasp the concept, discuss the fact that different sizes of balls and different thicknesses will produce different sounds. Have some examples of fired clay medallions that differ in thicknesses. Let the children hear the different sounds made by hitting each medallion of different thicknesses. Have a damp paper towel or sponge on the left so that the child can moisten the clay when needed.

Evaluation

POTENTIAL OUTCOMES. The child has explored clay by making three or more different sets of marks in it using her hands. She has tried making repeated patterns by stamping in the clay with the hand, fingers, or found objects. The child has learned that different textures, i.e., more than one kind of stamped impression, can be made in moist clay. She has learned that texture is one of the basic art elements. The child has made at least one medallion which will be painted or glazed for a wind chime or mobile and has learned how to mix clay (water-based clay, salt and flour clay, or both).

CLOSURE. Have the children share their texture explorations in their clay tray and tell how each pattern was made. Those who are making wind chimes or mobiles can do the same. The mobiles will be finished by glazing. The wind chimes will be finished by painting or by using shoe polish, wood stain, or coffee, and then displayed in the classroom. The concept of texture can be reinforced in many other class experiences. This concept will continue to grow as the teacher points out and describes textures in other art activities that the class will be doing.

TEXTURE HERE, THERE, AND EVERYWHERE

Purpose/Rationale

These three activities are designed to help the children discover that they have a sense of touch and can discriminate between different textures. Texture is an important part of the child's world. So is the sense of touch and the ability to discover the varieties of textures at the tips of one's fingers.

Materials

Crayons, large with paper peeled off
Drawing paper or newsprint about 9 by 12 inches (*c.* 22 by 30 cm)
Masking tape
Varieties of textures (burlap, cloth, corrugated cardboard, metal screen, sandpaper, etc.)

The textures should be flat items cut into various shapes. Small paper sacks and masking tape are also needed for the second activity.

Motivation

Bring in some obvious texture opposites, such as coarse sandpaper, grainy wood, cloth, metal screen, or other items. Make two piles of these: a rough and a smooth pile. Hold up the items or, better yet, pass them around asking for class reaction. Or have one child come and place a texture shape on the rough or smooth pile.

Procedure

Rubbings

The children select textures (three or more, one at a time) and make rubbings with them. A rubbing is done by placing the object under a piece of newsprint or thin drawing paper and rubbing across it with the long side of a peeled crayon. The pressure should be even, and the area rubbed should be at least one inch square so that it can be easily seen. The item can be taped down for easier rubbing. The children should have a choice of crayons. Have the children try and match up their rubbings with the objects afterwards. This should take about one-half hour.

Texture Hunt

The same rubbing procedure is used, but the children are instructed to go on a texture hunt or safari in the room or outside. Give some guidelines about how many and what kinds of textures are to be hunted. This should take about one-half hour.

Texture Game

Texture bags are made for each class member and one for the teacher. Each bag (small sack) contains four or five different texture items—for example, a square of screen, a piece of sandpaper, corrugated cardboard, a piece of bark, a thick piece of yarn, and a thin string. As one texture is pulled out, pass it around the class. Without looking, each child is to feel in her bag and find the same textured item. Then the child makes a rubbing of this. The procedure is repeated until the bag is empty. This game should take about one-half hour to play.

Adaptations

CHILDREN WITH MENTAL RETARDATION. The slower, younger, or less developed children may desire to stop with the first part of these texture activities. It may be an important opportunity to reinforce vocabulary. Select a few key words (see list under section on children with hearing impairments), and use many examples and a lot of repetition.

CHILDREN WITH LEARNING DISABILITIES. Set specific ground rules so that each child knows when it is her turn to match up textures. The children can cut out their own texture rubbings and make a collage from them. (A collage is a picture made with only different kinds of textured papers.) Some children may need some suggested topics for their collages.

CHILDREN WITH BEHAVIOR DISORDERS/EMOTIONAL DISTURBANCE. Set ground rules, especially for the texture hunt; otherwise the children will collide. Perhaps have the children hunt one at a time or in teams of two. Allow only one group at a time on the hunting ground. The children can bring in a favorite object that has lots of texture and share it with the others. A texture hunt outside may reveal lots of unusual discoveries. A group texture mural can be made.

CHILDREN WITH PHYSICAL DISABILITIES. Tape down the item to be transferred, and tape the newsprint over it. Use a bulldog clip around the crayon

The author wishes to acknowledge Larry S. Barnfield as the source for this concept.

so that the child can more easily grasp it. A crayon that is thick and is flat on one side works best. The crayons can be flattened with a knife. With the texture hunt, it may help to work in teams, as some children will have more use of their hands than others. Remember that feet can always be substituted for hands. The crayon can be taped to a foot or shoe and the paper taped to the floor. With the texture game, tape the open side of the sack that *touches* the table so the child cannot look into the sack.

CHILDREN WITH HEARING IMPAIRMENTS. This activity is an excellent chance to build language. Key words, among others, would be *touch, texture, feel, rough, smooth, press, rub, same,* and *different.*

CHILDREN WITH VISUAL IMPAIRMENTS. A bulldog clip around the crayon will help the child to grasp it. Use a no-roll crayon (flat-sided). Tape the sack to the table so that the child can reach into it. On the texture hunt, it may help to set aside one part of the room for this purpose and **plant** some interesting textures. The children may want to work in teams.

Evaluation

POTENTIAL OUTCOMES. The child has expanded her sense of touch by discovering one or more different textures and sorting them into rough or smooth piles. The child has learned the word for texture and can define it verbally or by pointing to different textures. The child has learned how to make a texture rubbing. She has completed one or more rubbings, demonstrating her knowledge of the process and correct use of materials. During the texture game and the texture safari the child has followed directions and has given appropriate social responses three out of four or more tries.

CLOSURE. The class can match or write the words for the textured objects they have rubbed. This may become a class display, and a collage can be made from the collected rubbings. The texture game may be expanded by having the children bring in some of their own objects. A texture table with class contributions can be set up in the room. The textures may be sorted according to a variety of categories.

WHAT'S IN A FACE?

Purpose/Rationale

This will be a series of suggested activities aimed at familiarizing the child with her face and its parts and learning the names for each part. At the completion of one or more of these activities, the child will have a better concept of her face and will have experienced success with a number of different media. The child will be able to use these media in imaginative ways.

Simple Faces

Motivation

Have several mirrors in the room and have the children look at themselves in the mirrors. Ask them to point to their eyes, noses, ears, mouths, and hair. Ask for a volunteer to come forward and point to her facial parts as the rest of the class names them. (Most children love the chance to be teacher in front of the class.) Discuss what the facial parts do. Make several sounds while discussing ears. Have some items with distinctly different scents to try while discussing the nose. Have sweet and sour items for the children to taste. Another kind of motivation would be to have the children express different emotions by making different kinds of faces, such as *happy, sad, angry,* and *funny*. Have the class guess each other's facial expression.

Materials

Buttons

Construction paper and other kinds of paper scraps

Old newspapers

Paint shirts or smocks

Paper plates, 1 or 2 per child

Pipe cleaners

Seeds in medium or large sizes

Synthetic foam packing pieces are used in packing items for shipment. Have the janitor or school school staff save them for you.

White glue in squeeze bottles or small tins with 1/4 inch (*c.* 1/2 cm) brushes

Yarn scraps, including yellow, brown, red, and black

Procedure

Have the children construct a face. They might want to make one that expresses an emotion. Demonstrate how to put just a little glue on the area to be glued and then place the items down to make the facial parts. This activity should take about 30 minutes.

Adaptations

Children With Mental Retardation. Provide a choice of materials to use and choose those that can be easily picked up. A mirror will help the child in using her own face as a reference point. If a child omits something, go over the parts with her and point them out in the mirror or on herself. Key words are all the facial parts. Also, each child can make a sentence about faces, i.e., "everybody point to their noses." A song may be sung about faces that includes the various parts.

Children With Learning Disabilities And Behavior Disorders/Emotional Disturbance. Facial gesturing can be emphasized before beginning this activity. Discuss some things which make the child laugh, smile or frown. For example, some items that might make the child smile or laugh are candy, or pictures of the zoo or a circus. The child's classroom teacher will have other insights about these ideas since she should relate to each child in her class. Avoid having too many choices of materials, as this may be confusing for the child. The child can finish one part of the face with one material before going to the next part.

Children With Physical Disabilities. Do not use especially small items but rather items that can be easily picked up. Place these buttons, synthetic foam packing pieces, and cardboard pieces in distinct rows so that the child can easily grasp them. Instead of using glue in a bottle, put some in a weighted container and use a one-half-inch stiff brush. The brushes should have short handles. Long-handled brushes may be shortened by cutting. The surface of the anchored plate can then be painted with white glue, and the child can drop the items into the surface. The child might want to use a cardboard funnel to assist in placement. If the child has very limited use of her hands, she can use her feet or a stick held in her hand or teeth to push the objects around to form the face.

Children With Hearing Impairments. Suggest that the children construct their faces using a particular expression. Discuss the words for these expressions using many concrete examples. Tell the children that their work should be secret until they are finished. After the activity, each child in turn can share her creation.

Children With Visual Impairments. Tape the plate down. It will be helpful to have different sizes of buttons, seeds, and synthetic foam pieces separated and set in a muffin tin that is taped or nailed to a work board. Have the child handle all of the items in the tin first so she knows what is available. Pipe cleaners might be used instead of yarn, as they may be easier to manipulate.

Evaluation

POTENTIAL OUTCOMES. The child has named facial parts correctly, missing less than two parts. She has made a simple face with the art materials and demonstrated appropriate use of glue. She has made her own decisions about which materials to use so that her face has at least one thing that is different from the others in the class.

CLOSURE. The class can review the facial parts by pointing to their own faces and to the correct part on their artwork. The class may do some simple dramatics by holding up their faces and talking behind them. This activity is preliminary to the mask activity that follows.

MASKS

Purpose/Rationale

Let a child make a mask and marvelous things start to happen. Put her mask on her and the ham within emerges. A mask is a license to play and to express all sorts of feelings and emotions which would not ordinarily emerge. A mask is an opportunity to reinforce what the child knows about a face and to be creative in putting that face together. Since different types of masks are best suited to different types of disabilities, these will be discussed under "Adaptations."

Motivation

Halloween is the natural time for mask making, but it should not be the only time in the year for the activity. A reading story can be the beginning for a mask and for some spontaneous drama. Capitalize on this occasion and develop a short play around the masks which each child makes. On a simpler level, each child can be given a chance to say or do something in front of the class as she wears her mask. Finally, have the children draw a story about themselves in their masks or make paper costumes to go along with the mask.

Materials

Boxes, large enough to fit over the head	Sacks, large enough to fit over the head
Brushes, 1/2 inch (*c.* 1 cm) wide	Scissors
Buttons	Seeds, large and medium size

Containers for glue, paint, and water
Crayons
Ice cream cartons, round, 3 or 5
  gallon size (*c.* 20 l)
Matt knife or sharp kitchen knife
Old newspapers
Paint shirts or smocks
Paper scraps in various sizes and
kinds

Stapler
Synthetic foam packing pieces
  (shaped like peanuts, popcorn,
  O's)
Tempera paint
Water-color markers
White glue
Yarn scraps, including yellow, red,
black, and brown

Not all of these materials will be needed for each of the mask activities. Read through the adaptations, and then decide what is needed from this list.

Adaptations

CHILDREN WITH MENTAL RETARDATION. Consider the level of difficulty in making the types of masks and the physical abilities of the children before deciding the types of masks they will make. The paper plate mask is the least difficult, followed by the sack, and the box. The class may only be able to do one type of mask. This is fine. Again, be sure each child has a choice of materials even if it is as simple a choice as using a marker or a crayon.

It may be best to use only drawing instruments on the masks the first time the child does the activity. This would take only about 30 minutes. Then repeat the activity, introducing other materials that can be used on the mask. If the children cannot cut paper to use, have them tear it. This activity will take 45 minutes.

CHILDREN WITH LEARNING DISABILITIES AND BEHAVIOR DISORDERS/EMOTIONAL DISTURBANCE. The decision on the type of materials for making masks depends on the interests, abilities, and attention span of the children. The paper plate faces easily become masks when eyeholes are cut or punched out, and the plate is stapled to a heavy strip of cardboard so that the child can hold the mask up to her face. Paper sack masks are also appropriate. Always provide some choice of materials for the child, even if it is only a choice between two items. Remember that for some children, two choices will be as many as they can handle.

Place the sack over the child's head and mark where the eyes should be. Some children may become frightened when the sack is placed over their heads. Demonstrate what is going to happen with one of the class who would not get upset with the sack on her head. Have a classmate mark where the facial parts go on the mask. Then remove the sack and cut out the eyes. Depending on the abilities of the child, she may or may not be able to cut out the eyes on the mask. Be prepared to do the cutting for the child.

Decorate the mask with the materials provided. For small children, it may be necessary to cut out a place for the shoulders. This is done by cutting a half-oval in each of the small sides of the sack.

As important as making the mask is what the children do with their masks when completed. Have each child show and do something from behind her mask. Another possible starting point is to have a series of one-line situations like, "I'm a monster and am going to eat up everybody! Snarl! Snarl!" Or, "I'm Superman and I'm going to protect you from the monster." Assign these judiciously to the members of the class.

CHILDREN WITH PHYSICAL DISABILITIES. Again, the ice-cream carton or another box that is a substantial stationary type (as opposed to one with a flimsy base such as a paper sack) is recommended. If the child wants to incorporate construction paper into her mask, use a tearing board and let her tear the pieces or strips herself. A tearing board is a flat board placed on top of the paper that leaves exposed the section that is to be torn. The child places one hand on the board and tears with the other hand. Let the child decide whether it is best to tear away from or toward herself.

Instead of gluing all parts, the child may choose to paint the mask. Avoid letting the child use too many different materials, as the result may look chaotic and the child may become confused herself. Depending on the abilities of the individual, this kind of mask should take between 45 minutes and two hours to make.

CHILDREN WITH HEARING IMPAIRMENTS. Any material or type of mask can be made. It will be important to teach the concept of masks. Language can also be tied into the lesson. Some examples might be "cutting *out* the eyes" and "pasting *on* the hair." The choice of words depends on the level of the class. It is also crucial to demonstrate the type of mask the child will make (paper plate, sack, or box). The box masks are discussed in the visually impaired and physically disabled adaptations sections. Do not show completed projects that the child will be tempted to copy. Emphasize that each child is to do her *own* work. Have the child act or do something wearing her mask. This facilitates spontaneous language expressions.

CHILDREN WITH VISUAL IMPAIRMENTS. The best materials for masks are ice-cream cartons (round, three or five-gallon size). They work best when they are empty, so have a party first! Help the child locate the spot for eyes and mouth. The child can brush glue (using a stiff half-inch brush) on the items she is to attach. It is best to put the glue on the item and then press the item onto the carton.

Some of the same items which were used for the face plates will work well. Add one or two other items to the pile. Small bottle tops, pieces of string, wood shavings, or synthetic foam packing pieces are some suggestions. Give the child a reference point by tearing a hole in the carton or gluing on a piece of material so that the child knows where the front is. Other types of boxes may also be used. It should take about one hour to complete the mask.

Evaluation

POTENTIAL OUTCOMES. The child has named facial parts with complete accuracy. She has made a mask with the art materials provided. She has selected materials and used them to demonstrate appropriate gluing and/or painting skills eight out of ten times. She has demonstrated her creativity by (a) not making a copy of anyone else's work, (b) having something uniquely added, and (c) uniquely using materials. (Unique is defined as a response that is different from all others in the class.) The child has put something on the mask that corresponds to some attribute she has herself (used the same hair color or same eye color, etc.). If she is making a mask of something else, such as a favored character, animal, or person, she makes it in such a way that it can be easily identified by others in the group or the teacher or therapist.

CLOSURE. The children can give a brief play wearing their masks. Have them put on their masks and say, do, or act at least one line for a brief time for the rest of the group. They can trade masks and create another short play. Costumes may be made to go with their masks. The masks may be used in other classroom activities. Masks of other persons or animals may also be made and used to dramatize social studies or current events.

PUTTING IT ALL TOGETHER: THE LIFE–SIZE PORTRAIT

Purpose/Rationale

Although this activity may be done at any time in the series (as can all of the other activities), it is designed as a culminating experience in body awareness. Many children are not aware of how tall they are. This is especially true for children with physical disabilities who are confined to wheelchairs and for blind children who need a point of reference about their height. Additionally, some children have difficulty in putting all the parts of the body together to form a comprehensive whole. This activity is geared to solving these problems. Since it requires teamwork, this activity facilitates cooperative skills. Decision-making skills are also involved in the choices that the child must make as she dresses her figure.

The author wishes to acknowledge Larry S. Barnfield as the source for this concept.

Motivation

For the younger children, start by simply asking them if they know how tall they are. Older children may be given a choice of their self-portrait or dressing themselves in the form of a famous person (from entertainment, politics, and/or literature or history). Or have a hatful of suggested names and let the child choose one. Be sure the names in the hat include famous persons of the same race and sex as the child. (It may be easier for the child to relate to the famous person if that person is the same sex and race as is the child.) Typically, younger children will choose to do a life-size portrait that is very similar to themselves. The portrait often will have the same clothes as the artist and will be the same race and sex. If a child obviously chooses to do a life-size figure of someone of the opposite sex and/or a different race, this *may* indicate confusion of sexual identity and a lack of acceptance of her race. When these choices occur, the adult may need to gather more information about the child and ask her reasons for the choices she made. If the reasons given suggest sexual role confusion or negative self-concept about race, then the child may need some special counseling.

Procedure

The child picks a partner (or one is assigned), and they take turns drawing around each other on separate sheets of paper. Mathematics may be tied in by having the child measure how tall she is. Then the paper is unrolled to match the newsprint, adding on an extra foot at the top and bottom. The child draws in her face and decides how she is to dress the figure. This is then cut out and put up in the room. It will take about one-half hour to measure and one-half hour to paint the figure. If cloth is used, it will take about one hour to complete the figure. To make a pattern for a piece of clothing, take sheets of carbon and newsprint paper and place these underneath the area to be covered. Next, tape the carbon paper and newsprint to the table. Trace around the area to be covered by cloth using a ballpoint pen. Remove the carbon paper and newsprint. Cut out the pattern on the newsprint and use it to make clothing from cloth or construction paper.

Materials

Brown wrapping papers, in lengths about 1 foot (*c.* 1 m) longer than each child

Brushes, ½ inch (*c.* 1 cm) wide

Old newspapers

Paint shirts or smocks

Paper scraps of various kinds and sizes

Buttons

Cloth scraps that can easily be cut or
  torn

Containers for water and glue

Crayons

Masking tape

Measuring tape or yardstick
  (meterstick)

Pencils

Scissors

Yarn scraps, including yellow, red,
  brown, and black

Water-color markers

Not all of these materials will be used on each life-size portrait, but the
choices can be made from this basic list.

Adaptations

CHILDREN WITH MENTAL RETARDATION. These children may not have the
attention span for an involved dressing of their figures. Be sure they add the
facial features, and give them a choice of coloring them in or making them
with construction paper. (Give them very large sheets of construction paper
to dress their figures.) This experience is an excellent chance to teach
clothing words to the children. If they dress their figure with cloth, be sure it
can be easily cut or torn. Have them brush on white glue as opposed to
squirting it out.

CHILDREN WITH LEARNING DISABILITIES AND BEHAVIOR DISORDERS/EMOTIONAL
DISTURBANCE. Think carefully about the materials choices given to the
children. Some children who become easily frustrated will not have the
patience to cut out the cloth to dress their figures. Other children will need a
choice of only two types of materials, as they may well become overwhelmed
by too many decisions. Different textured material and paper may be preferred choices for the learning disabled child.

CHILDREN WITH PHYSICAL DISABILITIES. If the child wishes to use cloth, be
sure it can be torn or easily cut. Some children can use electric scissors. If
the child prefers to use tempera paint instead of cloth, be sure it is thick
(cream consistency) and that she uses a wide brush. The brush should be
about one inch wide and have stiff bristles. It should have a short handle.
Since this child probably cannot cut too accurately, it is suggested that her
life-size picture not be cut out.

CHILDREN WITH HEARING IMPAIRMENTS. This is an excellent opportunity
not only to reinforce language of the body but also to introduce clothing
words. As the child dresses her figure, give her the words for the clothing
parts she is adding. The question form can also be reinforced by asking
"Where is the shirt?" or "How many buttons are there?"

CHILDREN WITH VISUAL IMPAIRMENTS. Trace around the child with white glue that will leave a raised line. If the child has some sight, use a heavy black line that is easily seen. Provide a choice of materials. Have the child use paper, construction paper, cloth, and/or yarn. If she is using cloth, be sure that there are differing textures and that it is easy to cut or tear.

OTHER ADAPTATIONS. This activity may be done several times during the year so that the child can check her growth. Another alternative is to have the children choose a community helper or famous person from history and then make themselves as this person.

The life-size portrait may be done on strong cardboard and a freestanding picture made out of it. This may become a coat and hat rack for the child. Finally, the class can go out on the paved playground and use chalk to trace and finish their portraits on to the paved surface. Tempera paint can also be used on the playground after the children are traced. Permission to use the playground should be obtained.

Evaluation

POTENTIAL OUTCOMES. In figuring how much paper to use, the child has measured accurately leaving less than 10 inches as a margin. By tracing around another classmate, she has shown she can cooperate. The child has named all the visible body parts and included them on her life-size portrait making less than three mistakes in naming and positioning the body parts on her paper.

She has related at least three things about herself to her portrait. For example, she has added to her figure the same hair color, eye color, or the same color of clothing that she has. She has shown her independence and creativity by making her own choices of materials and by not copying others' work. She has gained an appreciation for others' work by spending time looking at a display of their completed work.

CLOSURE. Display the finished portraits either in the room or in the hall. The class should have some time to view the completed figures. Names of body parts and clothing may be reinforced by choosing one child to lead the class by pointing to various parts as they are named. The rest of the class can be the umpires in this game. Discuss the way materials have been used. Encourage *each* child by saying something *positive* about her work in front of the class.

REFERENCES

Colchado, J. (1979). The effects of an art program designed to enhance the self-concept of Mexican-American children. (Doctoral Dissertation, Illinois State University, 1979). *Dissertation Abstracts International, 40,* 617–618A.

Deske, K. (1987). *The current status of art in programs of service to children in the domestic violence agencies of Illinois.* Unpublished master's thesis, Illinois State University, Normal, IL.

Erickson, J. (1979). The arts and healing. *American Journal of Art Therapy, 18,* 75–80.

Fitts, W. H. (Ed.). (1971). *The self-concept and self-actualization. Dede Wallace Center Monograph III.* Nashville, TN: Counselor Recordings and Tests.

Hamacheck, D. E. (1971). *Encounters with the self.* New York: Holt, Rinehart & Winston.

Harris, D. (1963). *Children's drawings as measures of intellectual maturity.* New York: Harcourt Brace.

Kramer, E. (1971). *Art therapy with children.* New York: Shocken.

Larose, M. E. (1987). The use of art therapy with juvenile delinquents to enhance self-image. *Art Therapy, 5*(4), 99–104.

Lowenfeld, V. (1957). *Creative and mental growth* (3rd ed.). New York: MacMillan.

Mattil, E. L. (1972). *The self in art education.* (Research Monograph No. 5). Washington, DC: National Art Education Association.

Omizo, M. M. & Omizo, S. A. (1988). Intervention through art. *Academic Therapy, 24*(1), 103–106.

Perez, J. (1989). Abstracts on research in arts used with children who are handicapped. Unpublished paper.

Piers, E. V., & Harris, D. (1959). *The Piers-Harris Self-Concept Scale.* Nashville: Counselor Recordings and Tapes.

Rubin, J. A. (1978). *Child art therapy* (2nd ed.). New York: Van Nostrand Reinhold

Steinhardt, L. (1985). Freedom within boundaries: Body outline drawings in art therapy with children. *The Arts in Psychotherapy, 12,* 25–34.

Ulman, E. (1977). Art education for the emotionally disturbed. *American Journal of Art Therapy, 17,* 13–16.

Williams, G., & Wood, M. (1977). *Developmental art therapy.* Baltimore: University Park Press.

Wylie, R. (1974). *The self-concept* (Vol. 1; rev. ed.). Lincoln: University of Nebraska.

AUTHOR INDEX

A

Aach, S.R., 142, 179, 180
Aach-Feldman, S., 152, 153, 156, 157, 179
Allan, John, 249, 250, 253, 257, 268
Allen, J.P., 98
Allen, J.R., 39, 93
Alpert, 270
Altschuler, R., 134, 139
Anderson, Frances E., ix, x, xi, xiii, 4, 31, 48,
     55, 61, 93, 135, 162, 163, 179, 185, 186,
     211, 230, 231, 256, 268, 272, 275, 276, 279,
     281, 284, 286, 288, 310, 311
Anderson, S., 250, 268
Appel, L.S., 17, 93
Arnkoff, D., 168, 181
Arrington, Doris, v, xvii, 37, 232, 233, 244, 268
Ash, L., xiii, xv, 4, 186, 211

B

Babier, Charles, 84
Bagarozzi, D.A., 250, 268
Baker, L., 24, 93
Balla, D., 95
Bandura, A., 41, 93, 168, 169, 179, 180
Barnfield, Larry S., 271, 281, 315, 341, 348
Barnhart, E. N., 130, 140
Barraga, N.C., 80, 87, 93
Batshaw, M.L., 53, 54, 58, 93
Bates, 16, 93
Baumgart, 304
Beck, A.T., 168, 180
Bedrosian, R.D., 180
Bel, 270
Bergman, A., 269
Beres, D., 234, 268
Beria, E.P., 80, 93
Bergin, A.E., 181

Bigge, J., 58, 93
Binney, 311
Blackhurst, A.E., 82, 98
Blandy, D., 3, 4, 93, 297, 302, 305, 306, 311
Blaylock, J.N., 87, 96
Blythe, D.A., 120, 139
Bowen, M., 233, 268
Bradway, 270
Braille, Louis, 84
Brigance, A., 190, 230
Brill, R.G., 68, 93
Brittain, W. Lambert, 95, 99, 104, 106, 111, 115,
     124, 126, 128, 130, 134, 140, 181
Brown, Susan, 297, 299, 301, 303
Bruscia, K., 236, 268
Bryan, T.H., 24, 93
Brydon, I., 93
Burns, R., 247, 268
Bush, Janet, 219, 220, 221, 222, 230

C

Cain, S., 297, 303, 311
Callan, E., 278, 280, 281, 282, 285, 286, 291, 311
Cane, Florence, 269
Canter, D.S., 295, 296, 311
Cardinale, R., 31, 48, 93
Carkhuff, 241, 242
Castrup, J.A.E., 101, 106, 139
Chapman, L., 124, 131, 132, 139, 190, 230
Church, J.A., 60, 93
Cirlot, J.E., 251, 269
Clements, C.B., 162, 165, 180
Clements, R.D., 162, 165, 180
Clements, S.D., 23, 93
Cohen, E.P., 218
Colchado, J., 185, 230, 288, 311, 314, 351
Cole, L., 6, 95
Collins, M.E., 80, 93

SUBJECT INDEX

A

Accidental causes of physical disabilities, 59–60, 66
Adaptive approaches to art therapy, 159–166
  approach of Anderson, 163
  approach of Clements and Clements, 165
  approach of Gonick-Barris, 164–165
  approach of Jungels, 163–164
  approach of Mayhew, 164
  as key concept, 271
  basis of, 159–160
  case example, 162, 165
    artwork of child illustrated, 166, 167, 168, 169
  categories of, 271–296
    adaptations in the art media and tools, 276–292
    adaptations in the instructional sequence, 292–295
    adaptations in the physical environment, 272–276
    technological adaptations, 295–296
  children with disabilities responsive to, 162
  mainstreaming special children, 161
  mandate of P.L. 94-142, 160–161
  "normalization" theory
    definition, 160
    effect on special education, 160
    principal of, 162
  principles of, 162
  role of adaptive art therapist, 162
Adaptive Behavior Inventory for Children (ABIC), use of, 6
Adaptive Behavior Scale (ABS), use of, 6
Adaptive devices for the handicapped
  computers, 62, 66
  drawing board, 272

for the physically handicapped, 64–65, 67
  physical adaptations of art media, 64, 65
  work on the floor, 64–65
head pointer, 278, 283
orthoplast use, 277
orthosis, 62, 66
prosthesis, 62, 66
scissors mounted on a board, 290
Velcro wriststrips, 278
Aggression, as a learned behavior, 41–42
AIDS, incidence, 59–60
Alcohol, congenital malformations due to, 58–59
American Art Therapy Association, training programs approved by, xiii
American Sign Language (Ameslan), 72
Americans With Disabilities Act & Adaptations, 310
Anxious and withdrawn children, 36
Aptitude-treatment intervention (ATI), use of, 27
Architectural Barriers Act, 85–86
Art
  and therapy as a partnership, 223–224
  adapting for children with disabilities, 271–310
  art programs (see Art programs)
  art therapy (see Art therapy)
  as a reflection of personality, 134
  as a second language, 153, 243–244
  as an index of intelligence, 134
  as essential to the quality of life, xiii
  based on memory, 134
  factors in considering children's artwork, 135
  importance of, xiii
  Individualized Education Program and (see IEP)

359

Normal development in art (*Continued*)
  explanations of child development in
    art as a reflection of personality, 134
    art as an index of intelligence, 134
    art based on memory, 134
    art production, 134
  gang age, 115, 117, 119–120
    color use, 117
    growing chart, 121
    illustration, 118, 119
    schemata as more representation, 115,
      117
    spatial representation, 117
    subject matter, 119–120
  high school art programs, 124–128
    adolescent art growing chart, 129
    illustrations, 127, 130
    purpose of, 124–125, 128
  influence culture on, 135
  late schematic art, 113–115
    illustrations, 113, 114, 115
  methods of study used, 128–134
  new findings from developmental
      psychology, 137
  preschematic stage, 102–106
    art skills and content, 106
    counting skills and art, 103
    growing chart, 107–108
    intellectual functioning and art work,
      103–104
    motivation, 105–106
    schemata and color variance, 104
    schemata emerge art, 103
    social interactions, 105
    word recognition and art, 103
  schema defined, 106
  schematic stage, 106, 108–112
    baseline and skyline appears, 108
    color use, 110–111
    growing chart, 116
    illustrations, 109, 110, 111, 112, 114, 115
    relationship art to reading, 111
    spatial representation, 108–109
  scribbling stage, 100–101
    art content, 101
    art skills, 101
    controlled scribbling, 100
    growing chart, 102
    named scribbles, 100–101

random scribbling, 100
stereotyped schemata, 112–113
Nystagmus, definition, 79, 80

O

Optacon, use of, 86, 92
Orthopedically impaired
  definition, 52
  number in special education programs,
    53
Orthosis
  definition, 62, 66
  examples, 62
Osteoarthritis, 57–58
Osteogenesis imperfecta, 58
Osteomyelitis, 58

P

Peer Acceptance, 41
Perceptual disabilities (*see* Learning
    disabilities)
Personal construct psychology, 173
Petit mal epilepsy, 55
Phenylketonuria, 6–7
Photography, adaptations for use of camera
    by physically impaired, 299
  adaptations for use of camera by
    physically impaired, 299
  cue hierarchies for operating camera, 306
  use of camera, steps in, table, 304–305
Physically challenged, new terms for, 4–5
Physical disabilities, 51–67
  accidental disabilities, 59–60
  adaptations for children with, 299
  adaptive devices, 62, 66
  art programming, 67
  body awareness through art
    artwork illustrating, 323, 324, 325, 327,
      328
    finger and foot stamping in clay,
      338–339
    making a life-size portrait, 350
    making simple faces, 344
    making hand and foot prints, 335
    making masks, 347
    sense of touch using different textures,
      341–342

S

Schizophrenia, time of appearance in
  children, 51
Scoliosis, 58
Seizure disorders (*see also* Epilepsy)
  causes of, 54
  description, 54–55
Sense of self development through art,
  313–351
  artwork of children illustrating, 315, 316,
    317, 318, 319, 320, 321, 322, 323, 324,
    325, 326, 327, 328, 329
  awareness feet and hands, fingers, and
    toes, 332
  body awareness through art (*see also* Body
    awareness through art)
  development of, 313
  measures of self-concept, 314
  relationship body image to self-image,
    314
Severe mental retardation (*see also* Mental
  retardation)
  art programming focus, 15–16, 19
  educational programming focus, 15, 19
  learning objectives for, 15, 19
  range intelligence scores for, 5, 18
Severely emotionally disturbed
  art therapist as part of clinical team,
    224–225
  art therapy for, an experience, 219–223
  use of puppets with, 225–226
Sign language, 72
Snellen Chart, use of, 80
Socially aggressive children, 36
Sonicguide, 85
Speech Plus Talking Calculator, 86, 92
Special education, categories physical
  disabilities necessitating, 52–53
Speechreading, 72
Spina bifida, 55–56, 66
  description defect of, 55–56
  hydrocephalus, 55–56
  IEP for art for child disabled due to, case
    study, 196–201
Spinal cord injury, IEP for art for child
  with, 206, 208–210
Starter sheet
  evaluation results, 332

footprints, 320
handprints, 320
illustrations, 315, 316, 318, 319, 320, 321,
  323, 324, 325, 326, 327, 328, 329
materials, 327
purpose/rationale, 316
procedure, 329–330
uses of, 331–332
Strabismus, definition, 79

T

Teacher Observation Progress Sheet
  (TOPS), 194–195
  artwork evaluation categories, 194–195
  examples, 201, 207, 212
  use of, 194
Tennessee Self-Concept Scale, 40, 314
Thalidomide, 58
Thematic Apperception Test (TAT), uses of,
  40
Traumatic brain injury, as separate category
  under IDEA, 52

V

Verbalism, definition, 80–81
Vineland Social Maturity Scale, 40
Visual impairments, 78–92
  adaptations in art tools and media for,
    290–295
  adolescent and adult educational issues,
    87–88
  body awareness through art
    artwork illustrations, 322, 329
    finger and foot stamping in clay, 339
    making a life-size portrait, 350–351
    making hand and footprints, 335
    making masks, 347–348
    making simple faces, 344
    use of starter sheets with, 331
  causes of, 79
  changes in work tray, 290
    illustration, 291
  characteristics of, 80–84
    academic achievement, 83
    Doppler effect, 82
    intellectual functioning, 81
    language, 80–81